PAUL & HARRIET

831-684-1401

Crashing the Party

Also by Ralph Nader

Ralph Nader

Crashing the Party

TAKING ON THE

CORPORATE GOVERNMENT

IN AN AGE OF SURRENDER

THOMAS DUNNE BOOKS
ST. MARTIN'S PRESS
NEW YORK

THOMAS DUNNE BOOKS.
An imprint of St. Martin's Press.

www.stmartins.com

"What I Voted For" by Tim Robbins, from *The Nation*, August 6, 2001, reprinted
with permission.

FDR Letter to the Democratic Convention reprinted from *Working with Roosevelt*
by Samuel I. Rosenman (New York: Harper & Brothers Publishers, 1952).

Library of Congress Cataloging-in-Publication Data

Nader, Ralph.
    Crashing the party : taking on the corporate government in an age of sur-
render / Ralph Nader.
        p. cm.
    Includes index.
    ISBN 0-312-28433-0
    1. Nader, Ralph.   2. Presidents—United States—Election—2000.   3. Po-
litical campaigns—United States—History—20th century.   4. United States—
Politics and government—1993–2001.   5. Presidential candidates—United
States—Biography.   6. Greens/Green Party USA—Biography.   7. Political
activists—United States—Biography.   8. Consumer affairs directors—United
States—Biography.   I. Title.

E889.N33 2002
973.929'092—dc21
                                                                2001054338

First Edition: January 2002

10 9 8 7 6 5 4 3 2 1

To those who devote themselves to building self-renewing, democratic societies for the fulfillment of human possibilities through peace and justice.

And to Rose B. Nader and Nathra Nader, who taught me the difference between justice and charity and the importance of both.

CONTENTS

PREFACE

Great societies must have public policies that declare which rights, assets, and conditions are never for sale. Such policies strengthen noncommercial values, which, nourished by public enlightenment and civic participation, can provide wondrous opportunities to improve our country. Guided by such values, we can better use our wealth and power to benefit all Americans. Applied beyond our borders, these values can help us astutely wage peace and address the extreme poverty, illiteracy, oppression, environmental perils, and infectious diseases that threaten to jeopardize directly our own national security as well as that of the rest of the world. Broad, humane values also advance the legitimate needs of workers and peasants who yearn for greater democracy and global stability.

Unfortunately, a working, deliberative democracy has few real champions in the Republican or Democratic parties. These parties see their self-perpetuation in the narrowest of dimensions—largely by allowing business interests too great a say in local, state, and national agendas. There is a relentless lobbying industry that enlarges the privileges and immunities of corporations as compared with individuals and makes sure that governments leave the people defenseless and feeling powerless. "Everyone is afraid to talk about poverty," said historian and commentator Doris Kearns Goodwin after the 2000 election. There are many patterns of injustice and abuse of power that the investigative best of the major media have exposed—corporate crime, corporate welfare, anti–worker labor laws, giveaways of commonwealth assets such as the public airwaves, the domination of corporate executives over the shareholders who own the company. Nonetheless, most elected officials are afraid to address these abuses. The absence of public sector resistance is especially troubling because the public sector, led by Congress, the White House, and the state governments, has given away the store to corporations through deregulation, privatization, subsidies, reduced law enforcement, and limitations on civil lawsuits. Still, these coddled companies demand more, more, and more. Enough is never enough.

The convergence of our country's two major parties is a widely noted phenomenon, even though the remedies of political competition from the outside are largely ignored. Third parties, which were the first to raise the seminal issues of our past—from slavery's abolition to the status of women, minorities, labor, and farmers—are now deemed "spoilers." Imagine, the defenders of the spoiled political-electoral system, which is rigged in favor of the two major parties, describe political participation by a new party in this derogatory way. There is little objection by otherwise sensitive reformers. Many would agree that nature cannot be regenerated without giving seeds a chance to sprout, nor can an economy be more innovative and efficient without giving entrepreneurs or small business a chance to compete. Somehow this axiom is not applied to the removal of the many hurdles to third parties wanting to regenerate politics.

A "democracy gap" discourages people from shaping a future for our country that is "of, by, and for the people." It prevents us from sovereign participation in the decisions and directions that can provide the necessities, address the injustices, and solve the problems afflicting our country, domestically and in its relations with the rest of the world. What led to this condition is what our forebears Thomas Jefferson, Abraham Lincoln, Theodore Roosevelt, Woodrow Wilson, and Justices Louis Brandeis and William O. Douglas, among others, warned about—the excessive concentration of power and wealth. Brandeis argued that such concentration is incompatible with a democratic society.

Today, much of this economic, political, and technological power is in the hands of global corporations wielding immense influence over our government in very intricate ways. One industry after another, not the least being the mass media, is dominated by increasingly fewer giant companies. The trajectory of this power is to centralize control—using our own government, wherever necessary, against its own people—and advance short-term commercial interests at the expense of the elevated living conditions and realizable horizons that should be the just rewards of all people.

The democracy gap is associated with the corporatization of our society beyond any and all boundaries established by previous generations. Commercialism has permeated nearly every nook and cranny of our society. It conditions the corruption of politics by vested-interest money, it propels the diversion of public budgets from human need to corporate greed, and it distorts the declared purposes of our universities. It spills into formerly taboo regions of our society, including the planned seduction of childhood from parental authority and the invasions of privacy with unheard-of velocities in medical, financial, and genetic areas. It strips people of control over their commonwealth—the public airwaves, the public lands, the pension funds, and other "commons" inherited from their forebears. The corporate quest for sovereignty over the sovereignty of the people is an affront to our Constitution and our democracy. Indeed, in their largest and most transnational form, the global corporations reject allegiance to nation or community.

This flood of corporate power over government feeds the rationalization of futility among concerned citizens. Our campaign reminded people that corporations, which, in their modern form, were created by state charters in the early nineteenth century, should be our servants, not our masters. What is out of mind is often out of sight, even though the needs are there to be seen. And so our campaign stressed that putting people first means that elections should be first about the responsibilities of the voters to think about the full consequences of their votes. Our campaign also stressed that people should play active roles in shaping the electoral agenda and ensuring varied, open debates. In short, democracy is not a spectator sport.

Civil society advocates have been excluded from the corridors of decision making in Washington, D.C. Belatedly, I realized that an external political energy was required to replace the dashed hopes of genuine reform. I ran as the Green Party presidential candidate to broaden our political horizon, to produce more leaders, not more followers. The Green Party encourages people to develop a higher estimate of their own significance in their communities, states, nation, and world. During the Civil War, Abraham Lincoln's words transcended even that epic divide when he said: "As our case is new, so we must think anew and act anew. We must disenthrall ourselves, and then we shall save our country."

Small political starts start small, as did the Green Party. In a big country it is not easy to start small unless the starters are willing to work incrementally. Building a progressive party dedicated to "liberty and justice for all" has many collateral benefits—citizens taking heart to correct an injustice, recommend a solution, lend a helping hand that lifts the civic morale for a peaceful march, rally, or get-out-the-vote drive. The benefits come from a deeper understanding that daily democracy requires daily citizenship and that a society that has more justice needs less charity for social ills and deprivations.

Seeing the Green Party in this multidimensional manner is not difficult when one sees Greens between elections connecting with civic justice initiatives in one community and neighborhood after another. Reclaiming our democracy means, to Greens, displacing the concentrated commercial powers and intolerant attitudes that keep America down, as America has been kept down by the forces of greed and power in so many areas. Our country has more problems than it deserves and more solutions than it deploys. New political and civic movements are the two pillars upon which a better society can be built.

This book is my story of the campaign. It is only one lens on this effervescence of Green politics and its overall interaction with the presidential campaigns of 2000. It draws on the activities of many people who made this campaign possible: Winona LaDuke, vice presidential candidate, the staff of Nader 2000, the volunteers, contributors, and voters who helped launch a long-term political reform movement for a strong and just democratic society. A selected bibliography provides further documentation for interested readers.

I thank Tarek Milleron for his encouragement, patience, and exceptional intelligence with regard to the substance of this work. Special appreciation is also due Claire Nader, John Richard, Theresa Amato, Steve Cobble, Jay Acton, and Laura Nader for their support and critical commentary. Any deficiencies are my responsibility.

Crashing the Party

One

BUSINESS AS USUAL:
THE BEST CONVENTIONS MONEY CAN BUY

The seat next to me on the stage was reserved for George W. Bush, but on that afternoon of August 2, 2000, it remained empty.

For months, a nonprofit, nonpartisan group called Youth in Action tried to have that seat filled in Philadelphia's Drexel University auditorium. The event was part of the National Youth Conventions, which involved thousands of high school students and other young people contributing to a National Youth Platform, and coincided with the Republican and Democratic national conventions. The platform covered ten subjects of concern to youth—political involvement, community involvement, education, human rights, health, drugs, juvenile justice, environment, violence, and poverty—and offered solutions in well-written, concise presentations.

As the presidential candidate for the Green Party, I was asked to listen to each youth panel summarize its points and then respond, which I did in some detail. Our interaction was one of the most stimulating exchanges in the campaign. I was pleased to hear young people in their teens and early twenties articulating a political agenda separate from the tactics, fund-raisers, and fluff and bluff surrounding the major-party candidates.

These Youth convocations were intricately planned and promoted. They were supported by major foundations, such as the Pew Charitable Trusts, and major nonprofits, including the League of Women Voters and the YMCA and YWCA. These conventions give young men and women a voice and involvement, when so often they are alienated from presidential campaigns that ignore their existence, except for the occasional scripted photo op.

By demonstrating a serious engagement with the presidential

campaign of 2000, as well as their deep stake in America's future, Youth in Action was hoping and desperately believing that it could lay claim to some personal attention by George W. Bush and Al Gore, just as large campaign donors had done throughout the year. Its schedulers made sure that there were no conflicts with the big events at the two conventions. Mr. Bush and Mr. Gore had their platform fights behind them and their nominations cinched, and they were more than capable of bringing their ever-hovering media a few blocks away for an hour to talk with a diverse group of fact-immersed, solution-oriented young people from all over the United States.

It was not to be. Mr. Gore matched Mr. Bush in declining to appear. The two candidates had more important events to attend— lavish parties where politicians shook down corporate lobbyists and fat cats, while the latter in turn were pleased to pay off their political friends for past and future favors.

The day after the gathering at Drexel, there were no stories in the major media, no mention of George W. Bush—the self-described education candidate who pledged to "leave no child behind"—being absent from an event that he could have turned into an advantage over Al Gore. Why? Because Bush and Gore's supposedly savvy staffs had polls showing that young adults do not vote in large numbers and their interests are more universal, unlike elderly voters whose demands are more particular and insistent, such as prescription-drug benefits, preserving Social Security, and patients' rights. Older voters have money. Older voters have influence. Younger voters tend to have neither. Then there are the less inhibited questions young people tend to ask and a risk of being caught off guard or being embarrassingly out of touch. Why should the candidates deviate from the carefully constructed script and emerge from the force field erected by their political consultants and handlers? How sad, empty, and shortsighted, I thought. Later I learned how disappointed the youthful panelists really were.

Leaving the Youth in Action event, I went to find NBC for an invited interview by Maria Shriver on the premises of the Republican National Convention. The area was like a military encampment without the tanks. Security personnel, police cars and vans, high fences, multiple checkpoints, and trailers with security equipment were omnipresent. Demonstrators were not allowed within a Hail Mary pass of the fenced encirclements.

Inside, I was driven in a golf cart to the NBC installation. I asked the driver where the interview was to take place, and he pointed skyward. There before us rose a forty-foot red scaffolding, slightly swaying from a vigorous wind. At the top were perilously perched Ms. Shriver and her camera crew. To reach them, I climbed the stairs of this rickety structure, greeted them, and asked why—why this Tower of Pisa? She pointed to the view of the Convention Center bathed in a spotlight as the one and only reason. A quick three-minute interview on MSNBC followed, allowing only for short answers to complex questions. I climbed down the narrow staircase, wondering how reporters like Shriver can take year after year of what they believe are shallow formats with ever shorter sound bites heading, it seems, for a future of sound barks.

Over at the Convention Center, the delegates were settling down to listen to Dick Cheney's acceptance speech. I walked over to the entrance where crowds of reporters were milling about, jabbering with one another and anticipating nothing much to make their day less routine. The formal sessions of these conventions, with their foregone conclusions, seem simply practices in applause and bore reporters silly (as they've told me countless times). The mind-numbing routines of the campaign trail with a major candidate become a source of cynical jokes and tedious logistical small talk. The convention, however, takes media redundancy to new levels, as every four years the major parties turn out their robo-candidates. I asked one British reporter what could possibly occupy him hour after hour, and he replied, "Well, you try and garnish the dullards a bit as best one can." At the Republican convention, the real action took place outside the main hall in the streets with the demonstrators and in the hospitality suites and parties in Philadelphia's luxury hotels and Main Line mansions.

But for me there was a little excitement during Cheney's monotonal address: I met Amy Goodman, arguably the most tenacious radio interviewer around (ask Bill Clinton, who called Pacifica and sparred with her in a memorable October 2000 exchange for twenty-six minutes). She invited me inside the building for a peripatetic interview. Amy presented our credentials, then we passed the typical bevy of security and were led down the runway to where the Florida delegation was sitting and restlessly listening to the vice presidential nominee. A score of reporters followed us down with mikes, cameras, and pads and began hurling the obvious questions about what I was doing there and what I thought of the goings-on. The Florida delegation was becoming more agitated at the commotion. But I managed to observe that while more than $13 million in taxpayer funding had gone to this convention because an earlier Congress viewed such gatherings as civic affairs, the Republicans had added to that millions of corporate dollars. Elections, I told the reporters, are supposed to be for real people—the voters—not for corporations, artificial entities that cannot vote (at least not yet).

Ultimately the head of the Florida delegation, Al Cardenas, had enough of what he saw as a rapidly expanding embarrassing situation and asked us all to leave. So back up the runway we went, then down another runway to sit with the Michigan delegates, who were astonished to find me—the auto makers' number-one nemesis, in their minds—in their midst. While I was again talking with reporters, a wandering corporate fellow, having overheard my remarks about the convention's corporate omnipresence, blurted, "It's free speech, Ralph." I responded, "Sure, money talks freely, doesn't it?"

And business money donated to the Republican Party and its convention made even more public money gush in its service. While visiting Leaven House, a large homeless shelter and soup kitchen in the severely impoverished city of Camden, New Jersey, I heard a frustrated shelter director refer to the nearly $50 million that the states of New Jersey and Pennsylvania spent to spiff up the Camden waterfront and remove retail eyesores, such as by-the-hour motels and topless joints on Admiral Wilson Boulevard, for the welcoming ceremonies of the convention on Camden's waterfront. The shelter director wistfully described what he could do for his beloved shelter with the mere $300,000 he had requested but not received from the state.

As for the waterfront, then-governor Christine Todd Whitman readily approved this expensive window dressing for four miles of dilapidated buildings so that Republican dignitaries would not be offended by scenes that are all too prevalent in many other less visible parts of Camden. "The first impression is important," said this latter-day Marie Antoinette. In the meantime, this city is not even eating cake. A devastated place of eighty thousand people, it is an economic and living disaster. Indicative of the devastation in Camden is the absence of a single supermarket, motel, or movie theater within the city limits. Camden's woes are hard to exaggerate: two thousand debris-filled vacant lots interspersed between thirty-five hundred vacant buildings and block after block of poor families trying to send their children to run-down schools with dropout rates soaring over 50 percent. Property values are so low that Camden's tax receipts can't begin to meet school and city government expenses; the bulk of the dollars come from the state. Street crime and drug addiction surge through much of Camden's 210 miles of roads. The state, which is the largest employer in Camden, has finally taken over the city's finances, while the mayor joined two of his predecessors in being convicted of political corruption.

In 1990 census figures put Camden, now the nation's fifth-poorest city, in destitution land. One-third of its people lived below the poverty level. Ten more years of decay have made the situation worse, with more companies "evacuating" Camden, as one executive put it. The eleven-story RCA building, which goes back to the Victor Talking Machine company when the city had a manufacturing base, is deserted. But the city does have a championship high school basketball team.

Campaigning in Camden, political consultants say, is a waste of time. For me it put human faces behind the government's statistics; it made clear the difference between charity and justice. Speaking at the Rutgers University Camden campus, I learned how local students saw their education as vocational in order to escape the city.

Camden is emblematic of a systemic collapse in our smaller inner cities, with across-the-board unemployment, non-living-wage jobs going nowhere, pulverized lives of addiction, and serious crimes of violence and ghetto exploitation by loan sharks and unscrupulous merchants and landlords. People who can make a difference leave for greener pastures so that they can put hopelessness behind them. Remaining are churches, nonprofit organizations, and dwindling public welfare programs offering stopgap assistance for food, housing, medical care, and counseling. Visiting a church on a low-income residential block, I heard the usual outspoken indignations, dreams of improvements, and the daily ministering to the poor souls who dread each day.

Who did Camden in? It wasn't always this way. Ordinary folks do not work overtime to ruin their lives. What brutish conditions lead to brutish behavior? Racism, top-down class warfare, political betrayals, concentrations of economic power? These questions are rarely asked and especially not during political campaigns. Instead, Camden is described with phrases of conclusions: "a disaster area," "chronic decay," "a basket case."

There are many Camdens in America—the world's richest and mightiest economy. Not just entire cities like East St. Louis and Bridgeport, Connecticut, but large areas of just about all our large cities. People left behind in the tens of millions with only the urban renewal of gentrification available to push them out. Nearly abandoned farm towns and villages, former factory towns with shuttered plants dot the scarred, contaminated landscapes and join with the longtime poor regions of Appalachia, the Ozarks, Indian reservations, the bypassed rural South, former mining and textile towns. These places represent the "other America" so graphically described by Michael Harrington, who helped motivate Lyndon Johnson's War on Poverty in the mid-sixties.

"It's a casualty," Rev. Michael Doyle, a priest in South Camden, told the *New York Times*'s Matthew Purdy, "and America is to blame for Camden. They don't see it that way. It's like a drunk on a grate, and people say, 'It's not my problem.' If you can't save Camden in a powerful economy, then when will we be able to make it livable? When?"

Just across the Delaware River, lavish parties were setting spending records for national political conventions. In addition to the sensual pleasure they afford, these events are the "convention behind the convention," as described by Republican functionary Dan Matton. The business discussed, casually or intently, while imbibing, strolling, or backslapping, has very little to do with the other America.

The talk almost always centers around big-business demands— contracts, permits, grants, subsidies, giveaways, tax breaks, bailouts, and reducing or eliminating regulation. Paying for these concessions with ever-larger campaign donations gives new meaning to what the wry Will Rogers once said about Congress: "the best money could buy." So when the corporate greasers and persuaders finished their work at the Republican convention, they took a few days off and then flew to Los Angeles for the opening of the Democratic convention. For them, it was the same racket, just different coastlines.

Ruth Marcus, an energetic graduate of the Harvard Law School who went to work at the *Washington Post* in the late eighties covering important but often dry legal subjects, observed both "conventions behind the conventions" for her newspaper. She rose to the occasion:

> The nonstop festivities had a certain end of the Roman Empire feel, from cruises on the Amway corporate yacht in Philadelphia to lunches at the Beverly Hills mansions of Hollywood moguls, where contributors chatted with senators as they strolled among the topiary animals and artificial waterfalls.
>
> Democratic National Committee donors who gave $50,000 enjoyed a private reception and shop-op at the Giorgio Armani clothing boutique on Rodeo Drive, receiving $100 gift certificates as they entered.
>
> The biggest donors watched the action from private skyboxes far above the floor, while a sold-out post-convention fundraiser—featuring Barbara Streisand's rendition of the Democratic anthem—"Happy Days Are Here Again"— brought in more than $5 million in valuable "hard money" contributions to the Democratic Party.
>
> It was a fittingly glitzy finale to the two-week orgy of revelry that began at the GOP bash in Philadelphia, paused briefly and resumed in full force as Democrats went Hollywood with a vengeance behind the scenes even as their candidates lashed the industry in their prime-time comments.

Not to be outdone, the *Washington Post*'s Mike Allen, a rising star with a flair that earned him a profile in *The New Yorker*, delivered his scrutiny of the Republican digs:

By one official estimate, there were 900 separate events at this year's gathering—candidates' fund-raisers, thank-you spreads laid on by the party for its biggest donors, and corporate-financed tributes to lawmakers who hold sway over their businesses.

One senior Republican official called the four-day convention, which ended tonight, "the biggest orgy of hedonism in the history of politics," a marathon of rock and blues concerts, golf and fishing tournaments, yacht cruises and shopping excursions.

Another GOP official said one party cost about $500,000 and three ran around $400,000, all paid for by corporate sponsors with business before the congressional leaders who were honored at the extravaganzas. . . .

One Republican official, after a reporter was physically barred from a lavish hospitality suite, explained that some of the guests might have people "on their arms" who were not their spouses.

Press coverage of conventions delights in pointing out the political styles of the rich and famous with a flair usually reserved for the sports or style pages. One of the themes reporters relish is candidates saying one thing and doing another. John Broder of the *New York Times* led his story on August 17 from the Democratic convention with this focus: "Barely an hour after Vice President Al Gore issued a call for reforming the ways political campaigns are paid for, he headed back to the fund-raising circuit for a concert that raised $5.2 million for the Democratic Party. In his acceptance speech tonight, Mr. Gore vowed to 'get all the special-interest money—all of it—out of our democracy. . . .' "

Politics, as it is practiced, is the art of having it both ways. One party—the Democrats—regularly says all the right things about campaign finance reform but does nothing. The other party—the Republicans—rarely says the right thing about the corruption of our elections and does nothing. Both use the same ready cliché when asked why one party doesn't lead on reform by example: "We do not believe in unilateral disarmament."

There are two lessons to learn from these political conventions, which *Dallas Morning News* reporter Richard Whittle called "just a television show for most Americans these days." One is that our nation's political leaders are chosen by one big entertainment extravaganza. Roger Simon called his book on the 1996 presidential race *Show Time: The American Political Circus and the Race for the White House,* with artwork on the cover reflecting the hoopla. That's the way it really is, and everyone knows it. Voters are left with only limp imagery, hackneyed slogans, and the omnipresent thirty-second propaganda advertisement. Dr. Pavlov soon becomes the patron saint of the political horse race.

The 2000 Democratic and Republican conventions hit the top of the banality curve. They ceased to shock, instead producing amusement or cynicism. Both avoided thinking about what politics should represent and failed to advance a deeper, functional democracy. Much to their chagrin, journalists, in a scramble for a newsworthy morsel, are turned into gossip-mongers, and readers are unable to make informed judgments.

Second, even when the press does its job, nothing changes. When House Majoriy Whip Tom DeLay (R-Texas) was subject to a devastating page-one exposé in the *Washington Post* five years ago, nothing happened. The article cited instances of DeLay bordering on making extortionate demands for money from special interests, and the House Ethics Committee did not even open an investigation. At the August Republican convention, Congressman DeLay became a veritable talent agent reportedly offering lobbyists packages starting at $15,000 and rising to $100,000 in terms of how exclusive one's meetings could be with the elected bigwigs.

Like most congressional districts, DeLay's is one-party dominated, and he wins by large majorities with only nominal opposition. This is typical. In about 90 percent of the 435 congressional districts, there is one-party rule. So choice is effectively denied to a vast majority of voters.

But the major party conventions in 2000 did not occur in a vacuum. At the same time, Ariana Huffington's shadow conventions in both Philadelphia and Los Angeles brought together large audiences of thoughtful people to hear and discuss with prominent speakers the subjects of campaign finance reform, the widening income gap, and the war on drugs. These gatherings received some national media coverage through C-Span and other cable and independent press outlets but little attention over the leading television networks, which all cut back sharply on their convention coverage. Outspoken legislators like Senator Russell Feingold (D-Wisconsin) did come over to speak their minds ("The big story at the Democratic convention was the political payoffs and influence-peddling") with a candor that had no scheduled time at the big conventions.

And certainly the most interesting events at these conventions took place in the streets, parks, and parking lots near the convention halls. But the story here incredibly became one not of protest but of crowd control and police preparation. Unlike in the sixties and seventies, peaceful mass demonstrations no longer receive much media coverage. Many a weekend march of fifty thousand to two hundred thousand people for women's and labor rights or for arms control and the environment receives little more than a picture and a caption in the *Washington Post* or *New York Times*. A movie premiere or socialite benefit earns many more column inches in the Style section.

Consequently, demonstrators began to figure that nonviolent civil disobedience or, in some frustrated instances, controlled violence against property, would mesh with the television media's mantra, "If it bleeds, it leads." Studious, well-prepared news conferences, absent these demonstrations, don't make the grade with the eyes and ears of the fourth estate. The reaction of course is for the police to organize massive counterforce against what is perceived as a giant safety problem.

The Philadelphia police prepared for thousands of arrests and detentions with so much manpower that the police outnumbered the demonstrators. In addition, they employed helicopters, motorcycles, patrol cars, full-body armor, sprays, tear-gas canisters, rubber bullets, plastic handcuffs, night-seeing cameras, and who knows what else that was not observable. Seeing this land-based armada, the demonstrators countered with their cries of civil rights violations.

And within this mock war, the message is lost. Reporters described the assemblage as a motley crowd with a grab bag of causes having no seeming connection to one another. What, pray tell, were they protesting that the media found so difficult to describe? Here's what: poverty in an era of great concentrated wealth; corporate welfare; globalization through the WTO, NAFTA, and the

World Bank; corrupt money in politics; bloated military budgets; global warming and other ecological degradations; genetically engineered foods without labeling; Occidental Petroleum's plans to drill on the sacred homeland of the U'wa tribe in Colombia; the prison-industrial complex; the widening income gap; sweatshops; the need for mass transit; tobacco industry and its lavish $1,000-a-plate event for "Blue Dog Democrats"; and the giant media conglomerates. Simply put, the entire agenda for progressive liberal politics. In a brief aside, William Booth got it right for the *Washington Post* when he reported that the slogan "Human Need, Not Corporate Greed" served as "a unifying march and rally for the disparate protest movement." The vast majority of the demonstrators were nonviolent, many trained in nonviolent civil disobedience, which has a great American tradition. Some were deliberately provocative of the police, but then press reports pointed to some pretty severe police overreactions and excessive use of force.

In Philadelphia, 420 people were arrested, mostly on misdemeanor charges. During the postconvention hearings and trials, the great majority of cases were dismissed for lack of evidence or other prosecutorial failings. Consolidated mass trials brought forth widespread testimony of violations of civil liberties and discriminatory police actions. Defense lawyers convinced Municipal Court Judge James M. DeLeon that a group of protesters were arrested simply because they were conveying an unpopular message. The judge threw out the misdemeanor charges against five protesters. In an especially egregious abuse, police arrested John Sellers and Terrence McGuckin of the Ruckus Society, singled them out as ringleaders, charged them with a combined total of twenty-one misdemeanors, and set bail at an unheard of $1 million and $500,000, respectively. Later, the prosecution withdrew the case against Sellers, and McGuckin was acquitted of most of his alleged misdemeanors. The arrests of these men constituted, in Sellers's words, "a war on dissent." They were kept in jail until the convention was over, which was the point of these "preventive detention" arrests. Someday there may be a law review article on these mass arrests, the costs imposed on a judiciary that found them baseless, and the suits for damages filed against the city by those arrested for violation of their rights. But in another city, the same thing will happen and cost the taxpayers millions of dollars—all to relearn that we have free speech, the right to assemble, and the right to petition our government.

There is an undeniable pathos associated with these rallies and demonstrations, and the power structures know that these "we protest and demand" rallies are harmless venting of steam. I spoke at one such rally, on July 29 at JFK Park, next to Philadelphia City Hall, that focused on demanding universal health care and an end to the HMO tyrannies over patients, physicians, and nurses.

Rallies and marches were the mode of protests of the nineteenth century, and they still are today. In the meantime, giant corporations have accumulated all kinds of modern technologies, techniques, and manipulations to exercise their influence. There is a huge imbalance between the forces of democracy and the forces of plutocracy, and it is increasing, along with the alienation, withdrawal, and powerlessness of ever-increasing numbers of people. All this results in low voter turnout and more powerful corporate influence.

Ted Hayes, an advocate for the homeless, was proposing a detailed Marshall Plan for the homeless around the country. He invited Mr. Gore to go two blocks from the Staples Center—the Democratic National Convention site—to visit the Dome Village homeless encampment, but with no success. He shouldn't have been surprised. What he wanted to say to Mr. Gore was: "Don't just come into our neighborhood and pretend we aren't here. It would be an incredible gesture for these super-rich to walk over the two blocks and say it is time to take the hand of the homeless with some real solutions, but not give them a handout. Hold a news conference with us. Do something."

What effect does this all have? In a decorous and orderly forum in late July in Cleveland, the Gore campaign resoundingly rejected each and every progressive proposal offered before the Democratic Party's platform committee. The challenge came from a newly constituted Progressive Caucus, led by Congressman Dennis J. Kucinich, California State Senator Tom Hayden, and Los Angeles civil rights attorney and radio commentator Gloria Allred. They were hardly extreme ideas. Platform rules require fifteen concurring members of the same 180-member committee to allow a debate on any amendments. The progressives could not muster more than five votes on any of the following: universal health care for the entire population; fair trade, not slave trade, which included requirements for decent working conditions and minimum pay along with environmental safeguards; narrowing the gap between rich and poor by eliminating tax breaks to corporations that pay "below living wages"; opposing "fast track" authority for trade agreements and democratizing the World Trade Organization tribunals; a moratorium on the death penalty and the unworkable, provocative, costly missile defense system. No discussion was permitted, no dissenting reports issued. The Gore forces were so imperiously dominant that Gloria Allred couldn't obtain the fifteen votes for a discussion. "People wouldn't even look up at me," she recounted. "They talk about a big tent," declared Ohio Congressman Dennis J. Kucinich, "but this tent just got a bit smaller." Tom Hayden tried to appeal to their political antennae, saying that the platform "will send liberal Democrats running to Nader's ticket" and warning that the platform, as approved, could damage Gore's support from labor unions. So whose interests, or monetary contributions, were being served here? After the session ended, Kucinich noted that these proposals by the progressives actually enjoyed majority or near majority support among the people. He called them "mainstream issues." Lila Garrett, president of Southern California Americans for Democratic Action, was more pointed, saying, "When it comes to the people's programs we are dangerously close to sounding like Republicans." Once again, what Jim Clarke, secretary of the California Democratic Party, acidly referred to as the "Democratic wing of the Democratic Party" got the back of the hand by the DLC-dominated Democrats who knew that progressives had nowhere to go and had to swallow hard and bear it.

Listening to accounts of this platform meeting and the sharply deteriorating vistas of the Democratic Party that it reflected brought back memories of the liberals' arch-reactionary—Richard M. Nixon. Between twenty-seven and thirty-one years ago, President Nixon put forth a national minimum incomes plan as a start in the abolition of poverty in America. Congress rejected it, and the comprehensive national health insurance plan he offered, and the proposal to emphasize rehabilitation of drug addicts instead of such heavy reliance on incarceration. With glowing words, Nixon signed into law the Occupational Safety and Health Agency, the National Environmental Protection Act, NEPA, and legislation creating the Environmental Protection Agency and the Consumer Product Safety Commission. Nixon sent legislation to Congress that would have given the District voting representation in Congress—a goal verbally supported by the Democrats but never backed by any serious campaign during the past three decades. Would any Democratic politician in 1970 ever have predicted that Richard Nixon would be a favorable standard for comparison with today's party leaders? History allows us to discern the long, deep slide into the political pits that is obscured by daily coverage.

Not surprisingly, the forty-eight-page Democratic platform was a model of avoiding both the spiraling power of big business and the economic disconnect between the rich and the rest of us. This is the party that abjectly surrendered for eight years to the super-profitable auto industry on fuel efficiency, safety, and pollution control—jeopardizing the global environment that Al Gore so feels for—sacrificing lives, limbs, and health. Accordingly, the committee rejected a thoughtful plea by one witness to include a sentence advancing auto safety. Fifty years after Western European nations, coming out of the rubble of World War II, provided universal health care for their people, Al Gore's platform described his vision for the world's richest country as "step by step" toward full coverage with no specific attainment date.

Page after page of the platform became a conceit of self-congratulation about the "prosperity" of the previous eight years. Credit was taken for quantitative economic expansions and their consequent public revenues, as if the coincidental technology boom of the nineties was a result rather than a cause. The document declared the party's intention to move ahead on many fronts. "You ain't seen nothing yet" was the ironic slogan, which Republicans used to their advantage. Efforts that a future Gore administration promised to initiate recalled very similar generalities long ignored in the Clinton platforms.

Omitted from any caressing lip service was a tribute to the Democratic Party's enlarging list of unmentionables—consumer protection, exploitation of the taxpaying poor, the destructive war on drugs, protection of the civil justice system and reform of the criminal justice system, solar and other renewable energy, doing something about corporate crime and corporate welfare, and, above all, supporting ways to encourage the people's participation in government. Without mobilizing the political and civic energies of the citizenry, even with the best of intentions, the Democrats cannot deliver. So long as they continue to reward the very power brokers whose avarice contributed to the destitution and perpetuated social injustice, the Democrats might as well be Republicans.

When it was time for the Democrats to have their convention, the marchers were again trying to get the attention of the media. Logistically they were helped by an ACLU lawsuit that persuaded U.S. District Judge Gary Feess to deter the Los Angeles Police Department from keeping protesters very far from the delegates. This is a common technique used by mayors and city police to render protesters invisible and demoralized. Judge Feess's ruling optimistically stated: "When it's convenience versus the First Amendment, convenience loses every time." Well, at least in his sensitive judgment.

Among the marches and gatherings were the Ministers Against Global Injustice—a new coalition of African-American ministers from around the nation that organizes communities of color to oppose international trade agreements that deplete African economies and weaken domestic inner cities. They aim to represent "those bearing the brunt of the adverse effects of globalization." Their rally was addressed by TransAfrica's Randall Robinson (see Appendix A) and Representative Maxine Waters. Then there was the National Chicano Moratorium Committee's "deport the two-party system" rally and a "beach party" sponsored by Global Exchange and other groups that "want to make the Democrats aware that people they say they represent—workers, immigrants, environmentalists—are locked out of the convention." Students Against Sweatshops, anti–death penalty and prison reform organizations, and Peace Action associations also made their presence known outside the convention.

Hugh Jackson, writing for the Las Vegas weekly *City Life,* compared what was going on inside and outside: "The ideas forwarded within the party convention's security fences were tired. The enthusiasm, the passion and hell, for that matter, the intellectual firepower outside those fences were far more intense than anything on display while party hacks and party hack wannabes delivered focus group tested sound bites within." In demonstration after demonstration, Jackson observed, the protesters' message "was completely ignored by the media," except, it seems, "when they're getting the shit beat out of them by baton-wielding helmeted troops." While inside, he added, "Money and inertia have put a stranglehold on the party."

At the Shadow Convention in Philadelphia, I chatted with Ben Cohen of Ben & Jerry's. There I also met Jonathan Kozol and Jim Wallis. These three gentlemen represent what the party should be all about—Cohen for socially responsible business practices and his activism for a reduced military budget delivering a Peace Dividend, Kozol for his three decades of striving for genuine educational reforms for poor children through stunningly graphic books and articles, and Pastor Wallis for mobilizing the religious community around issues of economic justice, disarmament, racism, and helping inner-city youth. Mr. Wallis, author of *The Soul of Politics,* earlier that spring joined with other members of the clergy in an appeal to both Gore and Bush and received no response to their broad-based, hands-on program of community revival and reconciliation.

In his acceptance speech at the convention, Al Gore surprised the DLC crowd with his announcement that, besides being his "own man," he would fight "for the people, not the powerful," and then he named the poll-tested industries of least popularity—big oil, big insurance, and big drug companies—that he would counter on becoming president. Immediately, his polls surged and my polls declined. Immediately, the big businesses named started making their calls, especially to running mate Joseph Lieberman, who spent the next few days reassuring these indignant callers that Gore was, of course, pro-business. Bob Davis of the *Wall Street Journal* wrote a remarkable article less than a week after the convention recounting how Senator Lieberman was telling business that Gore didn't really mean what he said. Gore's words, embedded in the solemnity of an acceptance speech before tens of millions of Americans, were just "impassioned rhetoric," said his number two. And on that forked-tongue note, to be sounded again and again, the Gore-Lieberman ticket was formally launched for the drive to Election Day.

Two

THE MORPHING OF THE DEMOCRATS

Back in Winsted, Connecticut, when I was growing up, the family conversations around the dinner table were about public affairs and what regular citizens could do about them. My parents would take us to town meetings and point out the active townspeople who were challenging, urging, and proposing ideas to the selectmen, as the elected officials were called. Whether it was my mother reading us passages from history when we came home from school for lunch, or my father's vigorous discussions with the customers in our family restaurant-bakery, the emphasis was very much on citizens doing something and people taking on the big boys, be they in government or in business. One of my mother's favorite sayings to us was, "I believe it's you," whenever we complained about people in authority, meaning we had to do something about it and not expect others to make the changes or address the complaints.

One day—I must have been about ten—my father took me for a ride. He drove around our town of ten thousand people—a typical New England mill town crossed by two rivers that helped power the factories—to point out what local philanthropists had given to their community. As we drove past the high school, the town library, the first hospital in the county, and a park, he described the people who made these services possible in the late nineteenth and early twentieth century. Then came the main point of the drive. He told me that by his estimate there were at least one hundred other affluent families over the past hundred years who could have provided something of comparable value through their donations or bequests. Imagine how much better a community it would have become, and imagine how much less of a community it would be, were it not for the half dozen benefactors who made their money last, decade after decade, for the townspeople.

I was brought up to aspire to advance justice as an active citizen, not as an elected politician. Not that there was anything wrong with running for office. It was just that my parents instilled in me a sense of social justice that wore no party or political brand. My graduation speech in the eighth grade was devoted to the life and accomplishments of John Muir, the great naturalist whose efforts led directly to the establishment of Yosemite National Park in California. And in high school, I became absorbed by the history of the muckrakers and crusaders of the early 1900s—Ida Tarbell, Upton Sinclair, Jeannette Rankin, Lincoln Steffens, and others absorbed my interest. I was fascinated by bold and persistent outsiders constantly challenging the systems of power. My father used to take me the short distance on Main Street from our restaurant to the county court to watch the judges, lawyers, and jurors perform their duties. Watching this precious drama unfold, I knew I wanted to be a lawyer. In my youthful idealism, being a lawyer meant representing the downtrodden, fighting for just causes, and laboring as a voice of dissent—again from the outside.

I mention this personal background because I never intended to run for elective office. I have always been an engaged citizen in a democracy, fighting to make things better. Find a cause, write a book, article, or pamphlet, expose the abuse, and motivate people to demand change. It worked for Thomas Paine, Thomas Jefferson, and Frederick Douglass, as it worked again and again in American history. The outsiders taking on the insiders. The abolitionists, the suffragists, the union effort, the farmer-progressive movement were all outsiders who transformed this country more than any president, as did those who came after them in the past century to lead the fight for civil rights, consumer protection, and environmental regulation.

So when I took the bus from Connecticut to Washington in 1963 to bring the reckless, unsafe, hyper-horsepower-minded automobile industry under the rule of law, it was a large ambition, to be sure, but one grounded in my reading of the best of American history. Which also meant I believed it was doable, though clearly a very uphill struggle.

I had lost too many friends in high school to highway crashes, too many college classmates lost their promising lives in collisions between vehicles that were unsafe at any speed. On the road with the truck drivers, who picked me up hitchhiking many thousands of miles, we came upon grisly pileups with some occupants very silent and others screaming for help. The more I learned about the simple safety features—seat belts, collapsible steering columns, padded dash panels, stronger door latches, head restraints, break-away rearview mirrors, less injurious windshields—that could make crashes survivable, the more I was driven to press for mandatory vehicle safety standards.

My book *Unsafe at Any Speed* came out in November 1965, and by September 1966, Congress had passed and President Lyndon Johnson had signed the Motor Vehicle and Highway Safety Acts, bringing the giant auto industry under federal regulation. In those ten months, the book created an uproar in Detroit. General Motors even hired private detectives to get "some dirt" on me to discredit my message. These peerless gumshoes were caught following me into the U.S. Senate. The Senate subcommittee chaired by Connecticut Senator Abraham Ribicoff was holding hearings on auto safety for which I was an unpaid consultant and a possible witness. General Motors executives were summoned by the subcommittee to a congressional hearing room packed with media and forced to apologize for hiring the detectives. The momentum from this widely publicized sleuthing carried the legislation through Congress in record time. Congress and the president, under regular media scrutiny, responded to overwhelming evidence that safer cars could greatly diminish highway casualties. Isn't this the way our political system is supposed to work?

More than a million lives have been saved and many millions of injuries prevented or reduced in severity over the past thirty-five years because of implementation of these laws. The system worked—government responded to an engaged citizenry, and the fatality rate declined from 5.6 deaths per hundred million vehicle miles in 1966 to 1.6 in 2000. The sixties and early seventies were the years of the "outsiders," when one civic movement after another was banging on the doors of the power structures and demanding social justice on a broad spectrum of subjects.

By conventional aggregate economic yardsticks, the sixties and nineties were prosperous decades, though in both periods there were serious consumer, environmental, and racial problems. Too many people then and now felt that nothing could be done about these situations and the powers that be, but active citizens and groups disagreed. The latter got much further in the sixties and seventies. In about ten years, enough determined citizens made the impossible happen. Jim Crow laws were replaced by civil rights laws. Conservative lawmakers, such as Senator Warren Magnuson, the powerful chairman of the Senate Commerce Committee, changed from being business lobbies' senators to consumer and environmental champions and passed a series of laws that regulated polluters and reckless manufacturers. Washington declared a war on poverty even while being immersed in the brutal and draining Vietnam War. Medicare and Medicaid were passed to provide health insurance coverage for the elderly and impoverished. Corporations were confronted with the regulatory rule of law and could no longer recklessly pollute or escape accountability for faulty products. Companies had to share such decision making with public regulators in a more open, standards-setting process.

Not a year went by without dozens of new citizen action groups opening their doors in the nation's capital and around the country. There was a heady atmosphere that abuses could be remedied, that power could be more widely shared, that democracy could be, in the word of the day, "participatory." Newspapers, magazines, and television stations, along with new community media, covered events as if "the whole world was watching."

Yet somehow that spirit, little by little, slipped away, and big business stepped in again to seize more influence on our government. Over the course of my work in Washington, both Democrats and Republicans have drawn so close to the monied, corporate interests that the citizens are shut out.

This is why I ran for president.

As the sixties unfurled their turbulent times, leading into the Nixon administration, the corporate grandees seemed at a loss, until they received one August day in 1971 what has come to be known as the "Powell memorandum." Lewis Powell, a corporate lawyer in Richmond, Virginia, and soon to be a Justice of the U.S. Supreme Court, delivered his analysis of the power balance in Washington and pronounced it a crisis for big business. The forces of reform had brought many industries under a variety of regulations, and business was on the defensive. Powell urged a fundamental expansion and strengthening of the corporate lobbying apparatus, using some of the very techniques that the consumer, environmental, and other citizen interests were deploying. These included corporate think tanks, aggressive use of the media, advancing business views on campus and in the curriculum, greater involvement in elections, and a mobilization of chief executives. It was time, Powell said, to mount an energetic counterattack to those who, he believed, would subvert the free enterprise system.

At the same time, two major "public servants" were urging the same. Treasury Secretary John Connally (he from the oil patch) and Federal Reserve Chairman Arthur Burns urged business leaders led by John Harper of Alcoa and Frederick Borch of General Electric to get their act together. In 1972 the Business Roundtable, composed only of big-time CEOs, was established. Many power lunches ensued, not only to eat beef but also to beef up the entire Washington infrastructure and outreach for the ascending power of the business sector.

The corporate government was determined to overwhelm the political government and bring it to bay as a service operation for business interests, on the one hand, and as close to an inactive manager of corporate law enforcement programs as Money Inc. can make possible, on the other hand.

It took a while to entrench this counterforce. These were the Nixon years, the Ford years, preoccupied with what was seen then as virulent inflation, price surges, an energy crisis, and Watergate. The momentum from the sixties and early seventies was not spent; the Democrats controlled Congress and were still effectively Democrats. Moreover, Jimmy Carter was campaigning around the country in 1975 and 1976 saying he would appoint the kind of regulators that I would approve of and that one of his top domestic priorities would be the creation of a consumer protection agency (CPA), another top item on our platform. He reiterated these points in August 1976, when he invited me to visit him in Plains, Georgia, during which time I joined the softball game between the Carterites and the press corps—as an umpire.

After Jimmy Carter was elected president, he did appoint some very good people to head some of these agencies, notably the Food and Drug Administration, the Federal Trade Commission, and the auto safety agency. He took on as his White House consumer adviser the estimable Esther Peterson, of labor, women's, and human rights fame. Ms. Peterson knew her way around Washington, having been Lyndon Johnson's assistant secretary of labor and consumer adviser. Carter and Peterson made the consumer protection agency bill their number-one agenda item for her White House tenure. There were 60 votes for the CPA in the Senate, but the leadership wanted the House to pass it first, where the vote was expected to be closer. Indeed it was.

With Jimmy Carter scarcely lifting a hand to press the bill through the House (he was all over Congress to pass natural gas deregulation, however), consumer and labor groups were defeated on February 8, 1978, by a vote of 227 to 189. Fully 101 Democrats, including many liberals, such as Tom Foley and Pat Schroeder, defected to the side of the Business Roundtable men and the largest business coalition to date opposing a bill. Because the CPA's mission was not regulatory, but rather advocating consumers' interests, just about every industry imaginable felt the potential heat of this tiny protective agency upsetting the cushy relationships they had greased with these so-called regulators.

The business coalition met regularly at the Madison Hotel in Washington to plot strategy, raise campaign money, and wildly exaggerate both the size and authority of the CPA with their media propaganda. Their victory emboldened them to suppose that even a Democratic Congress and White House could not withstand their extreme demands. For after all, these regulatory agencies were hardly prosecutorial zealots and consumers had been paying the price for the lack of law and order in this realm. One did not have to look back on the CPA's defeat and the unwillingness, over my objections, of its backers to try again the following year to sense that this loss represented the turning of the tide in favor of the business lobbies. The Democrats were faltering, not just with their reactionary southern wing but even among their more mainstream liberal members. The defeat of California dynamo Phil Burton for House Majority Leader in 1976 by a vote of 148 to 147 to conservative Texas Democrat Jim Wright occurred because liberals like

Max Baucus and Barbara Mikulski supported Wright against this effective, brilliant, and compassionate leader.

Temptation had even more lasting ambitions in the form of Tony Coehlo (D-California), who around 1980 persuaded the Democratic Party that it could raise piles of money from the same big-business contributors as did the Republicans. This was the beginning of the end for progressive Democrats. As the man in charge of raising money for House Democrats, Coehlo, and his associates, dove into this gigantic money pit big time, and the cash register rang louder and louder. PACs were proliferating by the month, and the mogul mint was responding, plying both parties with its lucre in the ultimate two-party hedge. It did not take much observational acuity for corporate lobbyists to sense that the pro-labor, New Deal Democratic Party was dying.

The labor law reform bill of 1977–78 was memorable in this regard. A mild attempt to reduce the barriers to union organizing, it simplified the election rules of the National Labor Relations Board, stiffened penalties on employers who violated existing labor laws, and provided "equal time" for unions to "address employees on company time and property prior to a representation election." The bill was at the top of the legislative agenda of the AFL-CIO, which mounted a major lobbying campaign. In October 1977, the bill sailed through the House by a vote of 257 to 163 and headed toward the Senate, where there was a Democratic majority of 61 to 39. There a filibuster led by Republican senators Orrin Hatch and Richard Lugar prevailed. The cloture effort to end the filibuster lost 58 to 41, in June 1978, two votes short of the 60 senators needed to close off debate. A massive business lobbying effort led to this defeat. The bill was sent back to the Labor Committee and, significantly, was not revived the following year or thereafter. This taught organized business that there was no fight-back capability or willpower by the Democrats—a lack of stamina that a trade association lobbyist can sniff with the sensitivity of a bloodhound.

The collapse of the Democrats' resolve became even more acute when the Reaganites arrived in town on January 20, 1981. Ronald Reagan had three missions: cut taxes, especially on corporations and the wealthy; greatly enlarge the defense budget; and deregulate companies based on industry wish lists. Even though the Democrats had lost several Senate seats, they were still confident that their stereotype of a light-headed Reagan would find Washington rough going. Tip O'Neill, the House speaker and veteran Boston politician, conveyed this condescension when he said that Reagan was in "the major leagues" now. If he underestimated Reagan, O'Neill overestimated his Democrats, including himself. It was not long before the Democrats outsmarted themselves, concluding that since a Reagan supply-side tide through Congress could not be stopped, they should let the president have his massive tax cuts, his massive budget deficits, his massive military dollars and civilian program cuts. With enough rope, the Republicans would hang themselves. That was the rationalization for the incredible surrender of the congressional Democrats, buffeted by poll-driven fear and the Iranian-hostage-induced Reagan landslide. Reagan's program passed easily, leading William Greider to reflect in *The Nation* twenty years later: "Ronald Reagan's great legislative triumph of 1981 destabilized federal fiscal policy for nearly two decades, creating the massive structural deficits that were not finally extinguished until a few years ago."

In Greider's famous private interviews with David Stockman, Reagan's budget chief, the number cruncher said, "Do you realize the greed that came to the forefront? The hogs were really feeding." Greider noted that both "Democrats and Republicans engaged in a furious bidding war to see which party could deliver more tax breaks and other boodle to the special interest hogs (Republicans won, but the Dems gave it a good try)." The Democratic Party was fast losing its soul, morphing into the Republicans to form one corporate party feeding on the same corporate cash, but still sprouting two heads, each wearing different makeup. The parties, after all, did have to present a different face to the voting public. The corporate takeover of politics is a daily accretion, a relentlessly driven motivation, given the endless rewards for such aggressions.

During the Reagan years we had a president whose hero was John Wayne—another actor—whose traits Reagan emulated in his official addresses of state. No president ever made more speeches condemning government deficits, and no president came within a light-year of producing more red ink. Indeed, his cumulative increase in the national debt was far larger than all the debt piled up by all previous presidents from George Washington forward. And here was a president who twice said—as a candidate and as president—that nuclear missiles once launched could always be recalled. And that 85 percent of air pollution comes from trees. His penchant for spurious anecdotes (remember the welfare queen who never existed) taught us how truly passive the press can be.

For all his surface charm, soft voice, and angled head, Reagan allowed his fervid turncoat ideology (he was once a liberal) to transform him often into a cruel man with a smile. Rigidly against government regulation of bad business, he furthered the business regulation of government. Applied to the health and safety regulatory responsibilities of the federal government, this political catechism can leave people defenseless—letting them die on the highways, in the workplace, and through toxic exposure in their environment. One of Reagan's first acts in this regard was to repeal what was known as the air bag standard, just before these dual-inflation lifesavers were about to go into motor vehicles. A few months earlier, Reagan had been campaigning in Michigan and accused the air bag of impeding the freedom of Americans. (In a sense, he was right—it impeded them from going through the windshield.)

Appointees take their cue from their boss in the White House, and what happened to 250,000 workers exposed daily to toxic hazards in their factories, mines, and foundries all over America is a case in point. For more than a decade, the Centers for Disease Control (CDC) in Atlanta had been collecting data on these workers. As they completed their massive study, the physicians remembered their calling. How could they know of the potential or real danger to these workers and not notify them? So the CDC asked Reagan's Office of Management and Budget (OMB) for funds to pay for certified, return receipt notification to all of these workers of what was in their workplace and suggesting that they might wish to see their doctor for precautionary screening or diagnosis. In 1984, the OMB turned them down flat.

Now comes a parallelism that has become all too frequent. I took this story to Walter Mondale's presidential campaign at the highest staff levels. Look, I said, the Republicans had their chance and blew it. What about Mr. Mondale going to a blue-collar industrial city such as Cleveland or Pittsburgh and, before a large assemblage of workers in the city square, making a major policy statement on the ravages of occupational trauma and disease and the enormous mortality and morbidity that occur each year? Graphic descriptions of corporate neglect could be included—such as coal miners' lung diseases, refinery explosions, injuries in chicken-processing plants— and the possible Mondale clincher:

> Let me tell you how callous this Republican administration can be. The Reagan government does not even have the decency to notify workers innocent of their peril after using their tax dollars to document their daily health-threatening conditions. Many of these workers were older veterans who fought for their country. But Mr. Reagan and his associates, who have anesthetized OSHA for four years, will not fight for their health. I call on President Reagan to spend the postage money and notify these workers and I am releasing the names of all the companies and their addresses where these workers labor for their livelihood.

The tepid Mondale campaign needed a steak with a sizzle. This was a way they could get some of the Reagan Democrats back.

The reply by the Mondale campaign was no thanks. Why, I asked? Because the campaign was on record pledging no increases in the federal budget—not even to save or lengthen many lives with less burden on federal Medicare, Medicaid, and other social service budgets as a result.

A short time later, I held a news conference, packed with media, to release the materials and names of the companies. National television, radio, and newspaper coverage ensued. A lead editorial in the *New York Times* strongly condemned the Reagan administration. The following day, local reporters made it another front-page story by visiting many of these companies in their communities. Still, President Reagan stood firm, as stalwart and determined as John Wayne. The workers were notified only indirectly, by the press, not by the physicians whose good work their tax dollars supported. There was a difference between these two modes of communication, but not between the two parties.

Following this, in 1984 my associates and I made our first determined effort to broaden the agenda between the two presidential candidates. We called this project The Difference. Our main office was located in downtown Washington, D.C. We had seven full-time people, led by Joan Claybrook, working the ideas. We also staffed field offices in six key states. As usual, the Republican and Democratic candidates—in this case Reagan and Mondale—managed to narrow the number of issues they would advance. The Difference challenged the candidates to take stands and debate subjects such as energy and consumer protection.

We furthered these issues by traveling across about a dozen key electoral states, holding news conferences, meeting with editorial boards, and fielding people in these areas to organize citizen and labor groups from many areas of community activity. It did not work. Sure, there was some good press coverage, but the candidates ignored our efforts and made it look easy doing so. No matter how much the hordes of reporters on the campaign trail grumbled, they and their editors were willing to be trapped by the routines and rituals of the candidates. "The boys on the bus" humdrummed their way across the country with the candidates and endured the numbing redundancy of photo opportunity crowds shorn of any participation beyond their applause or occasional heckling. Anyone trying to nourish a more responsive campaign from the outside was viewed as an interloper by the reporters, most of whom frowned on such attempts.

Voters were expected to be polled, to be spectators and to vote. Their participation in the whole election process as an active civic force shaping the substance and tone of the campaign—why, that wasn't the way it was done.

During the eighties, it became ever more clear that the Democrats were losing the will to fight. Business money pouring into party coffers melded into the retreat from progressive roots and then into an electoral tactic that argued for defeating Republicans by taking away their issues and becoming more like them.

The energy to strike out on a path extending the great American progressive tradition was quickly leaking out of the Democrats like a tire losing air. The party would address its Democratic critics by defining itself by the worst Republicans instead of becoming better. "Do you know how bad the Republicans are on this subject?" would be the standard reply. Buying into the lesser-of-two-evils argument simply meant that every four years both parties would get worse and be rewarded for it. Abhorring the Republicans, progressive voters had indeed nowhere to go. I noticed how the political language began to change. Democratic candidates almost never criticized abuses of corporate power or concentrated wealth depriving millions of workers of their just rewards. There was no modern language update for what Theodore Roosevelt called the "malefactors of great wealth" or what Franklin Roosevelt called "the economic royalists." References to "the poor" or to "justice" were out of style in major addresses by Democrats. The press chased Michael Dukakis around the country trying to get him to admit that he was a "liberal" during his 1988 presidential race. Finally, a few days before the election, they cornered him in the Central Valley of California and he confessed—grudgingly.

I knew when Democrats ran away from the word "liberal" and began to use the word "neoliberal" as an adjective—as in "neoconservative"—that this semantic shift reflected a fundamental abandonment. The storied history of liberalism and its achievements in our country receded from contemporary memory under the onslaught of aggressive conservatives, their think tanks, and associated media. These corporatists in conservative garb pranced arrogantly, sometimes sneeringly, on the public stage, as if they had much historical record to brag about. Self-described conservatives (Tories) opposed the Revolutionary War and with their business cohorts maintained slavery, opposed women's right to vote, and pitted their power against workers trying to organize trade unions. They sided with the banks and the railroads against the rising farmer populist revolt in the late 1880s and continued their war against this most fundamental movement for political and economic reforms for the next twenty-five years. In the twentieth century, reform after reform initiated by liberals found conservatives and the dominant business community consistently arrayed in opposition. These included forward progress in civil rights, civil liberties, consumer and environmental protection, Medicare, Medicaid, workplace safety, labor rights and women's equality rights such as equal pay for equal work and nondiscrimination in the marketplace. No matter how much these great initiatives improved the health, safety, and economic well-being of the American people, the corporatist-conservatives and their business lobbies never relented in their blocking, delaying, diluting, or repealing of any reform that was vulnerable to their reactionary influences. This intransigence was not always the case. Conservative legislators like Senator Robert Taft supported the GI Bill of Rights and public housing. For the most part, however, they were on the wrong side of our history.

If I had to pick a date for the beginning of the latest cycle of giant business's big-time resurgence, it would be in the last eighteen months of the Carter administration. Basically, the combination of oil price surges, gasoline lines, and inflation panicked the Carterites and froze any programs and policies that business lobbies viewed as inimical. The elections of 1980 were great tidings for this lobby. In addition to Reagan's victory, a number of key senators—Warren Magnuson (Washington), Frank Church (Idaho), Gaylord Nelson (Wisconsin), and George McGovern (South Dakota)—lost their seats, Democrats who championed issues centered on abuses by companies through detailed and publicized public hearings and legislative actions.

An unanticipated pattern began to emerge in that turnaround period between 1979 and 1981. It was an incremental pattern that was unforseen by most and therefore not given to forestalling. Emboldened corporations on the ascendancy observed their opponents inside and outside of government moving from resistance to retreat, losing even the sense of trumpeting their successes of the prior fifteen years in making America a better and safer place to live. Once on the defensive, it is very hard to go on the offensive. It was not lost on the numerous trade associations and corporate law firms that senators, representatives, leaders of labor unions, and citizen groups were experiencing ebbing energies. Unlike Ronald Reagan, either they no longer knew who they were or were confused about where they should be going. Historians often describe the engines of such ebbs and flows between contesting constituencies to be the rise of new ideas, dogmas, ideologies, or perceptions. In this case, it was more a flood of propaganda repeated with daily determination by business-sponsored institutions (the American Enterprise Institute, the Heritage Foundation) through reports, conferences, and media programs attacking regulations and other allegedly "failed" government programs while touting so-called free-market solutions for what traditionally have been public responsibilities.

The doctrines of corporate supremacy filled a concentrating media, itself increasingly corporatized, led by those propaganda bullhorns—the *Wall Street Journal*'s editorial pages and *Forbes* magazine. Instead of refining their programs, many established liberals were busy reinventing themselves as corporatizers to go with the Reaganite flows, getting along by going along. More and more business money flowed into their coffers as a continuing reward for their transformations. Noticing political decay, a weakening democracy, and an overwhelmed civil society in Washington, D.C., is not the stuff of headlines. But if they are not noticed and aggregated, illusion sets in and citizen groups find themselves working harder for less and less progress and justice within an ambiance of lowered expectations.

In between their daily struggles, retreats, defeats, and occasional defensive victories, citizen groups might have paused to reflect on how many liberal Democrats, once defenders against both the incursions of large corporations and arbitrary government violations of civil liberties and civil rights, were replaced by members of their party who took up the cudgels for capital punishment, for weakening habeas corpus, for corporate prisons, for the failed war on drugs, for the secret evidence practices of the INS and its runaway powers against due process of law. These replacements included Bill Clinton and Al Gore. While there remained some stalwart liberals in the grand tradition, such as Congressman Henry Waxman (D-California), the "new guard" reflected a political shell seduced by corporate money and overtaken by corporatists who viewed government as a "large accounts receivables" for business interests and as an instrument to be deployed against its own people.

What happened is the triumph of what Jefferson called "the monied interests." Here are a few examples from many that illustrate the chain-link consequences of this power grid.

In the eighties, *Washington Post* and *New York Times* reporters started responding to our reports and testimony exposing business abuses by saying, "We don't cover reports." That was not entirely accurate. They did cover the reports and studies of the Heritage Foundation and the American Enterprise Institute because these right-wing groups had allies in the White House and Congress. Unlike previous years, our consumer and environmental associations did not have such governmental support. Therefore, the major press deemed them not newsworthy.

My recollection of one such interchange involved a young, congenial *New York Times* reporter, the late Nathanial Nash. In the mideighties we tried again and again to raise the warning signals among the Washington press corps about the looming savings and loan collapse. After one news conference, I called Mr. Nash, who was covering banking matters, and asked why the *Times* was not there. Sighing, he said there would be coverage if we could show that there was support for our positions among influential members of Congress. It was not sufficient that the *Times* and *Post* were receiving these early alerts to a major, long-lasting savings and loan story that both were late in covering. I advised Mr. Nash that with this newsworthiness standard, he was likely to miss some important scoops over time. Hewing to power journalism, however, was not a reporter's discretion—it usually came from the editors and publishers.

The chain link extended also to the trade unions. Weakened by a shrinking membership and a shirking leadership, the unions' national headquarters in Washington spent the eighties looking for crumbs. They convinced themselves of their comparative powerlessness; some even supported a weakening of the federal regulatory laws to head off a worse shredding by business groups. Consumer and environmental communities fought hard and managed to block this corporate agenda, however. There were other noticeable defaults, most remarkably the large labor unions' posture on their most hated law, the notorious Taft-Hartley Act of 1947, which obstructed the formation of new trade unions and hampered the efforts of existing unions. Imagine the business community being chatteled by a similar law and not mounting a relentless, annual drive for repeal. Well, most Americans under fifty years old, and not related to the labor movement, have never heard of this statutory grip on American workers, unprecedented in any other Western democracy.

In 1997, the fiftieth anniversary of Taft-Hartley, I had an idea. Why not have the trade unions plan a whole series of events—marches, town meetings, rallies—to mobilize their base and educate the citizenry about the impact of this law on their wages and living standards and their freedom to organize? After all, the majority of American workers were making less in inflation-adjusted dollars and working longer hours than workers had in 1979 or

1973, despite a growing overall economy. I called two reporters covering labor for the *Washington Post* and the *New York Times* and asked them three months ahead of the anniversary month if they were planning on writing about Taft-Hartley, given the penchant for anniversary journalism these days. Both of them said they would if there were events to cover. So I wrote to a dozen national union leaders and urged them to plan events. Nothing doing. A few said they had other, more practical priorities. The second-highest AFL-CIO official, Richard Trumka, sympathized but said nothing was planned. What could be more practical than trying to repeal nine Taft-Hartley provisions that obstructed organizing by American workers?

The chain link erodes expectation levels and signals weakness among labor's allies in Congress. Intimidated by both corporate PACs and the giant corporate trade associations, these legislators helped to take the fight out of the unions, even though many of them could not win reelection without union money and get-out-the-vote efforts. Union membership in the private economy continues to slide—now under 10 percent of the workforce, the lowest in sixty years.

The chain link reaches into the civic community. Having lost key committee chairs and the Congress to the Republicans and Republicrats, some Washington-based environmental groups persuaded themselves that they could maneuver or outsmart polluting companies through private deals with them. One such deal, involving the Natural Resources Defense Council (NRDC) and their West Coast representative Ralph Cavanagh, resulted in California's electricity deregulation fiasco. This idea was the brainstorm of John Bryson, CEO of the Southern California Edison Company and NRDC. The latter thought that competition in generating and distributing electricity would bring more conservation, more renewable energy on-line, and cheaper prices for consumers. Deregulation unanimously passed the California legislature in 1996 with very little public awareness or discussion. Our attempt in 1998 to repeal parts of this bad law by a statewide referendum—Proposition 9—failed by a wide margin due to a $45 million television campaign by the utilities. Having given up on the prospect of regulation, California turned over regulatory power to the electric companies, their holding companies, and the large out-of-state power generators that have turned electricity into a speculative commodity. The harshest price consequences for consumers and taxpayers have resulted, shaking the state's economy and increasing costs to business. Any regulatory authority to stem this crisis was given up in 1996 to corporate supremacy.

After Clinton's reelection evaporated the notion that the old progressive Bill Clinton (whenever that was) would return, I decided to try two additional tests of the Democrats' resolve. It was May 1997, and Congressmen Bernie Sanders and Peter DeFazio were kind enough to invite me to address the House Progressive Caucus, made up of more than fifty progressive representatives. About six of them showed up. I presented them with nine fully drafted bills that would empower consumers, workers, taxpayers, and voters at virtually no cost to the taxpayer, reminding them that thirty years ago a few lone conservatives in the House had filed their long-shot bills to the amusement of most Democrats. No one is laughing now. Bills filed with a number become a nucleus of discussion and rallying point around the country. They are seeds that nourish an emerging agenda. Their sponsors talk them up, release statements, and attract support from other members of the House, interested columnists and citizen groups, and constituents back home. The cluster of bills was distributed to all the members of the caucus. I waited. Two months passed, six months passed, one year passed, two years passed. Reminders were sent. To date, not one member of the caucus has introduced a single bill. So much for the progressive cream of the crop launching a democracy-empowering agenda, whether ours or their own.

Not long after the meeting with the Progressive Caucus, I had lunch with Steve Grossman, the cochair of the Democratic National Committee. Grossman runs a family business from Massachusetts and probably would have been a John Kennedy Democrat had he been older in 1960. For two hours, my associate John Richard and I plied him with similar empowerment proposals and additional legislation of a more substantive nature in the health and safety, corporate welfare, and corporate crime enforcement arenas. He was wonderfully engaging and said he would take our materials and give them to the DNC's research unit for study and response. Before leaving, I handed Mr. Grossman several copies of a humorous little paperback titled *Dogs Are Smarter Than Republicans*.

A few days later, a DNC staffer called our office and asked if we could spare more copies of the *Dogs* book. We sent them right over. Alas, we're still waiting for a call from the DNC about the rest of the proposals, admittedly none of which were very satirical. Are dogs smarter than Democrats, too?

Even less humorous was the DNC's role in the 1990 reelection of Newt Gingrich. In 1989 members of Congress voted to raise their own salaries 25 percent, always a touchy issue with the citizenry. Neither party wanted this issue to emerge during the 1990 campaign, so, remarkably, they announced an enforcement scheme for a gag order at a joint news conference. Any candidate who used the pay raise topic against an opponent would lose his or her party's campaign funding. It just so happened that one David Worley, a thirty-two-year-old lawyer, was running for the House seat held by Newt Gingrich—easily the Republican most disliked by the Democrats. Worley was a candidate of little budget but great verve, especially for the Georgia Democratic Party. He was breathing down Newt's neck, and Newt knew it. Polls had them running neck and neck.

What was so exciting about the Worley-Gingrich race was not only who was involved but also the rarity of a contested congressional race against an entrenched incumbent. The two parties that always speak so pompously about "our two-party system" have managed to reduce this system down to a one-party domination in about 90 percent of the congressional districts and in many of the states on the Senate side. Worley had one problem—no money for ads on television. Gingrich was all over television, in the news and in his own advertising. In the last weeks of the campaign, Worley asked Tom Foley and the DNC for some television money. He insisted that he had a chance to upset the Democrats' nemesis, the man who caused Speaker Jim Wright to resign from the House. He even went to see Foley in Atlanta when the speaker was in town politicking. But no contributions flowed from the national Democratic kitty. Worley had violated the gag order. He was making the pay raise and the hypocrisy of the Republicans in holding down the minimum wage for millions of Americans a regular and resounding theme of his campaign. Without any television ads to help voters become acquainted with this bright new political light on the horizon, Worley narrowly lost by 950 votes.

Gingrich returned to Washington with a renewed mission to take down another Democratic speaker. And to do this, in 1994 he recruited a candidate, George Nethercutt, funded him, let him press the theme of six-year term limits (then popular in Spokane), and even journeyed there to campaign personally against Foley.

Voters woke up the next morning to hear the astonishing news that Foley had been defeated and, even more portentously, that the Republicans had swept away the Democratic majority and taken control of the House of Representatives. Newt Gingrich replaced Tom Foley as Speaker. This Republican victory was generally credited to Gingrich, who could have been retired in 1990 were it not for the personal and tyrannical pettiness of the Democrats. Turning horizon into myopia, the Democrats were no longer capable even of defeating people from the extreme wing of the Republican Party. They had run out of gas.

Three

CITIZEN CLOSEOUT: THE MORAL IMPERATIVE

Citizen groups, accustomed to some significant victories and the chance to take on the economic vested interests, were being shut out of the process, squeezed out of forums, rendered more voiceless and powerless with each year of rampaging corporatism over elections. There are various ways to illustrate this closing out of the civil society. One way to clarify the merger of business with government is to list the major departments and agencies in Washington, D.C., and simply ask who is the overwhelmingly most powerful influence over each of them. Seasoned reporters and commentators would scarcely be surprised by the following list: Treasury Department and the Federal Reserve (banks), Department of Agriculture (agribusiness), Department of Defense (military weapons companies), Department of the Interior (timber barons and the mining industry), Food and Drug Administration (food and drug companies), Occupational Safety and Health Administration, inside the Department of Labor, no less (corporate employers), General Services Administration (business vendors to the government), NASA (space industries), Federal Aviation Administration (airlines and aircraft manufacturers), and so it goes.

Of course, this has been the case for decades. The difference today is that these agencies have become more symbiotic with their clientele companies, often being led by former executives of these very industries. The difference is also that Congress is far less a countervailing force than a cheerleading crowd. The judiciary, composed of corporatist judges, is more prone to roll over on economic issues. Moreover, industry and commerce have become far more organized, more media-aggressive, and richer at the same time that organized labor's influence had declined as an opposing force across the spectrum of public decision making. When this severe imbalance of power becomes institutionalized, the sovereignty of the people is diminished.

Still, the citizen groups plod on, as if riding a treadmill that keeps slipping further behind. They cling to dwindling hopes: the remaining progressives in Congress, a defensive court victory on the environment, a new Clinton administration in 1993, a major investigative report on national television or in a major newspaper or magazine, a push from Western Europe on global warming or genetic engineering, a successful labor-organizing drive for janitors. It has been said that hope springs eternal, but for these groups, hope has been springing many contemporary leaks. They could never imagine, if told in the 1970s, that the economy was going to double in thirty years yet the problems of energy, poverty, lack of health insurance coverage, inadequate housing, real wages, consumer debt, the savings rate, criminal justice systems, disrepair of public works, family farms, wealth inequality, trade deficits, food safety, and others would either be at a standstill or sliding backward at the beginning of the twenty-first century. All this in a period of restrained inflation, booming corporate profits, surging stock markets, massive capital accumulation (heavily from pension and trust funds), and more recently a period of federal and state government surpluses.

The historic American ideology of continual progress has received its comeuppance, along with the impression that a rising tide lifts all boats. The major political parties have not delivered on their populist responsibilities. Rather, as proxies for big business, they have become the gatekeepers who let the powerful slam the door in the face of the people.

I remember as a student reading the words of Thomas Jefferson regarding how long people should tolerate an unresponsive government. His message was that when the situation becomes intolerable, go into politics and take back the government. This was a message that I resisted, notwithstanding the urgings that I run for elected office as early as 1970. Gore Vidal, no less, wrote an article for *Esquire* in 1971 recommending me as a presidential candidate. George McGovern, the Democratic nominee for president in 1972, called me when his running mate, Senator Thomas Eagleton, withdrew after a biased response to the disclosure that he had received electric shock treatment. McGovern asked if I would be willing to be considered for the vice presidential nomination. I thanked him but said that my role was in the citizen arena. In 1991, Carl Mayer, a New Jersey law professor, and Matthew Rothschild, editor of *The Progressive* in Madison, Wisconsin, repeatedly tried to get me to enter the presidential race. Others added their concurrence. So insistent and so determined were they to start working in New Hampshire that I suggested not officially running in the state's primary but standing as a write-in candidate with a progressive set of mobilizing issues to be discussed in town-meeting formats around the state.

This, of course, did not satisfy them. Nonetheless, hoping I would move later into a real candidacy, they opened a storefront campaign office in Manchester, right next to those of the other primary candidates. Bursting with enthusiastic volunteers, most of whom had little idea of how difficult it was for voters just to get write-in ballots to mark in most precincts, they worked late into the evenings.

The general goal of the campaign was to meet with people in one assembly after another throughout the state to hear and discuss a broad prodemocracy agenda. The subjects were contained in what I called the "Concord Principles," having released them one very cold winter morning on the steps of the state office building. The principles were essentially a "new democracy toolbox" replete with election reforms, such as public funding of elections, more convenient voter registration rules, binding none-of-the-above (NOTA) lines that would cancel that election and order a new election with new candidates if NOTA won the most votes, and twelve-year congressional term limits. The principles also offered simple strategies for consumers, workers, and taxpayers to band together with membership organizations and work for universal health insurance, trade union growth, an end to corporate welfare, renewable energy, and safer food and other products, and to try to avert future perils and injustices on the horizon.

While it is hard to procure a write-in ballot in New Hampshire, it is in other ways an ideal state for this type of personal, grassroots campaigning. Local democratic traditions tend to linger longer in New Hampshire than in most other states. As it is the first primary state in the land, New Hampshire residents like to look over their candidates. It is not unusual, when asked his or her opinion of a presidential candidate, for a New Hampshire voter to answer, "I don't know yet. I've only met him twice."

New Hampshire recalls the old days of campaigning before television sound bites and inaccessible candidates. People in many small towns that are distinct communities with large gathering halls and auditoriums expect the candidates to visit them and stay long enough for some back-and-forth exchanges. The dozens of dark-horse candidates who would be brushed off as nuisances elsewhere find New Hampshirites bemused by their single-issue efforts.

We strove to meet New Hampshirites with our town meeting–style gatherings. The turnout was impressive, and the people often stayed for three hours. Word of mouth works better in this state. The veteran political columnists Jack W. Germond and Jules Witcover, who have covered so many presidential campaigns marked by massive voter indifference that they wrote a book titled *Wake Us Up When It's Over,* started their syndicated column on January 9, 1992, with some astonishment:

> It was, in a word, extraordinary. In a state where much-courted voters have long been inured to the appeal of political candidates, most candidates are encouraged if 50 or so folks turn out to hear them.
>
> So it was an eyebrow-raiser here the other night when upwards of five hundred New Hampshire citizens of all ages showed up to hear Ralph Nader, the nation's foremost political scold, introduce himself this way: "Hello, I'm none of the above, and I'm not running for president."

Well, why was it so extraordinary? I was amazed by the reporters' astonishment. Christine Gardner, writing in *USA Today* on January 27, observed: "Three weeks ago he drew 1,000 in Exeter at Phillips Exeter Academy prep school. Last month, at the University of New Hampshire, where Arkansas Gov. Bill Clinton attracted 100 to a free talk, Nader pulled in 300."

Why was I attracting such assemblies and interest? First and foremost, people felt at the time, and even more so today, that they were losing control over everything that matters to them—their jobs, their governments, their marketplace, their environment, their communities, their privacy, their ability to get their calls returned, their children. It doesn't matter where they are coming from— right, middle, left, Republican, Democrat, Independent, blue-collar, white-collar, small business, commuters, pedestrians, carnivores or vegetarians. The complexity of modern life and the increasing remoteness of the decision makers feed this sense of powerlessness.

Politicians then have the nerve to come before the people and flatter them so as to calm them or, more often, bore them. Even the well-intentioned candidates cannot deliver on their sincere promises, because once they are in the White House or Congress, they are in a cocoon spun by thousands of corporate lobbyists.

One man leaving one of our meetings was overheard saying to a friend, "He's showing the politicians that the people can be a force to be reckoned with." Exactly. The Greek word for "people" is *demos,* and "democracy" means rule by the people, in contrast to "plutocracy," rule by the wealthy and powerful. If political candidates do not speak to ways that enable citizens to be more powerful individually and together to shape the future of their society and address their current grievances, what is left of their campaign other than platitudes, resolutions, and assurances that they conveniently assign to limbo, whether they win or lose the office they are seeking?

As we motored through one town after another in the fifteen or so days of the NOTA campaign, we made a point of addressing fundamental issues. Although candidates for national office readily nod at Tip O'Neill's adage that "all politics is local," few ever really take a stand on the state of New Hampshire. I did, whether standing with opponents near the Seabrook nuclear power plant— a massively expensive boondoggle that still doesn't know where to safely put its deadly piles of radioactive waste—or speaking out against a two-hundred-ton-per-day Wheelabrator trash incinerator in Claremont that was posing pollution and financial liability nightmares.

The lesson directed to the other candidates was to campaign *with* the people, not parade in front of them as if they were onlookers rather than participants. Nonetheless, the Democrats and the Republicans kept track of their holy trinity of campaigning—how much money they could raise, how many TV spots they could buy, and how many hands they could shake. Clinton specialized in look-ing intently and directly into people's eyes while he shook their hands, thereby breaking away from bland politicians or candidates who shake hands in a crowded room or restaurant while looking for the next person's hand to shake. This turned into a big plus for the governor of Arkansas. Thankful for small favors, people would say afterward, "He made me feel like I mattered."

Such low public expectation in 1992 was one of our campaign's themes. "You should be in charge," I would say. "You should develop your own policy recommendations, summon the candi-dates to your own get-togethers, invite the press to cover them, have a fully unscripted back-and-forth with the candidates, and insist on commitments. To do this, you have to spend more time knowing and acting. Give yourself a chance. You might be sur-prised by what happens when you and your neighbors collaborate in these ways. If you don't do it, who will? You can't have a daily democracy without daily citizenship."

One evening in February, Carl Mayer and I drove deep into the New Hampshire woods. We were en route to the tiny northern hamlet of Dixville Notch. New Hampshire primary candidates of-ten go to this remote village because its thirty-two voters gather at midnight on Election Day to vote at the Balsams Grand Resort Hotel. Within seconds, their votes are tabulated and the results sent to the wire services to launch the presidential primary campaign. Any candidate who wins or places well receives a little early psy-chological lift.

A light but steady snowfall accompanied our journey and, sur-rounded by dense roadside tree cover, made us feel that we were moving through one of James Fenimore Cooper's "primeval for-ests." Earlier that night Clinton's philandering was what people wanted to talk about. Curiously, the Gennifer Flowers uproar helped Clinton attract attention. Flowers became Clinton's spot-light, and he made the most of it. I'm almost certain that he and his close associates knew it was coming, especially after they planned and then postponed a presidential run in 1988. Clinton knew how to stay on message, and nothing was going to get him to take a stand on President Bush's NAFTA proposal before Con-gress, or on nuclear power, or on the failing banks in New Hamp-shire. He evaded questions from our supporters regarding the

Concord Principles, which were pretty simple ways to give people more power, more voice. (Jerry Brown became the only candidate to endorse these principles.)

For most of the Dixville Notch trip, Carl and I just enjoyed the quiet scenery and recalled some of the characters of the state's primary season. There was an old friend from Pennsylvania, Gene Stilp, who arrived late one day in Manchester, went down to the headquarters basement with a load of lumber, and emerged at dawn with some fifty giant pencils that he had fabricated to symbolize, atop motor vehicles, our write-in campaign. Soon a caravan of cars with the Andy Warhol–like artifact assembled in front of our storefront campaign office and, to noisy hoopla, they streamed away in different directions. The festival nature of the New Hampshire primary and the amused tolerance that people brought to its events were illustrated by the circulation of the minor or "dark-horse candidates." There were sixty-three aspirants on the ballot in this category.

Actor Tom Laughlin, of *Billy Jack* fame, campaigned actively as a "nonpolitician" and received considerable press notice. Back again was former Senator Eugene McCarthy at seventy-five years, saying he was as "serious" as the rest and stressing his foreign policy experience. One of the nation's finest mayors, Irvine, California, Democrat Larry Agran, delivered a serious set of proposals ranging from electoral reforms, urban revitalization, citizen engagement, and shifting to domestic programs the $150 billion that was being spent each year to pay for U.S. forces in Europe and Japan. Carl and I would meet Agran on the hustings, and the way the Democratic Party treated him reflected their rejection of any opportunity for internal reform of the party.

Carl and I arrived at the Balsams in Dixville Notch just before midnight, and the next morning we were met by the Barbas, the husband-and-wife hotel managerial team with distinct personalities and views that they did not hesitate to show. Gail Barba was the chairwoman of President Bush's reelection campaign in the Notch but said that she had decided to vote for me. "It wasn't so much that I was fed up with Bush as with Congress," she said.

One reason for New Hampshirites' enthusiasm during primary season, aside from the break they get from wintry cabin fever, is their awareness that the results of their kickoff primary can launch a winner or shape the dynamics of subsequent primaries arc the country. Their time slot is special, and because of that attitu New Hampshire has surprised the nation with its major party winners time and time again. Candidates temporarily learn not to trust the polls. They learn that the voters would cheer lustily for candidates they had no intention of voting for on Primary Day. Editorial writers for the various papers single out minor candidates if one or more take a stand on an issue that the paper favors (as with Nackey Loeb, publisher of the extremely right-wing *Manchester Union Leader,* who praised my proposal for a binding none-of-the-above option on all ballot lines). Independents abound. The chairman of a local Bush-Quayle reelection campaign quit in late January 1992 to support me, saying, "I cannot in good conscience cast my vote for the Republican Party." The *Monadnock Ledger* in western New Hampshire editorially endorsed Paul Tsongas on the Democratic side and me on the Republican side. The *Ledger* wrote that it wanted to send a message that citizens want "real change."

Well, as it turned out on Primary Day, February 18, I received 3,054 write-in votes on the Democratic side and 3,257 on the Republican side—almost a fifty-fifty split whose size was not as significant as its bipartisan appeal. During the day, people would come into our Manchester campaign office to complain bitterly over their inability to overcome the precincts' indifference or hostility to requests for write-in ballots.

Before I left the state, a woman whose eyes and demeanor suggested long experience with justice struggles, admonished me, saying that I should have run as a Democrat with my name printed on the ballot. "You lost a historic opportunity," she sternly remarked. Hers was not a lone voice. Many of my fellow agitators thought the same: Go all the way, express your desire to be president within the Democratic Party. I would remind them where I was coming from. Citizen movements make real changes. Informed and organized citizens can shape and direct the campaigns of politicians. They said I was dreaming, that the late twentieth century, with liberal safety nets in place, was very different from bygone eras, with their domestic turmoils and desperation. The political beast was too insulated, too fortified, and too rooted in the established interests to be changed unless you get inside it, they said.

"Maybe you're right," I replied, "but in that case you need another candidate."

For 1992, the irresistible force became Bill Clinton, whose broken field running took him to victory over President George Bush and ended a twelve-year White House drought for the Democrats. In short order, Clinton defined what a "new Democrat" was like. Over the next four years, he so favorably astonished the business lobbies that the head of the National Association of Manufacturers, Jerry Jasinowski, told me after a cable television taping that we shared, "We like Clinton more and more."

And why not? The boy wonder from Arkansas pushed through the greatest surrender of local, state, and national sovereignty in U.S. history to those corporate-inspired systems of autocratic governance called NAFTA and the revised GATT's World Trade Organization. Clinton signed the megacorporate legislations involving the telecommunications and agribusiness industries, ballyhooed phony welfare reform for the poor while creating new models of corporate welfare, and undermined civil liberties in signing three criminal bills, all while losing a health insurance package in a Democrat-controlled Congress in 1994. For good measure, he further delighted the Jasinowskis of the corporate world by losing his party's congressional control and handing it over for the duration of his term to the extreme right wing of the Republican Party.

Come 1996, Clinton thought only of his reelection, for which he brought on board the switch-hitting consultant Dick Morris, fresh from advising Trent Lott, to guide him on the nuances of political hermaphroditism. For reasons that certain White House assistants told me they never could understand, Clinton was mesmerized by the irrepressible Morris, with whom he would strategize for hours at a time. There was a reason. Ever since Clinton lost his reelection run for governor of Arkansas, it seemed he was determined never again to lose an election by sticking to principles. Morris fit that resolve perfectly, with his triangulation approach—which I understood as beating the Republicans by taking away their issues and becoming more like them. Economists call this behavior in the business world "protective imitation."

During Clinton's first term, I had no illusions about any progressive agenda other than universal health insurance, which he and Hillary botched. They overcomplicated both the process of drafting the legislation and the bill itself due to his penchant for trying to secure support of the big HMOs, the drug companies, the hospital chains, and the AMA—or at least neutralize their opposition. In the end, the health plan collapsed of its own weight. But if I did not expect advances, neither did I envision so many retreats, such as on campaign finance reform and, especially, on corporate regulation. The White House fed these agencies sleeping pills. Clinton thought so little of the federal government's auto safety mission that he let a Reagan holdover run the National Highway Transportation Safety Administration for eight months until he found someone who shared his vision of turning that regulatory agency into a consulting firm for Detroit. Clinton, deciding against his Department of Transportation's own projections of casualties, went along with the lifting of the federal interstate speed limit for trucks and cars to 65 miles per hour (effectively 70 miles per hour without a citation). I called the Oval Office, asking for a telephone appointment to speak with him for five minutes, to try to dissuade him on safety, energy waste, and air pollution grounds. It was the only time I made such a request, and it was declined. On November 28, 1995, Clinton signed legislation that ended the 55-miles-per-hour federal speed limit that had been in place since 1974.

According to a 1998 study by the Insurance Institute for Highway Safety, which was based on casualty experience after the law went into effect, thousands more Americans will die every decade on federal highways where the speed limit was lifted. The number of highway deaths was unchanged on the highways where the speed limit stayed the same.

Toward the end of Clinton's first term, I received a letter from California, signed by several prominent environmentalists, led by the great David Brower and Democratic political analyst Pat Caddell, urging me to place my name on the California presidential ballot. They were seriously upset with the Clinton-Gore nonrecord on environmental matters, and it was increasingly clear that no progressive Democrats were going to challenge Clinton—not Jesse Jackson or Paul Wellstone or any outsider. So, on November 27, 1995, I accepted their invitation to place my name on the Green Party ballot in California. My brief statement read: "I intend to stand with others around the country as a catalyst for the creation of a new model of electoral politics, not to run any campaign.

Californians deserve a campaign that will practice taking the corrosive impact of special interest money out of politics at the same time that it preaches campaign finance reform. This effort will focus on removing such money from elections, and ending the corporate welfare and other privileges that it buys. I will not seek nor accept any campaign contributions."

The Green Party of California was, to put it mildly, a fledgling association of several really energetic people that claimed eighty thousand registered voters. Right at the outset, I made clear to them that this was not about me seeking to become president. It was about helping to focus the initiatives of growing numbers of people who want more political choices. So don't expect a traditional campaign, I told them. There will be no fund-raisers or appeals, no hoopla rallies, just opportunities for people to start the difficult process of shaping the future course of our beleaguered democracy.

My friends and associates, remembering the noncampaign in New Hampshire back in 1992, moaned about this latest political suspension zone I was entering. My corporate-fighting California buddy, Harvey Rosenfield, who overcame with my help the powerful auto insurance lobby, told reporters that while I would "draw people from all sides of the political spectrum, he's got to be out there doing it. And I don't think he gets that yet. Ralph has not given the word to everybody that he's serious." And here I thought I was going further than my civic-indentured mind ever thought possible.

Whether I was serious or not, the reporters jumped on the issue that they and the Democrats thought was very serious: Would I take enough votes away from Clinton-Gore to cost them California, their crown jewel of fifty-four electoral votes? The hawkeyed *Wall Street Journal* started the horse-race question on January 3, 1996, with an editorial titled "Nader vs. Clinton":

> What Democrats should focus on . . . is the real danger that Bill Clinton could lose vote-rich California if liberal activist Ralph Nader is a Presidential candidate. . . . No one can come up with a plausible Electoral College scenario that re-elects Bill Clinton without California's 54 electoral votes. A Field poll gives Mr. Nader 11% of the vote in a three-way race

against Mr. Clinton and Bob Dole. Even a minimally funded Nader effort would end up with 3% to 5% . . . almost all at the expense of Mr. Clinton.

When I read these words, I burst into laughter. Clinton at risk in California? Why, Bill could have his $200 haircuts on the LAX tarmac every week and not lose to Kansas Bob. Anyone who knows anything about California knows that Bob Dole doesn't fit there. From the get-go I always believed that Clinton would have little trouble with Dole, who himself seemed resigned to losing. While Dole would tell audiences that he had to leave the auditorium because he wanted to fly back home that night, Clinton would shake every last hand. Besides, Californians historically get cold feet for third-party candidates when they enter the voting booth.

But Bill Clinton did not share my certainty over his reelection. Again and again in the early months of 1996, Dick Morris told me, Clinton queried him about whether I could be persuaded to drop out of California. Clinton was really worried. Both his cautious political antennae and articles in the *New York Times, Washington Post,* and other papers raised the prospect of tipping California into Dole's column. Morris knew better. "Boss, don't worry. Nader's voters come from both Democratic and Republican voters," he told the president. Morris, quite to his credit, remembered what had happened in New Hampshire four years earlier.

Starting in February, letters began arriving from Greens in other states asking me to place my name on the ballot. New Mexico, Oregon, Colorado, Alaska, Hawaii, and the number kept increasing until twenty-one states had my notarized acquiescence. C-Span started to cover my addresses at places like Haverford College and the University of Colorado at Boulder as part of their "Road to the White House" series. I did lots of talk radio shows and responded to feature reporters from around the country for interviews. But my travel was restricted because under the Federal Election Commission rules, raising and/or spending $5,000 or more made you an official candidate under a matrix of official rules, and I could not afford to cross that threshold. But by driving and finding the cheapest airfares, I did manage to visit more than a dozen states and help galvanize enthusiastic audiences around the neglected areas of health care, the trade "über alles" agreements of

NAFTA and GATT-WTO, environmental foresight, and consumer safety.

The California Nurses Association, and their tough-minded, sensitive executive director, Rose Ann De Moro, were running a statewide initiative (Proposition 216) on health insurance for all, and I campaigned with them across the state. Nurses are held in such politically high regard in our country, largely for good reasons, that joining with them was obvious. These were no ivory tower theorists or thumb-sucking columnists. Real grievances for their patients turned these nurses out into the streets to protest. Unfortunately and predictably, they were defeated at the polls by overwhelming HMO television dollars.

The Green Party nominating convention in August reminded me of an Earth Day gathering. It was held in Los Angeles, where Mike Feinstein, making his first and successful run for Santa Monica City Council, together with John Strawn and Greg Jan, were busily attending to the myriad details and a surprising number of reporters in attendance from around the world. MTV's Tabitha Soren, in particular, continued to cover the Greens. Winona LaDuke, a Harvard-trained economist, author and organizer, mother of two children, working farmer, and member of the Ojibway tribe in Minnesota, was chosen as my vice presidential running mate. At the age of thirty-six, Winona had already been chosen by *Time* magazine as one of the fifty forthcoming leaders in our country. She was well known among progressives at conferences and rallies around the country. A few weeks earlier, I had met with her in Minnesota and was struck by her spirited seriousness and warm sense of humor.

In an otherwise somnolent Clinton-Dole campaign, our unofficial campaign, which gave new meaning to the word "bare-bones," kept the flames of a people's politics flickering. At the time, I was busy with numerous civic projects as well as helping to start and build new citizen groups, including two involving my Princeton class of 1955 and Harvard Law School class of 1958, which mobilized "alumni for systemic justice," as we phrased it.

Come Election Night, we received just under seven hundred thousand votes, coming in fourth after Ross Perot on the Reform Party ticket. The only state where the Greens may have cost Clinton was Colorado, which went for Dole. I remember wondering whether the Democrats would get any message from this small signal on the horizon. In the months that followed, it was hard to detect any.

There was a strange letdown at the White House after Clinton's reelection. Instead of starting a new four-year term with some larger visions and objectives, he offered, in his adviser Bill Curry's words, "the politics of small gestures," often announced on Clinton's Saturday-morning radio message. The president paid attention to the little things that linger in the beneficiaries' minds. His favorite columnist, Ron Brownstein of the *Los Angeles Times,* was naturally pleased when Clinton sent his young son a birthday card. These recognitions poured out of the White House regularly, and their transformation into treasured mementos paid both intangible and recognizable dividends.

Bill Curry became restless and then incredulous at the absence of presidential initiative, leadership, and sense of priorities. It was too easy, he said to me, to blame a Republican-controlled Congress run by Newt Gingrich and Trent Lott for doing next to nothing. It was too easy, I replied, for Clinton to bask in the sun of a growing private economy, corporate profits, stock market surges, and declining unemployment while ignoring the grossest disparities in economic justice. Clinton, though cognitively capable, had no public philosophy, no guiding standards of what merits public enterprise. If he knew the proper lines between business and government, which he further blurred, or of what safeguards are needed when public assets are given to private companies, as with scientific and medical research results, he did not communicate them to the public at large.

When it came time in 1996 for Clinton to decide whether he was going to renominate Alan Greenspan as chairman of the Federal Reserve, the decision was an automatic yes. It did not matter to Clinton that this powerful agency was controlled not only by the banking industry but by a man who still is for the abolition of the minimum wage and still maintains his antiregulatory beliefs honed as a member of Ayn Rand's inner circle forty years ago. Although Greenspan is sworn by his oath of office to enforce numerous laws that protect the financial borrowings and savings of consumers, he still has not disavowed his view that regulation "of dishonest and unscrupulous business" is "welfare statism," "illusory," and based on "armed force." One would think that Mr. Greenspan had some explaining to do about his regulatory inaction before receiving another term as chairman. Instead, Clinton, the Republicans, and all but seven Senate Democrats gave him a coronation.

Clinton's second term overlooked a cascade of concentrations of corporate power. It seemed that every Monday morning I opened the newspapers to read of one or more giant merger announcements, with no mention at all of its effects on workers, consumers, and communities. There even was no coherent antitrust policy other than approval or at times requiring minor sell-offs of dealerships and subsidiaries. It almost seemed that the widely publicized Microsoft case, brought by the Department of Justice, was a fig leaf hiding this astonishing abdication by the Clinton administration.

Clinton even signed legislation that encouraged such consolidations. The notorious Telecommunications Act of 1996 was a case in point. It was promoted by both parties as a fundamental stimulus to competition that would benefit both consumers and innovate small firms. At the White House signing ceremony, President Clinton was enthusiastic, promising that the law would bring consumers "lower prices, better quality, and greater choices in their telephone and cable systems." Listen to the *Wall Street Journal*'s assessment five years after the act's passage:

> For consumers, the competition never got started. Now, with many startup phone companies faltering or folding, it looks unlikely that it ever will. The Baby Bells and the cable TV operators have the country pretty much to themselves, enjoying lucrative monopolies in most areas. . . . Lacking competition, incumbent cable and phone companies have been raising prices, and they have relatively little pressure to improve shoddy service. Nobody has a sure answer for how to fix it.

Eisenhower's Republicans would have blushed at what Bill Clinton gave up to large corporations. It reached the point where it was a waste of time talking to the White House about any change of course or new direction. Before becoming Secretary of the Treasury, Clinton's Wall Street adviser in residence, Robert Rubin, became apoplectic when Labor Secretary Robert Reich spoke of corporate welfare being unfair and draining public monies from public needs.

All we were left with during our occasional meetings with White House staff were pleas to hold firm on opposing federal erosion of the civil justice system traditionally reserved for the states. Clinton and Gore never stood firm on tort law, which protects the rights of people injured by defective products, toxins, and other harms. While telling their large campaign contributors in the trial bar one thing, they were busy negotiating deals with the tortfeasors' lobby on Capitol Hill. Clinton signed eleven mini–tort deform bills into law in such areas as aircraft manufacturing and biomaterials, which gave slices of immunity to these industries. In 1998 he was willing to sign the first general federal preemption of a portion of state tort law, but a bitter dispute over the sufficiency of the corporate immunities between two industry groups left the bill languishing in a Senate ready to pass it. This was the same Bill Clinton who as presidential candidate in 1992 gave leading trial attorney Phil Corboy at a Chicago fund-raiser his patented direct eye contact and firmly said, "You'll never have to worry about me restricting tort law."

The petitions, appeals, letters, testimony, meetings with Clinton's so-called regulators, with the exception of Dr. David Kessler, head of the FDA, on tobacco matters and Arthur Levitt, chairman of the understaffed Securities and Exchange Commission, were met with veritable blank looks, interminable delays, or rejections. Again and again, the citizen groups would try, and again and again they were shut out, albeit with occasional sweet talk. The regulatory agencies were more than captives of the industries they were supposed to regulate—they became their camouflage, material for auto, aviation, food, drug, railroad, and other industries' advertising bragging that their products met or exceeded federal safety or other standards—standards often written by industry lawyers and immediately obsolete when they were issued twenty or thirty years ago.

Our elders used to urge us on with the words, "If at first you don't succeed, try, try again." So a few months after the election in 1996, we made the first of numerous attempts to sit down with Vice President Al Gore and run by him a number of significant policy initiatives. My assistant, Caroline Jonah, started what turned out to be an extraordinary process of accessing the vice president. At first his staff requested a written letter with the topics we wanted to discuss with him. Fair enough. We sent the letter and followed up with another call. Then another call. And another. Soon the days turned into weeks and the weeks into months, until finally Caroline received the reply: "The vice president has no time to meet with Mr. Nader." I called him directly to see what was amiss. He called back in a few days, and I recounted our frustration with his staff giving us the runaround.

"They have?" he asked, as if surprised.

"You weren't aware that they were not letting us meet?" I asked, reminding him of a constructive meeting we had in 1993 at his office. "Then can you give me a time when we can get together?"

"Well," he replied, "let's talk now."

"There are several major topics," I said, briefly listing them, "and I doubt whether you have the time or whether it is best to discuss these on the telephone. Can't we find a time to meet?" I fully expected him to agree and refer me to his scheduler.

"Well, I'll see," he said and politely ended the conversation.

That was the last I heard from Al Gore, until he began telling crowds in the closing days of his 2000 presidential campaign that a vote for Nader was a vote for Bush.

Gore's disingenuousness had become more profound over the years, in part because he had never lost an election because of it and in part because, except for a few "misspokes," he had gotten away with this sleight of mind. But Jamie Love and Act Up made sure in 1999–2000 that he did not get away with drug industry dualism. Gore always portrayed himself as someone who had spoken truth to the medicine makers.

Unbeknownst to just about everybody was a private drama between these companies and South Africa involving Gore as a central character. Gore was the co-chair of the U.S.–South Africa Binational Commission along with President Thabo Mbeki. Gore used this position to pressure Mbeki, whose parliament was considering changes in its Medicines Act that would promote competition, liberalize rules for important drugs, and encourage the greater use of generic drugs, to lower the prices of medicines. About 4 to 5 million people in South Africa were HIV-positive, and at ten to twenty thousand dollars per patient per year for the multiple AIDS drug treatment, only a very few would receive this chance to save their lives.

As documented extensively in a February 5, 1999, State Department report to Congress (available on www.cptech.org), Gore had meetings with Mbeki, declaring that such legislation would constitute a violation of the revised GATT trade agreement and should be withdrawn. It was most demonstrably not a violation of the GATT treaty. Fronting for the U.S. drug industry, it was not easy for Gore to be credible. Without the full protection of Merck, Pfizer, and other companies' intellectual property, he and his staff argued, there would not be the billions necessary for further research and development. Gore, of course, would have seen no need to inform Mbeki that the growth in the industry's advertising and marketing expenditures is greater than the growth of their research budgets, or that many of the most significant drugs were financed through tax dollars by the National Institutes of Health and the Pentagon, along with gobs of federal tax credits.

In 1998, for example, Pfizer made more than $1 billion in profits, paid no federal income tax, and even received a $100 million refund, due to generous tax credits drug lobbyists secured from Congress. Jamie Love exposed Gore's role, and the press responded with several articles. Meanwhile, Act Up moved into a direct voice mode, culminating in a loud interruption of Gore's carefully scripted presidential announcement from his hometown of Carthage, Tennessee. After a few similar Act Up confrontations, Gore began backing down without admitting it. Starting in 1997, I sent him three detailed letters urging him to reverse his stance and support the South African legislation (which is now law) from a standpoint of compassion, if nothing else. He assigned an aide to provide a pro forma response.

Ignorance was rarely a problem with Gore. However, after eight years of Clinton, his hide-and-go-seek games bordered on amateurism. In many ways, Al Gore is the symbol of a Democratic Party that has become too corporate.

Indeed, the corporate influences on our political parties and the media have dulled our imaginations about what the agenda should be for creating a better society.

Unfortunately, the system is not working and our democracy is at risk. The debate about what we, as a people, should do to advance justice has narrowed, and it has become more difficult for people to challenge abuses of power.

It is an important function of the electoral process to spark thoughts about what our country could be if the public interests were paramount and to encourage actions by people to reclaim our democracy.

Four

CAMPAIGN LIFTOFF:
AMERICA, WE'VE GOT A PROBLEM

Starting in early 1999, the questions about whether I would run a real campaign in 2000 started and with each passing month became more insistent and frequent. The inquiries provoked my usual reluctance to move from citizen activist to an electoral candidate. But the more I tried to persuade myself that becoming a candidate for president was contrary to my habit of civic independence, the more I realized I was indulging myself. Besides, no one else was coming forward to advance progressive politics—except perhaps Warren Beatty.

The Warren Beatty phenomenon lasted about four months and must have amused Warren and his estimable spouse, Annette Bening. Warren floated the idea in the summer of 1999 that he might be interested in going for the Democratic nomination. Senator Bulworth got the celebrity writers into excitable overdrive. Is Beatty serious? How could he withstand the inevitable probing into his lothario years? Would the Democratic Party faithful accept his entry into the race? Articles, features, and editorials poured into print. Larry King went into supercharge mode. Beatty running? Made to order for the king of celebrity politics. Beatty got a good run of media on his principal issues, led by campaign finance reform—a "slow-motion coup d'état of big money," he declared.

All along, when asked, I said that Beatty never was serious about running but was very serious about his issues. Just imagine him going from one state to another, one fund-raiser to another, one Marriott to another, with reporters hounding him on every trivial tidbit in his past and bystanders grabbing for his autograph. Beatty is many persons, but a masochist he is not. After an impassioned speech at the Beverly Hilton Hotel on September 29, he declared that he would not run.

It was now November, and I had to make a decision soon. Running for president requires a level and intensity of political ego that I do not find congenial. Day in and day out, your sentences are expected to tout you: I did this, I promise that, I was there for you, I have a better plan, I've been everywhere, I've visited there, I'm for all of you, and on and on. If you feign self-effacement or humbleness as a regular style, the press sears through what it senses is a personality pretense. After the 2000 election, at the annual spring dinner of the exclusive Gridiron Club in Washington, D.C., the reporters serenaded Senator Joe Lieberman with these lyrics to the tune of "Mrs. Robinson":

Thank God for me, for Joe Lieberman,
A man of such amazing modesty.
Me, me, me.

Then there is the flattery. Long, long ago, politicians realized this. Show me a politician who does not flatter the people and I'll show you one who is out of a job. It comes with the territory and has many faces. Violate this tradition and the press will pounce, as they did on President Jimmy Carter when he made his hardheaded "malaise" speech to the American people.

Associated with flattery is another highly prized trait—charisma. This can be dangerous in dictatorial societies, as the twentieth century has taught us often, but in a modest democracy beset by an apathetic electorate, charisma can camouflage or carry a candidate. One need only remember the popularity of Ronald Reagan.

In 1996, friends chided me for rarely mentioning the achievements that I have registered over the years. They were to repeat these points later in the 2000 campaign. My approach was to focus on bad conditions and how to diminish or prevent them in the future. This required considerable detail over a wide range of subjects, which contradicted the conventional political advice of sticking to a few themes and slogans and repeating them ad nauseam.

But sound-bitten reporters dismissed anything substantive. As in

1996, but even more in 2000, more than 90 percent of their questions were "how do you feel" inquiries about my effect on the two-party horse race.

All these ambient sideshows that are brought to center stage raced through my mind in the days before deciding to run for the Green Party nomination. Then Winona LaDuke, expecting her third child in February, generously agreed to be my running mate, at no small discomfort to herself and her family. Understandably, she told me that she could not pursue a heavy travel schedule.

The decision to run a full campaign came to five principal reasons rooted in disturbing realities. I jotted them down over Thanksgiving weekend.

1. The "democracy gap" had widened and deepened over the past twenty years. Citizen groups were working harder and harder and achieving less and less. It mattered less and less which political party was in putative power. Both were morphing into each other.

2. Solutions to our nation's injustices, needs, and unfilled promises abounded. They were being applied, as with inner-city schools or organic farming, on the ground in a few places but without any engines of diffusion behind them to overcome bureaucratic, avaricious, or nontechnical obstacles.

3. In their finest hours, however infrequent, the major newspapers, magazines, and television shows repeatedly headlined investigative stories about the failings of big business and government, but nothing was happening. This was a telltale sign of a weakening democratic society unable to provide the linkages that bring serious misdeeds reported by the major media toward a more just resolution.

4. Having to spend so much time and so much of one's conscience and dignity raising money from interests you don't favor or like has turned away too many good people from running for office in America. A political system that turns

off good candidates can hardly be in a position of ever regenerating itself.

5. People's expectation levels toward politics and government had reached perilously low levels. Why try? Why bother? These words become the mantra of withdrawal.

Those of us laboring in the civic vineyards of Washington, D.C., really had two choices: suffer the daily lockouts from all three branches of government and the official source brand of journalism, or pack it up and go to Monterey to watch the remaining whales. Neither was palatable. It was time to toss the myths, get off the treadmill, and break out of the mold. A new long-range political reform movement was needed that would be accompanied by quickening and organizing the combined political and civic energies of like-minded Americans—people who were serious, not merely concerned, who sought fundamental structural shifts of power and accountability, who saw their role in history and who sought to look their descendants in the eye without blushing with shame.

It was now December 1999, and my decision was now an overwhelming yes. I set about finding experienced people to run the campaign. My first choice for campaign manager was Joan Claybrook, but she could not leave Public Citizen (see Appendix B). Steve Cobble, a seasoned professional who had run or participated in a number of political campaigns, demurred. He could not devote the kind of time required, given his family responsibilities. Mike Dolan, the chief organizer of the global trade coalition at the Seattle meetings that November, was receptive but wanted to be the campaign manager, not the field director, which was truly his forte. Human-rights lawyer and Harvard Law graduate John Bonifaz of Boston, after some contemplation, decided he could not leave his organization and move to Washington. John Passacantando, founder of Ozone Action (and now head of Greenpeace), was unwilling to uproot himself from his fight against global warning. All of them were excited about the campaign, as were many of my former colleagues, but everyone had immediate professional commitments, a family situation, or a disinclination to disrupt present routines for nine months of intensive campaign work. Some of those friends had told me years ago that if I ever made a serious run, not like 1996 or 1992, they would be on board. When I reminded them of that previous assurance, they said what they meant was if I ever ran as a Democrat.

Listening to all this feedback reminded me how many times over the past seven years I had listened to their sharp denunciations of one Clinton-Gore policy or refusal to act after another. Whether it was Dr. Brent Blackwelder of Friends of the Earth bitterly complaining about Clinton-Gore covering for the biotechnology industry, or labor leaders disgusted with OSHA's inaction on workplace toxics, or consumer champions furious over Clinton's positions favoring banks, insurance companies, and the telecommunications industry, I never heard them soften their rage with the words "Well, at least the Democrats are not as bad as the Republicans." That rationalization was to come later.

It was getting late into December. I gathered some close advisers to discuss the campaign. Its substantive proposals were well known, but what timing, resources, strategies, and tactics were appropriate to establish a solid, progressive third party were in large part still to be decided. We knew from past elections that participating in the presidential debates, ruled by the Commission on Presidential Debates (CPD), was probably the best and only way to reach tens of millions of American voters. It was the Khyber Pass to the electorate. By contrast, a fifty-state campaign would only personally reach the population equivalent of several large football stadiums.

Although we planned and met our objective of campaigning in all fifty states—the only candidate to do so—by June 2000, only a small fraction of the audience was reached, compared to the forty to ninety million people who were expected to watch each of the nationally televised debates. The CPD was the barrier, and for obvious reasons. Organized as a private corporation in 1988 by the Republican and Democratic parties, this supposedly educational organization was actually an exclusionary mechanism to keep out third-party competitors. Funded heavily by companies such as Philip Morris, Anheuser-Busch, Ford Motor Co., and AT&T, the CPD decided all the rules, including the number of debates, their location, the format, and who would ask questions. No one close to this hybrid had any doubts that the two nominees were the final decision makers.

To make the barrier even higher, the CPD's cochairs, corporate lawyers Paul Kirk (Democrat) and Frank Fahrenkopf (Republican), held a press conference in Washington on January 6, to announce that no third-party candidate would be invited if he or she did not reach a 15 percent average in five designated major polls by September 2000. This, of course, creates an intentional catch-22. Since all these chosen polling companies were owned by the major media, such as the television networks, the *New York Times,* the *Washington Post,* CNN, and the like, and if their editors and reporters did not cover third-party campaigns, there would be little chance of rising in the polls. Moreover, if these candidates were not high in the polls, the media would say they were not important enough to merit regular coverage. So the media gives the CPD a monopoly, and the circle is complete. I made all these pointed criticisms at the time, but to no avail. The varieties of autocracies in human societies are numerous.

During these deliberations and interviews, the primary season was maturing with Bush and McCain and Gore and Bradley locked in daily struggle. I was not part of the media-intensive New Hampshire primary or of any other primary, except for California, where Professor Joel Kovel was also running in the Green Party primary. When there are major parties with numerous contenders in state primaries, the media pays even less attention to third-party candidates. Moreover, with limited financial resources, I thought it prudent to shorten the campaign and eschew the primary treks in which there was little Green Party involvement anyhow.

Observing the insurgencies of McCain and Bradley against what Bradley called "the entrenched party interests" did afford me some appreciation of how the major parties ward off compelling and modest challenges to the apparatchiks. Senator John McCain, and his symbolism, should have taken George W. Bush. He was a military P.O.W. with undeniable self-discipline and bravery. The North Vietnamese, on learning the prominence of his military forebears, offered to free him after many months of captivity. He would not leave without the American prisoners under his rank. So he stayed with his men. I recount this because at one point Bush partisans started floating malicious rumors about McCain's instability. They should have a quarter of his iron discipline under the pressure he endured from his captors.

McCain had numerous other appeals. Everyone noticed and appreciated his humility, sense of humor, and soft voice during crowded New Hampshire town meetings. His openness with the reporters left their mouths agape, and his "Straight Talk Express" bus concentrated the press's admiration for McCain. But what made McCain stand out as a Republican were his repeated statements about dirty money in politics—what he called the "incumbency protection racket."

Then came the electrifying words. When I first heard them, I said to myself, "You gotta be kidding." This was a Republican talking, a Republican who for all his genuine charm had taken more than his share of special-interest money and unwise corporate positions. However, when you hear these words day in and day out, the effect becomes like what a novelist described: Repetition of wish-fulfilling words works a trance on its listener. Here are McCain's words:

> We have squandered the public trust. We have placed our personal and partisan interest before the national interest, earning the public's contempt for our poll-driven policies, our phony posturing, the lies we call spin, and the damage control we substitute for progress. And we defend the campaign finance system that is nothing less than an elaborate influence-peddling scheme in which both parties conspire to stay in office by selling the country to the highest bidder.

All said in McCain's custom-made soft voice with a mezzo-urgent tone. Remarkable!

After McCain handily won the New Hampshire primary, money poured into his campaign—$1 million in one peak day including matching funds. So why didn't he win the nomination? Because the Republican Party politicos, along with key Republican governors in key primary states, had already chosen Bush. Republican primary voters were not the representative sample of people to whom McCain's reformist language appealed. They view themselves more as conservatives than reformers, and Bush's mantras repeated ad infinitum were harmless: "compassionate conservative," "I trust the people, not the government," and "leave no child behind."

Many of these voters thought McCain was too far out precisely because of his appeal to independents and Democrats who, in states that allowed it, crossed over and voted for McCain in the Republican primary.

After New Hampshire, McCain thought he would win the nomination. Instead, he lost to an inarticulate Texas governor with a sorry political record. McCain was extremely disappointed and hard on himself privately. After the November election, NBC's Tim Russert asked him whether he thought about being in George W. Bush's shoes. Slightly laughing, McCain replied, "Every day." When someone like McCain, who had a fair record of opposing wasteful pork barrel projects and supporting campaign finance reform, cannot upend the pols in his own party, it goes to show how extremely rigid the GOP can be.

On the other hand, Bill Bradley had his own unique set of appeals. A Rhodes scholar and former star forward with the New York Knicks, he had widespread name recognition before serving three terms in the Senate. He did not have the political baggage that Al Gore carried because of his eight years of Clinton association. The press and pundits viewed him as "clean." His statements calling for racial unity and tax reform were forged from much thinking and work while in the Senate. His fund-raising prowess startled even the old pros for the party—amassing in a few months more than ten thousand donors who each contributed a thousand dollars or more to his primary campaign. But "Dollar Bill," as his basketball fans used to call him, had vulnerabilities that showed in his debates with Gore, who has fairly been described by political writers as vicious in debates. At the memorable Apollo Theater debate in February 2000, Gore repeated his distortions of Bradley's health insurance proposal—a subject of considerable Gore denunciation by news analysts and opinion reporters. However, Gore had a more basic purpose in repeating his fallacious riposte. He wanted to rattle Bradley into submission, knowing that Bradley had promised he would campaign above the mudslinging fray. He also knew that Bradley would be shaken if accused of advancing health insurance changes that would hurt the poor and minorities. Knowing all this, Gore got down and dirty at the Apollo, which he clearly packed with his supporters against the popular former Knick.

In the monotone voice immortalized by *Saturday Night Live*'s

Darrell Hammond, Gore framed Bradley as implying that the Congressional Black Caucus was naive or worse: "You know what? In my experience, the Black Caucus is pretty savvy. They know a lot more than you think they know. . . . Congressional Black Caucus is not out there being led around, you know. They know what the score is. And they also know that their brothers and sisters in New Jersey said you were never for them walking the walk, just talking the talk." All this holier-than-thou speech from a man who did not lift a finger to protect African Americans and Hispanics from harmful commercial exploitation in the ghettos, who led his administration's phony welfare reform, tried to bully the president of South Africa into maintaining sky-high drug prices, and did not walk his talk about toxic pollution where the poor live.

Bradley seemed unable by temperament to slug back, and he sounded weary and besieged. Though possessing arsenals of material against Gore, Bradley could not or would not use them. He avoided going after Gore on high drug prices because the ex-senator from New Jersey was very close to the large pharmaceutical companies in his state. Bradley's staff early on had received what came to be known as the Dorsey Memorandum, after Michael Dorsey, the Sierra Club board member who wrote it. Offered as an internal discussion paper, but sent to Gore, it listed fourteen areas where Gore had undermined or abandoned environmental goals. Bradley sat on the memo. Brent Blackwelder, who heads Friends of the Earth, eventually endorsed Gore as the lesser of two evils. Prior to the endorsement, though, Blackwelder told me that Bradley had damaging material on Gore's failure to protect wetlands.

Although Bradley spent more time and resources than did Gore in New Hampshire, he lost that primary and went downhill until he abandoned his campaign after the Super Tuesday primary on March 7, and, loyally holding his stomach, endorsed a triumphant Gore.

Throughout the primary campaign, the media obsessed over the tactics of the candidates and other horse-race aspects such as the polls, endorsements, stumbles, momentum, staff turnover, and the like. This has become a professional addiction and a contagious one at that, providing mind-numbing renditions. Fortunate exceptions to these quadrennial seances were the independent community press and radio—their coverage plumbed depths uncontemplated by their larger and wealthier brethren.

We scheduled the announcement of my candidacy for Presidents' Day, February 21, 2000, at the easily accessible Madison Hotel in downtown Washington. Most, if not all, candidates would have avoided a Washington location like the plague. You are supposed to announce in your hometown or at least in your home state, since you had to be seen as an outsider ready to take on Beltway insiders. I chose Washington simply because the driving goal of our campaign was to turn our nation's capital into a servant of its people instead of a corporate puppet. It was appropriate to make that point in situ.

Because February 21 was a national holiday, the day was almost guaranteed to have little news competition for the announcement. Our advance notification efforts seemed to produce results. Sure enough, many television, radio, and print reporters showed up to make us think that the coverage would be at saturation levels. All three networks and Jim Lehrer's *NewsHour* were there.

That evening, we gathered to view the national television news. There was not a single sentence about my announcement on any of the three major networks. The networks' cameras at the Madison registered zero that evening and succeeding evenings. The *NewsHour* camera did not do any better. Its tape of our news conference found not a split minute on Jim Lehrer's show that evening. Was I surprised by this uniform blackout on four networks? Of course. Usually the media will give the smaller third-party candidate some attention on his coming-out day. It could be expected that a candidate with a visible thirty-five-year record of consumer, environmental, and worker advocacy would merit at least fifteen seconds on the nightly news. The *Washington Post* reserved a two-inch squib, but the *New York Times,* after intercessions by Michael Oreskes, its Washington bureau chief, used a sizable wire story. The *Wall Street Journal* came up empty. Clearly, the Commission on Presidential Debates' polls were not skyrocketing for me given such inattention by their media giant parent companies. Although there was good coverage throughout the independent media and community newspapers, and the talk radio and cable shows I managed to do afterward, we quickly realized that our "democracy gap" campaign had fallen into a big-time "media gap."

My remarks at the news conference that day were structured for wide-ranging substance, historical context, and specific recommendations around known solutions and contained more than a few usable sound bites in the question period if that was what the editors needed. But you, dear reader, can judge for yourself. The entire text of my prepared remarks on that Presidents' Day is printed in Appendix C. You can read it, if you did not see it on C-Span, the only medium left for unedited national television coverage of civic and political events in the world's oldest continual democracy.

Media coverage of a campaign's launch is important beyond the next day's news, and its absence can have a disastrous ripple effect that we had to overcome. Also, this was the year 2000, a bleaker media period than previous presidential election years when, for instance, Phil Donahue would have the candidates on before a large nationwide audience, or the network news shows would devote considerably more time. In an interesting twist, large radio talk shows had offered standing invitations to Gore and Bush, which were ignored. In speaking with these extroverted hosts, I got an earful of bitter recriminations against the major candidates who in their view were too cowardly to go on the unpredictable stage of rock-'em-sock-'em call-ins. "Gore and Bush complain about the media editing them. Well, they are unedited on radio and still they won't return our calls," said one host.

In a campaign, you've got to keep moving. There is no time to cry in your beer. Before March 1, when I was scheduled to launch the campaign journey with a news conference at the LA Press Club, there were all kinds of campaign office details to tend to rapidly. Our campaign manager was Theresa Amato, a graduate of Harvard and NYU Law School, who bravely but reluctantly agreed to take a leave from her position as head of the Citizen Advocacy Center in Elmhurst, Illinois. Theresa certainly had the temperament for the job—energetic, hardworking, hard to discourage, able to juggle lots of duties at one time, and with the help of our excellent attorney Michael Trister, willing to navigate the treacherous regulatory waters of the Federal Election Commission.

Theresa did an excellent job and soon started recruiting a staff that eventually grew to include more than sixty young people. What they lacked in experience, they tried to make up for in enthusiasm.

Vendors descended upon us—very specialized ones at that. Software firms offer FEC-certified programs that overcome the pitfalls and pratfalls of complying with the agency's reporting requirements. Tailor-made and ready to go, they asserted. How much? Just five thousand dollars a month! That kind of charge is enough to encourage small-party candidates to set even higher fund-raising goals. The FEC staff has little choice but to proliferate regulations and interpretations because a thousand dutiful attorneys around the country are always thinking of ways to find loopholes or escape clauses for their candidates' schemes and avoidances, which the FEC has to block or anticipate.

And just about every move required a call to Michael Trister. A few examples will give a sense of the FEC thicket that had to be cleared. Mr. Trister, if we do not have any authorized committees in the field, beyond the general and primary ones, how do we pay for things at the state and local level? His reply: Send checks everywhere or give small field advances for which we must receive accountings. Okay, when does our primary season end if the Green convention is in June? It was important to determine the cutoff date for primary, as distinguished from general election, contributions. Contributors could give no more than one thousand dollars to a candidate in each time period. We required an FEC opinion on this question and were formally advised that our primary season ended either on the last day of the major-party candidates' convention or the last date that we were seeking the nomination of a state party convention, whichever was earlier. Back to Mr. Trister. Can we have an event in a union hall (since corporate and union contributions are prohibited)? His answer: Yes, if we pay for the hall and it is regularly made available to all candidates who seek to rent the space.

More questions. Can someone voluntarily drive the candidate to and from events without converting it into a dollar contribution for gasoline and mileage expenses? Yes, if he is using his own vehicle or even renting a vehicle for himself and the candidate rides in it, but the volunteer jitney cannot overdo it—say, spending above one thousand dollars for fuel, etc. What expenses are primary and what expenses are general election ones? What is the difference between a coordinated expense and an independent expense? Do we have to put "Paid for by the Nader 2000 election committee" on our buttons? Answer: No, there is a *de minimis* rule for items that are too small. Can a photographer donate photos? Answer: Yes, artists can donate their services if the campaign pays for all attendant costs, i.e., the processing charge, the mailing charge.

One day I picked up a half-inch-thick FEC volume called "Guidelines for Presentation in Good Order." These innumerable pages, filled with codes for how to treat various checks and other forms of contributions, are the rules for obtaining matching funds for the candidate from the U.S. Treasury. Matching funds start when the candidate raises five thousand dollars in each of twenty states in denominations of $250 or less.

If you are finding the above listing tedious, try studying the guidelines and then transferring them into operation among the headquarters staff, field people, and everyone else they have to guide. Try explaining why things cannot be done the way staff and volunteers believe logically they should be done because the FEC rules the roost. Full public financing of public elections would remove the vast number of regulations. The FEC thicket has become another barrier to entry by small parties that simply cannot afford the cost of clearing a path toward fund-raising.

But there was little time to contemplate all these corrosions and erosions of the electoral system. We had staff and expenses to pay for. We had to confront the nasty challenge of simultaneously raising money and maintaining our principles at the same time. Not since I was a schoolboy swallowing cod liver oil before leaving for school did I have such a taste in my mouth as when I started dialing for dollars.

Five

FRIENDS, FUNDS, AND FORMIDABLE HURDLES

I made it easy for myself with my first call. It was to Jerry Mander out of San Francisco, a man of many insights, causes, and networks. His provocative books on communications, advertising, and corporate globalization predisposed him to new political frontiers, and he did not disappoint. Next call was to actor Ed Begley Jr., an electric car and solar energy enthusiast and all-around good guy. He hadn't gotten much work, of late, he related, while recalling that he supported me in 1996. Uh-oh. Last year, he had agreed to support Al Gore, not knowing that I intended to run. He was very sympathetic but didn't "want to be like a windshield wiper." He did offer to give me some names from his database. My old friend Bill Haddad, generic drug crusader and collaborator on exorbitant pharmaceutical prices, was blunt. "You must be crazy to do this," he joked, after saying that he was "locked into Al Gore" inasmuch as his father, the first Senator Gore, was a friend and ally.

 Despite these two turndowns, I kept dialing and finally reached Dr. Quentin Young, prominent in medical reform circles for half a century and former president of the American Public Health Association, who said he would contribute and offer leads to other potential supporters, as well as attend any event in the Chicago area. Then on to law professor Michael Tigar, who quickly and generously responded with the maximum contribution. That was followed by a non-money-raising call to Jim Hightower to discuss preliminary strategy about launching the campaign. On the other line, classmate and labor law professor Paul Tobias was returning my call. Paul is a genuine pioneer, blazing the pathways for non-union employees to secure workplace rights. He came to his life's work after realizing how difficult it was to unionize employees (he is pro-union) and someone had to help them in their nonorganized state—now numbering 90 percent of the private workplace.

After thanking Paul for his contribution, I called Edgar Cahn who, with his late wife, Jean, roared out of Yale Law School in the midsixties and worked tirelessly for legislation that established the Legal Services for the Poor programs all over the country. Edgar is the creator of the Time Dollar service credits program now operating in more than two hundred communities here and abroad. These allow people who are poor and have free time to volunteer hours and earn time dollars. Then they can receive valued services in return when they are in need. He was finishing his book *No More Throwaway People* when we spoke and he said he would both send a donation and help in any way he could. On the campaign trail I had numerous occasions to speak about his Time Dollars as one very practical and doable way to arrest community disintegration.

Harry Berkowitz, my Princeton classmate who was in the clothing business and later ran the Yale Co-Op, was his usual encouraging self. Yes, he would give, adding, "You have always been willing to step into the breach. I hope you can have some fun at it as well."

Such words do charge one up to continue the calls. The next was to Anchorage, Alaska, and Peter Gruenstein, an attorney and former head of our Capitol Hill News Service. Peter agreed to make a donation and promptly launched into a critique of the Democratic Party wanting to pay off the entire national debt without dedicating substantial surpluses to health care and education. We're in the "twilight zone of politics," he muttered, advising me that it was a "complete, utter waste of time to come to Alaska." He said the governor was in the oil industry's pocket, the educational system was awful, streets weren't cleaned, and people didn't give a damn and were in a surly antitax liberation mood. "No matter," I said. "Alaska is on my wavelength. I'm going there." He replied, "Well, you might as well have some fun when you're here."

Maybe this was going to be fun. I rang up Jerry Brown, now the elected mayor of Oakland. "You don't have to convince me, I know," he rapidly said. "Will definitely give you my best list and will help in other ways." I thanked him, noting that according to the FEC rules we would have to rent the list, and he said he'd get back to me about other ways he could help. A few days later, on February 25, 2000, I was mildly astonished to read that Jerry had endorsed Al Gore at the Oakland Union Hall as "a man of vision"—a subliminal touch of irony for anyone who knew the former governor of California. Gore, who was there, thanked the mayor, saying "he did not have to do this" so his endorsement meant even more. I left a message at Jerry's office, recognizing that it may not have been Jerry Brown but *Mayor* Brown who endorsed Gore.

The telephone conversation with Rob Glaser, founder and CEO of Real Networks, was supersonic. Glaser's mind is not just multifaceted, it's greased lightning. I always thought that this former Microsoft executive, who retired in his early thirties a multimillionaire and later started his streaming technology firm in Seattle, was, one on one, Bill Gates's match. His mind began to click: "global warming, dinner with Bill Bradley, Bradley made Gore run better, new generation of politicians, Paul Wellstone, Russ Feingold, lots of expertise available, issues of globalization incredibly important but most Americans don't get it, except when it relates to democracy, taking on globalization issues without letting jingoism take over . . ." I asked whether he had suggestions of how the new technology could help our campaign and whether he would sponsor a fund-raising event in Seattle for us. He mentioned some entertainers like REM who might do this if the global warming issue were at center stage. "Let me think about these things further," he said, and pledged personally to contribute the maximum legal amount. He said he would think about raising fifty thousand dollars when that figure was suggested and said he'd call back and talk campaign strategy the following week.

Wade Green, the longtime adviser to and representative of several of the Rockefeller "cousins" (often described as the progressive generation of Rockefellers descended from John D.) picked up his telephone. I wanted to know the attitude of his clients toward my campaign. Alida Rockefeller, whom I have long admired not just for her courageous support of controversial environmental causes but also for her straightforward and inquiring personality, was not happy. Back in 1996 she was concerned that critical votes might be drawn away from Clinton-Gore who, disapproving as she was of them, were not as bad as the Dole-Kemp bunch. This time she was even more unhappy, Wade related. Ann Bartley, another "cousin," did not want to speak with anyone from our campaign.

After that exchange, I was ready to speak with Tom Geoghegan, a Chicago labor lawyer who has represented steelworkers, nurses, teamsters, and carpenters. A 1975 graduate of Harvard Law School, Geoghegan broke into the literary world seventeen years later with his sterling book *Which Side Are You On?* In Bill Greider's words, this book "tells of labor's tragedy with an intimacy that is full of pain, humor, anger and honesty." Geoghegan agreed to contribute and also suggested that I call the progressive Chicago labor leader Jerry Zero, who was outraged in his charming Irish manner over Gore ignoring the fired employees from the Honeywell plant in Mexico. When I called Zero, he noted with understatement how NAFTA's so-called labor standards were not very meaningful. After recommending someone in California with fundraising experience who, he believed, would help us, he remarked how Clinton's welfare reform was driving down fair labor practices and shafting the middle class.

Putting down the phone, I reflected how useful calling people for their contributions and listening to their suggestions and complaints were becoming to our campaign. Running with the Greens was proving to be liberating in a unique sense. Nobody I called wanted anything in return, which frequently would have been the case were I running as a Democrat. People gave because they wanted to help cleanse politics or better our country or world. They knew my record and my commitments. If there was any conflict between my stands and their business or occupation, they switched and put on their citizen hats and responded accordingly. This is why I always like to speak with Peter Lewis, the CEO and dynamic builder of Progressive Insurance, the nation's seventh-largest auto insurance company. I knew him as a shy classmate at Princeton but, in a remarkable transformation, he has for years been an iconoclastic, flamboyant executive, philanthropist, ladies' man, and political player in the Democratic Party, with which he has become more than a little disappointed. "Can you max out, Peter?" I asked. "That I can do," he replied, and indicated that his son would also give.

George Riley, my next call, was out of this world. He is a patent lawyer with a large California law firm and had recently become the firm's chief attorney for Steve Jobs of Apple Computer. George worked for us before and during law school at Harvard, coauthoring one of our books on the public lands. George always talks about coming back into the public interest law, but he is too successful taking on the giants like Intel on behalf of smaller competitors. "I'll be glad to contribute the maximum," he declared and offered to make additional calls. He agreed to try to raise fifteen thousand dollars in response to our usual request for the "maximizers" to raise an additional sum over time.

I had met Jack Dangermond on a flight to Japan. He and his wife, Laura, had established a very successful company devoted to software applications for Geographic Information Systems. Jack and Laura were immediately responsive to my request, maxing out and agreeing to host a dinner later in the campaign.

Jean Carper, author of bestselling books about food, nutrition, and health, was ever so kind ("Thanks for doing this for all of us") and sent the fullest contribution permitted right away and declared she would raise more from friends. Gary Sellers, an early "Nader Raider" lawyer, who worked with me to lobby the OSHA legislation through Congress in 1970, was customarily vague when it came to specifically agreeing to contribute. He thought my announcement statement "was brilliant," having gone to the Madison Hotel that morning. I was to find out months later what was behind that hesitation in one of the weirdest phenomena witnessed by the campaign.

My call to Michael Dorsey of Dorsey memorandum fame was fascinating for more than one reason. As a director of the Sierra Club, he added a list of Clinton misdeeds, from banking legislation to welfare reform. "So much is worse than ever," he remarked. He said he could contribute $250 and leaned toward raising more in due time after some reflection. Dorsey ended up voting for "the least worst" in the fall when the Sierra Club gave an actively soliciting Gore its endorsement. Just another example of why the Democrats need to be challenged.

So the large-denomination fund-raising continued with people I have known for years, people whom I knew about but never spoke to, and entirely new people with whose accomplishments I became acquainted. All these calls were made from Washington, almost never on the road, a few hours at a time during the days between travels. Most pro-Gore individuals were candid and opted out, like Mimi Cutler, who once headed our Aviation Consumer Action Project. Some did it by implication. My boyhood chum David Halberstam, usually so warm and friendly, was polite and a little terse and simply said good luck. Later he told a college audience in Ohio that this was not the year for a third-party challenge. John Kenneth Galbraith, one of the clearest, wittiest, and most contextual economists of the twentieth century, was his usual gracious self. He wrote on March 10, noting his long friendship with me but concluding that "as the candidates scrambled, I endorsed Al Gore, a good man and a long-time family friend."

There was one gentleman, however, whose phone call took me on quite an odyssey. Never underestimate Warren Beatty, the many-splendored reactor-actor. It was said in the eighties of his close friendship with Senator Gary Hart that the reason they got along so well was that Hart wanted to be Beatty and Beatty wanted to be Hart. Fictionally, at least, Warren got his wish with his politically satiric but very telling film *Bulworth*.

My first call to Beatty in late February instantly elicited his view of the announcement, which he viewed over C-Span. He pronounced it "great" and noted that I was "funny once in a while." When I asked for his support, he replied, "Let me put my head together," though of course he and Annette would max out at two thousand dollars each.

As for going beyond that, he wanted to think about the "publicity implications or ramifications at this time. This is a longer conversation," he continued. "But you are an undervalued asset that could be altered in four months. You have a record and a consistency that are unmatched. Do you really want to be president the way Jimmy Carter wanted to become president? I'm an I, I, I sort of guy." Just listening to him, how can you not be intrigued?

Two weeks later, I extended my conversation with Beatty. A lifelong Democrat, he allowed that he hadn't yet "thought through the consequences of being opposed to the Democratic Party. I don't want to support you in a half-assed way. I haven't thought through whatever influence I have. I have been thinking of doing a lot for you, but there are ramifications. If you were to run as a Democrat,

I'd give my full attention. I'll call you in about a week and see if I'm a dud or not."

Next week another Beatty, the helpful, almost touching micro-adviser, calls. "Get someone to put light on you during your press conferences to produce a more cheerful kind of look—otherwise, one has the feeling of a suspense movie. The studio interview with Rosendahl [the most popular serious cable talk show in California] was perfect—humor, wit, more easygoing, easier to take for people who feel guilty or are alienated from you. You've never been better—fifty times more lucid and funny than the others . . . a little too honest . . . all you need is one light from the front directly in front of you, not over your head and not lower."

Whew! This could have given me a swelled head, a virus my parents inoculated me from many years go. The next time we spoke, Beatty said that McCain and he talked frequently and that Larry King called him often to invite him on the show. What do I say? Beatty is hard to get. I gently mentioned that his contributions had still not arrived. He reassured: "Of course I'll do that. I told you so." Talk of a suspense movie—our office staff was taking bets about whether the legendarily frugal Beatty would ever send checks. When they finally came, a cry of approval was followed by a rush to the copying machine.

The fourth conversation with Beatty was a tour de force. He commented on everything, including Gore's widely viewed comment on Elián Gonzalez that sent a wrong signal to Beatty. Then he did a friendly analysis of John McCain, who had called him after *Bulworth* and struck up a friendship.

Is Beatty torn by nuance or racked by indecision? Whatever it may be, he did not show up at several fund-raisers near his home thrown for us by friends who invited him and Annette. He resolved how much he was going to do to help our campaign by not re-solving it. While he said many nice things about our efforts on the phone to friends, such as Pat Caddell, who Beatty said makes me look like a moderate on the Democratic Party, nothing jelled. He stayed with the party, yet always the needler and iconoclast. Did I waste my time and patience? No. Talking with him was educa-tional, like tapping into an oracle that never moves as it ponders and ponders.

Raising money quickly for start-up costs was crucial. The basic office and field staff could not wait on cold mailings to prospective lists or fund-raisers that require long lead times. I had put in forty thousand dollars of my own funds at the outset, but the fiscal launch, so to speak, came from the people who could afford to contribute the maximum one thousand dollars for the primary season, along with another one thousand dollars for the general election period. Had I contributed more than fifty thousand dollars, we would not have been eligible for matching funds.

After fund-raising, our next priority was getting on the ballot in every state. In no Western democracy are the hurdles for candidates to access the ballot anywhere near as high as ours. Another obstacle for smaller parties to challenge the duopoly.

Because the Libertarian Party has been around for so long, it has the process down pat, using seasoned signature gatherers to get on all or nearly all the state ballots. The other way to do it is to pay firms to provide paid signature gatherers. But that can become very expensive, as Pat Buchanan found out. The cost to his 2000 campaign was more than $200,000 just to get him on the North Carolina ballot.

Georgia illustrates the deplorable situation I and other third-party candidates have to confront. Officially, 39,094 verified signatures are required for a place on the presidential line. Actually, many more signatures are needed in all the states to protect against nitpicking by election officials, either Republicans or Democrats, who disqualify many signatures through some quite arbitrary methods.

Early in 2000, a coalition of third parties, including the Greens, and supportive Georgia legislators backed a bill that would significantly reduce the number of required signatures. The bill actually passed out of the House committee, with the controlling Democratic leadership officially neutral. Late one afternoon, the day before the bill was to be considered by the whole House, I placed a call to the number-two Democrat under the venerable speaker Tom Murphy and asked whether he would be supporting this legislation. He said that he had the short bill in his briefcase and would take it home and read it that evening. This was the first sign of trouble, since the proposal had been in the news over the previous days.

I related to him that about two years before, the Republican governor of Pennsylvania, Tom Ridge, had vetoed legislation passed by a bipartisan vote in Harrisburg that would have raised the number of required signatures from 37,500 to 98,000—the highest in the nation. Ridge rightfully said in his veto message that such a barrier was unjustified and antidemocratic. The Georgia majority leader listened. He then volunteered that in recent informal discussions among Democrats, the question was raised as to why they should be encouraging their own competition by passing such legislation. I replied, "You know, sir, there are some fellows in countries overseas who have taken that kind of philosophy to the next level of repression." The bill lost in the House, though not by a big margin, and that ended any such efforts before the election.

Take a brief scan at some of the more onerous state statutory hurdles. Texas requires 37,713 signatures to be collected in just seventy-five days. Moreover, no one who has voted in a primary that year is permitted to sign any petitions. In North Carolina, 51,324 signatures are needed by May 15. In reality, candidates get more than 90,000 for a safe margin. By law, the petition for Greens and others reads, "The signers of this petition intend to organize a new political party," which scared potential signers away with its neo-McCarthyite tone. Signing your name is one thing. Intending to organize a new party is quite another. To have write-in votes counted even requires a petition beforehand with hundreds of names. In Virginia, the lawmakers require ten thousand signatures, four hundred from each congressional district. Anyone who circulates a petition in a county must live there or in an adjacent county. Oklahoma is the record holder at present with the highest per capita total of signatures in the nation—36,202 signatures in a state with a population of 3,350,000. By Oklahoma law, write-in votes there cannot be counted. New parties in Illinois have to get 25,000 verified signatures to get on the ballot, while established parties are on with 5,000 signatures.

Other bipartisan barriers also paint a shameful picture. In West Virginia and Georgia, the filing fee is four thousand dollars. Pennsylvania stipulates that signature forms have to be on special colored paper. Officials would provide only four hundred forms when our volunteers needed more than two thousand. Downloading the forms from the Internet was prohibited.

And of course there is the unofficial harassment on the ground.

Local authorities evicted our volunteer petitioners from one state park. The mayor of Tupelo, Mississippi, stopped petitioners from gathering signatures in the town square on the Fourth of July. Circulating petitions in a public market in West Cleveland was halted by local police.

As third parties succeed in surmounting these fences, higher fences go up during the next legislative session. This happened in Illinois, South Dakota, and Utah after the 1996 presidential election. It was not always this way. In the pre–Civil War period, candidates had only to help pay for the printing of the ballots in order to place themselves on it. I wrote my first article on ballot access barriers in 1959. And matters have in many states only gotten more burdensome. For decades, third parties have had to spend time and money confronting ballot barriers. Judges have, on occasion, found certain ballot access restrictions arbitrarily burdensome and therefore constitutionally invalid. Unfortunately, state legislators stand ready to pass new laws that continue to present third parties with legal obstacles that must again be challenged.

To bolster the efforts of our field staff and its director, Todd Main, we brought nine lawsuits in several states against one or another slice of these obstructive statutes. The results were mixed, although we attained more positive than negative outcomes. For example, we did not prevail in North Carolina at the trial court level, but we were able in Illinois to call attention to an unconstitutional provision requiring petition circulators to be registered voters. So we did not get on the ballot in seven states. But we made it on the great majority of state ballots long after the campaign began.

Six

HITTING THE ROAD

Not getting on the ballot in places did not change our commitment to campaign in every state. It was suddenly March 1. The start of the long road was the L.A. Press Club. Our press people did the requisite advance work. The Press Club has seen better days, but it is conveniently located and spacious for a news conference. That morning we walked into the room and wondered whether we were in the right place. Besides some sympathizers, there was one TV camera (Fox), a small radio station, and a community newspaper. The leading elected Green in Southern California, Mike Feinstein, a vigorous Santa Monica councilman, was absent. There was, however, some finger food and soft drinks.

I conducted the press conference as if it were filled with reporters. The L.A. media absence was the first sign that unless you're engaged in a flamboyant spectacle or are a celebrity with a charity, restaurant, or premiere, you can forget about coverage. This is, after all, a city where the three major TV stations—profitable ones, at that—shut down their Sacramento offices a few years ago, figuring that they could rely on remote feeds to cover their state government. But where was the *Los Angeles Times*? My associate Tarek Milleron called the *Times* political editor, Massie Ritch, right after the news conference and politely asked why there was no reporter in attendance. Ritch seemed genuinely understanding and explained that the sprawling mass of *Times* reporters were all taken up with the Gore-Bradley debate that evening.

We headed upstate to Laney College in Oakland, where we were told there was a large, modern auditorium for my midday address. I turned into the room, which must have had five hundred seats, to find a crowd of eight people waiting for my appearance fifteen minutes later. I doubled over in laughter. At this scale, to say the least, it was a friendly and intimate occasion, with seventy in attendance.

I dropped by to see Jerry Brown in his mayoral lair. He gave me a rapid-fire verbal tour of Oakland, remarking on how inert downtown was in the evening and how there was not a single construction crane on the horizon. He spoke about the $21 million annual subsidy the city had to pay the Oakland Raiders for the stadium taxpayers built, how he was trying to get upscale professionals to take advantage of the low rents in downtown to invigorate urban life and generate needed tax revenue. He also wanted to change the terms of the upcoming cable contract to reflect broader civic programming and rebutted critics who took him to task for inviting the U.S. Navy to engage in some exercises around the port of Oakland. He then took a host of suggestions from me, which we chewed over, and I went out of City Hall into a light rain on the way to a union hall on the outskirts of Oakland to have a news conference and endorse a human dynamo, Rebecca Kaplan, who was running at large for Oakland City Council on the Green Party line. Rebecca was full of ideas for improving life in Oakland and made sure that the press turned out. Meanwhile, some members of the carpenters union local gave us an earful over what they viewed as the dictatorial behavior of their union president in Washington, D.C., whom they vowed to picket if he ever came to the Bay Area.

That evening, we experienced the first real sweaty Green rally, in a stifling hot middle school auditorium in San Francisco. In the hallways outside, there were all kinds of attended tables piled with pamphlets, newspapers, buttons, and pennants, and citizens were arguing or pleading their causes. Inside were seven hundred people packed and cheering one speaker after another. Waiting outside by one of the tables, we met—yes, it is true—a *New York Times* reporter who was covering the rally. Evelyn Nieves had covered lots of events in New York and other cities before coming to the *Times*'s San Francisco bureau. I answered a few of her questions while waiting for my turn to speak and then entered the hall to view the Greens at their most distasteful task—fund-raising. One of the California Green Party's founders, Ross Mirkarimi, was on the stage calling on anyone to come up and give five hundred dollars. Very soon, Ross was down to asking for one-hundred-dollar offerings when a man mounted the stage. Before the sweltering crowd, the man dramatically pledged half of all his wealth, upon his demise, to the Green Party. The assemblage both hushed and gasped, perhaps wondering what fatal disease afflicted him. In his next breath, he declared that he had an invention and was seeking marketing partners. Some in the audience cringed slightly. After a few more donors came up, I delivered my remarks in the humid atmosphere.

The next night in Sante Fe, New Mexico, was different in composition but the same in substance. Arriving in Albuquerque, I was joined by Green activist Carol Miller, who garnered almost 20 percent of the vote in a congressional race in 1998 and shook the Democratic Party there. Also present was lawyer Rob Hager, who argued effectively for my 1996 ballot placement. We drove to a café in Sante Fe that was filled to capacity. Like the Greens in San Francisco but with different backgrounds—more artists, youths, retirees, and Latinos—they wanted change. They believed that people mattered, that authentic cultures and natural environments counted. What would it take to start us resolutely in the right direction, I asked, then replied: one million Americans devoting one hundred volunteer hours a year and raising one hundred dollars a year for the cause. How many here, I inquired, would join such an association? At least one-third of the audience raised their hands.

How many of you are undecided, I asked, and would like time to think it over? Another third raised their hands. I thought this was a useful exercise to encourage people to contemplate what quantity of human initiative and resources it would take to make change, because many people have a hunch that it takes an overwhelming number of engaged citizens to achieve goals such as universal health insurance or renewable energy or cleaner elections.

Next stop was Austin, Texas, where on a grassy slope I was introduced to a couple hundred people by Jim Hightower, the finespun, homegrown, and hilarious Texas political philosopher.

It was sobering to hear reporters stationed in the state capital telling us how Bush would finger reporters who asked semi-tough questions by having his aides come around after news conferences and ask them where they were coming from. They admitted that the tactic was intimidating. After all, Austin was where Bush's record contradicted his rhetoric, where researchers like Craig Mac-Donald were documenting the almost knee-jerk surrender of government—all three branches—to corporate interests at a depth extraordinary even for Texas state politics.

Back in Washington, partisan Democratic pundits predicted that Gore would tear Bush apart on his Texas record, and he started to do just that in an address before the National Society of Newspaper Editors in April. In a strange way, Gore and many other politicians feel more comfortable zeroing in on one or two Achilles' heels of their opponents than on the kind of smorgasbord offered by Bush. It has its reasoning—too many attacks become negative overkill and turn the opposition into an underdog, as happened with Reagan.

But there was another reason the vice president could not press his attack regarding the Texas governor's record on pollution, poverty, prisons, and plutocracy. Gore's federal government was doing little to ameliorate air and water pollution. Clinton and Gore drove NAFTA through Congress in part with the promise of investing heavily to clean up the horrendous border regions with Mexico. Like many of Clinton's promises, this one died on the vine, and the border's contamination, congestion, infectious diseases, smuggling, and abject poverty got worse. So what would a pro–corporate prison, pro–death penalty administration official like Gore say to the mirror-image state administration of George W. Bush? Also expected from Clinton-Gore's many giveaways and subsidies was Gore's silence on the lucrative corporate welfare deal for the Texas Rangers, which netted part-owner Bush $14 million off the sale of the team. (See Appendix D.)

Two-party complicity makes for difficult arms-length political competition. Add Gore's unwillingness to stand up to Bush and the emergence of Gore's own corporate straitjacket—so evident during the October presidential debates—and it becomes clear why Gore's "message" was so ineffectual.

Following our trip to Austin, we traveled to Boston. With the storied wall of Fenway Park, home of the Red Sox, as background, neighborhood groups and I held a Saturday-afternoon news conference opposing a yet unapproved neighborhood "feeder" proposal under which a new ballpark would be built, replacing a fifteen-acre piece of downtown Boston with one of those private-public partnerships that make business moguls tearfully joyous on the way to the bank. In the past dozen years, these deals had built new stadiums and ballparks for sports zillionaires in major cities all over the country. State and local officials team up with the sports teams and their corporate lawyers to expropriate land, level neighborhoods, build skyboxes for corporate bigwigs, raise ticket, parking, and food prices beyond the range of working families, and then send the bill to the taxpayers.

But this swindle doesn't always work. In 1998, the owner of the New England Patriots, Robert Kraft, met secretly with Republican Governor John Rowland of Connecticut in a small airport hangar near Hartford. There they worked out one of the biggest taxpayer giveaways to a sports team yet: a $500 million package to get the New England Patriots to move to Hartford. When announced, there arose a "the Patriots are coming, the Patriots are coming" frenzy among the press and politicians. It was a boosterism that would have startled Sinclair Lewis while writing *Main Street*. Rowland repeatedly said that this was not just about football—it was about the spirit of the community. A few months earlier, Rowland did not support a proposed multimillion-dollar appropriation to repair Hartford's legendarily crumbling school buildings. The Patriots deal, it was claimed, would create jobs, and the team, shown on *Monday Night Football* nationwide, would presumably inspire owners of businesses to locate in Hartford by the Connecticut River. Except for one thing. A business that is open eight days a year does not create many jobs, except for professional football players and their handlers, and is hardly an incentive for hard-boiled business relocators. As Professor Andrew Zimbalist, a sports economist, has testified and written over and over again, these expensive subsidized arrangements are structured in ways to assure that there is very little return on investments either for taxpayers or for the surrounding private economy. The Patriots deal was laughable in its extremism. Connecticut's taxpayers would build the new stadium and a special practice field, and guarantee unsold skyboxes, among other open-ended commitments.

Leaders of both parties in the legislature swooned over the NFL coming to town and rammed the legislation through in a special December session with the most perfunctory of public hearings. Within four months, the deal, exposed relentlessly by a Green Party–led coalition that included Greenwich stockbrokers, blue-collar workers, public-interest lawyers, environmentalists, conservative taxpayer groups, and talk-radio skeptics, collapsed. The stadium site had serious toxic saturations deep underground, the deal needed yet more money from the legislature, and the media started doing its job of informing rather than propagandizing the public. Kraft journeyed to Hartford in April and, with a red-faced governor, informed the public that he was going back to build a stadium near Boston with private investment money.

So it was with some experience that I, a Yankees fan, could challenge the emerging Red Sox deal. The economics of $135 million in state funds and $140 million in city funds for new land and site preparation toward this $627 million Fenway Park project did not come close to sustaining a return on investment, apart from inevitable cost overruns. But self-described capitalist sports owners expect, even demand, that there be a deep public trough for their hands to dip into, while they write checks to the political campaigns of politicians who have the final pro-forma say and who will receive numerous invitations for skybox viewing.

In my statement at Fenway, I said that "taxpayer money should be used for serious public purposes, not for schemes by rich corporate socialists who reject capitalism in favor of corporate welfare handouts." Share in the costs, but not in the profits, say the owners to taxpayers. The community groups know what these public needs are—affordable housing, citywide after-school programs, and repairing the schools, as well as clinics and other sundry public works. Boston city officials had been saying there were no funds available, which was just the contradictory nerve point that makes politicians squirm.

While the Red Sox franchise got the proposal through the state legislature, with the help of high-powered lobbyists like ex-Senator George Mitchell, the Boston City Council was quite another cup of tea. Council members, like Mike Ross and Mayor Tom Menino, worried about the disruption, displacement, and lack of economic benefits raised by all kinds of community groups, including a newly formed local coalition called Citizens Against Stadium Subsidies, which organized the Fenway press conference. Under this umbrella group were Save Fenway Park, which argued for renovation rather than demolition, the Fenway Action Coalition, ACORN, Fenway Community Development Corporation, and Citizens for Limited Taxation. Each of these and other groups had their favorite neighborhood uses for this tax money and they represented real angry votes. The Red Sox needed nine out of thirteen council votes and were not able to achieve their goal.

Standing with energized citizen groups on localized issues about which we are knowledgeable was a theme of our campaign. It worked very well that day in a city not known for its media coverage of citizen events. The story led or was prominently featured on the evening television news, on the radio, and in the next day's major newspapers, including the *Boston Globe*. When we left Boston, we were persuaded of two predictions—that we would be staying in touch with the citizen groups as they invigorated their grassroots base for sensible budget priorities and that neither Gore nor Bush would ever touch this stadium issue, anywhere, not even in Democratic Massachusetts, which was not a contested state. At this community level of people's concerns, the national parties are nowhere. They are hollowed out.

Another example of this was witnessed in our trip to Toledo. We visited a nearly demolished neighborhood of more than seventy houses and numerous small businesses bought out for meager sums by the city under the threat of eminent domain. The purpose: to clear a triangle of land given to the Chrysler Corporation in 1998 for a new, expanded Jeep plant. This neighborhood in particular would be used for shrubbery and landscaping, with the bulk of the other acreage devoted to the factory and staging areas.

We were met at the Detroit Metropolitan airport, a gloomily forbidding display of labyrinthine architecture, by two of the most give-'em-hell, congenial women you'll ever meet: Julie Coyle, the ever-pleasant cabaret singer and civic networker extraordinaire, and Kim Blankenship of Kim's Auto and Truck Service, who with her husband was the last holdout against Toledo Mayor Carlton Finkbeiner's demolition service for DaimlerChrysler. The hour-and-a-half drive to Toledo offered us an opportunity to catch up with the news and meet with Wyatt Andrews from CBS's *Eye on America* for an interview to be included in a segment he was doing on the local controversy.

Long before the campaign commenced, I had been traveling to Toledo to help the people oppose a city government determined to take their property and give it to Chrysler. When that effort failed, I met with the homeowners and local counsel, the redoubtable Terry Lodge, to seek a fairer buyout price. So attached were we to these Toledans that they dubbed themselves "Nader's Neighbors," and the dozen or so who held out got a much better price a year later through Terry's efforts.

It was devastating—elderly people, friends and relatives, families—uprooted for corporate landscaping. Houses were demolished as they were purchased, leaving the community pockmarked with debris. DaimlerChrysler stayed discreetly in the background and let the city officials do the dirty work and take the heat. But that did not divert Mel Robie, who died heartbroken after having lost his home. He told his son: "I fought the Germans in World War II and now they are taking my house."

The Toledo-Jeep story needs to be backed up a bit. When Chrysler decided to expand, it did what many other big companies do—dangled the prospect of putting the new plant out for bids from various municipalities and states.

So when Chrysler opened up the bidding among Ohio, Illinois, and Michigan, Toledo Mayor Finkbeiner was the most desperate and essentially panicked. Toledo was in bad financial shape, but he managed to rustle up a combined federal, state, and local subsidy package of nearly $300 million to keep the plant expansion, which would of course further impoverish city finances. Part of the freebie package was allowing Chrysler a property and sales tax holiday for a dozen years and squeezing city funds to buy and clear land, prepare the site, and absorb any potential environmental liabilities, and then give it to Chrysler. Here were the small businesses and homeowners in Toledo paying their fair share of taxes for their town's services, but giant DaimlerChrysler, with $20 billion in cash at that time, was freeloading its privileges and immunities on their backs.

And what did the giant auto company do in return for all these definite dollar benefits? Just retain, not expand, forty-nine hundred jobs in its old and new plants under a nonbinding promise. The written contract with the city was not released until well after the deal was announced by the mayor, and on perusal it was essentially a one-sided contract for DaimlerChrysler, with all manner of escape clauses and contingencies.

In 1999 I called up Lou Goldfarb, an acquaintance, who was one of Chrysler's high-level in-house attorneys, and asked how he could justify small taxpayers having to pay their share but not a big taxpayer whose Jeep plant, no less, had produced immense profits with a very diligent, productive labor force. At first he said that a new plant would produce more economic activity, which would result in more tax revenues. To which I replied, The same could be said of any business, small or large; so if you're big enough, you can get away with a tax holiday and other kinds of subsidies, including the cost of buying a neighborhood and demolishing its homes for landscaping. Lou is a smart fellow—his final defense was that all large companies did this and his company had to stay competitive.

In 2000 the bloom started coming off the DaimlerChrysler merger, and it became clear that it was more an acquisition of Chrysler than a merger of equals. Plant shutdowns and layoffs began to be announced as profits and the stock price plummeted. Toledo was apprehensive, and for good reason. Though the new plant was spared, the total employment roll was now expected to go below three thousand. Mayor Finkbeiner was embarrassed and angry, and he resolved to take the company to court to enforce the agreement. Alas, the mayor had no cards. The agreement had enough loopholes to drive a minivan through. There were no "clawback provisions" that would reduce the subsidies proportionately to the job reductions. Chrysler was never asked to post a bond, as some had suggested, to support its promise to retain forty-nine hundred jobs.

Being on the road day after day, most politicians boil down their presentations to a few paragraphs, largely poll-driven to address concerns and present a vision of the future, mixed with flattering local political personages onstage. Then on to a local fund-raiser. One week, Vice President Dick Cheney followed us by a day up the coast of California with this tightly disciplined approach. In

Santa Barbara, he had an exclusive dinner for supporters or plead-ers—$25,000 a plate. The next day, there was a reception around Ventura, where it cost $5,000 to shake the candidate's hand.

My approach was to deliver remarks that provided a history of major advances in justice and then to dissect the consequences of the concentration of corporate power over our society. I ended by proposing ways to better our nation, explaining that these are within our grasp if we strengthen our democracy for voters, work-ers, taxpayers, consumers, and small investors. As is his quadren-nial practice, one English professor graded my language at the twelfth-grade comprehension level, Gore at eighth grade, and Bush at sixth grade.

A lengthy question-and-discussion period followed. Sometimes there was a suggested contribution at the door, but most times no such effort was made. Occasionally we would schedule fund-raisers at private homes or halls, but the chief purpose of these trips was to get our message across to audiences, media, and prospective volunteers whom we encouraged to sign up. Giving our Web site address—votenader.org—made it easy for people to contact the campaign after our departure.

So localism was an added task but a necessary function of my campaign. We held daily news conferences, sometimes more than one. Gore went months without a news conference. At our sessions, we had to know about and refer to local situations or controversies just to receive any coverage. When Gore and Bush passed through a locality, chances were good that people had seen them on na-tional TV many times. That meant they could be winners. Sup-porting local people on their chosen struggles, associating with poor people's activism, although important, does not by itself get votes. Being seen as a potential winner beats all other communi-cations. That is why the polls assume such importance and drive the coverage.

Long after the election, in a Kansas cab, the driver delivered a confession. He said he intended to vote for me on Election Day, knew that Bush had Kansas in hand handily, but once in the voting booth, he voted for Bush. By the time he got home, he said he was ashamed of himself. I asked him gently why then did he vote for Bush. He replied, "At that moment, I wanted to be with a winner."

In a system with proportional representation, there can be many winners, but in our electoral system, it's a winner-take-all jackpot. People react accordingly. More than they are willing to admit, people vote for a candidate whom they think many others will vote for as well. In any event, I campaigned in areas of great injustice to get a feel for the people, their conditions, and what can motivate them to act. Sometimes we helped by referring them, for example, to Lois Gibbs's National Clearinghouse on Hazardous Waste or to an occupational safety organization or to a foundation that may be of assistance. Besides supplying names, addresses, and Web sites, and showing how they can demand service from their government regulatory agencies or get help from some pro bono lawyers, campaigns are run on such a frantic schedule that they cannot lay the basis for community organizations, as I hope someday can be the case. That kind of deep campaign builds democratic institutions as it goes and can always be a winner in this respect. Understanding the forces of community disintegration is perhaps the most difficult question confronting a wanna-be functioning democracy.

Just past mid-March I addressed the annual legislative conference of ACORN, one of those needed community institutions that started in Arkansas and has since spread to many states. Its mission is to organize and represent lower-income people. The room at the 4-H Complex outside of Washington, D.C., was filled with African-Americans, who were the real organizers and leaders on the pavement, in the projects, and throughout the ghettos. I could see that they had been through much, and I delivered a formal written speech. "There is a lot of lip service paid to the poor and to community investment," I said, "but when the chips are down and when the interests of the financial powerhouses are in the balance, the legislative and regulatory scales are invariably tilted toward the corporations, not toward communities." I went over some statistics that the people gathered in the hall have to live with daily. There are more than five million families who are in desperate need of affordable housing and, according to congressional testimony by Clinton's HUD secretary Andrew Cuomo, six hundred thousand homeless Americans, many of them working poor, who don't know where they are going to sleep tonight.

It is difficult for Americans who are well off enough not to live in urban poverty to appreciate the daily business crime waves that sweep over these ghettos with unchallenged ferocity. Payday loans, rolled over to payday after payday, can reach annual percentage rates of 400 percent. Rent-to-own rackets proliferate. Predatory lending is a booming business from high-cost automobile financing to home equity and refinancing scams.

Behind this shady world of exorbitant interest rates are some well-known Wall Street investment and commercial banks that provide the capital to fuel these operations. In the seventies, the financial lobby secured the repeal in most states of the usury laws, so the sky's the limit as far as interest rates are concerned. It can be expensive and often dangerous to be poor in America. The poor pay more and receive less law enforcement against these merchant predators. There are far more full-time pet therapists for affluent clients in the United States than there are prosecutors to bring these exploiters to justice. Needless to say, not many politicians running for office discuss doing something about crime in the suites. But the sheer scale of predatory lending in the country and its distinct ties, through subsidiaries and other intermediaries, to major banks and insurance conglomerates is beginning to worry some government officials. Alan Greenspan, the chairman of the Federal Reserve, is one of them.

I asked him in the spring of 2000, at an elaborate social occasion in New York City, about rumors that the Fed was going to crack down on predatory lending. He looked at me knowingly, nodded, and said, "Enough is enough." The poor are still waiting.

As is true for many widespread abuses, there are solutions. Community development credit unions, of which there are at present only four hundred operating in low-income regions, are a fair source of credit, including home mortgages. They provide those essential small loans for workers temporarily laid off from their jobs or when the family's wage earner falls sick without medical insurance. Credit unions are cooperatives, owned by their member depositors. Together with community development financial institutions, thousands more of these credit unions would do much to drive the sleazy credit predators and their Wall Street backers out of inner-city neighborhoods.

However, without a sensitive political movement directed toward these desperate Americans, there will be no enforcement of many laws already on the books. There will be no rapid expansion of these community institutions that are critical in binding together low- and moderate-income people.

I dwell on this unconscionable condition in America's poverty belt, where tens of millions of people reside, because so few political figures even mention it. For Gore-Lieberman, the mentions were overwhelmingly for "the middle class"—shrinking though it is—and for Bush-Cheney, well, they trust the crooks, not the government.

At the end of my remarks, which went unreported, and after discussion with the ACORN audience, I felt sadness in the room. There was outrage long before I came to them that day, but it was associated with a weariness from having to battle these and many other unmentioned cruelties by themselves with little or no help, even from minority lawmakers elected from their neighborhoods. They want action.

Our groups have been working with ACORN and other associations for years. We grind out the maps and testimony documenting the redlining and other abuses. But the chain has not been broken—not in the marbled offices of the financial corporations or at the other end in the squalid ruins of ghetto misery in America.

In mid-April, the misery of billions of humans in the Third World was given prominence during the mass demonstrations in Washington, D.C., against the economic models pushed by the WTO, the World Bank, and the IMF. I spoke at one of the major rallies and again that evening before a highly articulate audience at the Foundry United Methodist Church, where the Clintons worshiped. A fund-raiser at Andy Shallal's restaurant brought out a packed house of some two hundred people. You could hardly move your elbows to dip a chip. I was gratified to see so many familiar faces, which told our campaign that many progressives in Washington, D.C., at least, were supporting the Green Party. We chose Andy's Luna Grille as our location because of his widespread reputation for hosting charitable causes of a wide variety. It makes it especially easy for people to decide to go there when they have already participated in previous occasions advancing good works. If there were more restaurateurs like Shallal, combining social conscience with business acumen (he's started four successful restaurants in fifteen years), all over the country, the citizen movement would have more than a culinary base from which to proceed.

———

The distributional deficiencies of our huge economy are quite clearly demonstrated in Atlanta, the bustling crown jewel of the South and center of an enormous sprawl that extends 110 miles from end to end. It is downtown, however, where the business community is putting the squeeze on a large, well-run homeless shelter.

My day started with a call on the editorial board of the *Atlanta Constitution*. As with most visits to editorial boards, the atmosphere around the large table was cordial and curious. The candidate is expected to make his case briefly and then answer questions. Near the end I mentioned the Peachtree-Pine Homeless Resource Center and its problems with the city and the downtown business association. For the editors, this was old news, and they did not let on where they stood. As I was taking leave, it never occurred to me to inquire of the news desk, as we passed by, whether it was going to send a reporter a few short blocks away to cover our news conference. I should have. No one from the *Constitution* showed up.

At the press conference, I was joined by Steve Gaskin, winner of Sweden's Right Livelihood Award, along with the famous people's architect Hassan Fathy. Gaskin was also running in the Green Party presidential primary. Also there were Hugh Esco and other Greens working to get the party on the Georgia ballot. The shelter has been controversial ever since its founding. The downtown business association would like to have it out of sight so it can be out of mind. For two years, the city licensing agency had failed to issue a food license that the shelter's administrators need to help feed the homeless. It surprised me to learn that 37 percent of the men sleeping at the shelter are working, many of them in labor pools for minimum wage. Given the price of housing in Atlanta, they would have to earn twice the minimum hourly wage of $5.15 to afford a one-bedroom apartment. To the few reporters who attended the part rally, part news conference, I took the city to task for making it difficult for the shelter to do its job, chided those in the business community for their hostility—some of those probably were long on corporate welfare themselves—and urged a national affordable housing and universal health care program and a minimum livable wage standard.

The recent history of how the homeless are treated in Atlanta goes back to before the Olympics were held in that city. As an angry Anita Beaty, executive director of the Atlanta Task Force for the Homeless, which is in charge of the shelter, recalled, Mayor Bill Campbell declared his goal was to "sanitize" downtown, in preparation for the '96 Olympic Games. In just the year before— 1995—9,500 people were arrested for their homelessness under the city's ordinances, for, Beaty said, "not having a place to be. Jail costs fifty-five dollars a day. Imagine the solutions that money could fund." She added, "These criminalizing policies are designed to make Atlanta safe for commerce—for profit." Privatizing the commons and the criminalization of poverty in Atanta was how B. Wardlaw, a key founder and funder of the shelter, once described the scene.

After my speech, I met with Ted Turner at his office to renew our acquaintance, discuss the campaign, and maybe focus his customary legendary impatience (years ago there was a sign on his desk: "Lead, follow, or get out of the way") on the shelter problem. Entering his very spacious and well-decorated office, I encountered Turner on one of his down days. He was feeling under the weather, which meant that he could deliver only a pungent two-hundred-word excursus on the world going to hell. He also was feeling powerless, confessing that he had little influence these days at AOL–Time Warner, where he was a vice president. When I suggested that he call City Hall, he didn't say yes or no, just shrugged wearily.

As a university and law student, I wrote papers and articles about my travels in poverty-stricken places around the country. Seeing these inhuman conditions afflicting mothers, fathers, and children, significantly due to age-old exploitations, provoked an urge for justice that did not dim.

I've found most reactions to poverty by the better off to be unconnected to any public philosophy of action. Except for what George Soros calls "market fundamentalism," we are a society without organizing theories of social action in any accepted mainstream sense. We organize charities that are very empirical, lessening symptoms but not going all the way toward removing causes.

And these charities cannot keep up. New York City has a telephone-book-size list of names and addresses of all kinds of charities. Like the rest of the country, New York is losing the charity race as the deprivations mount and become endemic and more complex.

There hasn't been a poor people's movement since the days of Martin Luther King Jr., Cesar Chavez, and George Wiley, who started the rights movement of welfare mothers. The poor have been strangely silent for a long time. Someday, the poor will be heard from in a sustained way. But until that happens, the established powers will not listen.

I write these words on a day when the *New York Times* features an article titled "Fear and Poverty Sicken Many Migrant [Farm] Workers in U.S." and prints two deservedly glowing reviews of Barbara Ehrenreich's new book, *Nickel and Dimed: On (Not) Getting By in America.* She portrays her experiences trying to make it "during the best of times" in a variety of unskilled jobs that pay between $5.15 and $7 an hour. The reviewer, Dorothy Gallager, ends her piece by thanking the author "for bringing us the news of America's working poor so clearly and directly, and conveying with it a deep moral outrage and a finely textured sense of lives as lived. As Michael Harrington was, she is now our premier reporter of the underside of capitalism." The underclass grips one out of three full-time workers in the United States.

Apropos of the Greek saying that "fish rot from the head down," this gross inequality of income has flashed off the charts when CEO pay is compared with workers'. *Fortune* magazine, no less, featured a cover story on June 25, 2001, titled "The Great CEO Pay Heist," describing it as "highway robbery" and then, astonishingly enough, adding, "Why the madness won't stop." *Fortune* was referring to the 350 or so of the largest companies by revenues in the U.S. where the average CEO's compensation has gone from twelve times the entry-level wage in their company in 1940, to forty-two times in 1980, to about five hundred times by the year 2000!

The wealth of the Forbes 400 in the three years 1998 to 2000 increased on the average for each of them by a total of $1.9 million per day! The economy has more than doubled in per capita output since the sixties, yet the working poor, the working near-poor, and the just plain destitute are everywhere. What has changed is that the rich have become superrich and, unlike the stagnant federal minimum wage, the compensation package of the well-insured and pensioned members of Congress is keeping well ahead of inflation, thank you.

Leaving Ted Turner's office, I flew to Birmingham and, as usual, met with petitioners and some citizen group representatives. Our Green Party contact, Johnny Ardis, said that they needed to collect five thousand signatures by the end of August, but he was taking no chances. My speech at the University of Alabama's Bell Theater made mention of the South's populist tradition—a long time ago, admittedly—and that what the American people own as a commonwealth (the public airwaves, the public lands, worker pensions in the trillions of dollars) is overwhelmingly controlled by corporations.

Todd Main and I spoke long into the evening at Lanny Vines's home, where we spent the night. Mr. Vines is a successful plaintiff's attorney, a generous philanthropist, and a longtime civil rights fighter in Alabama politics. As a political strategist, he had much to say to us. We were off the next morning just as the planners for a local charity association arrived for a function at the Vines home, which he generously made available for such receptions.

Arriving in Jackson, Mississippi, I was interviewed by the *Jackson Clarion Ledger* before traveling to Louisiana to speak at Loyala University. Louisiana has always had a uniquely corrupt politics along with some very flamboyant populists, including Huey Long, whom Franklin Delano Roosevelt feared in the thirties as a political competitor. For presidential campaigns, Louisiana requires no signature, just a check for five hundred dollars—the only state where you can buy your way onto the ballot. The next morning I met with members of the editorial board at the *Times-Picayune*, who were quite lively for that early-morning hour. The newspaper has printed some weighty articles by some first-class reporters like Tyler Bridges, now with the *Miami Herald*. At editorial board meetings around the country, I tried to open my remarks with the reasons I ran. The ones that resonated most were the shutting out of the civic groups by the convergence of the two parties (and in Louisiana they have had Exhibit One—Senator John Breaux) and how good investigative stories by newspapers usually go nowhere in terms of generating change.

Off to Nashville via Atlanta's sprawling airport, to Fisk University's Memorial Chapel and a joint press announcement of Tom Burrell's senatorial candidacy. Burrell is one of the more remarkable new Greens.

It was 4:45 P.M. and our advance work was not successful. Only a few dozen people showed up, although there was a fair press turnout. Mr. Burrell is an African American who grew up in rural west Tennessee on a small farm his family had owned for three generations. He served in Vietnam with the Eighteenth Engineering Corps and on his return went to work in a Michigan auto plant. He soon returned to his roots in Tennessee to run the family farm, which, with additional rented land, cultivated thirty-five hundred acres of cotton and beans.

That's where Burrell learned the tragic history of the black family farmers. The U.S. Department of Agriculture's Farmers Home Administration would routinely deny, through local lending boards, their crucial operating loans. From one million black farmers in 1900, there are now only eighteen thousand, a decrease five times that of white farmers.

Burrell became a leader for the black family farm, spearheading demonstrations and sit-ins and helping to launch a national movement in 1981, which built upon our research on the Department of Agriculture dating back from 1969. Having joined a class-action suit against the USDA and alleging severe racial discrimination regarding crop loans and other practices, and then objecting to the ridiculously low monetary settlement to the black farmers, Burrell is calling for a new federal agency to deal with the problems of minority farmers, whether black, Hispanic, or Native American. With materials from Tom, I carried the cause of the black farmer to several states, as part of the overall subject of depressed rural poverty beset by aggressive agribusiness giants and the federal agencies they control to advance and subsidize their profits.

Afterward, we drove four hours along a beautiful highway to Lexington, Kentucky, where we visited the *Lexington Herald* and learned that some major disputes were erupting at the nearby University of Kentucky. And it did not have anything to do with basketball.

By the time we arrived for a press conference at the Singleton Center for the Arts, the anti-sweatshop student activists were all over us about their being harassed, denied fair procedures, and threatened with dismissals for a sit-in protest. Having worked with this campus movement, we assured them that they were not alone, and should it come down to a judicial proceeding, we could help find them counsel. These students were fact-filled and on fire. It was an inspiring group that reminded me of their forebears in the sixties, taking a local issue and moving their frame of reference toward the whole phenomenon of corporate globalization.

Earth Day, April 22, is an event I have participated regularly in since its inception in 1970 when some fifteen hundred events on college campuses and other sites put the environmental issue on the front burner. I had committed to spending the day in California for a series of events around the Bay Area. Our supporters did not consider this to be the best venue for either maximum press or audience. They recommended Washington, D.C., where Denis Hayes, the venerable manager of Earth Day celebrations, was presiding over the largest expected outdoor gathering. There had been behind-the-scenes politicking over whether political candidates would be allowed to speak to the assemblage. Denis Hayes did not want candidates. That was understandable because every candidate would argue for equal time, and most candidates also tend to drain away the civic spirit of the occasion. But if Al Gore was invited to appear, our campaign staff (see Appendix E) was determined to get time on the platform. Al Gore was so invited. But, by that time, I was not about to break my commitments to California, so Winona LaDuke took my place.

A few weeks earlier, I had called Carl Pope, the director of the Sierra Club, to discuss the club's decision process on the presidential candidates. Speaking as an individual, Pope said he disagreed with the Greens—not their goals, but their strategies. He referred to Green Party candidate Carol Miller, whose 19 percent of the vote, he believed, helped elect a Republican to Congress. (The Democratic candidate in that race was also a hardened reactionary as well.)

If the Green Party can field candidates where it makes sense, well, he could get more enthusiastic, which I took to mean where it doesn't complicate the election of Democrats. He added that the Supreme Court matters greatly, whether or not Bush wins. As for the Sierra Club endorsement process, that would be made by a two-thirds vote in July based in part on a close review of the candidates' responses to their detailed, but I thought incomplete, questionnaires about their environmental positions. Who knows, said Pope, the board "could endorse both Gore and you."

The Dorsey memorandum and internal dissent aside, there was not a chance this would happen. Pope later said on TV that I had a very good environmental record but couldn't win.

Knowing this about similar proclivities of other major environmental groups that allow the Democratic Party to take them for granted, I was intent on showing where Gore's environmental record had come up very short in the past eight years. The outdoor Earth Day rallies in Sacramento, Berkeley, and San Francisco were not the best occasions because speakers were not expected to be so directly partisan. The contrast became quite clear, however, when I mentioned a few differences, such as the administration's backing down on pesticide regulation, its near silence on a needed solar energy mission, its continuance of long-standing taxpayer subsidies for the profitable coal, oil, gas, and nuclear industries, and its surrender of environmental leadership to the trade supremacy mandates of NAFTA and GATT. Moreover, no one would have predicted in 1993, the auto companies included, that Clinton-Gore would not propose any higher fuel efficiency standards. This position not only allowed the average miles per gallon to decline during their eight years in office, it also set the stage for Bush-Cheney to define their energy crisis in 2000 as requiring a push for supply drilling and expansion, instead of pressing for demand reductions through engineering improvements.

The atmosphere at these rallies was relaxed—family picnic style—on the grass. The Sacramento-owned electric utility—SMUD, as everyone calls it—had a large exhibit showing its work for solar energy and conservation. Little did I know how directly and shortly relevant this exhibit would be during the 2001 California power blackouts and supply manipulations. Both Sacramento and Los Angeles have owned their electricity companies for years. Both are not gouging their customers, have a surplus of power, and unlike Pacific Gas and Electric, Southern California Edison, and other private utilities in the deregulatory fiasco, are not being diverted by worries about their stock prices, executive stock options, or investments around the world. They are owned by their communities, who expect them to deliver electricity reliably and ever more efficiently.

At Berkeley, two remarkable women shared the stage with me. The first to speak was Medea Benjamin, co-founder of Global Exchange, which monitors international corporate misbehavior. She was the Green Party Senate candidate whom Senator Diane Feinstein aloofly treated as a nonperson as she floated to reelection on an ocean of cash. Medea is a very motivational, concise, informed, hell-raising speaker. She had worked in some of the most poverty-stricken areas of the world and is no armchair observer. She did not disappoint her sun-drenched audience.

Nor did twenty-five-year-old Julia Butterfly Hill, the next speaker. All Julia had to do to highlight the destruction of the giant ancient redwoods by lumber companies was to live, under harrowing conditions, two years and eight days high up in a thousand-year-old redwood she called "Luna" in Humboldt County, California. This is what it takes these days for the media to turn one into a civic celebrity. Her message was a mixture of poetic, aesthetic, cultural, natural, and environmental testimony for sustaining and restoring the life of Earth.

We drove to the main square in San Francisco, which was only half filled with people listening to speaker after speaker. By the side of the stage, sitting quietly in his wheelchair, I saw the last half century's greatest practicing environmentalist. David Brower was very ill with cancer, but he would never miss a beat in his bulldog determination both to enjoy and protect the rivers, the public lands, the forests, and the parks. "Let the forest breathe for us," he told me the last time I saw him at his Berkeley home.

I asked him how he felt. He replied with a wan smile, "Better than I have any right to expect." Before and after I spoke, I thought to myself how different Earth Day 2000 and even Earth Day 1990 were from the first indignant, focused, raucous Earth Day gatherings. It is not simply that dozens of major corporations have moved in on Earth Day, appropriating the language of environmentalism in their ads and sponsoring and funding events. It is that the spirit has been sucked out of Earth Day by this steady process of co-opting harmony.

Of course, credit should be given where credit is due, as with the Interface Corporation's giant strides toward zero pollution and maximum recycling from the manufacturing of their extensive tile and commercial carpet products. However, when companies use Earth Day as a fig leaf for their daily pollution damage and their regular lobbying against stronger environmental standards, they do not deserve a seat of honor at the Earth Day parade.

Too many of the Earth Day events have lost their focus. Instead of naming names and assigning accountability—as with the Dirty Dozen in Congress—Earth Day has gotten too soft, too imprecise, and it has been losing its attendance and enthusiasm. Increasingly, it is leaving behind only footprints in the sand, and public relations benefits for corporate polluters that are unlikely to attract the hope and zeal of future David Browers.

Seven

As we campaigned in one state after another, back in Washington, D.C., Theresa Amato, our campaign manager, was putting together the elements of a campaign staff. As I mentioned earlier, it was extremely difficult for seasoned citizen advocates to break away from their institutions and join a political campaign. Steve Conn was a luminous exception to that immobility. A longtime fighter for Alaskan and other indigenous people's rights, Steve took a leave from heading the twenty-five-year-old Alaska Public Interest Research Group (AKPIRG), and flew to Washington when our campaign was really bare-bones and while Steve's mother was seriously ill in New York City. I could only imagine the pressure and pain he was under, for there was no closer relationship than that between Steve and his mother, Gertude. On one occasion, I called Steve when he was at her apartment by her bedside, and he gave her the phone. The clarity and sensitivity of her words were overwhelming. Steve and I had worked together for years, and she treasured that cooperation. And I now understood where Steve's unwavering principles, cool, intense concentration, and strength of purpose were coming from. "I'll go to sleep tonight smiling," she said. A few days later, she passed away, but not her legacy or her example of a life lived justly. Campaigns are flooded with mundane details and strains, but there are those rare moments, as this one, that elevate the larger perspectives and keep them ever in mind.

The necessity of multiple perspectives, as with a series of concentric circles, is particularly appropriate for presidential campaigns, where, try as we did, politics cannot be heavily local. People expect some contemporary proposals, especially bread-and-butter ones, but they also want the candidates to express a vision for America, demonstrate character, and champion values. All this lends itself to a variety of abstractions and slogans, which the major candidates' wordsmiths are particularly adept at creating. George W. Bush is the most transparent at this: "I am a compassionate conservative" (repeat on the hour), "I will restore honor and dignity to the White House" (this reminds the public of Clinton), "I will change the tone in Washington," "I am a uniter, not a divider" (whatever you say, say nothing), and "Leave no child behind" (taken from the motto of the progressive Children's Defense Fund).

Slogans and images, kept simple and repeated often, go unchallenged. They meet the presumed short attention span of people, most of whom say they do not care much about politics anyway. It is a package designed for sound bite journalism, which, if you are a possible winner, knows no limits to repetitious broadcasting. Couple all of this with pictures that convey those slogans and you've got a double punch.

Quick, ask yourself what comes most to mind when you think of George W. Bush, the presidential candidate in the year 2000? For me it's pictures of Bush with little children, usually two or three up close, often minority children. Bush must have set the all-time record for such placements.

Year after year of such formulaic campaign strategies by major presidential candidates produces a numbing phenomenon. With their expectations and guard down, voters come to expect what they are given to expect—a kind of conditioned response that makes it very difficult for a campaign like ours to break through. I am a "Brandeis brief" type of person who believes that factual reality counts, that candidates' records matter greatly, that arguments need to be rooted in evidence, and that robust debates with challenging reporters provide the most level playing fields. I do not like posed photo opportunities. A campaign should not be a vehicle for an ego. Rather, it is an opportunity for other articulate voices to be heard. By way of illustration, I listed many names of such individuals in my announcement address. When the Green Party conventioneers in 1996 started chanting, "Go, Ralph, go," I immediately changed the phrase to, "Go we go," and it caught on to a surprised but delighted audience. Social change occurs when "we" come together to create a just and democratic society. It's as simple as that. If you want a society that embraces both "visions and revisions," to use Mark Raskin's felicitous phrase, then the motto must be "Together we can make a difference." That leaves little room for "ego tripping" or people who are so egotistically fragile that they can be blistered by moonbeams.

I began my activism many years ago as an undergraduate and law student against "discriminatory injustice" regularly suffered by women, blacks, Hispanics, and the first Native Americans. Later I turned my focus onto the areas of "indiscriminate injustice" that affect all the people in varying degrees, such as unsafe automobiles and other consumer products and malpractices or environmental toxins, workplace hazards, corporate crime, and looting of the public budgets and public assets. Our citizen groups focus on many facets of corporate abuses, which includes working against discrimination. Like Harvard professor Cornel West, I believe that race matters, and like him I believe that class inequities are very much related to racial injustice. Over the years, we have documented how abuses against all people abuse the poor and minorities even more.

Our groups have been in the forefront opposing bank and insurance redlining in low-income neighborhoods, mostly populated by people of color. Our computer maps of cities all over the country, which graphically document bank redlining, are used by community groups to fight back under federal laws that prohibit such lending discrimination. Environmental pollution affects all, but especially the poor. The poor pay more in rip-off markets and die earlier due to environmental racism and shoddy medical and other services rooted in racial inequities. Again, we have been very involved in these struggles to protect children from lead poisoning in crumbling apartments and the poor from incinerators and toxic dumps operating where they live. The "discriminatory injustice" movements have had greater success in getting their points across to both the media and elected officials, compared to advocates against "indiscriminatory injustice." Still, the champions of the former demand that progressive candidates emphasize what has already been emphasized at the expense of what is almost never emphasized in political campaigns—namely, the giant corporate takeover of our society.

Black Americans and their leaders are properly incensed over illegal use of police violence, racial profiling, and the violence that comes from sharply discriminatory enforcement of laws against minorities, who often have to rely on incompetent or rushed defense counsel. But there is also the silent violence of lead poisoning of little children, asbestos ingestion, medical malpractice, air and water toxics, contaminated foodstuffs, crumbling housing and slumlords, and other afflictions that mark life and death in the ghettos. A poor neighborhood does not get its calls returned, while the Upper East Side in New York City, or Scarsdale, does. Guess which area suffers more from the above damages? So focusing on economic and political inequities that flow from severe imbalances of power between the corporate wealthy and the downtrodden classes sends civic energies in both directions—human rights and corporate unaccountabilities—and unifies the aggrieved peoples across racial, geographic, and occupational boundaries.

Later in the campaign, when some liberal Democrats began actively campaigning against Nader-LaDuke, this kind of bickering was used to score some cheap political points. Congressman Barney Frank ignored our basic work with Act Up, our criticism of the exorbitant price of medicine, and our stands on gay and lesbian rights, which were far superior to those of Gore-Lieberman. Gore himself was picketed by gay rights groups who reminded him not just of his fronting for price-gouging drug companies and taking their contributions but also of his antigay votes as a member of the House of Representatives. Gloria Steinem went around the country touting her "ten reasons not to vote for Ralph Nader," while forgetting our groundbreaking work on women paying more in dollars and injury because of marketplace discriminations, not to mention founding a leading women's policy group in the early seventies. While Jesse Jackson and Congressman John Conyers tried to elevate Gore's civil rights record by deprecating my efforts in these fields, the record shows that I led in critical areas of educational testing bias and life-taking and budget-busting consumer abuses aimed at minorities and exposed the Democratic Party's neglect of racial injustice behind its civil rights rhetoric and oratory.

Being a progressive presidential candidate meant far more than being an identity politics candidate. It meant going to the roots of the power abuses of our political economy. If I made one mistake in addressing the identity politics adherents, it was not putting forth a detailed record of my past writings and involvement against racial and gender discrimination going back to the midfifties.

Going into May, we felt that the campaign was beginning to shape up. The national pollsters started to include Nader-LaDuke in their polling. Led by the Zogby surveys, the polls started to break past 5 percent on occasion. We had a big map on the wall at campaign headquarters where we marked the states in which we had achieved ballot status. Individual contributions began flowing into our empty coffers, which enabled us to hire more people to deal with the mounting work. We glanced at the other campaigns, but we were almost totally absorbed with our own fledgling formations. Democratic Senator Harry Reid took notice and assailed me for "not respecting the process"—one of the more puzzling comments we had to decipher and one Jim Hightower satirized in his speeches. But the Gore campaign had a more standard response to press inquiries about our campaign. They would say repeatedly, "We're not losing any sleep over Nader." To which I replied, "Slumber on, Al Gore, slumber on."

May 2000 was in many ways the most pleasurable month for campaigning in the entire eight-month stretch. Summer is traditionally not a good time to be on the road. People are on vacation, heat waves keep people away from sweaty gatherings, there are fewer events to attend, colleges are out, and the big political conventions absorb the media. Moreover, June through August is the last opportunity to get work done on position papers, to go on Washington-based cable shows on CNN, Fox, and MSNBC, to raise funds, and to discuss strategies and schedules for the final, nonstop eight weeks of the campaign.

Increasingly, people would ask me what it is like running for president, how wearisome it must be, and so packed with pressure. I would reply that the traveling was nothing new, even in its intensity, inasmuch as I have been civically campaigning for thirty-five years all over the country. Of course, presidential campaigning is a different dimension—there is no comparison to the wide array of subjects that must be considered. Polls become straitjackets on one's reach, people have far more hereditary prejudgments and stereotypes on "politics" and "parties," and there is a set date for votes to be counted.

Building a political movement, in contrast to advancing a civic or consumer issue, requires constant lobbying for media attention. One local opportunity that recurred again and again was meeting with editorial boards of major and community newspapers. I tried to have such sessions in every state. A surprising number of newspapers agreed to these meetings. From Columbia, South Carolina, to Concord, New Hampshire, to Los Angeles, Seattle, Lexington, Des Moines, and Las Vegas, my associates and I would sit around a large table with the editorial writers, a columnist, and a political reporter—and sometimes a cartoonist—and they would serve coffee, soft drinks, and snacks as they listened to my opening soliloquy. No matter what the paper's ideology, the custom across the board was that they were there to listen, not to browbeat the candidate. Unfortunately, their demeanor with us was one of curiosity rather than any consequential interest in our drive.

Their questions were the same, predictable inquiries: Are you at all concerned that you could take enough votes from Al Gore to cost him the election? How would you feel if you woke up the day after the election to learn that you helped elect George W. Bush? You know you can't win, so why are you doing this? Do you really believe there is little difference between Al Gore and George W. Bush?

With an inaudible sigh I would respond: Would I be running if I were concerned about taking votes from Al Gore? Isn't that what candidates try to do to one another—take votes? Would they ever ask a start-up company whether it is worried about taking sales dollars away from two dominant competitors? We're trying to build a new progressive politics in this country, that is our priority. It has to start sometime. If George Bush is elected, I would say that Al Gore blew it. He had every advantage over Bush, a bumbling Texas governor with a terrible record flatly contradicting his rhetoric. I would continue: Yes, there are a few but nowhere near enough major differences between Bush and Gore, and the converging similarities relating to corporate power's entrenchments tower above the dwindling real differences over which the two parties are willing to contend. Sure, the Democratic Party may register a D+ and the Republican Party a D–, but in my book they both flunk.

But I did long for editors prodding me with searching questions about my proposals, such as "Mr. Nader, you often say that you are running with the aim of giving more power to voters, taxpayers, workers, and small investors. What is your plan to do so? Has there been any success to date with any of your proposed tools having been adopted? How would you deal with an uninterested Congress that you hope will pass these facilities to bind these constituencies together into voluntary civic associations? What makes you think they wouldn't fight each other on certain policies?" Alas, these questions and many others that could have enlivened and broadened what politics should be dealing with were not forthcoming. If political discourse does not ask the big questions about the nature and uses of power, then it is very unlikely that it will ever reach the big answers.

The other regular interfaces with the media were the daily news conferences, whenever the schedule permitted, and reporters or columnists, joining us for a day or two and then returning home to write their stories. May 1, 2000, started at the Baltimore airport with John Judis of *The New Republic*. There was no surprise at the twisted piece that resulted. The publisher/owner of *The New Republic* was Al Gore's professor at Harvard and has made sure that his longtime protégé received first-class touting in his publication. So the dour and sour John Judis, who probably would still call himself a liberal, read our campaign as harming our own causes by undermining Democrats. Judis has strayed from any fundamental grip on the question of corporate power in America and was satisfied with marginal etchings in his portraits of the politically feasible in the country. It was no surprise then he was so distinctly unimpressed with us because his mind was already made up.

From Baltimore we flew into rainy Detroit and soon arrived at Solidarity House, the United Auto Workers' storied headquarters, to spend half an hour with UAW president Steve Yokich. Yokich was not pleased with the Democrats and didn't hesitate to say so. On May 23, 2000, he publicly said, "America's working families need and deserve a president they can count on to stand with them on their tough issues, not just the easy ones. That's why we have no choice but to actively explore alternatives to the two major political parties. It's time to forget about party labels and instead focus on supporting candidates such as Ralph Nader, who will take a stand based on what is right, not what big money dictates. Supporting those who support us is our political agenda, not just a slogan."

The mere mention of my candidacy by Yokich agitated the Gore campaign, which was continuing the party's tradition of expecting organized labor to lockstep with its politics and get out its vote. Even within the UAW's circle of leaders there was dismay at Yokich's remarks. It is not that these people were happy with the Gore-Lieberman ticket and the Clinton regime in general. It is—there they go again—that the Republicans were worse. I never expected the UAW to bolt from the Democrats, but at least there was a stirring, a caveat to that party's continuing choice of organized corporations over organized labor. Would that Clinton-Gore exercised a fraction of their political capital and energy in Congress over raising the lagging minimum wage that they unleashed on behalf of the corporate lobby behind NAFTA and GATT.

Yokich was especially worried that day about the upcoming congressional vote on permanent trade relations with China. He foresaw entire factories, such as those of Delphi Automotive, closing down and opening up in China with thirty-cents-an-hour workers in newly equipped plants producing products for shipment back to the States. This is a little-publicized impact of NAFTA and GATT.

After meeting with Yokich, I went over to speak to the newspaper guild, whose members were locked out in a lengthy dispute with the city's two merged newspapers. Several years have passed since the *Detroit News* and the *Detroit Free Press* merged and locked out hundreds of workers, but thousands of Detroiters were still refusing to buy the paper, circulation was way down, and the locked-out workers were still defiant.

We flew out of Detroit in the late afternoon for Madison, where I joined a picket line of unionists in support of workers subcontracted from Aramark Corp., who were not earning a living wage at the University of Wisconsin's Fluno Center.

The majority of Americans have been falling behind, notwith-standing twenty years of economic growth: losing ground in real wages, losing ground in home mortgage payments, health care, and consumer debt, burdens all, taking a much larger percentage of family income, losing ground to the increased costs of commuting to work and, with the near end of the extended family, increased consumer bills for day care and other services the family used to provide that now have to be purchased in the marketplace, and working longer hours than twenty-five years ago in a low-wage economy with a shrinking union base.

We then rushed over to the Rathskeller at the university for a speech and attended a fund-raiser at the home of Matt Rothschild, the editor of *The Progressive*. There, at least, I spied some nutritious food on a large table and managed to consume a portion. Around the country, at times, we thought the Greens took this solar energy issue a little too far. Maybe they assumed that being Green meant we photosynthesized and did not need any food to keep us going hour after hour. Madison is always special for any progressive candidate. Out on the back lawn of Matt's house, our supporters needed no explanations—it was all about building democracy, the sovereignty of the people, rolling back corporate power, and looking ahead. On our way to the airport for the flight to Chicago, I recalled the great speeches of "Fighting Bob" La Follette from Wisconsin, who led the progressive movement in America in the early twentieth century. Were he here now, what would he say?

On to Columbia, South Carolina, where we headed straight to the state legislature and met with Gilda Cobb-Hunter, the minority leader of the House. An African American, Cobb-Hunter, upbeat and effervescent, gave us the impression that she was surrounded by a battalion of courtly, smiling white sharks. She wanted to introduce me to the legislators in session, but their business ran long and I had to settle for a few sideline chats with some of the lawmakers. Then, in quick succession, we met with twenty citizens working on our campaign, attended an editorial board meeting with the state newspaper, and appeared on a radio talk show on WVOC, the largest AM station, with Kevin Cohen, a confessed conservative who railed against big government and regulation and attracted Rush Limbaugh followers. (Welcome to talk radio, so dominated by right-wingers who day after day attack our government, which doesn't advertise, and applaud the business world, which does.) If you are a guest, you can get your licks in, but callers are attracted to like-minded hosts, so not many progressive callers telephone or get through the screeners. Then on to a press conference at the statehouse, a meeting with *The Free Times,* a community weekly, and then a speech and discussion at the Unitarian Universalist Fellowship before leaving for the airport and the flight back to Washington, D.C.

The next day in Washington included several hours' fund-raising on the phone, a telephone conversation with Michael Lerner, author of *Spirit Matters,* about his fervent belief that the campaign should emphasize the more spiritual dimensions of justice, and an interview with *U.S. News and World Report.* Afterward I went to Capitol Hill for a meeting I arranged between Major General Parker, M.D., and naval researchers on global infectious diseases with Congressman Sherrod Brown and his colleagues. The government's only "drug company" is in the Department of Defense, where army and naval medical scientists with incredible efficiency have discovered and tested major anti-malarial drugs, along with other drugs and vaccines now used throughout the world. This remarkable story of amazing successes with first-class science on tiny budgets, extending over three decades, shows up the exorbitant major drug companies that have no interest in investing in malaria, TB, and other infectious disease research, because they don't see enough money in it for them.

In discussing foreign policy initiatives on the campaign trail, I would repeatedly stress the need for the United States to launch a major program against these scourges, coming toward the United States with drug-resistant strains, which take millions of lives a year, mostly in the Third World. The Pentagon's tiny enclave at the Walter Reed Institute of Health is one of the best-kept secrets in Washington. The press had never heard of it, nor had anybody in Congress, nor had Bill Clinton's White House aides. The latter, led by Sidney Blumenthal, did meet at the White House earlier with the same army and navy scientists and me to discuss what more could be done.

Returning to our headquarters, I met with the Hillsman media group from Minneapolis and our staff to go over the prospect of their doing some political messages for a modest television buy in selected cities. Bill Hillsman is a fresh voice, who produced award-winning ads for the first election of Senator Paul Wellstone and later for Minnesota Governor Jesse Ventura. Hillsman's trademark is generating news coverage of the ad either because it is unique and funny or because it provokes controversy. Of course, such news coverage usually entails replaying the ad as part of the news story. I told Hillsman that I didn't like the idea of spending money to enrich television stations that should be covering the campaign as a news story. Moreover, there was very little money available for that purpose anyhow. He said that he could work within those parameters and that such adroitly placed ads, conveying content and comparisons with other candidates, would reach, amuse, and arouse the voters and get the word of mouth under way. Hillsman is very clever, but we never expected that he would return to his North Woods Advertising Agency in Minnesota and create what turned out to be two of the most talked-about and award-winning political ads of 2000.

Next stop, Pittsburgh, where I spoke before the Pennsylvania Credit Union convention. The performance and promise of credit unions was to become a topic of my campaign remarks in low-income communities and whenever the subjects of consumer, bor-rowers, and big financial institutions came up.

There are twelve thousand credit unions in the United States with over fifty million members who own them. Consumers receive auto loans, personal loans, some home mortgages, and other credit at reasonable costs. Credit unions and other cooperatives are old so-cial and economic innovations that meet human needs. Unfortu-nately, the astigmatism of the two-party electioneering is illustrated when candidates ignore these working institutions.

The credit union delegates in Pennsylvania were worried about the sharply increasing concentration of banks and insurance com-panies through mergers and the political lobbying power often used against credit unions that flows from the emergence of such super-conglomerate giants as Citigroup.

The scene shifted dramatically when we arrived the next day in Charleston, West Virginia. There, in the office of my old friend Ken Hechler, secretary of state, the topic was the dynamiting of mountaintops by coal companies. Yes, in the year 2000, King Coal was blowing off mountains and choking rivers and streams with tons of sludge and debris. Both parties have done little to curtail this destructive activity.

West Virginia can teach you a lot about politics in America. Heavily reliant on the coal industry, it has sacrificed itself on the avaricious altar of the coal barons. Tens of thousands of its sons over a century have given their lives for their companies, succumbing to black lung disease and mine disasters. Wide swathes of its beautiful hilly countryside look like moonscapes from strip mining. Its rivers and streams have suffered acid runoffs from coal mine slag. Decades ago, the large coal barons, many situated in London, New York, and Chicago, bought or pressured local politicians. They escaped paying most of their property taxes for the schools and other local services by getting absurd underassessments of their coal lands. During the unusual hard times of the twenties and thirties, the barons' lawyers created the notorious "broad-form deeds" by which they obtained from the impoverished and desperate people of Appalachia, for fifty cents per acre, the right to all coal, oil, gas, metals, and minerals, the right to divert and pollute water— and immunity from all liability. This included immunity from responsibility for causing the people's homes to cave in dangerously due to the hollowed-out underground.

I mention these predatory actions because more than thirty years ago, my associates and I worked intensively to secure congressional passage of the coal mine safety law and the coal miners' pneumoconiosis act, which has provided billions of dollars to the widows and orphans of these sacrificed miners. In my earlier travels throughout that battered state, from the towns to the hollows, I met the workers and families who benefited mightily from these laws. Collaborating with a young, dynamic lawyer, David Grubb, I helped start the West Virginia Citizen Action Group in Charleston, which was a great fighter for consumer, worker, and environmental justice.

For years, the *Charleston Gazette,* under the Chilton family, championed our efforts in their editorials and reported them in their news pages. But memories dim as the years pass, and our campaign presence in West Virginia was too sparse to remind people of the times when key members of Congress, such as Congressman Phil Burton, were around to move legislation that was needed, no matter how loudly the coal and steel moguls bellowed.

Our work for the people of West Virginia was matched by the national recognition that we gave to the state's unique problems.

On November 7, however, we received 2 percent of the West Virginia vote. Obviously, electoral politics is a soup of many ingredients, and vote tallies on Election Day don't necessarily correspond with what a candidate has done for the electorate.

Back at headquarters, from Saturday, May 6, to Friday, May 12, my days were filled with fund-raising telephone calls, contacting civic leaders, some of whom were celebrities like Willie Nelson and Susan Sarandon, to ask if they would join our citizens' support committee. I answered other calls, which requested appearances at future dinners, like the industrial hemp dinner—yes, hemp food—in the San Francisco Bay Area in June. Then there were press calls to return from regional newspapers such as the *Lincoln-Star Journal* in Nebraska, C-Span's "Road to the White House" series, and, most significantly, the first invitation to go on Tim Russert's *Meet the Press*. For a person who broke into the news business in his forties, Russert has both a news sense and a smiling, tough questioning mode that leaves his competitors far back in the pundit pack. Early on, Russert sensed that the balance between Gore and Bush could be affected by the Greens. The polls bolstered his hunch, and that got me in the door. Russert asked and challenged me about my positions and my criticisms of the major candidates and then shared some sandwiches with me after it was all over. Not a bad way to spend part of Sunday morning, I thought, and I left thinking how those twelve interview minutes were more exposure than days on the road.

The China trade vote was coming up in the House, which gave me an opportunity to visit Representatives Henry Waxman, Paul Kanjorski, and Peter Deutsch and Minority Leader Dick Gephardt. Kanjorski is a legislator who engages you in a dialogue, which I appreciated. Too many legislators just sit and listen, sometimes with a perfunctory nod or with glazed eye contact, never letting you know what's lurking in their minds.

Waxman's meeting was difficult. He is a perfect argument

against twelve-year term limits—maybe the only such argument left in the House. With a superb voting record, including reasoned votes against NAFTA and WTO, he was undecided on China. He told us that Clinton, who spearheaded the WTO though Congress, called to lobby him, starting the conversation with the beguiling words, "Henry, I know the WTO sucks," and then giving his pitch as to why Waxman should vote yes, which he eventually did. Gephardt, as the leader of the Democrats, was against giving up the annual congressional review of whether to grant China most-favored-nation treatment, for reasons of human rights, worker abuses, and trade violations. Some Democrats thought that Gephardt took this position but didn't twist arms because he really didn't mind losing, which would get the corporate interests and the White House off his back. I was unable to judge the accuracy of this widespread belief in anti–corporate globalization circles that went back to the struggles over NAFTA and GATT. Certainly, Gephardt did not restrain his energetic deputy David Bonior, and it is not Gephardt's personality to be a Sam Rayburn or a Lyndon Johnson. When I asked Gephardt why Clinton continued to fight his own party in the House on these unfair-trade matters and side with the global corporations against labor and environmental groups, he replied without hesitation, "Because he is selfish." As for our campaign, Gephardt did not seem displeased at all, knowing what we knew at the time, that control of the House would be decided by about a dozen very close House races and that a Green spillover vote in those districts, where Greens were not running, would likely help the Democratic incumbents or challengers.

On May 12 we flew to New York for interviews with the impressive Beth Gardner of the Associated Press and her energetic photographer, who spoke almost as fast as she clicked the camera. All we could manage at the *New York Times* was a meeting with the paper's chief political writer, Jim Roberts. No reporter was assigned, and the editorial board, which invites candidates for various federal, state, and local offices for Q and A, did not invite me. This was just the beginning of the high-hat treatment from the folks on West Forty-third Street.

The next interview was pure substance and pleasure. It was conducted by Bob Kuttner, co-editor of the *American Prospect* magazine and a columnist for *Business Week* and the *Washington Post*. Kuttner is a liberal political economist who appears congenial to insurgencies as represented by the Greens, but always returns to the Democratic Party fold of which he is often a strong critic. He later wrote that he'd "hold his nose" and vote for Gore in Massachusetts.

That evening we went to two fund-raisers in New York, one by young adults who read *The Nation* and *Village Voice* and the other by young adults who read *The Economist* and *Wall Street Journal*.

We flew out of Baltimore on Southwest Airlines to Providence, Rhode Island. Two round-trip tickets cost a combined total of $294. Southwest Airlines saved our campaign money and was our preferred airline everywhere we went that it had routes. Its passenger mix is diverse, boisterous, and friendly. When people on the plane expressed astonishment that we travel Southwest, which is all coach, I gave them so many reasons, it sounded like a promotion for the company. It is a low-cost airline with good service, and relatively new and well-maintained planes; it gives its employees discretion and stock; it has a few seats facing backward, which I like for conversation; and it shows the nation that without this airline, the mindless scope of deregulation would be more of a disaster. With all this, Southwest, by charging less and providing good service, made more profits in 2000 than United, US Airways, and Northwest Airlines combined. I also like the way Southwest usually answers its phones at all hours immediately with live, responsive human beings.

The grind continued, but it was exhilarating. On May 15 historian Richard Walton of the Providence Greens met us at the airport and drove us to the State House Building for a press conference with Greens Greg Gerrit and Tony Affigne. We then went over to the State House Rotunda, which, as a backdrop for a political speech, is without peer in the country. Picture a two-level rotunda, split by stairs, where your voice is amplified and enhanced. Then pack it with scores of cheering partisans and a full brace of television cameras and reporters. What an incredible experience! Every time I made a point, the folks roared in response. When I spoke out against a local corporate welfare scheme to build yet another mall on the backs of taxpayers, the roar broke the sound barrier. Looking up at the assemblage of people of all ages, holding posters and banners, with eager and hopeful expressions on their faces, ready to volunteer and spread the message for a responsive politics, I thought of the great murals of yesteryear depicting such rallies against the entrenched interests.

Eight

ON THE ROAD TO FIFTY STATES

I most like campaigning in New England. Being a New Englander, I know the land, the towns, the history, the lore, and the life. Sure, the region has a few big cities and their sprawl, but in terms of sheer acreage and the number of distinct towns, New England has held on right into the twenty-first century. Places like Vermont, western Massachusetts, and Connecticut, the coastal towns, and the lake country still have the potential of recovering and enhancing their finest traditions with more local economies, local husbandry, and community self-reliance.

From Providence we drove to the Boston Commons, where a rally organized by high school students against the M-CAS standardized tests in Massachusetts and the looming privatization of public schools was under way. From afar, one could think that those youngsters just didn't like tests. But these youngsters had done their homework. Created by consulting firms that saw the corporate management of public schools as a profitable objective, these tests appear to be designed to show that public education was not working because so many students flunked. Experience in Texas with such manipulations led to high dropout rates for high school students under Governor Bush. This testing tyranny forces the schools to teach to the tests, which themselves are narrow-scoped and misleading yardsticks. There is plenty of evidence to show that behind these tests is a commercial ideology panting to take over more and more of the $320 billion spent annually on public schools.

A goodly number of high school students and their parents were planning to boycott these tests. I explained my support for the students, but unlike in Providence, the large Boston media rarely covers such rallies or citizen gatherings. Coverage is left to community papers or the large alternative weekly, the *Boston Phoenix*. Crossing the Charles in a hurry, we were late for an address at MIT arranged by Professor Jonathan King, a well-regarded microbiologist and civic activist on many fronts. He is in regular support of the M-CAS rebellion. King had a National Science Foundation grant to work with high school students on developing their scientific curiosity. Now, with pressure on teachers to produce good multiple-choice-test scores, he saw his program being shunted aside in favor of repeated classroom test preparation. He took us to a room at MIT where we met with the petitioners and members of the Green Party steering committee, which had the task of getting ten thousand verified signatures in order to get our candidacy on the state ballot. They did.

That afternoon my remarks at MIT's Wong Auditorium included observations on technology and health, and academic science versus corporate science, with references to the struggle for auto safety, and the necessity for science to rein in a runaway biotechnology that is lacking both an ethical and a legal framework. I recounted a story from my law school days at Harvard when I was doing research on unsafe automobile designs and the law. In my innocence, I went to MIT looking for the department of automotive engineering, or a professor or even a graduate student researching auto safety. There was no one at arguably the leading engineering university in the country. The motor vehicle transport system was only the largest engineering system in the land, and crashes on it were causing the fourth-largest category of fatalities in the country. Generating knowledge to nourish lifesaving policies and practices was not part of MIT's mission, certainly not when it conflicted with a major industry's practice, I suggested to the largely student audience. I asked them to reflect on what other contemporary deficiencies or corporate biases exist in MIT's curriculum or research activities.

There was not much time for extended discussion because we had to motor to Concord, where Richard N. Goodwin was hosting a fund-raiser. It was a memorable drive, keeping in mind America's revolutionary history and driving over Concord Bridge as the sun was going down and spring was breaking out. Dick Goodwin— special assistant to Presidents Kennedy and Johnson, author, and political strategist—was a law school classmate. Although he continues to be a tough Democrat and receives invitations to the White House, nothing can compromise either his independent thinking or his unerring retention of the fundamental ends of politics in a democracy. Governor Clinton, running for the presidency in 1992, praised Goodwin's *Promises to Keep* as "an extraordinary and brilliant book." His message was an eloquent reminder of how America's promises to its people, rooted deeply in American history, have been stalled and even reversed by greed and corruption. Clinton as president promptly forgot this admired analysis. Years later, Goodwin summarized the Clinton administration as one where "to mention it is to accomplish it."

Our short-term objectives were threefold: to achieve ballot status in as many states as possible, to participate in the presidential debates, and to receive more than 5 percent of the popular vote. This meant that we had to conduct a fifty-state campaign to attract our hard-core votes and then spend more time in states, such as California and New York, where we expected to do well. They were challenging but reachable goals, and my New England tour that May generated the enthusiasm that we could do it.

The next morning we left Boston and journeyed by car to Dismas House in Worcester, an unusual alternative to incarceration, which had inmates and college students working together. This was followed by a speech and rally at Assumption College, a meeting with signature gatherers, and a news conference. If Worcester was uneventful, the Phillip Metropolitan Christian Methodist Episcopal Church common room in Hartford brought home the grim realities that African-American pastors connect with daily.

Six reverends belonging to the interdenominational Ministerial Alliance and members of the inner-city community gathered to convey their concerns and hear my views. Reporters were present. Hartford was not unknown to me. It was twenty-six miles from where I grew up. I practiced law there for a while after law school and taught a few courses at the University of Hartford. All this did not mean that I was familiar with *their* Hartford—now one of the poorest inner cities in the United States, suffering violent, drug-ridden, devastated schools, crumbling houses and tenements, high infant mortality, and a stunning asthma rate among black and Hispanic children reaching 40 percent. But as I stood by the church, one sight, one glimpse, caught the tale of two cities that is Connecticut's capital. There over the horizon rose the gleaming office buildings and hotels of the insurance companies, with their tens of billions of dollars in assets and their well-compensated executives, who at the end of the day leave for West Hartford, Simsbury, and other lovely suburbs west of the city. There also were the banks that for years found reasons to abandon low-income areas, redlining them into sure decay.

Inside the church, the pastors knew about the two Hartfords, but they had more immediate matters on their mind. They grilled me for forty-five minutes on what I would do about police brutality, racial profiling, economic development, health care, failing schools, drug use and crime, and the hopelessness and human tragedies they minister to day after day with compassion and very few resources. I regretted that Elizabeth Norton Scheff, the first elected African-American Green in the United States, was not present due to a previous commitment. In 1999 I campaigned for her election to the Hartford City Council, and her widely publicized battles to reform the city's schools were not forgotten by the voters who chose her. Ms. Scheff is one of those rare urban/civic warriors who are pure empiricism—intensely focused on mobilizing and taking on the injustices with no detours. Therefore she is seen as an irritator. It would have been a fascinating, instructive mix of exchanges had she been at the church that afternoon.

I knew from their comments that the ministers were backing the Democrats, but they were under no illusions about any party making much of a difference. I reminded them the Democrats have run Hartford's city government for decades and asked what they had done with few exceptions beyond presiding over decay, kowtowing to the corporate powers that be, and sweet-talking folks like them. It seemed that my words made a connection, going well beyond political correctness, and they concluded the meeting by forming a prayer circle with hands clasped and prayed for our campaign and its sensibilities. How do they keep their spirits up? They simply have faith that someday their just causes will overcome. I took leave of them, thinking once again, as little children innocently scampered around us, just how far politics and its smugness have gone in our country.

In the late afternoon we joined the striking workers who were picketing the Avery Heights Retirement Community on busy New Britain Avenue. The moving circular picket line did not have much physical space to maneuver, but the spirit of the workers was uplifting. They knew that the chain owners of this retirement community were making big money and could well afford assuring their workers just rewards for their labors.

Hartford being a compact place, it did not take long to reach the fund-raiser for the Connecticut Greens at the Hartford Brewery. I wouldn't call it a happy hour, but when I entered, it certainly sounded like one. The Connecticut Greens have been among my favorites and not just because they hail from my home state. The core of the party is small in number, but they are hardworking and choose important issues, like stopping the Patriots football deal, the living wage, the troubled and risky Millstone atomic power plants, the pitfalls of electricity deregulation, and numerous environmental damages. They keep a steady eye on the objective of building a progressive political movement by tapping into any and all potential supporters, organizers, or leaders. Warming up an already warmed-up crowd were Mike DeRosa and Tom Sevigny, both early founders of the state Green Party and both candidates for local office as well. I reviewed some of the Green Party's accomplishments and took to task Connecticut's two corporate senators, Democrats Chris Dodd—the opponent of state civil justice systems who wants to diminish the rights and remedies of injured or defrauded plaintiffs—and Joe Lieberman, who has not seen a weapons system, an insurance company, or a drug company he doesn't like. They both have nice smiles, though.

The Greens and I then went to the Hartford Public Library auditorium for the evening discussion, where cable TV and other press reporters were waiting. The place was packed and my polls were hovering around 10 percent in Connecticut. But I knew better than to count on all those votes because many people tend to get cold feet in the voting booth, regardless of other Connecticut polls showing Gore in a landslide.

The next day found me giving individual interviews with the

New Haven press at Barrie's Booters. We then walked to the Yale
Co-Op, which had been run and defended against encroaching
chain bookstores by my Princeton classmate Harry Berkowitz, who
met me with a campaign contribution. Speaking in a large bookstore is a bit disconcerting, what with the aisles and shelves and
different angles making eye contact a kaleidoscopic sport, and I
wasn't at my best that day—the nature of the room, the kind of
podium, the lighting all affect my delivery. I've heard many other
speakers say the same. For instance, a high platform stage looking
down on the audience really affects the audience's intangible response as well as the sense of feedback the speaker gets while the
audience is listening. I like rooms where the speaker is on the same
level or just slightly elevated. Not good at all are those medical
school–type lecture halls that are built as if they were on a hillside.

With a smooth, rapid-fire Connecticut trip behind us, thanks to
the Greens' Peter Ellner, that evening I found myself in New York
at Paul Newman's apartment, where he graciously hosted a fund-
raiser. There seems to be no end to Newman's talents. At the top
of his craft as an actor, he entered professional auto racing at the
age when most racers complete their careers. He's a smart and
effortlessly charming figure who was so steeped in military weapon
policies that one would have felt sorry for Gore or Bush had either
had to debate him. A longtime advocate of international arms control, Newman for years has taken this issue to television talk shows
and the like.

A little earlier, I had spoken to his daughter Nell, who lives in
California and is a leader in the organic food movement and critic
of unlabeled genetically modified foods, which more than 90 percent of the American people want the government to label. Paul
Newman was not turning Green. He was and still is a Democrat
and has endured much evasion, cowardliness, and dissembling by
Democratic politicians without splitting from the party. But he and
his celebrated wife, Joanne Woodward, seemed to be near their
limits and saw my candidacy as at least shaking up the stagnation
of the Democrats and broadening the political debate on issues
about which they cared deeply.

I stood by the piano before some forty people in their living
room, and Newman started to introduce me. He recalled a Mike
Nichols impersonation of Tennessee Williams as he is questioned

by a reporter: "Tennessee, can you tell us something about your new play?" Tennessee replies, "Well, as the curtain rises, our heroine is being accused of many heinous crimes such as public fornication, sodomy, corruptions of minors, money laundering, and puttin' on airs." "So," says Newman, "Ralph is safe on this last charge." Everyone roared with laughter. Among the people present were Katrina vanden Heuvel, editor of *The Nation*; Russian specialist Professor Stephen Cohen; Victor Navasky; Dr. Warner Slack, the pioneer in computer medicine; Judith Vladeck, civil rights lawyer; Joan Claybrook; and Phil Donahue. They knew very well that basic changes were needed. What was on some of their minds, especially Victor Navasky's, was why I thought the pluses of a Green candidacy would not be canceled out by the risk of costing Gore a close election. Navasky and some others in the room would have liked Gore to win plus a significant Green Party turnout to push Democrats along a more active, progressive path. In addition, the composition of the future Supreme Court concerned them very much.

I described how bad the past twenty years have been for civic groups, how the Democrats chose not even to oppose Antonin Scalia. Indeed, every Democrat, including Senator Gore, voted for Scalia, who was confirmed by a vote of 98 to 0. When they had control of the Senate, the Democrats gave Clarence Thomas eleven decisive votes, in a 52–48 victory for President George Bush. My point: The Democrats, who are quick to say that these two justices are their least favorite, knew this going into the nomination process but did not have the fight in them that they had earlier displayed against Robert Bork and other rejected Republican nominees. Besides, who nominated Earl Warren, William Brennan, Harry Blackmun, John Paul Stevens, and David Souter? Republican presidents.

I mentioned another reason for running: the increasing reluctance of good people to become candidates for public office. This is more than an immense loss of talent. It leaves too much of the field to the rascals. I told them of a conversation I had with Gerry Spence, a trial lawyer of great skills and a prolific author from Wyoming. The Senate seat was open in 1996, following the retirement of Republican Alan Simpson.

"Gerry," I said, "why wouldn't you throw your hat into the Senate race?"

"Ralph, I am better known here than any politician," he replied. "But why would I want to do that? Who in his right mind would want to go into that pit?"

"But what an eloquent voice. Who can better communicate to the American people than you? You would be the conscience of the Senate."

"Ralph, listen. I'm sitting in my office and looking out at the Grand Tetons. I'm happy where I am now," he said.

"Gerry," I replied, "the country needs you. It's just that patriotically simple. There are too few champions of the people there. What if a few days from now I filled a truck with manure and in the middle of the night dumped it on your front lawn? Next morning you get up and see it there. Would you turn around, go to your study, and look out at the Grand Tetons? Or would you clean it up?"

"You bastard," he declared.

I could just as well have mentioned Phil Donahue as an example. Donahue is a man of conviction, daring, compassion, and enormous awareness of the need for society to exercise its First Amendment rights. For nearly thirty years, his national television show gave voice early and consistently to the grievances and the rights of women, minorities, workers, consumers, gays, lesbians, antiwar advocates, children, and the downtrodden. He had the Reverend Jerry Falwell on the show thirty times. In right-wing circles, it used to be said that you're more likely to get on the Donahue show if you loudly condemn and criticize him.

This was a great compliment to Phil's fervent belief that advancing free speech must include giving it to those you disagree with. Is there a better listener? Was there a better speech on the mass media than the one he gave at the Newseum in 1998? Well, I thought that Donahue could run for the U.S. Senate seat from Connecticut as an independent in 1998 and become a superb senator. We had a group of people urging him to do so. Senator Dodd was up for reelection, and one poll had a sizable percentage supporting his retirement. The Republicans were putting up a candidate they knew did not have a chance—defeated Congressman Gary Franks. A three-way race would help Donahue win. Money would not have been a problem. Phil has honesty, character, and an unblemished record in a talk-show industry that swells heads.

Name recognition was high. Imagine town meetings in just about every town in Connecticut, and he could be back home in Westport every night. Ten years ago, Donahue would openly say how he would like to be a senator someday. This time it was nothing doing. To Donahue and many other potential candidates, the political process had turned squalid, myopic, and beholden. His polite refusal further fueled my sense that those of us striving for a clean politics could no longer be on the sidelines and self-indulgently recoil from diving in to be members of the cleaning crew.

At Paul Newman's house that night, I had no inkling of how involved and important Phil Donahue would become later in our campaign. He was quiet at the fund-raiser, other than suggesting that I not neglect the many cable television news and interview shows that were satisfying a demand for political expression.

The next day we were in Concord, New Hampshire, with Dick Ryan of the *Detroit News* accompanying our party. Along with New Hampshire Green leaders to greet us was Richard Grossman, who has pioneered the rediscovery of American corporate charter history. Indefatigably, he has launched citizen committees of discussion and local action throughout the country, challenging the legitimacy of corporate sovereignty.

A spirited press conference in the lobby of the legislative building and a meeting with Green Party petitioners was followed by a brief address to the New Hampshire Senate. The senators were very cordial, and a few expressed their support as I was walking to the speaker's podium.

I decided to use my few minutes that day to speak about the unspeakable—that the large corporation is the dominant institution in our society. This very assertion was made way back in 1959 by William Gossett, then a vice president of Ford Motor Company and later president of the American Bar Association. Forty-two years later, the global corporations have ascended to far greater power over our elections, government, workers, and consumers, including children, jamming commercialism into just about everywhere.

I mentioned how public budgets are being massively distorted by the proliferating array of taxpayer subsidies, giveaways, and bailouts (known as corporate welfare) to corporations. And I described how these transnational companies have no allegiance to any country or community other than to control them. Company executives have yearned for years for their company to be "anational"—outside any national jurisdiction. While this literally has not yet transpired, corporate globalism is creating its autocratic systems of governance under the guise of global or regional trade agreements such as the World Trade Organization and NAFTA. Increasingly, these modes of governance that subordinate nontrade standards, such as consumer, environmental, and worker conditions, to the supremacy of international commerce, will avoid and thereby undermine local, state, and national sovereignties. All this I said quickly because I wanted to revisit some New England history with them.

In the early 1800s, Massachusetts began legislating charters for the nascent textile factories that created their corporate form of limited liability for their investors. These charters constituted tight rein, stipulating what the new company wanted to manufacture, the term limits of the charter, which was then up for review and renewal, and the public purposes—standards—incumbent on the company.

People in those days were wary of these artificial legal entities called corporations having too many privileges and immunities. There were vigorous debates in the legislature and other forums. When companies misbehaved, their creator—the state government—could and did revoke their charters. The attorney general of Ohio revoked the charter of Standard Oil Company of Ohio late in the nineteenth century. Then came the corporations' single greatest legal victory. In the case of *Santa Clara* v. *Southern Pacific Railroad,* the Supreme Court of the United States ruled, in 1886, without even being asked by counsel, that a corporation was a natural "person" for purposes of the equal protection clause of the Fourteenth Amendment. Today, the modern corporation has all the rights of real human beings, except for the Fifth Amendment right against self-incrimination, and all kinds of privileges and immunities that human beings do not or cannot have. Until we come to terms with this issue of "personhood" and the grave imbalances that follow, the warning of Supreme Court Justice Louis Brandeis in the 1930s about these big companies becoming Frankensteins in our midst will be more prescient than ever.

I don't think these lawmakers had ever heard such words. Some appeared thoughtful as they listened. Others were bemused, and still others—probably hard-core corporatists themselves—just wanted to resume their legislative business. Richard Grossman was standing in the back of the chamber listening. As I was leaving, I said to him, "Well, Richard, this must be the first time that any legislature has been spoken to about these issues of corporate charters and personhood." He nodded knowingly.

On our way to Vermont, we stopped at Keene State College in Keene, New Hampshire, where I spoke to a gathering of local citizens. I emphasized local democracy and the need to resuscitate the town-meeting tradition—possibly the most pristine form of democracy anywhere in the world today. I noted how large corporations, whose predecessors used to rip off consumers (monopolistic price-fixing and shoddy, unsafe products), now have expanded to take away tax dollars while they also become adroit tax escapees. Tax dollars were supposed to meet public needs—like the public works, schools, medical research, parks, public safety, and the like—that private enterprise was not interested in putting their investment capital into. Now, with their power, large companies, in direct and subtle, complex ways, siphon off large portions of the local, state, and public budgets via corporate welfare. Or as Ronald Reagan put it back in the mid-seventies—by having their "hand in the trough." Only small business has the freedom to go bankrupt, I quipped. Green Party materials were passed out, and I left for the Green Mountain state with a good feeling that basic populism was not contrary to the beliefs of conservative New Hampshire.

The next day we were in Burlington, Vermont. A noon press conference at the City Hall auditorium evoked the obvious question: Would Congressman Bernie Sanders, former Burlington mayor and now officially independent, support our candidacy? I said that Bernie's endorsement would be welcome, but they would have to ask him. Earlier in the campaign, however, Bernie had told me that while he sympathized and agreed with our pro-democracy agenda, he could not come out officially for us. The reason was that his modus vivendi with the House Democrats would be ruptured and he would lose much of his influence, including a possible subcommittee chair. Fair enough. He did agree to introduce me before an assembly that night at Montpelier High School.

But first there was a sit-down lunch at the Society of Friends building with Ruth Coniff, a reporter for *The Progressive*. Following this unaccustomed luxury, we met at two P.M. with the signature petitioners for their kickoff drive to get us on the ballot. These good citizens, like others of their avocation around the country, are the unsung heroes of third-party candidates. They are the rebuttals to the ugly collaboration between the Democrats and Republicans in state legislatures who do whatever they can to exclude competition. Some states are much worse than others. Little Vermont was in the modest barrier category, requiring only one thousand signatures for a presidential candidate.

The fund-raiser that followed at the home of environmentalist Crea Lintilhac was not much in terms of dollars, but made up for it with the dazzling presence of Vermont's activists of all ages and incomes. Of course, the location also helped to dazzle. Crea's home and the expansive landscapes around it are a splendid reminder of why people love to visit Vermont.

That sunny afternoon, the star of the show was Anthony Pollina, the gubernatorial candidate of the Vermont Progressive Party. Pollina was a longtime civic leader in Vermont, heading the Vermont Public Interest Research Group with illustrious results. He knew Vermont upside and downside. Taking the podium, he stated right off that his was a campaign to win, not just to make a few points. He quickly distinguished himself from Vermont's Democratic governor, Howard Dean, by listing the governor's positions and neglects and adding that Vermont's Democrats and independents would have been outraged at these same policies were Dean a Republican.

Pollina then launched into a concise, articulate description of what Vermont needs and what he would accomplish as governor. At the time, I said to myself, this is a real political comer. Pollina had it together. Moreover, Vermont's campaign finance reform law had just taken effect. This meant that Pollina would qualify for the maximum matching funds, which totaled just over $300,000. This brought the state toward a little more level playing field.

As the guests started to leave, I was so impressed with Pollina that I asked him to join me in Montpelier. He agreed to come, though I sensed a hesitancy, which was explained that evening. Driving through the bucolic countryside—and it verily defined "bucolic"—I made a call to Steve Yokich, the United Auto Workers' president, urging him to get the Democrats to give labor a better agenda in return for the UAW's probable endorsement of Gore.

When I arrived at the bustling high school auditorium, with its tables, volunteers, and incoming audience, Bernie Sanders took me aside and in grave tones expressed his concern at my having invited Pollina to speak with us. Clearly he was worried that the Democrats, who had agreed no longer to seriously challenge Bernie (with one exception in 1996), thereby sparing him a three-way race, would see his association with Pollina as a hostile act to their party and their governor.

I expressed surprise. "Bernie," I said, "Anthony was once your staff member, and there are no positions that I know where you are in disagreement."

He acknowledged that but repeated his displeasure nonetheless. Going up to the stage with Bernie, I thought to myself that an Independent should not have to worry about such matters. Bernie graciously introduced me and described our work together. But he left the stage and departed in the middle of my speech before I asked Pollina to come up and give his precise, factual stem-winder. He was a great hit with the crowd. There was very little time after the question and comment period to circulate with the Greens. It was late. We had to drive that night to Portland, Maine, which was nearly five hours away.

It was a fast-paced tour and I have to admit that I started counting down the states left.

Maine is one of two states—the other being New Mexico—where the Green Party first started getting the attention of the press and the dominant parties. This is in no small part due to the energy and intellect of John Rensenbrink, who, until retirement, taught politics at Bowdoin College. He came very early to Green politics in the eighties, convening or actively participating in its raucous conferences and meetings and giving as good as he got. In 1997 he published his book *Against All Odds,* a history of the U.S. Green

Party, with emphasis on its ecological and political reform stands. John is insistent, always exhorting people to surpass any of his own previous efforts. I visited Maine three times during the campaign, but that was not enough for him.

On this trip, following our daily press conference near Brunswick, we attended the Maine Green Party nominating convention at Noremega Hall in Bangor. I spoke for a few minutes and then Nancy Allen placed my name in nomination. In a field of three, I was voted their nominee. The Associated Press and MSNBC were there. Our numbers in the polls were still inching upward. What more could one ask?

The next morning we stopped for Sunday breakfast with a jam-packed crowd of Greens at the Mesa Verde restaurant in Portland. For nine A.M., these people were sure charged up. Two Green Party candidates for the state legislature, Derrick Grant and David Palmer, spoke about their first-time plunge into politics. I went over some local issues, reminding some of the old-timers of our book *The Paper Plantation,* which exposed the enormous power of the giant paper and pulp companies in Maine. These mills literally controlled and ran major rivers, and the struggle over the legendary Maine woods was still ongoing with rallies, statewide referenda, and lawsuits. If there was ever a state for the Greens to thrive in, it was the land of the Mainers.

That evening I stayed at the home of Herschl and Selma Sternlieb and discovered again what political campaigning finds—talented, engaged citizens who hold up far more than their share of democratic society. A successful, semiretired businessman, Mr. Sternlieb is a clear-eyed progressive moored in fundamental principles of candor, justice, and resolve. He is a satirist of both right-wingers and wobbly liberals, and you can't stop laughing at his myth-puncturing poetry and prose.

The next morning we were back in Washington. I went to the ABC studios to do a Webcast with Michael Oreskes, Washington bureau chief of the *New York Times*, and Josh Gurnstein of ABC News. No news organization wanted to be left behind in this new medium, though I have to ask if Webcasts are worthwhile. The next day I did a similar Web interview with MSNBC, and there were more upbeat assurances about audience size.

All the presidential and vice presidential candidates used the Internet with elaborate, heavily worked Web sites. They enthusiastically counted the millions of hits. They poured out notices and messages and got replies back. Millions of voters purportedly got more engaged in watching, reacting, and commenting on these campaigns. The Internet age, a hundred pundits predicted, would greatly change political campaigning and fund-raising. Well, it proved to be a very cheap fund-raising medium that encouraged small givers. But for increasing voter turnout—another frequent prediction—it was disappointing.

From virtual reality we set out for our West Coast journey that included Alaska and Hawaii—two states that major candidates treat as off-limits—too far away, populations too small, and too politically predictable. But first we attended a fund-raiser held in Berkeley, thrown by my nephew Tarek Milleron's close friends Stacia Cronin, a pediatrician, and David Wilson, a home builder, wife and husband. Stacia and David, somewhat less than impressed with the major choices in the election, had generously offered their help to our campaign. Despite a few heated phone calls, the turnout for the fund-raiser was healthy indeed. The house, high in the Berkeley hills, was filled with professionals who would ordinarily be skeptical of Green politics and even a few of whom would ordinarily be voting Republican. Tarek introduced me, feeling at home in his hometown, and recounted memories of fielding the fly balls I used to hit to him when he was a kid. It was a stark contrast to the campaign we were now waging. Two years earlier, Tarek told me he would be with me in 2000 if I ran. Now he took time out from earning a graduate degree in tropical rainforest ecology to hit the campaign trail—a different sort of jungle, to be sure.

The next morning, accompanied by reporters from *Business Week* and the *Los Angeles Times*, we flew to Portland, where I spoke at Portland State and met with the anti-sweatshop students who were incensed that Nike CEO Phil Knight had pulled the plug on a $30 million contribution promised the University of Oregon because of their protest. Then in rapid succession, a fund-raiser at Julie Lewis's home, which included a marvelous exchange with eighth graders, an editorial board meeting with the *Portland Oregonian*, and an address at the First Unitarian Church before leaving for Anchorage, landing there at eleven P.M.

We arrived late in Anchorage and groggily made our way the

next morning to an event at Cyrano's Bookstore. I was amazed that the reporters, camera crews, and radio hosts managed to squeeze into the available room. The questions ranged over a multitude of Alaska matters, including oil, timber cutting in the Tongass Forest, and regulation of the fisheries.

The state is a quarry for raw materials extracted by American, British, and Japanese corporations with very little value-added industry. Alaskans were having to purchase imported finished products or fish that actually originated in their state. A far cry from Alaska's early Democratic and progressive years, the state is almost completely dominated by Republicans, as are most other low-population western states defaulted by the Democrats. The only exception is the kindly Democratic governor Tony Knowles, who tries hard to be a Republican on matters such as restrictions on tort law, overcatering to the oil companies, and openly voting for the Republican senator Ted Stevens.

I received good media coverage that evening and the next morning on the day's activities. From the news conference we joined a protest march outside a hospital by the self-help coalition Alaska Injured Workers. It was a beautiful warm day. Drivers passing by would honk their horns in support of the demonstrators. The insurance companies were bringing in physicians from outside the state who deny workers' compensation claims and then return to California or elsewhere. The stories told to me by the marchers were heartrending. Serious back, neck, knee, or other disabilities kept them from working but did not keep away the bill collectors. Even for most tort attorneys, the whole workers' compensation system is off their screen because the fixed fees are so small they cannot make much of a living representing these workers. Tens of thousands of workers are thus herded into a backwater of American law with meager benefits when their claims are accepted. Workers' comp lawyers call these payments a meat chart—so much for a leg or an arm, with laws not permitting pain and suffering compensation.

During my campaign I spoke often about the avoidable violence of occupational deaths, injuries, and diseases from the factories, mines, and farms. According to OSHA, about fifty-eight thousand work-related fatalities occur in the United States every year. This figure exceeds by a considerable margin the number of fatalities on the highways and is almost four times the number of homicides in the United States. But these are not media-attracting casualties save for some collective tragedy such as a big coal mine collapse. The workers die in their beds, one by one, often from long-term exposure to toxic chemicals or lethal particulates. These losses are almost all preventable by the companies in charge. Yet this subject is almost never a campaign plank or a debatable condition of American life.

From the picket line we went to a fund-raiser for AKPIRG at the Snow City Cafe. The turnout was great, with old friends like Peter Gruenstein, Hugh Fleischman and Steve Conn present. The spirited response to a great little citizen group heightened when I started to match dollar for dollar contributions beyond the ones made at the door.

This was followed by a full-length address before six hundred people, an impressive turnout, since it was Memorial Day weekend. I took the occasion to critically comment on the record of the two Republican senators and representatives from Alaska whose seniority had given these arch-reactionaries—Ted Stevens, Frank Murkowski, and Don Young—powerful chairmanships of key committees relating to public lands, energy, and appropriations. The once-dominant Democratic Party and the once-powerful Teamsters Union had both lost influence to the Republicans and the large oil and gas companies. I urged the audience to strive for a strong progressive movement in the state that would have considerable leverage to limit the damage done by their legislators in Congress. The Alaska Green Party, as it turned out, got Winona and me 10 percent of the vote, the highest percentage of any state.

Alaska is the trustee for a very large portion of America's natural resources, including fisheries, yet it receives a disproportionate amount of inattention from national environmental and other citizen groups—not to mention the Democratic Party.

That night I thanked the Garas family for hosting us and got to the airport just in time for the flight to Seattle en route to Honolulu. It was, as I said, the Memorial Day weekend, but the Hawaii Greens succeeded in arranging a meeting of union representatives and environmental leaders on a Sunday. Following that, I did one-on-one interviews with reporters from the major Hawaii media that focused on these beautiful Pacific islands and their growing battle with air, water, and solid-waste pollution.

Hawaiians are very sensitive to the problem of "pollution in paradise" due to their reliance on the tourist industry. More than twenty-five years ago, I sent a young man, Davitt MacAteer, from West Virginia coal mine country, to Hawaii to shake up the complacency among the ruling classes. He spent a few weeks there and created an uproar that older Hawaiians remember to this day. Davitt's strategy was to send mass mailings to travel agencies on the mainland showing pictures of raw sewage being dumped into the Pacific not far from Waikiki. Not very appetizing fare for your average family vacation plans. Some of the raw sewage problems have since been taken care of, but judging by our public meeting with a couple hundred people that evening at the Harris United Methodist Church, the environment was very much on their minds. Folks were also hard-pressed by exorbitant prices for food and other necessities. Hawaii has long been beset with large importers who did not like competition. After all, this island for years was dominated by what was commonly referred to as the "Big Five" corporations—AMFAC, C. Brewer, Alexander & Baldwin, Castle & Cooke, and Theo H. Davies & Co. Also present at the church were advocates of the Hawaiian native movement, which seeks a stronger cultural identity and autonomy.

The highlight of my visit to Hawaii was just outside of Honolulu on a large fenced-in lot. Inside was a small area of less than half an acre surrounded by barbed-wire fence and klieg lights. Our group included Woody Harrelson, the actor and Hawaii resident, and Dave Frankel, an attorney and industrial-hemp activist. As we approached the internal fence, we were greeted by Dr. Dave West, a plant geneticist, who was in charge of the only federal legally licensed plot to grow industrial hemp—a long-fiber, versatile plant domesticated five thousand years ago by the Chinese.

When the Marijuana Tax Act of 1937 was passed, industrial hemp fell into the category of a similar prohibited product. It helped that the paper industry wanted this to happen because industrial-hemp producers would be an undesirable competitor. But the U.S. military used industrial hemp throughout the war effort ("Hemp for Victory" campaign) because of its strength in the manufacture of rope and such items as webbing in parachutes. Perhaps the best summary of the position held by President Clinton and his drug czar, retired General Barry McCaffrey, was that "industrial hemp is a stalking horse for marijuana." This comes as a surprise to agronomists who know that industrial hemp, at one-third of one percent of THC (the psychotropic component), would cross-pollinate and dilute any nearby plot of marijuana. Moreover, both General McCaffrey and Bill Clinton could smoke (even inhale) a bushel of industrial hemp every day and not get high.

So there I was walking toward a clump of the "dreaded" industrial-hemp plants, which Hawaiian state and legislative officials and the University of Hawaii had urged the Clinton administration to allow as an experiment to test varieties of industrial hemp. They all saw a potential multibillion-dollar industry emerging in the United States, which would increase the income of many hard-pressed farmers. Like their counterparts in numerous other states, such as Kentucky, North Dakota, and Wisconsin, they could not understand why it was legal to import industrial hemp from France, China, Romania, and recently Canada, but it was illegal to grow the crop in the United States. They also agreed with former CIA chief James Woolsey that industrial hemp could reduce our reliance on imported oil and was a national security plus.

Back to the tour, where Dr. West patiently explained how this industrial-hemp experiment had resulted in lots of paperwork and incessant reports to Washington. For example? I asked. Well, he said, the other day some birds flew over the barbed wire and ate some hemp seeds. He had to report this. I asked whether the birds flew away in a shaky fashion. He said of course not.

Woody Harrelson, months earlier, had gone to Kentucky and announced that he was going to plant some industrial-hemp seeds. He was immediately arrested. In late 2000 a court threw his case out, but his civil disobedience generated quite a bit of publicity and public attention to the cause of legalizing industrial hemp. I told him how I once spoke to two dozen midlevel employees of the U.S. Department of Agriculture and asked if anyone believed industrial hemp should continue to be banned. Not one person raised his or her hand.

Little did I realize standing by that industrial-hemp plot the extent to which the Clinton regime would go in its war on this issue. Five thousand miles away on the impoverished Pine Ridge Indian reservation in South Dakota, Alex White Plume was carefully and openly cultivating industrial hemp plants, which had grown to ten feet in height. Two years earlier, the Oglala Sioux tribal council had passed an ordinance reviving the legal distinction between industrial hemp and marijuana to encourage what tribal members called "land-based economic development." They knew that there would be a legal challenge by the federal government to both the ordinance and tribal sovereignty in federal court. But what they never anticipated was what happened on the hot early-summer morning of August 24, 2000.

About twenty-five federal law enforcement officials from the DEA, FBI, and the U.S. Marshall Service, wearing bulletproof vests, in twelve vehicles, two airplanes, and a helicopter, swooped down on this isolated land north of Wounded Knee. They carried automatic weapons and large Weed Eaters that were instantly turned on the tall plants. More than two thousand plants were chopped down or uprooted.

White Plume watched the raid in a state of shock, later telling a reporter from the *Lakota Nation Journal,* "This crop was going to be the beginning of our future, we followed all the criteria of the tribal legislation, we were totally open with everyone." The DEA agents were friendly, he said, revealing that they had gotten some leaves from his crop earlier and tested them and found they were below 1 percent THC content. Meanwhile, a few hundred miles to the north, Canadian farmers stood ready to legally export their industrial hemp to the Sioux or anyone else in the United States who wanted to buy it.

I'm going into some detail here because our campaign believed that industrial-hemp growth has great environmental consequences, eliminating the need for chemicals such as chlorine and lots of dangerous byproducts like dioxin associated with cotton and other fibers and fuels. But this issue also pointed out in the clearest fashion how hard it is to break through with a new proposal in a presidential campaign. Not one national reporter, to our knowledge, wrote about our detailed position on industrial hemp except AP's Eyn Kyung Kim, covering our press conference in Washington after the Pine Ridge raid. Not one reporter ever asked Bush or Gore about industrial hemp—a product that millions of Americans and the nation's farmers want to be grown in the United States.

On short notice I had a quick lunch with Governor Ben Cayetano. He is my favorite of all incumbent governors. Without much organized citizen support, he, more than the other state chiefs, stands up for workers and consumers when companies overreach or bully them. For years he has taken on the rapacious auto insurance companies, often against a hostile legislature controlled by his own conservative Democratic Party. When I mentioned Clinton's recent announcement on restoring Hawaii's reefs, Governor Cayetano shrugged and said, "Just talk."

We also broke some bread with the pride of Hawaii's Greens—the compelling Keiko Bonk, who, having been elected to the Big Island's council, was running for mayor. Polls had her leading the race and she was causing the Democrats real concern. Although she did not win in November, she'll be back.

Woody Harrelson must have noticed how sleepless we looked after days on the road. So he and his wife, Laura Louie, invited us to join their family for an excellent Thai dinner. Since I can count on two hands the number of leisurely, sit-down dinners we had on the road, this dinner was a godsend. Afterward the Harrelsons gave me a handsome industrial-hemp shirt, which I am wearing right now as I write. Woody said I could wear the shirt but I could never wear it out. We'll see how it resists on the elbows.

Back—to the mainland and Los Angeles. A few press interviews and then over to the beach at Santa Monica, where in full view of the tourist hotels, I joined a living-wage rally with hotel workers, labor leaders, and members of the Santa Monica City Council, including Kevin McKeown and Michael Feinstein, who that election year became one of five Green mayors in California.

A major fund-raiser was planned that evening at the home of Betty and Stanley Sheinbaum. We expected to raise about thirty thousand dollars—a big deal for our campaign. When we arrived there around six, the living room and outside terrace were already full with many friends, including Les and Sherry Frumkin and Lila Garrett, and newcomers who were curious to hear what I had to say. The Sheinbaums were not endorsing the campaign. They were longtime real Democrats upset with the direction of their party, for which they had raised millions of dollars. Stanley is an institutional economist of the old school and a dedicated public citizen. He has had a major supervisory role on an official commission looking into the behavior of the Los Angeles Police Department and for years has spent much time working for an Israeli-Palestinian peace settlement. I asked Pat Caddell to say a few words, and he delivered an impassioned indictment of the Democratic Party. This descendant of Democrats who had held high elective office listed one betrayal after another by the Clinton administration and the Democratic Leadership Council. A party that for now is beyond redemption, he declared. Whatever I had to say about the Democratic Party was an anticlimax, so I stressed the pro-democracy message and the many improvements in our country that were being held down by business lobbies and their political servants. We need a new progressive political movement to change the dynamics and expectations of politics in America, to push the major parties in the direction of renewal and revival, or begin to replace them. I emphasized the defensive collapse of the Democrats who were making a habit of losing to the right wing of the Republican Party in both state and federal elections. Some listeners voiced their concern about the Greens costing Gore the election. I told them again that it was Gore's election to lose.

Nine

"WE, THE PEOPLE"

By June our campaign had reached William Jefferson Clinton's political consciousness and calculation. On June 13, he attended a fund-raiser at the palatial Washington home of his close friend attorney Vernon Jordan. The large contributors were assembled there to finance the shoo-in campaign of longtime District of Columbia's nonvoting delegate to the House of Representatives, Eleanor Holmes Norton. One of the big givers approached Clinton and asked whether the Nader campaign would hurt the Democrats in California. Obviously, Clinton had thought about this matter. He said, "It's weird, he really wants it. But when people get into the voting booth, they usually move away from third-party candidates because they want their vote to count." Then the president began to show his grasp of the political numbers. He said that the Green Party could affect the Democrats' chances in New Mexico, Oregon, and Washington State. But this, he added, wouldn't be the case in the blue-collar states of the Midwest.

This was the source of the Democrats' confidence—that the Green Party polls, as with other third parties, would sink once people were in the voting booth. Voters want to be with winners, they asserted. But as civil rights attorney Sam Riddle told a rally in Flint, Michigan, some weeks later, "They keep telling us to vote for the winners, and we keep losing." But as the campaign wore on, this "cold feet" syndrome in the voting booth was seeming less likely, and the thousands of people who told us they were supporting Nader-LaDuke never gave a hint of any such indecision.

Back at campaign headquarters, the staff was nearing the end of two drives. The first was qualifying for federal matching funds by raising at least $5,000 in contributions of $250 or less in each of twenty states, and the second was completing ballot access in as many states as possible. Already, Georgia and North Carolina were lost, and a few other states weren't looking good. We got tens of thousands of signatures in Oklahoma and Indiana, but fell just short of numbers needed to get on the ballot. South Dakota was also out despite a lawsuit brought by our pro bono lawyers at NYU Law School's Brennan Center. So was Wyoming. In Idaho, someone swiped a clipboard full of signatures while it was being circulated in a restaurant. That unfortunate theft resulted in our being kept off the ballot, though we received a remarkable twelve thousand write-in votes. All in all, we ended up with our names on forty-three state ballots as well as the District of Columbia ballot. This was achieved almost entirely by volunteers, whose efforts were truly heroic.

One of my favorite examples was Dr. Frances Mendenhall, a Nebraska dentist, who periodically closed her office and drove far and wide across the state collecting a large share of the two thousand signatures from each of three congressional districts. On August 1, she, Tom Rinne, and their fellow Greens rallied on the steps of the state capitol with 10,700 signatures.

Nebraska is a big state. When Dr. Mendenhall learned that I visited Chadron in western Nebraska, where farmers and ranchers were having a tough time economically, she drove hundreds of miles there to pick up more names.

The role of volunteers in most campaign books is reduced to different ways of saying thank you. But volunteers have an effect on candidates and their staff that cannot be quantified in numbers of envelopes stuffed, calls taken, or data entered. Their effect on me starts with not wanting to let them down, to strive to set an example that illustrates my dedication to them. Late in the campaign, when Democrats and quite a few of my friends were urging or demanding that I step aside and let my voters go for Gore, my very first reaction to the press was, "Do you think I would ever let our volunteers down? They have given us a level of trust that can never be breached."

To whom am I referring when I reply this way? There were thousands. Let's start with Cesar Cuauht'moc Garcia Hernandez, a twenty-year-old native of McAllen, Texas, who worked his way to Brown University. Cesar translated our brochure and Web site materials into Spanish, prepared ten thousand flyers and distributed them on the Washington Mall during Fourth of July festivities, then returned to Brown in the fall, where he started the Brown Students for Nader-LaDuke.

And then there was Lauren Mooney, all of thirteen years old, who expected to be treated as a grown-up by adult volunteers at the office and certainly produced like one. Or imagine my handing votes over to Al Gore after Fred "the Phoenix" Mauney rode his bicycle from Salt Lake City to Washington, D.C., while trailing a huge VOTE FOR RALPH NADER FOR PRESIDENT sign on a contraption that he referred to as a buggy. He arrived at the office with many newspaper clippings of his journey across America. He became a superhuman volunteer right through and into the election's aftermath. One time he cobbled together a giant Fred-powered moving billboard that he would ride around town and at the rallies, including the biggest, at Madison Square Garden. The amazing thing about Fred was the least known. Back in Utah years earlier, he came down with a condition that led to partial paralysis. Doctors told him he would not walk again. But he was too determined to accept their verdict. There was no way I would ever let him down.

The same held for Sally, who came almost daily to our headquarters on arthritic knees and cheerfully took on what chores were needed to be done. Or the Communications Workers of America volunteer who came in on his days off, or the housewife who made hundreds of phone calls for us while her children were in school, or the carpenter from suburban Maryland who helped set up one of our adjunct offices in record time.

Thousands of e-mails and letters poured into our campaign from the widest variety of backgrounds and places. From Massachusetts, a young Jonah chose to make his contribution to Nader 2000 from the money he received for his bar mitzvah.

There are the images of people while we were on the road—people we saw expressing their feelings from a distance but whom we could not engage. Like the elderly man at a labor rally in Detroit handing out flyers while tears streamed down his smiling face. I was on the stage speaking and wondering what was going on in his mind—memories of the sit-down strikes, or perhaps joy at hearing Taft-Hartley denounced after decades of silence by candidates.

I could only wonder, but I could and did take heart from all these good people.

College students performed herculean tasks. In Pittsburgh, one student came up and told me how he drew a slew of media attention in his small town by hanging large, hand-painted Nader-LaDuke signs from highway rails. On Election Eve, with just a few hours' notice, a Boston University freshman mobilized his friends and filled the Armory with three thousand exuberant students and faculty for an eleventh-hour rally.

What was so touching were the many stories told me by elementary school children, in the company of their parents, who proudly described how they persuaded their teachers to include the Green Party candidate in any mock debates or straw votes conducted in the classroom and how many of their schoolmates they persuaded to go Green. So when I hear some people say, "Yeah, but you got only 3 percent of the vote," I urge them to consider the intangibles—the many people who will intensify their civic activities in their communities and the many more people who had intelligent conversations with their friends and relatives about politics, power, justice, peace, and strong democracy. And consider the children and teenagers too young to vote, but who thought more seriously of themselves and their future roles, whether running in elections or widening their horizon. Then there are the many fledgling Green candidates who will be coming forth at all levels of government. I saw the enrichment of the public dialogue and more than a little effervescence of many hitherto demoralized Americans. The volunteers were the vanguard of the intangibles, of these seeds and insights and awarenesses that someday may bear the fruits of more justice and revitalized political institutions. In my opinion, they were engines of inspiration.

It was also in June, while experiencing a sudden barrage of national media requests for interviews, that I realized the severe limitations of agenda alone in getting press coverage. New or rarely advanced ideas were not sufficient. No matter that the subjects and positions conveyed were specific, timely, important, ignored by major candidates, and related to the concerns of millions of Americans. Press coverage galvanizes a political campaign only when there are controversies or a murky perception of "momentum."

And the first sign we were moving was that the Democrats were getting fidgety.

The reason incumbent politicians do not welcome debating their opponents, or large corporations seek to ignore their critics, is that up to now, these tactics for the most part have worked. It takes "two to controversy" and invite media attention. My rolling criticisms of corporate power and its control of government fit those tactics of silence perfectly. The ability of entrenched interests not to reply over time is a genuine sign of their true power and fundamentally reflects the weakness of any democratic society and its supposed countervailing forces and systems of accountability. Citizen groups have realized that their investigative reports about pollution or fraud or corruption by companies have little effect if they are not followed by better business competitors, civil lawsuits, legislative hearings, or criminal prosecutions, which by their nature do produce responses. The media likes to see issues joined so that it can report on the contesting parties.

In an early June swing through North Dakota, Montana, and Idaho, I took a strong stand against any commercial logging in our national forests and on a beautiful day in Missoula I joined with a like-minded group from the National Forest Protection Campaign. At a press conference located in the sparkling Missoula Children's Theater, I made the arguments. About 3.3 percent of the nation's timber demand comes from the national forests, where the remnants of America's ancient forests survive the power saw. The taxpayers are subsidizing the timber companies for roads and other gifts at a level of $1.2 billion a year. Many of these logs have been exported from Alaska to Japan. Using that money to preserve and restore these precious forests would produce far more enduring jobs, enhance recreational and tourist activities there, and stop the extinction of species, soil erosion, floods, landslides, and water contamination. A forest full of stumps creates few jobs for loggers. A modest effort to recover the waste wood thrown in the nation's dumps would make up for any lost timber from the national forests.

Gore and Bush declined to support a ban on commercial logging on public lands, I noted, adding the names of the giant timber corporations whose executives were backing one or both of the other candidates. Aside from an occasional bark of disapproval from a newspaper columnist, there was no response either from the candidates or from the timber barons. No controversy, no press, no joining of the issues, no move toward resolution in the reasonable future. The issues continued to dangle, shorn of a dynamic electoral context. Even were there a clamor by the citizens, if it occurred in any of the forty states that were landsliding either for Bush or Gore, why would either of them care? In Idaho, people were resigned to being ignored by both candidates because the state was overwhelmingly Bush country. The lesson learned: Clamor needs contested exchanges to have an effect.

To prove this point, there was a great deal of clamor regarding coal companies blowing off the tops of mountains in West Virginia, over the preservation of the Everglades in Florida, and over the toxic emissions of a giant incinerator in East Liverpool, Ohio. We visited these states, which were closely contested between Bush and Gore. We took detailed environmental positions. There was no controversy generated because both Bush and Gore chose not to distinguish between themselves on these matters. The lesson learned: Clamor needs contrasts to have an effect.

Well, what about endorsements? There are two kinds. One is the celebrity imprimatur, which attracts attention to the candidacy and maybe some votes. Celebrity endorsers, including political celebrities, have historically produced few votes (recall Michael Jordan's declaration for Bill Bradley), but they do produce larger numbers of people who hear about what you are striving to achieve and can help in raising funds. We had very fine celebrity endorsers, people with a long record themselves of social justice activities: Susan Sarandon, Tim Robbins, Jackson Browne, Willie Nelson, Cornel West, Bonnie Raitt, Eddie Vedder, Pete Seeger, Barbara Ehrenreich, Ani DeFranco, Casey Kasem, Patti Smith, Studs Terkel, Randall Robinson, Richard N. Goodwin, Jim Hightower, Michael Moore, Barry Commoner, Ben Cohen (of Ben & Jerry's), Danny Glover, Linda Ronstadt, and Phil Donahue. Some of these declared supporters raised alarm bells with the Democrats, and they went to work to get them back. William Daley, in his first press conference in July after taking over from the money-tainted Tony Coelho as Gore's campaign manager, said as much. Common practice in politics, he indicated. Both

Al Gore and he calmly tried their persuasions with Phil Donahue. From *Air Force Two,* Al Gore made his arguments about keeping the Republicans out. Donahue replied, "Well, Mr. Vice President, I may have my head in the attic, but I'm going with the Green Man." (There are some memorable recountings in a political campaign, and this one caused a repetitive chuckle for us.)

The other kind of endorsement can be a membership or constituency kind, such as the cogent voter-turnout support of the Latinos for Better Government of Santa Barbara County, California. On June 14, the California Nurses Association, with more than thirty thousand members, led by President Kay McVay and executive director Rose Ann De Moro, came to Washington for a press conference announcement under the rubric "RNs for RN."

Favorable comment from an unexpected source came from Jimmy Hoffa Jr., the newly elected president of the large Teamsters Union. This event occurred at their union headquarters near the U.S. Capitol on June 22, at a media-filled press conference with Hoffa, other Teamster officials, and me. A few moments earlier I met with the Teamsters Executive Board, a seasoned team of union veterans from all regions of the country. It went very well while we were all concentrating on the power of multinationals, NAFTA, job safety, and labor law strengthening. It continued to go well when the discussion moved to the anemic labor policies of the Democratic Party and the need for organized labor—critical for Al Gore's chances—to insist that a firm labor agenda replace Democratic lip service. But then an upset board member raised the lawsuit that Public Citizen had filed on behalf of dissident Teamsters against the union. I reminded him of the longtime work that Public Citizen had done for truck safety and reform of the former corrupt ways of the union that seriously undermined internal union democracy years ago. Now, in the latter stages of the federal government's trusteeship over the union, I simply stated that the more honest a union is, the larger it will grow and the more beneficial effect it will have on workers. I assumed that all in the room shared this philosophy. We then walked over to the room with the cameras and reporters to begin the news conference, where the unionists were kind enough to give me a standing ovation.

Because the 1.4-million-member Teamsters, known for their comparative militancy, independence, and occasional endorsement of Republican candidates, had not joined the AFL-CIO in its early Gore endorsement, the major media reporters were in attendance. Hoffa did not disappoint them. "There is no distinction between Al Gore and George W. Bush when it comes to trade," he said, adding that Gore was "wrong on trade."

He continued: "No one in the political arena speaks stronger on the issues important to American working families than Ralph Nader. We agree wholeheartedly with what Mr. Nader has said." This event was only a few weeks after Clinton-Gore rammed through Congress the China Permanent Normal Trade Relations bill that organized labor strongly opposed. Also, the Teamsters were very concerned with the NAFTA agreement to allow eight-dollar-a-day Mexican truck drivers in heavy, poorly maintained rigs to take their cargo throughout the fifty states.

The next day, Richard L. Berke, the prolific political reporter for the *New York Times,* wrote a page-one story titled "Once Seen as the Odd Man Out, Nader Is Rocking the Gore Boat." Berke reported that Gore advisers told him "they had moved aggressively behind the scenes to try to keep Mr. Hoffa from endorsing Mr. Nader" and that other Democratic leaders, led by Senator Harry Reid, were contacting several labor leaders to discourage them from defecting to our candidacy. How seriously did I take all this? It was a breakthrough just to hear about some unions having doubts about Gore to this degree. But I was under no illusions. All the large unions, including the Teamsters, would endorse Gore, however unenthusiastically. One of the two major parties, they believed, would win, so they'd go with the least worst and once again be taken for granted. That said, Jan Pierce, former vice president of the Communications Workers of America and our "Labor for Nader" organizer, told me that our campaign had more union endorsements than Jesse Jackson had in 1984 and 1988 combined. Labor for Nader Committees were forming around the country, thanks to Jan and local leaders like Dan McCarthy of UAW Local 417 in Detroit.

The other audition, for an endorsement by Friends of the Earth, seemed more promising. This was like old homecoming week, or so I thought. President Brent Blackwelder, a brainy Ph.D. superactivist and severe critic of Clinton-Gore's environmental surrenders from biotechnology to NAFTA/WTO to pesticides to forest issues, joined many a collaboration with us over the years. He had gotten his board to break from the environmental groups and endorse Bill Bradley in the primary. So in a one-hour exchange with him and several members of the board and staff, we connected on what the two parties haven't done and what needed to be done to take the global, national, and local environmental missions to a new level of action. I left feeling confident and remained so even after Brent told me on the telephone that there was some division among the board members. I received a call on September 5 from a reporter saying that Brent Blackwelder had released an endorsement for Gore with a ringing resolve to campaign heavily for him, especially in close states where many residents favored a strong environmental enforcement stance. The bells of the duopoly's least worst syndrome rang in my ears. If the arch-critic Blackwelder could fall into line, the task of our candidacy to deal with what later became a full-fledged fear campaign by Gore suddenly seemed more formidable.

Earlier, both the Sierra Club and the League of Conservation Voters, knowing full well how early and pervasive my work on the federal environmental laws had been, nonetheless endorsed Gore. The grassroots environmental groups, such as the Center for Health, Environment and Justice, led by Lois Gibbs, did not have a political arm, so they could not legally endorse candidates. There was little doubt in my mind, though, that her seven thousand local chapters of people living and fighting on the toxic ramparts would have formally supported our candidacy. We had met too many of them who appreciated our work to think otherwise.

The Green Party nominating convention was coming up the weekend of June 23 in Denver's Renaissance Hotel. We wanted to do as much press as possible to raise visibility and enthusiasm and I began a series of press interviews that started with the *Philadelphia Inquirer* and included *USA Today,* radio programs, the giant Japanese newspaper *Yomiuri Shimbun,* Fox *Sunday News,* the *Village Voice,* the *Washington Post, Hardball,* the *New York Daily News,* and my first interview with Don Imus, who told his sidekick

Charles on the radio that he could see himself voting for me. People who are daily aficionados of Mr. Imus told me this was a big deal in getting voters because of his large following.

And on top of all that I had two more states to visit in order to make all fifty. I flew to Little Rock for a meeting with activists and petitioners and a press conference. It was one hot, humid day there. Then on to St. Louis for a fast-paced series of meetings, media, lectures, and a half hour with my favorite big-city editorial board at the *St. Louis Post Dispatch*. The Greens were sharply split in Missouri, with one camp in St. Louis and the other in Kansas City. So to reach both sides I flew to Kansas City and spoke at the Kansas Community College. Driving across the Missouri River into Kansas, our little party erupted in cheers at meeting our pledge of campaigning in every state.

It's always good to stop in Boulder, where they gave me a re-sounding liftoff for the convention the next day at the large standing-room-only Chautauqua Community House.

More than at any other event in our campaign, many of the major media organizations were represented at the Denver convention, including the *New York Times* and the *Wall Street Journal*. The foreign press, mindful of the many Green parties around the world, was also present, and I was pleased to find out that there were Greens attending the convention from five continents. Saturday, June 24, was devoted to one-on-one interviews with reporters, meeting informally with many of the delegates, and preparing for the modest nomination festivities the next day.

Once again, the Green Party, under the convention leadership of Dean Myerson and Annie Goeke, set an example that went un-noticed by the media. There were no hospitality suites for com-panies, no freebies with corporate logos plastered on them, no fund-raisers shaking down fat cats. The signs held by delegates were about organic agriculture, solar energy, opposition to the death penalty, and corporate prisons. Now, it could be argued that the Greens could embody such virtues and be this noncom-mercial because no companies would care to sponsor us. What, after all, would it serve them? But there are many companies of lesser size and greater conscience that would have been pleased to be associated with the Greens. Companies prominent in energy conservation, renewables, recycling, wind power, or nutrition, or businesses with social crusades on behalf of indigenous peoples or arms control would have been pleased to be there. So far the Green Party, which has debated this very matter of convention sponsorships, has held the line between the political and the commercial.

Freed from the vested interests, even good ones, the Greens were still in thrall to their own schisms, especially between the Association of State Green Parties and Green Party USA. Fortunately, both groups, which differ in personality, style, and some tactics and positions but agree on far more matters, including the Ten Key Values (see Appendix F), submerged their differences long enough to have one unified convention and support the ASGP platform coordinated by Steve Schmidt. This was accomplished by a few Greens in each camp who had the patience and vision to agree that a certain degree of unity advances the Green cause on a faster track and quickens the likelihood of it becoming nationally certified by the Federal Election Commission.

The convention itself was a serious and joyful occasion with about five hundred Green delegates in attendance at workshops, caucuses, and receptions, with some casual music. There was nothing casual, however, about our attention to the abuses of power and the denials of justice that the political system has been allowing or even profiting from to advance the careers of its practitioners. There was no blather, few clichés, and little flattery among the speakers who came to this age-old problem of oligarchy from different angles.

Jim Hightower regaled them with his factual, homespun satiric darts and metaphors. Hightower is the closest human being we have in this country to a progressive Will Rogers and he is much funnier. His books cover a range and depth of subjects belied by his colorful titles, as with his latest, *If the Gods Wanted Us to Vote, They'd Have Given Us Candidates.* Dr. Sidney Wolfe, head of Public Citizen's Health Research Group, shocked even these Greens with his descriptions of how the HMO-dominated corporate medicine machine treats, mistreats, or refuses to treat patients in our country. Labor Party founder Tony Mazzochi, representing the best in democratic union labor, spoke about the nature of work in America, how it is defined, how labor is relegated to the lower rungs of the American power structure, and the suffering that comes from a weakened unionism. Steve Gaskin and Jello Biafra delivered their inimitable declarations. They were both vying for nomination votes from the delegates.

The renewable form of energy known as Ronnie Dugger provided a wonderful introduction to my acceptance speech. By this time, the delegates had seen and heard some of the best political orators around and did not exert any effort to suppress their enthusiasm for my acceptance remarks. I have always found it more difficult to speak to a supportive or applauding audience than to one critical of my positions. This feeling comes from an aversion to anything that sounds like pandering, instead of my desire to foster concurrence, reinforcement, and extension. I like to meet the challenges of persuasion or rebuttal. On the modest convention stage, however, watching the banners, balloons, and signs held by people enthusiastically on their feet, I felt their energy.

Most presidential candidates would have their advisers jockeying for the specific concerns of swing voters who could spell the difference in one or more states or, more crassly, to give a nod to a constituency of donors. My associates had only one basic plea: Keep it short. Say, about forty minutes.

Well, ninety-five minutes later, the delegates were still cheering. Why did I speak so long? So much required predicates, facts, and connections made. Major-party candidates can speak in short paragraphs of conclusions because what they are saying people have heard again and again within the retread regions of political rhetoric. I recall MIT professor Noam Chomsky, when asked why he would not go on television during the Vietnam War to convey his pronounced views on that conflict. Sound bites favor the status quo, he said. A pro-Vietnam person can simply say, "Peace through strength." In contrast, Chomsky would have to lay down some predicates to explain his antiwar position. Time allotted would be less than ten seconds on an evening news program, and even a three-minute segment of question-and-answer would not suffice.

In my case, I set about to reach a broad spectrum of voters with a deep array of subjects rarely presented or discussed in political campaigns. I had to find a way between soaring sermons and the *Statistical Abstract*. There was a need for a combination of irresistible rhetoric and unassailable evidence. I was aware that the audience for my remarks, in snippet, in part, or in whole (C-Span was there), contained the diversity and concern with the subjects treated. Different issues touch people's temperament, experience, and sense of injustice differently. People often are moved much more by one topic close to them than a series of other topics. Third parties historically have been viewed as single-issue movements, which made their continuance fragile. I was determined that the Green Party be seen, at least through its nominee, as broad and as comprehensive as its platform, its key values, and its most hard-working supporters.

Opening my remarks with, "Welcome to the politics of joy and justice," I led with what could be the longest acceptance sentence yet delivered:

> On behalf of all Americans who seek a new direction, who yearn for a new birth of freedom to build the just society, who see justice as the great work of human beings on Earth, who understand that community and individual fulfillment can be mutually reinforcing, who respect the urgent necessity to wage peace, to protect the environment, to end poverty, and to preserve values of the spirit for future generations, who wish to build a deep democracy by working hard for a regenerative progressive politics, as if people mattered—to all these citizens and the Green vanguard I welcome and am honored to accept the Green Party nomination for president of the United States.

Right away, I wanted to lift expectations and civic responsibility levels. But a few moments later, after elaborating the meaning of a deep democracy in terms of structural objectives, I stated that such goals were also conservative goals, driving the point home that conservatives are not corporatists with several rhetorical questions:

> Don't conservatives want movement toward a safe environment, toward ending corporate welfare and the commercialization of childhood? Don't they, too, want a fair and responsive marketplace for their health needs and savings? Let us not in this campaign pre-judge any voters, for Green values are majoritarian values, respecting all peoples and striving to

give greater choice to all voters, workers, individual taxpayers, and consumers. As with the right of free speech, we may not agree with others, but we will defend their right to free speech as strongly as we do for ourselves.

Oratory specialists tell us that speeches on such occasions have to provide vision. I provided scenarios of what our collective futures could be like as a country and as a world and then spent some time on the critical point of voter motivation.

I have learned that reminders of heroic reform achievements in our nation's past and comparisons with nations that have moved ahead of us in important areas of public need give people today hope, inspiration, and energy. The past struggles against King George III, slavery, the disenfranchisement of women and blacks, the rapacious robber barons—to name a few—provide a rhythm to the march for justice that each generation, if its members are to become good ancestors, must join. Moreover, our status as the world's leading power has often led us to ignore how much we can learn from other countries and the ways they have dealt with universal health care coverage, labor rights, worker benefits, child care, public transit, and other public facilities. I spoke about the tightening exclusion of civil society in Washington by an ever-stronger corporate state that for the past twenty years has obstructed citizen groups from participating in their government. After all, as Cicero said, freedom is participation in power. The words of Woodrow Wilson nearly a century ago ring so true today: "The government, which was designed for the people, has got into the hands of their bosses and their employers, the special interests. An invisible empire has been set up above the forms of democracy."

I argued that this state of exclusion need not persist if we marshal the assets we already have into action. Besides bringing more nonvoters into the voting booth, we as a people legally own very significant assets that we have allowed corporations to control. For instance, we own the public airwaves (the highways for the television and radio companies), the public lands (one-third of the United States with the largest share of natural resources), and $5 trillion of workers' pensions funds. Imagine developing the mechanisms so that we can control what we own—a rather conservative principle. If we did, we would have our own radio and television stations, our own use and preservation of the public lands, and large shareholder leverage over the major corporations on the stock exchange.

Other assets are more intangible but no less motivating. I spoke about who controls our yardsticks that measure conditions in our country. If the yardsticks are those preferred by business economists—that is, profits, inventory levels, GDP, stock market levels, which we hear about almost daily—that will set the economic agenda. If we use more people yardsticks—e.g., child and adult poverty, affordable housing, hunger, the uninsured, failing schools, land erosion, environmental devastation, natural resource depletion, decaying public works, corporate subsidies, corporate crime, fraud and abuse against consumers, workers, and the government, nonliving wages, underemployment, child obesity, diabetes, and asthma—then our public agendas and discussions become quite different. We can begin focusing on the distributional nature of the quality of both our economy and its growth, on who is benefiting and who is not.

But I wanted to conclude the address with something other than an oratorical flourish. So I posed questions and punctuated my answers with that simple phrase from our Constitution's preamble, "We, the people."

"Who will achieve public financing of public elections and thereby remove many roadblocks to progress?" I asked the audience. "We, the people," they roared back. "Who will secure universal, accessible, and quality health care, with an emphasis on prevention, for all children, women, and men in America, at long, long last?" "We, the people." "Who will repeal restrictive labor laws such as Taft-Hartley, secure a living wage, enforce and strengthen the environmental, consumer protection, and job safety laws, end hundreds of billions of dollars of corporate welfare?" "We, the people," rang through the ballroom and out to many more Americans across the country.

This back-and-forth was going so well that I decided to plow new territory: "Who will discover the small and medium-size businesses that practice their belief in sustainable economies, like the Interface Corporation of Atlanta, so as to refute the chronic naysaying of big business? Who will elevate the many civil servants in our federal government above the demeaning stereotypes that politicians have pasted on them?"

Back and forth we resonated that "we, the people" will send bigotry and virulent intolerance into oblivion, expand the definition of national security and national purpose to drive back the global scourges of poverty, contagious disease, illiteracy, and environmental destruction, and support workers and peasants for a change instead of dictatorships and oligarchies.

Afterward, an associate told me that this sequence was overdone. I replied that repeating the civic obligations of "we, the people" can never be overdone, until it is done.

Some special groups of "the people" had to be addressed directly. They were the nonvoters whose varied objections to voting, I believe, were dissolved by the Green Party's platform of reform, empowerment, and goals. These include upper-income people, whose influence could be put to far greater good by giving voice to the majority of their fellow Americans who cannot exit from bad conditions as the affluent can, and the millions of retired Americans who have so much experience and perspective, which affords endless opportunities for applying their community-based patriotism and nurturing of the young. I urged the youth of America to avoid being trivialized by the commercial culture that tempts them daily. Because if they do not turn on to politics, the lessons of history are that politics will turn on them.

My remarks over, the Green assemblage erupted with cheers, as the balloons fell from the ceiling (a rare concession to traditional big-party hoopla). The person who made all this possible—my mother, Rose—came up and, holding a sunflower in one hand, gave me a big hug with the other.

That evening our United Airlines flight to Los Angeles was canceled. United rescheduled us for the next morning, but when we arrived, we learned that the 6:40 A.M. flight had also been canceled.

Presidential candidates prefer private jets. But if Gore and Bush traveled on commercial airlines, they would understand the outrage that airline passengers feel at the increasing delays, cancellations, poor service, cramped seats, and gigantic fares in many markets where there is little or no competition.

I have flown in coach for over forty years and coauthored, with Wesley Smith, a book on airline safety. In 1971 I started the Aviation Consumer Action Project, representing the rights of airline passengers with some success, especially in safety areas.

In the seventies, Allegheny Airlines (now U.S. Air) bumped me from a Washington, D.C., flight to Hartford, Connecticut, where a large audience was waiting to hear me speak. In the ensuing case, *Nader* v. *Allegheny Airlines*, our lawyer Rueben Robertson discovered that Allegheny, and other airlines, routinely overbooked their planes. The case went to the Supreme Court of the United States, where I won a ruling that later led to the airlines changing their overbooking practices.

Passengers, flight attendants, and pilots seemed to appreciate that I was flying coach with them, and a few said they would vote for me. If Gore and Bush had spent more time in coach class, perhaps consumer and safety complaints about air travel would become a priority for the FAA.

It was like another world the day after the convention at the William Meade Housing Project in South Central Los Angeles. It was just before noon under a blazing sun in the drab courtyard, and many little children and their moms greeted us with green and white "Nader for President" signs. A sizable contingent of press had arrived, including, and this is remarkable, two of the major Los Angeles television stations, as well as a very perceptive reporter for the *Los Angeles Times*. I was thinking back to the second day of our campaign, when we received almost no media attention at all.

The press conference lasted about thirty minutes as the small tots started melting. What wasn't melting was a major worry of the mothers—the toxic dust blowing off a nearby large pile of soil as part of the city's casual attempt to clean up contamination under the project. You see, these very modest apartments were built on top of a former oil refinery site, and the soil was soaked with benzene and other chemicals. So many people in the project, which housed more than eleven hundred residents, have died from cancer that the surviving tenants listed their names on a little memorial in the courtyard. I thought this occasion was an appropriate one for releasing our statement on impoverished children in California. When I first examined the data a year earlier, I was shocked. Children living in poverty greatly increased in number and percentage since 1980, when it was at 15.2 percent. That worsened to 21.9 percent by 1986 and 25 percent for 2000–2001. As documented in the annual California Children's Budget issued by Professor of Law Robert Fellmeth of the University of San Diego Law School, a respected Columbia University study places 48.9 percent of California's children under six years of age at "below or near poverty."

I went through some of the obvious health, education, child care, and higher minimum-wage recommendations. Naturally, the reporters were most interested in my views, which I gave them, on the current controversy between the residents and city housing project officials (the oil company is long gone). The residents were angry and resigned, telling us that even their elected representatives were not doing much for them. I wondered why in this rich country of ours anyone, much less innocent children, has to live in such conditions. Especially in a country whose politicians of all stripes endlessly mouth the slogan "children first." As we were mixing with the press and the residents, a helicopter hovered overhead, an LAPD police car cruised by, and an observing Housing Authority police car parked by the curb for a while. This is the atmosphere that these children are exposed to in broad daylight—even a press conference has to be monitored.

In any event, that evening and the next day the L.A. media produced some good television footage and column inches about the Meade Project's problem and child poverty. My departing impression was that the friendly people of Meade did not have any belief that Republicans, Democrats, or this newcomer, "El Partido Verde," was going to make any difference in their lives. Still, we wonder why half of the eligible voters don't bother to go to the polls. Grassroots politics will entail a great deal of work to fill vast vacuums bred by decades of political neglect.

Ten

THE MEDIA: AN ONGOING NON-DEBATE

There is a major problem for anyone who runs for president, especially a third-party candidate. No matter how long or extensively you campaign in every state of the union, no matter how large your audiences become, you cannot reach in direct personal communication even 1 percent of the eligible voters. In essence, you don't run for president directly; you ask the media to run you for president or, if you have the money, you also pay the media for exposure. Reaching the voters relies almost entirely on how the media chooses to perceive you and your campaign. In short, this "virtual reality" *is* the reality.

Since the media controls access to 99 percent–plus of your audience, it is not shocking that 99 percent of most candidates' strategies is born and bred for media play. The media is the message. When George W. Bush nuzzles next to two little schoolchildren, his handlers make sure that the AP and other photographers on his campaign have good positioning. When Al Gore stands near some national park in his L. L. Bean attire, his handlers know they succeeded only if the image and a few choice words are played throughout the country. There are very few rallies anymore. Instead there are carefully orchestrated photo opportunities that often leave some locals resentful, feeling they have been used. And, of course, they have been used, just as the candidates use journalism for their poses, or try to, and just as journalism uses them.

There can be, though, alternatives to such contrivances. The people could have their own media, a point I made repeatedly at my press conferences. The people own the airwaves. "The people are the landlords," I would say, "and the radio and television stations are the tenants. They pay us no rent to our real estate agents, the Federal Communications Commission (FCC), yet they control who says what and who doesn't, for twenty-four hours a day. What is needed are our own stations, well equipped, our own audience network, both controlled and funded by viewers. A portion of the rent that should be charged for this vast public asset, which since day one we have given away, would amplify the viewers' stations." The camera crews and attendant reporters first would appear curious, then amused, knowing that this was one long sound bite that would never make it onto the evening news. Neither did my words reach the newspaper columns. The media itself was never viewed as an issue in the campaign. A few years ago I asked a candidate why not? His reply stuck in my memory: "The media represents that part of my voice that gets through to the people. I'm not going after my voice."

There is another, much older and inexpensive way to reach people. Once under way, word of mouth is the most credible, quickest, and most lasting medium of all. It goes from friend to friend, neighbor to neighbor, worker to worker, relative to relative—between people who afford each other longtime credibility. Word of mouth goes on all the time, but it is very hard to escalate to high levels of velocity or intensity. It would take a veritable cultural revolution of civic interest, awareness, and engagement to change the tide. We are far from that nexus as a society, except for a few hot-button issues such as abortion and gun control, which possess their own intense grapevines.

In an age of deepening concentration of conglomerate media corporations, their executives have their own interests to defend and expand. More and more, newspapers, magazines, and television and radio stations are caught up in larger megacorporate strategic objectives, which shape the nature of campaign coverage. During the summer, on the television in my hotel room, I saw Sumner Redstone, boss of Viacom, which bought CBS, being interviewed about his reportedly strained relationship with CBS boss Mel Karmazin. "Nothing to it," replied Redstone. "Mel and I are both driven by our stock price." Shades of Herbert Hoover and Edward R. Murrow, who saw the public airwaves as a public trust. That being Redstone's yardstick means that hypercommercialism becomes ever more the governing standard. This results in down-

grading respect for the public service requirement of the 1934 ✓
Communications Act and its famous provision for licensees to reflect "the public interest, convenience, and necessity."

When they are not merging or joint venturing, these mass communications giants are in a frantic race down the sensuality ladder,
filling the airwaves with what John Nichols and Robert McChesney
call the "trivial, sensational and salacious." These authors published a little paperback in the middle of the presidential campaign
titled *It's the Media, Stupid*, where they illuminated the connection
between "media reform and democratic renewal." This little volume is a factually immersed brief for their thesis, best expressed by
their own words:

> The flow of information that is the lifeblood of democracy
> is being choked by a media system that every day ignores a
> world of injustices and inequality, and the growing resistance
> to it. No, the media system is not the sole cause of our polit-
> ical crisis, nor even the primary cause, but it reinforces every
> factor contributing to the crisis, and it fosters a climate in
> which the implementation of innovative democratic solutions
> is rendered all but impossible.
>
> The closer a story gets to examining corporate power the
> less reliable our corporate media system is as a source of in-
> formation that is useful to citizens of a democracy. Commer-
> cial indoctrination of children is crucial to corporate America.

It is at least permissible to assume that corporations such as
Disney, AOL–Time Warner, Rupert Murdoch's News Corporation, Viacom, Seagram (Universal), Sony, Liberty (AT&T), and
General Electric, which rely heavily on corporate advertising revenue for their expenses and profits, are not likely to go out of their
way to cover candidates who are critics of their major advertisers
who are big contributors to both the Republican and Democratic
parties. It's just simple business sense.

As these media giants become ever more global, along with
global advertisers, their self-importance and impact become almost
unreal. On the occasion of announcing Time Warner's merger with
AOL, Time Warner CEO Gerald Levin declared exuberantly that
the global media is "fast becoming the predominant business of the

twenty-first century" and is "more important than government, it's more important than educational institutions and nonprofits."

Even with fewer and fewer key individuals controlling more and more print and broadcast media properties (one company now owns eleven hundred radio stations), much of their power to frame the agendas and confine the issues is the result of a two-party default. Twenty-one years ago, the especially perceptive Duke historian James David Barber wrote about the "emergence" of mass communication

> to fill virtually the whole gap in the electoral process left by the default of other independent elites who used to help manage the choice. Their power is all the stronger because it looks, to the casual observer, like no power at all. Much as the old party bosses used to pass themselves off as mere "coordinators" and powerless arrangers, so some modern-day titans of journalism want themselves thought of as mere scorekeepers and messenger boys. Yet the signs of journalists' key role as the major advancers and retarders of presidential ambitions are all around us.

In Barber's view, the political parties failed because "their giant ossified structures, like those of the dinosaurs, could no longer adapt to the pace of political change. Journalism could adapt . . . journalism took over where the parties left off."

Well, maybe some Democrats and Republicans were reading Barber, because they decided to take back from the media the management of choice in one area of crucial importance to any political challengers to them: the presidential debates. Until the late eighties, the League of Women Voters sponsored these debates. In 1980, they allowed independent candidate Congressman John Anderson to join Jimmy Carter and Ronald Reagan, which helped Anderson considerably in national recognition and the polls. At one point he scored 21 percent in the polls, and he ended up with 7 percent on Election Day. The two parties did not like the League—a nonpartisan civic group—setting the rules and running the debates. So a private corporation was formed, given the official-sounding title of the Commission on Presidential Debates (CPD) and headed by co-chairs who were the former chairmen of the Republican and Democratic National Committees. Its phony purpose was voter education. The debates cost money, so the CPD found corporations to write big checks. These firms have included Anheuser-Busch, Philip Morris, Ford Motor Co., and other companies that also gave soft money to the parties' national committees.

In 1992, Ross Perot came on the scene, and his wealth and widespread polling support led to his being allowed to join the debates. His polls went up, too. He received nineteen million votes, shaking the political establishment with his Reform Party and his paid televised lectures. Never again, vowed the two parties. Fully ninety-two million Americans saw the debate among Perot, Clinton, and Bush, more than double the average of the three 2000 debates. Too destabilizing for the duopoly. Perot was barred in 1996 by a series of vague criteria based on interviews with columnists, pollsters, and consultants who concurred that he could not win. He was also barred by the national television networks from buying the same kind of thirty-minute time slots that brought his message of deficit reduction and political reform into the living rooms of millions of households.

Speaking with him after the election, I said, "Ross, at least you've proved that the big boys can keep even a megabillionaire off the air."

In the year 2000, the CPD revised its criterion for third-party candidates: 15 percent or more as measured by the average of five private polling organizations (which just happened to be owned by several major newspaper and television conglomerates). So if their parent companies did not cover the third-party candidate, the polls would not likely move up. Without moving up, there would be little media, and so a catch-22 was built in the CPD's entry barrier. How can a private company get away with this? By virtue of the mass media default, of course. There's absolutely nothing stopping the major networks and newspapers from sponsoring their own debates.

The televised debates are the only way presidential candidates can reach tens of millions of voters. Several polls during 2000 showed a majority of the voters wanted Pat Buchanan and me at the debates, regardless of folks' voting preferences. Larger audiences and ratings would almost certainly follow. People want a wide variety of subjects, viewpoints, forthrightness, and candidates.

They do not see the presidential debates as a cure for insomnia. However, the great default is now on the shoulders of the media moguls, and the major parties are back in charge of the ticket for admission to the public.

This is all about giving small starts a chance to have a chance. This does not mean that there be only three debates. It doesn't mean there are no criteria. An Appleseed Foundation project suggested in a report for campaign 2000 that candidates be included who meet one of two tests: (1) the polls show that a majority want the candidate included; and/or (2) the candidate has at least 5 percent support in the polls (the statutory minimum for receiving federal matching funds) and is on enough state ballots to theoretically be able to win a majority in the electoral college. Law professor David Kairys, who advised us on the debate matter, wrote in the *Washington Post*:

> The nation's broadcast media have so far been accomplices in this charade. CPD debates should at least be accurately labeled as Republican-Democratic campaign events, rather than as "presidential debates." ... [T]he rules of the debates should not be left to the major parties or their handpicked representatives, who have a history of excluding candidates and ideas the public wants—and deserves—to hear.

We did not take the CPD's autocratic exclusionary mission passively. Throughout the spring, summer, and early fall of the campaign, I denounced the CPD to one rally or audience after another. We encouraged citizens to communicate with the CPD, as we did, and demand the opening of its doors to competition. I sent letters to the major networks asking them to sponsor their own multicandidate debates. Two replied sympathetically but to no result. In September, I wrote the heads of the major industrial unions in the critical, close states of the Midwest urging that they cosponsor presidential debates with special emphasis on neglected labor agendas. No one from the Steelworkers, the Machinists, the Teamsters, or the United Auto Workers responded. I urged national civil rights organizations, including the major Hispanic civil rights association in Southern California, but to no avail. Granted, they had their reasons—the CPD debates were already scheduled, logistics, and the risk of being turned down and viewed as powerless. Now, with plenty of time until 2004, I call on people and institutions who want robust and diverse debates to join together and form a People's Debate Commission.

The newspapers take elections more seriously, comparatively speaking, than the broadcast media. Television and radio have many ready-made excuses for their shrinking coverage. A twenty-two-minute national television news program, excluding advertising time, is not sprung from holy writ. The format of the local television news, with its nine minutes of ads, with several leadoff accounts from the police crime blotter, four minutes of sports, four minutes of weather, one minute of chitchat, and the prescribed animal and medical journal health story, is not carved in stone. Apart from public radio and the few nonprofit community radio stations, commercial radio and television devote about 90 percent of airtime around the clock to entertainment and advertisements. News is sparse, abbreviated, and very repetitious. When radio is not singing or selling, it is traffic, weather, and sports with headline news spots. The number of reporters and editors has been cut to the bone. No more are there FCC requirements for ascertaining the news needs of the community. Gone are the Fairness Doctrine and the Right of Reply. In 1996 there was near silence on the tube regarding the congressional fight to block the giveaway of $70 billion worth of the new spectrum to the television stations—a giveaway opposed even by the Republican candidate that year, Robert Dole. The notorious Telecommunications Act of 1996 received the cold shoulder, notwithstanding its paving the way for a massive binge of mergers and further concentration of media power. In 2000 the FCC, under its chairman, William Kennard, started granting community radio licenses to nonprofit neighborhood associations. The formidable media lobby, led by the National Association of Broadcasters, descended on Congress. They pummeled into line a majority of Congress—Democrats and Republicans—to pass legislation, which Clinton reluctantly signed, that blocked the FCC from licensing these little stations, which could accept no paid advertising. A minor Hollywood celebrity's DUI received more television and radio coverage than did the FCC's attempt to give people a radio voice of a few miles' radius.

After dealing with reporters, editors, producers, and media honchos for nearly forty years, and being a reporter and columnist myself, I had few illusions about the difficulties in obtaining a fair quantity and quality of coverage for our campaign. Making any challenge to the existing two-party hegemony is akin to climbing a sheer cliff with a slippery rope. No other democracy in the world erects so many barriers and is so uncongenial to small political starts. From the starting gate, the major parties radiate the message to all the media that no one but them has a chance to make it a contest, much less to win. This easily convinces the media powers that a small-party candidate doesn't merit coverage because he or she can't possibly win. This produces the most insurmountable obstacle of all, which is the virtual lock enjoyed by the two major parties on coverage in the national media. We are left with the old chicken-egg routine. Waiting for poll risings to receive coverage means no poll activity due to little coverage.

We were quite aware of conventional media mind-sets and routines. There was, even among the more competent and experienced news reporters and columnists, what people inside the fourth estate have called "blackbird journalism." One blackbird takes off and the rest follow. This phenomenon is hardly counteracted by the smaller, community media or magazines like *The Nation* or *The Progressive*, which are so often ahead of the news curve. It is entrenched through horizontal peer dynamics. The *Washington Post* looks over the shoulder of the *New York Times* and vice versa, and the national networks read both papers every morning to see what is deemed significant. I came across a nearly perfect passage from James Barber's *The Pulse of Politics: Electing Presidents in the Media Age* that speaks to all of this:

> Journalism's strength is not theory but fact. . . . A war over the facts, every four years, could help journalism break out of its losing preoccupation with the nuances of hypothetical opinion, symbolic epistemology, electoral bookie work, and the tired search for someone to quote, and do what it does best: get relevant information, quickly and accurately. Citizens, now woefully mis- and un- and under-informed on the

way things work, . . . might begin to see through the fog of rhetoric to the shape of reality. The drama of revelation might grip the public imagination a good deal more firmly than do the campaign gossip and ideological chit-chat that now drone through so many eminently forgettable paragraphs.

That is the point, isn't it? Journalism should give at least equal attention to the messages as it does to the carrier, if not more. Abraham Lincoln once said that if brought the "real facts," the people "can be depended upon to meet any national crisis."

Take a simple numerical hypothetical. Suppose a first-time candidate for the presidency, running as an independent, marshaled ten thousand super-energetic volunteers to work on one objective: registering at least two hundred thousand voters a week, week after week. The candidate didn't show in the polls, had no track record of successful advocacy, and never held public office. Should the media give that candidate regular coverage? Surely, the difficulty of getting any significant number of the one hundred million people who stay home from the polls has puzzled everyone. This candidate seemed to be achieving something that has eluded very experienced and well-funded people and candidacies for decades. In so doing, dozens of interesting stories about this amazing performance were there for reporters to gather. Thinking outside the box may happen in some classes in journalism school but rarely at the news and editorial desks of the news business.

This is not to say that the major media organizations failed to cover our campaign. They did. But they consistently viewed it as an occasional feature story—a modestly colorful narrative dispatch from the trail with a marginal candidate—rather than a news story about our agenda. During the months when I was traveling throughout the fifty states, the local press usually reported on the visits. In contrast, the national print and electronic media was capricious. It would parachute in a reporter to travel with us for a day or two and file a profile that focused on the so-called spoiler issue. We were never a news beat, even when the margins narrowed between Al Gore and George W. Bush during the last month and made our voters very consequential. So much so that a radio reporter in Washington, D.C., about a week before the election preposterously asked, "How does it feel to be the most powerful politician in America?" I demurred and returned to our fourteen-seat van for reporters, which was more than half empty.

In April, the first poll (Zogby) came out and put us at over 5 percent nationwide. Our audiences were growing and we had an exhaustive agenda—much of which we had worked on for years—that was of compelling concern to millions of Americans. These were topics that, over the years, many news outlets had reported on, investigated, and editorialized about. Bush and Gore were either dismissing us or taking positions opposite ours. Their poor respective records gave further credibility to our agenda. We had a long track record, and we weren't offering easy rhetoric. And, as the weeks unfolded, the Nader-LaDuke ticket was qualifying on forty-three state ballots and the District of Columbia, far exceeding any potential electoral college majority.

I paid a visit in May to Jim Roberts, the political editor of the mighty *New York Times*. Unlike some reporters and editors at the *Times*, Roberts appeared genuinely open to our requests for more regular coverage. I asked him whether the *Times* had any overall newsworthiness criteria for covering significant third-party candidates. He allowed that there were no specific standards, implying that *Times* editors made judgment calls as events unfolded. When I asked, for example, what would qualify as a newsworthy event in our case, he replied, "If you do anything with Pat Buchanan, or when you campaign in California, I'd be interested." At the time, California was considered a must-win state for Gore's campaign and favorable territory for our candidacy.

I often asked newspaper editorial boards across the country what I had to do to be more newsworthy. The responses were either noncommittal or related to our effect on the Gore-Bush competition. One would think that merely to escape the tedium, the press would declare itself some holidays from the horse-race question. Imagine their business reporters interviewing the CEO of a corporate start-up like RealNetworks' Robert Glaser in competition with Microsoft with the query, "Mr. Glaser, aren't you worried about taking dollars away from Bill Gates and Microsoft?"

When a candidate attempts an appraisal of the media's performance, it is important for him not to confuse his worldly agendas with the world revolving around him. Of course, there are many important topics that reporters have to cover daily. But a huge amount of time and space also are given to just about anything but serious news. And what results is a cultural abridgment of imagination, plain laziness, and self-censorship. Editors, producers, and reporters stick by their journalistic traditions, and somehow politicians who campaign against big government receive more coverage than those who are critical of big business. In the nineties, Ralph Reed of the Christian Coalition was on the network Sunday news shows twenty times more than I was.

It's important to understand where the media is coming from and how its traditions and prejudices affected the coverage of my campaign. Here are a few stories that hint at what I mean.

The *Washington Post* was a puzzle even to some of its own people. In October we filled Madison Square Garden with donating supporters. The *Post* covered it with a paragraph two days later. Back in D.C., I held a news conference across the street from the *Post* at the Madison Hotel, which exposed the phony crisis of Social Security that Bush and Gore were peddling for different reasons. No one showed up from the *Post*. AP sent a story around the country. The *New York Times* wrote it up but did not print a story. However, unlike the *Times*, the *Post* invited me to meet with its editorial board and columnists, which I did. The next day, David Broder, their chief political writer, produced an accurate column-length article. Shortly thereafter, the paper invited me to submit an op-ed piece, which I did. It was the definition of running hot and cold.

Our press office became aware of this schizophrenic tendency early on, so when Dana Milbank called to say he wanted to travel with us and write a feature for the *Post,* we warily filled him in on our next California trip in late August. We started at Occidental College near Los Angeles, went to San Diego, and then went up to Santa Barbara, Salinas, Carmel, Santa Cruz, Berkeley, and Sacramento. The trip had great variety—people, geography, and issues. By the afternoon of the third day, Milbank had had enough. Arriving with us at an early-evening farm labor rally in rural Salinas, he announced that he was cutting out and driving to San Francisco to spend that time with some Yale buddies.

When his long Style section feature came out, we wondered whether we had traveled with the real Dana Milbank. His piece focused on the soy cheese quesadillas served at our San Diego fundraiser, and that we stayed overnight at a wealthy volunteer's house in Santa Barbara. Milbank made no mention of our detailed session with people in San Diego working on border issues, and since he headed for the city early, he missed our electric exchange with California's migrant farmworkers and their advocates in Salinas. It seems that Milbank developed a dislike for me when, at a Latino community center, I made a sharp comment on the media's often upside-down sense of newsworthiness and in passing referred to the *Washington Post* as one of many culprits. Milbank reddened, waltzed over to one of our campaign staff, disputed the charge, and stalked out of the room. Oh, well, have another quesadilla (they were pretty good).

In mid-September I was campaigning in Washington, D.C., when the *Post* coverage saga returned. I felt that a full day at D.C. events had to get us their coverage. This was its hometown, overwhelmingly Democratic and overwhelmingly avoided by previous presidential candidates of the major parties. I started with a news conference at a community center near the *Post*, sponsored by Scott McLarty and Gail Dixon, local Green leaders. I spoke in some detail of the terrible conditions in the "other Washington" where the tourists do not visit. The poverty of the District, the widespread poor health, record infant mortality, air pollution, uncertain drinking water, crumbling potholed streets and underground infrastructure, and malfunctioning governmental agencies and schools form just part of the picture in the nation's capital that resists basic improvements. It is truly a tale of two cities, between the well-to-do, who can afford to escape many of the city's ills, and the majority, who cannot. I urged a much stronger drive for statehood and democratic empowerment for its disenfranchised citizenry. While the District is recovering modestly, with the new mayor, Tony Williams, and a real-estate boom, many poorer people are being pushed out by gentrification.

We then walked through the Anacostia farmers' market in one of the city's most neglected areas. This is Ward 8, with sixty-five thousand residents, mostly African Americans, and not one food supermarket. If you live in Ward 8, you go to Maryland for your groceries, or to another section of the District—inconvenient, costly, and humiliating. There are many towns in the United States with less than a third of that population which have three or more large supermarkets. There are parts of Anacostia that look like Camden, New Jersey: abandoned buildings, debris-covered lots and structures, and schools badly in need of repair. Plenty of crime, too. The farmers' market was not doing too well. There were about five tables with some spare clusters of tomatoes, cucumbers, peppers, sweet potato pies, some fried foods, and a table of homemade soaps and balms. The vendors were properly proud of their enterprise, but the customers were sparse. We stopped by the Expery Barber Shop, where I picked up the friendly fatalism of the people about their community, though one man said that things were a little better than a few years ago.

Then over to Evans Middle School at 55th and East Capitol Street, N.E., where the principal, superintendent, and two eighth graders who were twins showed us what a determined level of cooperation among administrators, teachers, and parents can do to make an inner-city school sparkle. Equally promising was a visit to a large organic garden on an acre of land provided by St. Elizabeth's Hospital. The head farmer, flanked by Georgetown University student volunteers, was infectiously enthusiastic as he explained what they were growing and distributing locally. I just listened. There was nothing for me to say other than to point the accompanying writers to this thriving agrarian oasis in the middle of the city.

That evening, there was a high-energy rally for D.C. statehood in the auditorium of the University of the District of Columbia. Ambrose R. Lane Sr., journalist and radio host, and Sam Smith, publisher of the *Progressive Review* and District activist, were the cohosts and speakers. I noted in my remarks that while Democrats were for D.C. statehood and Republicans were against it, both parties for years have done everything they could to make sure nothing happened for D.C. statehood. I urged that sometime before Clinton left office there should be thousands of peaceful demonstrators around the White House demanding statehood and real self-government so that District residents can blame themselves for the city's deficiencies instead of having to blame Congress and the Financial Control Board that rules the disenfranchised.

Late that evening, I turned on the local TV to learn that I was the first presidential candidate ever to campaign in Anacostia. The only time the Democratic or Republican candidates appear in the uncontested D.C. on their campaigns is for fund-raisers at posh hotels or large homes of the rich and powerful. The next day, AP sent out on their national wire a photo of me talking with Malik Lloyd, who was getting his hair cut by Kevin Davis, as I toured the neighborhood promoting "community strength."

The day after, however, there was nothing in the bulging Sunday *Washington Post*. In fact the paper had not even bothered to send a reporter.

Still in the *Post*'s circulation area, the next morning I attended the annual Farm Aid rally in Bristow, Virginia. This is Willie Nelson's big event on behalf of family farmers. Thousands come every year from all over the country, making it the biggest such gathering in the United States. Naturally, Willie and Carolyn Mugar, executive director of Farm Aid, invited all of the presidential candidates. The only ones to show for this long-planned event were me and Pat Buchanan.

As I had sponsored a six-hundred-page report—*The Corporate Reapers*—on big agribusiness in 1992 by Al Krebs and had campaigned in farm country earlier, it was not difficult to summarize my position.

The family farm is at greater risk now than at any time in the past century. Today the threat is not drought, locusts, or plunging cyclical prices. It is industrial, vertically integrated, concentrated agribusiness backed by Washington. Traveling through the Midwest with an associate recently out of college, I advised him to view the farms we were whizzing by in our motorcar because someday he'd be able to tell his grandchildren that he once saw these long-gone farms with their barns, silos, and planted acreage. In 1999 *Feedstuffs* magazine wrote that "American agriculture must now quickly consolidate all farmers and livestock producers into about fifty production systems," citing agribusiness analysts as their sources. At Farm Aid, I called for a government policy to break up the excessive market power of the grain, meat, and poultry giants that is squeezing downward the prices paid these farmers.

In addition to antitrust enforcement, there has to be a promotion of new food infrastructures to market directly farm food, provide research for family farm preservation, and prevent pollution and the degradation of natural resources through strong conservation policies. By breaking the stranglehold that agribusiness has on the small farm economy, we could increase the share of the food dollar received by the farmer and facilitate a degree of price and quality competition for consumers. For further action, I referred the farmers to a group I helped start called the Organization for Competitive Markets (OCM), which organizes family farmers and academic specialists in these directions.

The farmers present did not take kindly to Gore and Bush being absent. Instead of asking Secretary of Agriculture Dan Glickman to represent his views, Gore sent as his spokesmen Congressman David Obey (D-Wisconsin) and Senator Byron Dorgan (D-North Dakota). This choice of emissaries reflected badly on Gore's character, because both Obey and Dorgan voted against the Clinton-Gore position on NAFTA, GATT, and the Freedom to Farm Act of 1996—often called the Freedom to Fail Act by farmers. Obey and Dorgan were popular with family farmers over the many years they served in Congress. When both held their breath and spoke in support of Gore, I could see they were playing the good soldiers. Gore was obviously exploiting their goodwill among farmers for his political benefit. But the farmers were not fooled and frequently voiced their displeasure. They wanted Gore to defend his positions directly.

And all of this might have made a good election-year story by the *Washington Post*. But the next day, readers saw nothing about Farm Aid.

Of course, the *Post* was always going to endorse Gore and believed that our votes would take more from Gore than from Bush. But after speaking with a number of *Post* reporters and editors and the publisher, Don Graham, I still cannot explain the chasms in their coverage.

The *New York Times* was different. It wore its biases on its sleeves and announced them dramatically on June 30, 2000, with a 618-word lead editorial titled "Mr. Nader's Misguided Crusade." In this article, written by Steve Weissman, under instructions from his superiors, the *Times* declared that since there was a clear-cut choice between Gore and Bush, my running as a nominee of the Green Party was a "self-indulgent exercise" driven by ego. The paper asserted that "there is no driving logic for a third-party candidacy this year, and the public deserves to see the major-party candidates compete on an uncluttered playing field. It is especially distressing to see Mr. Nader flirt with the spoiler role." Since the editorial board did not invite me to discuss the reasons for my candidacy, they were highlighting their own ignorance and dismissing the wide divide between Democrats and the Greens. The editorial concluded that the main economic issue dividing me from the major-party candidates was trade. To learn more, couldn't they at least have logged on to our Web site, votenader.org? Once again, those poor editorial writers could know little about our objections to GATT and NAFTA as autocratic governance from reading their own newspaper coverage since 1993. In 1995 I discussed the GATT agreement with a couple of their pro-GATT editorial writers at their office. I referred them to an unpleasant reality, which was that neither their reporters nor any other members of the public would be permitted to attend the WTO's tribunals in Geneva, Switzerland. Did you know, I asked them, that these tribunal proceedings, affecting not only trade but environmental, labor, and consumer matters, are conducted behind closed doors in secret? It is worth the price, replied one writer.

However, the *Times* editorial did praise my record and accomplishments over the years and how I could have "the effect of enlivening the public debate." Then came the 180-degree turn: "The only realistic role" I could play this year was to tilt swing states like California toward Bush.

This editorial astounded many readers. "So rough, unreasoned, un-*Times*-like," a patrician from the Upper East Side told me. Weissman reportedly was taken aback by the reader reactions that flowed into the *Times* during the following days. Reporters in the Washington Bureau of the *Times* were seen shaking their heads and laughing, according to one of them. I swore to one *Times* reporter that I did not pay for this editorial. In the aftermath, I expected the *Times* to increase its regular coverage, given its thesis of my spoiling Gore's chances. That logical and naive prediction never panned out.

John Anderson called me in high dudgeon. The *Times* had never treated his candidacy that way in 1980, when they must have discerned a major difference or two between Jimmy Carter and Ronald Reagan. Anderson wrote an op-ed piece in the *Times* a few days later defending our candidacy. I was given a little space to reply in the letters column.

The *Times* editorial against our candidacy was just the first on that page. There followed a critical column by Robert F. Kennedy Jr., two pieces by Anthony Lewis, a diatribe by Paul Krugman, and three more editorials from the *Times* board. Except for Krugman's piece, which contained errors and distortions, all this commentary did not disagree with our stands or positions, just with our effect on Gore's chances. In my attempt to respond to this onslaught, I learned that the *Times* has a two-month rule, holding readers to no more than one published letter every two months. The editorial page can attack and can mislead as Krugman did when he suggested I opposed passage of the South African constitution, and there was no chance for me to reply. Even concise letters from South African members of parliament correcting the record and a short letter replying to Kennedy by the preeminent ecologist Professor Barry Commoner were not printed. Unlike the *Washington Post*, the *Times* prohibits "taking exception" op-eds replying to previous columns or editorials. When I discussed this lack of fair play with the page's editor (now the executive editor), Howell Raines, he noted the scarcity of space and the many letters they receive each day. I responded by urging a larger space for letters. While the paper has grown in size enormously in the past thirty years, space for letters has remained the same. Again, by comparison, the *Washington Post* at least devotes an entire extra page on Saturday to letters.

The *Times* has some rethinking to do. For $34,000 a pop, it sells a corner of its editorial op-ed page mostly to corporations like Exxon Mobil or think tanks with pronounced ideological views. It then refuses to print any letters to the editor in rebuttal, thereby giving these propagandists an unchallenged access to the readers on this influential page. Again, in an earlier conversation, Raines explained that priority goes to letters responding to their reporters, editorials, and columnists as a matter of professional standards. When I suggested devoting that bottom right-hand space once a week to letters rebutting the other six days, he said they would consider this and other recommendations. That was more than three years ago. Newspapers and magazines devote too little space for printing reader feedback even though surveys show that the letters section is one of the readers' favorites.

Nonetheless, the important question is: Did the editorial position of the *New York Times* affect the extent (not the quality) of coverage of our campaign in the news and feature sections? No one is saying so at the *Times* (a newspaper well known historically for having its favorites, like Daniel P. Moynihan, and its nonfavorites, like Noam Chomsky or, earlier, George Seldes). But it certainly wasn't easy for filing reporters to receive space for our campaign. After a while, why should they even try against such odds? Suffice it to say that my many years of contact with *New York Times* reporters, especially in the Washington Bureau, has given me plenty of evidence of selective bias toward noncoverage, which is distinct from bias in any coverage that does occur. Once after twelve reporters over a period of many months told me that it was difficult to get their stories about our advocacy groups through the New York editors, I wrote then-boss Abe Rosenthal for an explanation. He did not think there was anything going on like that. But reporters in his Washington shop surely did.

And I can't overemphasize the influence of the *New York Times* and *Washington Post* in setting the scene for the rest of the media. They view themselves as agenda shapers for public issues, apart from any election, so it is not a big leap for them to know how important they are for candidates climbing uphill who are not annointed front-runners. After presidential elections, ambitious new candidates dream of a David Broder column in the *Post* touting this newcomer's attributes and chances. In addition, the television networks take their cues from what the *Post* or *Times* leads with. In this sense, the operational concentration of the media is greater than the market share ratios ever indicate.

None of this reality discouraged our small press office. Led by Texas populist and former longtime House Banking Committee staffer Jake Lewis, it came up with a panoply of good ideas. One of them was to respond immediately to major position statements by the major candidates. In September, Gore said he would tap the strategic petroleum reserve to lower the rising gasoline and heating oil prices. I instantly issued a statement summarizing the Clinton-

Gore record of surrendering to the demands of big oil companies, including rubber-stamping most giant oil industry mergers (which have concentrated markets and pricing power) and ignoring information about why the oil industry voluntarily closed down in the U.S. one hundred refineries during the past fifteen years.

Mr. Gore's too-little, too-late call for releasing the Strategic Petroleum Reserve to reduce heating-oil prices was primarily a political ploy. The reserve was established for national security/emergency objectives, not for helping a candidate whose long record of receiving oil industry political money and caving in to Big Oil has become an embarrassment.

We issued these kinds of prompt commentaries hoping that a sentence or two would get into the lengthy articles. That almost never occurred. Didn't we realize that this was a two-party election?

During the summer I learned that both *60 Minutes* and *20/20* were considering a feature segment on our campaign. The latter never surfaced, but Mike Wallace of *60 Minutes* was more interested. He wanted to know whether we were planning any trips that his camera crew could join. I pointed out a couple that I thought would have visual content for television, including the Labor Day parade in Detroit. When nothing seemed to be happening, I called him at his Martha's Vineyard summer home—to his credit he is very accessible. He still held out the possibility of a piece but said *60 Minutes* wanted to wait awhile and be sure our polls were not heading downward. When the program didn't go forward even after learning of our Madison Square Garden plans, I called Mike and asked him why. Is it Don Hewitt, I asked? He replied, "Call Don," the legendary founding producer of *60 Minutes*. I got Hewitt on the phone and asked whether he was the source of the hesitation. He said yes, adding that the proposed segment was on me the candidate, not me the consumer advocate, and was he going to be expected to do similar segments on other candidates? I said he was the boss on that decision and urged him to call Mike back for one more chance at being persuaded. He said okay. Later I called Mike and asked what happened. He said it wasn't going to happen. Hewitt is the last word. I asked Mike what was the best argument he made for such a program. He replied, "I told Don that the Nader campaign was the only one that had a pulse."

Months later, in June 2001, during a public debate, Mike said that he voted for me even though he had turned me down for a *60 Minutes* interview. My luck has been historically bad with *60 Minutes*. Back in 1990, Ed Bradley was commissioned to do a segment. The show's camera crews traveled with me to Florida, Moscow, and other places, probably spending more than $100,000, before I was told that there would be no show. When I asked why, the producers replied that they could get no one of any visibility to come on the program and criticize me, not even Newt Gingrich. Sometimes, you just don't gotta believe. In any event, losing out on *60 Minutes* meant losing out on reaching fifty times more voters than I reached in person during my fifty states campaign.

There were reporters, like Maria Recio of the *Fort Worth Star-Telegram* and Tom Squitieri of *USA Today,* who saw early on the significance of my campaign. They persuaded their editors to allow more regular coverage of the campaign. Similarly, Dan Harr of the *Hartford Courant* traveled with us in New England and New York and filed daily reports. Their sense of the campaign's news importance was preceded by Tim Russert of NBC's *Meet the Press,* who invited me on the show four times, and the fast-talking Chris Matthews of MSNBC's *Hardball,* who extended numerous invitations, including one at a wildly raucous town meeting with students at the University of Wisconsin.

I have no complaints about press photographers whose assiduousness drew no distinctions between small- and major-party candidates. They had a job to do, and some were nonstop clickers. I often wondered whether there was a correlation between the skill of a photographer and how many times he or she snapped a picture—as in the better the photographer, the fewer the clicks. A young newspaper photographer came with us one day and crouched in front of the podium like a big cat. I moved my chin four degrees to the left. *Click.* I raised my index finger three inches. *Click.* I looked down. *Click.* I arched an eyebrow. *Click, click.* I smiled slightly. *Click, click, click.* I raised my hand to my ear. *Click.* Moved it to my chin. *Click, click.* I felt a surge of power in singlehandedly increasing Kodak's sales. I had some fun with the photographers, especially the young ones who did not judiciously wait out trivial moments but ran wantonly through their inexhaustible click supply. I would tease them during the long days by announcing at events that "a photo op was imminent."

The media handlers for Bush and Gore knew that politics is theater and entertainment, and their candidate had to get on the late-night comic shows and some of the more sane daytime talk shows. So both Bush and Gore got on, at least once and sometimes twice, the Jay Leno and David Letterman shows, where they could deliver their well-rehearsed jokes or Top Tens. In mid-September, both Gore and Bush appeared on *Oprah*. Bush won that round among the pundits by greeting Oprah with a kiss and discussing his giving up alcohol at age forty. He told the audience that he was not "running on Daddy's name." And he showed tears in eyes when he discussed the joyous birth of his twin daughters. That was the point of appearing on these shows—laughs, emotion, a little self-deprecation, and very little on the issues. In previous presidential campaigns, invitations by Phil Donahue meant tough questioning by the host and by members of the audience if they so chose. Today, the main challenge is to be funny, to appear congenial, and to confess a little as if you are the interviewed celebrity on the cover of *Parade* magazine.

Well, I decided to make the trek and asked these shows to have me on. First was Bill Maher of *Politically Incorrect*, which Gore and Bush steered away from. I mean, could you imagine either of them exposing himself to Bill and three other wildcat guests? Bill is very perceptive—he voted for me.

Then I went on Jay Leno, who does go into the green room with the guests to chat, and David Letterman, who does not. Probably the latter approach makes for more spontaneity—at least it did for me. Both appearances went well. Then there was *Saturday Night Live*, my fourth visit since 1977, where I did my five-minute sketch about being excluded from the debates, with Rob Lowe and the show's originator, Canadian Lorne Michaels. The impersonations of Bush and Gore by Will Ferrell and Darrell Hammond were side-splitters and deserved the media's—and the candidates'—attention.

After learning that Bush and Gore were invited on *Oprah*, with its large afternoon following, our press office asked if there was a chance for me to go on too. After all, when Oprah was a lonely talk-show host in Baltimore, well before she made the big time in

Chicago, I gladly appeared on her small program. So we tried to penetrate the show's iron curtain. Like most of today's daytime television shows, just getting through to a live person, much less getting a response, is next to impossible. Oprah's people were no exception. Calls, letters—it didn't matter how or who—there was not the courtesy of a reply. Disappointing but not surprising. Oprah never replied after I wrote and spoke in her defense when she was frivolously sued by Texas beef businesses for her famous show on the negative side of eating meat.

A new entry to daytime television, the *Queen Latifah Show* in New York City, offered greater promise. The staff was responsive, courteous, and professional. With the added delight of being joined by Susan Sarandon and Phil Donahue, we had a serious and enjoyable half hour with Queen Latifah.

The *Charlie Rose Show*—one of the last serious national television interview programs—told us in May that they wanted me for a full hour. When we finally found a date of mutual convenience, they promised thirty minutes. When I got to the studio, it was reduced to fifteen minutes. Charlie loves to interview actors, actresses, prominent authors, diplomats, and corporate executives, but he doesn't much like talking about corporate domination of society. Once when I prevailed on him to have Jim Hightower, William Greider, and me—corporate critics all—on the show, he put us all together for fifteen minutes sandwiched between two new novelists whose works he probably could no longer remember three years later. There was a great response to our segment the following day. The show's producer, in a message inadvertently sent to us, told her associates that viewer reactions were probably orchestrated. Sometimes you can't win.

But we kept trying. One terrific success came through our first political advertisement. It was a parody of the MasterCard "priceless" ad. It received widespread accolades in the media for its accuracy, its humor, and its focus on my getting included in the debates. MasterCard's foolish lawsuit for $35 million alleging copyright infringement only focused more attention on the ad and the campaign it represented. When I read the MasterCard complaint, I was overcome with laughter, for they asserted that I was trying to lunch off the goodwill and reputation of MasterCard to advance my candidacy. I savored that argument, especially since I had been criticizing and exposing credit card gouges and deceptions for years. Still chuckling, I called the president of MasterCard, Robert Sealander, who was vacationing on some tropical island, and asked whether he knew what his attorneys were getting him into with the lawsuit. He expressed disappointment, thinking that my call was for the purpose of discussing a settlement. Settlement? The next morning I was at the National Press Club with Bill Hillsman, the producer of the ad, giving a news conference about credit card abuses and having our "priceless" ad played free over the television stations that were there. Sometimes corporate lawyers do the darndest things! Our fine pro bono attorney Anthony Fletcher from Fish and Richardson helped to prove how frivolous the MasterCard lawsuit was in its attempt to stifle political speech.

All along through the months of June, July, August, and September, I reached the public through several cable TV shows (CNN's *Crossfire,* Fox cable news, MSNBC, *Talk Back Live*), syndicated radio shows like Pacifica Radio, Chris Lydon's *Connection,* and Don Imus, the Sunday-morning news shows, *Business Week, Time, Newsweek, U.S. News & World Report,* and *Harper's* (they ran a cover story), community weeklies in cities from Los Angeles to Boston, which, like the *Village Voice* and the *Advocate* papers in Connecticut, analyzed the campaign in welcome detail. Conservatives George Will, David Brooks, and William Safire devoted columns to our race. There was a very occasional network television news bite.

Once, on the CBS Sunday show *Face the Nation* with Bob Schieffer, Pat Buchanan and I followed each other, and after it was over, before the remote cameraman unhooked me, Schieffer, not knowing he was still on our audio, told his producer, "That was a good show. It was refreshing. Different viewpoints." I thought it was too bad the debate commission czars and their cooperative TV networks did not think that way.

The most intense treatment of the Nader-LaDuke campaign appeared regularly in the progressive press, especially the local weeklies like the *Village Voice* in New York City and the national magazines such as *The Nation* and *The Progressive.* Back and forth the discussion would rage between editorials, articles, columnists, and reader letters arguing over Gore needing liberal voters' loyalty because Bush was worse, or Gore deserving a Green Party challenge for his broken promises. This was all very fascinating to read, and I especially enjoyed writers such as Lewis Lapham, Nicholas von Hoffman, Marc Cooper, Micah Sifry, Matt Rothschild, and Alexander Cockburn for their historical, contemporary, and futuristic perspectives on our efforts. It was quite motivating. These liberal-progressive debates were also a welcome relief from the daily drumbeat focus on the horse-race question.

Interestingly enough, talk radio was far more open to hearing and questioning the candidates through audience call-ins than all the other mainstream media combined. Whether on the Lydon, Imus, Bohannon, or other local talk shows like Ron Owens in San Francisco, and Michael Jackson in Los Angeles, this was one forum where sentences and even paragraphs could be introduced over the airways without the frenzied pressure of sound-bite cutoff. Certainly, one could not languish and drone on, but what a difference thirty minutes or sometimes an hour makes from television's three-minute quickeroos.

One of the major themes that the established commentators and reporters wrote about most often was what reformers call "dirty money politics." I read with appreciation one editorial after another in the Times, the Post, and the regional papers excoriating the soft-money binges, the lavish fund-raisers, the Niagara of money pouring into both major party coffers at countless events stamped by corporate logos. The press named names of fat-cat companies and what the expected quid pro quos were from the politicians. In spite of these relentless stories, the money corruption gets bigger and seedier. So one might expect that the reporters and commentators would add to their material by highlighting the one party that did it the way they would want the major parties to behave. Yet rarely, if ever, did our campaign or that of any other Green Party candidates receive any recognition by the major media for refusing to take soft money, corporate money, PAC money. We set an example that went unnoticed.

It became clear that, as we were fluctuating in the polls between 4 and 7 percent, we were receiving less than 1 percent of the print and broadcast space and time devoted to Bush and Gore. It became more evident that even with 5 percent of that kind of coverage not much would change. If the media did not view you as inside the two-party playing field, as it did Perot in 1992, there was no dynamic to the media you received. The campaign remained sidelined. Voters had to read about and see you in the big mix, just as fans have to see the underdog team tangle in the same arena with the favorites in order to decide who is best for them. There has to be interactive contrast, which is why getting on the presidential debates is so decisive.

In October we tried one more way of persuading editors and producers to pay attention to corporate power abuses that we were regularly highlighting. Our researchers compiled nearly 200 investigative articles and television exposés on subjects that were related to our agenda. They ranged from the brilliant 1998 *Time* magazine cover story on corporate welfare by Donald L. Barlett and James B. Steele to prominent stories about environmental, consumer, investor, taxpayer, and worker injustices committed by major corporations and reported prominently by the *Wall Street Journal,* the *New York Times,* the *Washington Post,* the *Los Angeles Times,* the Associated Press, *60 Minutes,* the *Boston Globe,* and others. We pointed out to these papers and programs that their own reporters had written these articles, which went nowhere in terms of changes. The public authorities of the three branches of government at local, state, and national levels were, for the most part, not following up on these finest hours of journalism. Moreover, the policy questions they raised had not found their way into the presidential campaign dialogue. I asked one *Time* magazine staffer why, given their cover story, their campaign reporters didn't raise the subject of corporate welfare with Bush and Gore. His reply was, "It is hard on the trail to reach the candidates, and when you do break through, they don't answer the question."

Well, what about when Gore and Bush were on the Sunday news shows or granting long interviews to major papers and magazines or answering their questionnaires? Or at the debates? Or during the more accessible primary season? There are opportunities for a determined press corps, particularly a press corps that demands regular press conferences to force answers on these questions, either from the candidates or from their press spokespersons. Instead, too many reporters settle for exclusive snippets or asides on the campaign plane. Even when they have great daily access, such as with Senator John McCain on the "Straight Talk Express," these questions are not asked. It has become a cultural rut.

After all the pages written about Bush and Gore—their youths, their early years in politics, their position papers, their daily sound bites, their sallies against each other—not very much came to the public's attention about their actual records, in contrast to their highly publicized rhetoric. On July 7, 1999, the *Post*'s David Broder wrote that Bush's "five-year record in public office is largely unexamined." He must have meant by the mass media. Certainly Molly Ivins cast a cold eye on his governorship in her book *Shrub,* and publications such as *Mother Jones, The Nation, The Progressive,* and *In These Times* made constant critiques. But Broder was writing about media that reaches large audiences and affects other opinion makers as well as the candidates themselves. Gore was a media escapee—except for his sophomoric gaffes—when it came to separating his speeches from his record on topics as varied as the environment, drug prices here and abroad, corporate subsidies, comsumer protection, and his continuing daily promise to fight "big oil," big HMOs, big insurance companies, and big chemical companies. His record is rich in surrender to big-business interests, including car companies, the biotechnology industry, and the banking, agribusiness, and telecommunications goliaths. Since corporate George W. Bush, marinated in oil and gas, would not point out these failings, it was up to the media to examine repeatedly these records of both Bush and Gore, which of course they neglected to do.

There is also a self-interest on the part of the major media conglomerates. They are, after all, businesses that rely on advertising revenue and the goodwill of the surrounding business community.

We heard fear of top management expressed in the voices of the reporters and producers in television studies. They feared losing their jobs in an industry laying off while increasing profits. A rattled producer at an Austin station, owned by Time Warner, came hurtling out of her cubicle and insisted on my repeating a short interview. Why? Because, as she stated, she was unable to edit out my comment on Time Warner CEO Gerald Levin's statement about the media being more important than governments, nonprofits, and educational institutions.

There is one unsung hero in this story. Brian Lamb, the creator of C-Span, convinced the cable industry years ago that serious events deserve unedited coverage. In all of the United States, the communications supergiant of the world, only C-Span covers entire events regularly during a presidential campaign. Although its audience is relatively small, C-Span repeats presidential campaign addresses two or three times over a two- or three-day period. To reach people unedited is a political candidate's idea of heaven.

There were other efforts to get the media to open the doors for coverage. The most relentless one was Morton Mintz's series of twenty-eight cogent and concise articles for TomPaine.com on a wide range of subjects "that powerfully affect us all." They were directed to "Mr. or Mrs. Presidential, Vice Presidential, Senate or House Candidate." Besides the Web site, the series received some major visibility when one of Mintz's pieces was excerpted in an advertorial on the *New York Times*'s op-ed page. Still, his work came largely to naught, other than reifying journalistic standards to guide future writers. "I didn't get a single reaction of any kind from any political editor or reporter involved in covering the campaigns," he told me after the election. The lesson of that silence is clear: No democracy worth its salt can rely so pervasively on the commercial media. And no seriously prodemocracy campaign will ever get an even break, or adequate coverage in or outside the mix, from that media.

It is not difficult to locate the media's own self-criticism by seasoned workers in its trenches. Even the celebrities who have benefited most from the status quo, Walter Cronkite, Dan Rather, Peter Jennings, and Tom Brokaw, have all commented on what's wrong with political coverage. Journalism reviews like Columbia's publish pointed critiques and concrete recommendations for expanding the political debate by the press. Underneath these evaluations is the sense that the media itself is up against what Lonnie Isabel of *Newsday* called "Trying to Scale the Impenetrable Wall."

Writing in the *Columbia Journalism Review*, Russ Baker observed that "by and large, what the public heard was what the candidates chose to talk about. Both Gore and Bush controlled the 'dialogue,' avoiding press conferences for great stretches (Gore hid out for a stunning five months) and adhering tightly to a script throughout. And thus political discussion was generally limited to the areas they believed most marketable (Social Security, taxes, public education, and the high cost of prescription drugs), and by their narrow framing of solutions." Even with these issues—as with national health insurance—the structural or systemic aspect was avoided and only a slice was highlighted: prescription-drug benefits but not prices. Baker went on to write, "We know that the candidates stayed to their script. But did the media do the same thing? If so, were we complicit in limiting the quadrennial national debate?" And the coup de grâce: "The focus groups assembled by the candidates often reflect what people have already heard in the media." "So," says David Dreyer, a former deputy communications director for the Clinton administration, "excessive polling by the media contributes to a narrowing of the campaign. There is a shared complicity."

All these and scores of other articles and books on media and political campaigns make for important cogitations, but what did all this mean to Nader-LaDuke?

We learned more about end-running the media during our visit in July with Governor Jesse Ventura. Friday was casual wear day in the governor's office, and he was wearing jeans. How did you reach the people of Minnesota to win the election? I asked him. He replied that he was at about 10 percent in the polls and then got on ten statewide debates with the other major candidates. Second, the state provided substantial public funding of election campaigns, and third, Minnesota had same-day voter registration. In about a month, Ventura went from 10 percent to 38 percent and won the governorship in a three-way race. Same-day registration led to a last-minute surge of voters for him that helped raised the total voter turnout to about 65 percent—almost double the national average in an off-year election. Our informal session over, we entered the press room where Ventura repeated his support for me and Buchanan being in the debates, for public financing of campaigns, and for ending many barriers that keep voter turnout down. Jesse is very plainspoken, in addition to having a flamboyant personality that gets him easy media.

In 1987 the veteran newspaperman and editor Martin Schram wrote *The Great American Video Game*, which left no doubt where he stands: "The instrument of television has taken control of the presidential election process. It is the single greatest factor in determining who gets nominated every fourth summer and who gets elected that fall." Schram, who has covered many presidential campaigns, believes that television is also the nation's greatest hope, "the only medium that can give the public what it wants most: the ability to take the measure of the candidates for president in those intangible up-close and personal ways that the newspaper can never fulfill."

Schram wants to open the public airwaves to all qualifying candidates: "Congress can—and should—require the networks and local stations to make available to all qualifying candidates a specific amount of airtime for commercials—free commercials. A new law should require that these ads feature the candidate talking directly to the camera—no slick ads, no actors, no narrators. Just the candidate speaking." Fourteen years later, the major campaign finance reform legislation, McCain-Feingold, has no such media access provision. That is where political reality resides in the year 2001.

I realized one visual necessity. Future campaigns by progressives must search for greater visual communication that is true and compelling. At the start of the campaign, I replied to a reporter's question and said I would not be kissing babies. Nor did I seek out photo ops with retired coal miners suffering from black lung disease who now receive critical compensation due in part to our legislative advocacy over thirty years ago, or photos of college students in their activities working for the betterment of their states, due to our organizational efforts. Or of people saved by auto safety devices now required on cars. In retrospect, not doing this was a mistake.

It all started to get interesting when the media couldn't help but notice our effect. On the last day in August, I started early with Matt Lauer on *The Today Show*. Lauer wasted no time getting to the core scenario: "If this candidacy comes down to a tight race and we get to California, a lot of those liberals in California are going to go for you maybe and it's going to cost Al Gore the race."

I responded that none of the candidates were entitled to any votes, that we all have to earn our votes. To Matt's credit, he went on to ask about ballot access and the presidential debates, but as all *Today Show* guests realize, four or five minutes for back-and-forth hardly leaves time for many complete sentences.

What followed is a tribute to convenience of corporate concentration. All I had to do was walk across Rockefeller Plaza to the GE building, where I held a press conference decrying the decades-long PCB contamination of the Hudson River by General Electric. GE continues, against rising opposition from citizens and politicians, and even Bush's EPA, to delay, dodge, and obfuscate its responsibility to clean up its poisons in heavily contaminated sectors of the Hudson River bed. A cluster of New York media was there, along with the most vociferous sidewalk kibitzers in the country.

I then braved midday Manhattan traffic to speak with restaurant strikers in Chinatown, which offered a splendid opportunity to highlight some labor issues. A Chinese-American reporter asked me why I was in Chinatown, did I come here often, did I like Chinese food, and so on. I responded with a few words of Chinese from my Princeton days. She didn't seem to know any Mandarin, given her nonplussed expression.

From there we taxied over to the bastion of global capitalism, the New York Stock Exchange. For many years, my Princeton classmate Mike Robbins, an Exchange member, had been extending an invitation for me to visit and see how markets are made. He said I would never forget the experience, and he did not disappoint. After a courtesy call with William R. Johnston, vice-president of the Exchange, Mike took me and my two associates down on the floor to see this amazing mixture of chaos and order, this nexus by the split second between the human brain of the market makers and all the computers, which I learned cost a total of $3 billion.

There was George Moerler, Jr., nearly fifty years with the Exchange, which he'd gone to right out of high school, and the rapid-fire market maker for General Electric stock. Fed by a cheery sidekick forty years his junior, Moerler was so seasoned he seemed to be on automatic, barking out buys and sells while he was discussing in detail with us the workings of his craft. He clearly enjoyed our astonishment, as did a growing crowd of specialists and aides who followed us from one "stall" to another.

I was about to hold a news conference at twelve-thirty on the steps of Federal Hall facing the exchange. So I decided to do a little "field work" and asked several specialists if they believed the Stock

Exchange bosses when they hinted about moving to New Jersey if they could not get a billion-dollar subsidy package from New York City to buy land nearby and build a new Exchange headquarters. If only there was a video of their reactions. One fellow was eating a bologna sandwich for lunch and almost dropped it, he was laughing so much. Move to *Joisey*? How would the "suits" stay close to their buddies in the securities industry, their lawyers, and their investment banker friends? Invite them on the ferry to Hoboken? With computers, members of this chorus added, there is less need for space, not more. But if they can get it free, it's a sure bet, isn't it?

Standing on the steps a few minutes later, I recounted the story of this billion-dollar boondoggle, the utter hypocrisy of this big apostle of free market and free enterprise, and suggested some dire public needs in New York City that could use $1 billion, such as the decrepit schools, deserving clinics, and libraries that are limiting their hours. Though it was a successful media day, even resulting in a *New York Times* Metro section article, the story did not, as would have been the case with the candidacies of Gore and Bush, move beyond New York to the national level.

There was a humorous analogy here. One day in early summer, I opened my *Washington Post* and saw a seven-hundred-word article with the headline "Gore, Family Taking It Easy in North Carolina."

I considered going to Vermont and really, flamboyantly relaxing. Maybe then the *Post* would take notice.

Eleven

THE SUPER-RALLIES:
NOT YOUR AVERAGE GARDEN PARTY

By late summer we were waiting for serendipity. Our candidacy was now solidly in third place. We had established all the major fronts—ballot placement, a firm phalanx of documented positions, fund-raising, media placement, visits to all fifty states, and an energetic field staff. Still, running for president against a two-party duopoly is not tennis. A player can be ranked fiftieth or eightieth in the world and still find Wimbledon's gates open. Our polls were fairly static—most ranging from 3 to 7 percent nationally. And under the present power system, the polls are a controlling process over people and not, as they purport to be, reflective of public opinion. This is so if only because of the choice of questions.

Earlier, I referred to the catch-22 between the media coverage and the polls, flowing in part from the winner-take-all system and other barriers that impede or deter the growth of small starts. Knowing this, two lawyers in Portland, Oregon, Greg Kafoury and Mark McDougal, and their friend Laird Hastay were thinking about taking the campaign to a new, higher level. They noticed that when I campaigned in Portland at the auditorium of Benson High School, all fifteen hundred seats were easily filled on a rainy evening. The lightbulb went on: Why not launch a round of super-rallies for the last ten-week stretch to Election Day? Greg and Mark have similar personalities in one respect. They enjoy impossible challenges and love to say to doubters, "Watch us go."

When they broached their proposal, our top staff was hesitant and doubtful. Filling the Portland Memorial Coliseum with more than ten thousand paying people was daunting enough. Risking about $65,000, when the campaign's checking account was always low and other pressing expenses high, was a big risk. But we had to do something to break out and create attention and harness the enthusiasm of our many supporters.

We gave the green light and secured the Memorial Coliseum for Friday, August 25, 2000. Kafoury and McDougal had twenty days to fill this giant arena. While Theresa Amato, our campaign manager, was expressing her cautions, I was remembering how easily we filled the Santa Cruz Civic Center, which had a capacity of twenty-five hundred. Portland is a much larger city than Santa Cruz. What's more, over many years I had worked with citizen groups in Oregon, starting with the successful Oregon Student Public Interest Research Group (OSPIRG), which got going as far back as 1970. I have joined with Oregonians on numerous statewide referenda, environmental struggles, the rights of injured people, and political reforms. Throughout its history, Oregon has had more than its share of firsts in the country with various reforms. So how could we not start the super-rallies in the Beaver State?

We came into Portland from our California tour and met Winona LaDuke, who grew up in nearby Ashland, to strategize over the Coliseum. We knew one thing for sure—however many people showed up that night, they would have been drawn by the politics of justice. This was a rally without any organized buses or celebrity bands. Winona and I comprised the "marquee" that evening.

By the afternoon of August 25, about six thousand tickets were sold. The vast arena seemed even larger than before. Banks of empty seats stretched up toward the roofline with each section of seats painted a different color. As the seats started filling up, no one expected the highest section of red seats to be occupied. But to our amazement, a massive line was forming outside as thousands of tickets were sold at the door. Some exclaimed, "Look, the red seats are starting to fill up." Soon, none of the red seats were empty. Other super-rallies followed, but no gathering was more reactive, vigorous, and robustly loud than these Oregonians. The sheer intensity, cheerfulness, and attentiveness of the thousands of individuals and whole families of all ages took us all aback. I came onto the stage to such an enthusiastic reception that all I could say by way of an opener was, "Wow, what a rousing Oregonian welcome!"

As I scanned the people from the podium, I was overwhelmed

and overjoyed. These were citizens who had many struggles for justice in their civicula vitae accompanied by young men and women who yearned for a new politics. They were fed up with props, posturing, and politicians with forked tongues. They wanted action, results, and practical solutions to chronic human needs and environmental devastations. This was an audience that left hundreds of bicycles chained up outside. Earlier that night with red, white, and blue lights beaming down on the stage, they resonated with Winona LaDuke's call for ending commercial logging in national forests and "breaching some dams to save some salmon." Winona then spoke about recovering the Great Plains, now being depopulated but in olden times the sustaining lands for the First Nations. She spoke of bringing back the buffalo and the natural ecological rhythms of the vast grasslands and turning the wind-swept plains into what she described as "the Saudi Arabia of wind energy." As usual, Winona's address was earnest, lyrical, and vivid. She held the audience with an intense intelligence, speaking as a leader for indigenous people's rights, a mother of three children, and a working farmer. Was there ever such a vice presidential candidate? Thunderous ovations followed her remarks.

Green candidates do not use TelePrompTers—at least not so far. This permits more eye contact with people in the front rows and gives a different texture to one's remarks. I was intent on two goals. One was to deflate Bush and Gore in ways that they would not do to each other. The other was to set forth explicit achievable goals for a political reform movement that serves the long-range, serious interests of the American people and their democracy. This is a tall order in a crowded sports arena. But I figured that if thousands of people took the time to come, I would take the time to explain what needs to be done and why and how. This was not the time for short attention spans.

On such occasions I find it essential to run through some American history and remind the audience about their heroic forebears who raised the levels of justice against powerful odds. Brief recountings of the antislavery abolitionists, the women's suffrage drive, and how workers and farmers threw off some of the corporate yokes on their backs—all ordinary people producing extraordinary history. It has to motivate people. Moreover, I hastened to point out that these nineteenth-century stalwarts broke through without electricity, phones, cars, faxes, or even e-mail! Just their hearts, their minds, and their feet.

Next I made connections between the economic stagnation that surrounds a majority of workers, despite the economic boom of the past twenty years, and the chronic American poverty that plagues tens of millions of people and their children. The continual decline of our democratic promise to shape brighter futures must be reversed. These debilitating conditions are not the natural order of things. We have the resources to do much better. So who is keeping our country back? Well, look and see who is saying no every day to universal health insurance, a living wage, clean money politics, environmental cleanup, the peace dividend, enforcement of consumer protection laws, and the prosecution of corporate criminals. The Kings of No are, first and foremost, businesses. To break the hammerlock on our government and "the republic for which it stands," the present-day corporate sovereigns must yield to the sovereignty of the people "with liberty and justice for all." If millions of Americans can articulate these words when pledging allegiance to the flag, I asked, then surely we can articulate them in deeds and pledge allegiance to a more functional deliberative democracy where the people rule. Take back the government.

The two major parties, I argued, are increasingly becoming look-alikes. The differences between the Democrats and Republicans are not contested enough; they're not broad enough or deep enough. Both parties are weakening our democracy and furthering the concentration of economic and therefore political power. And if I'm telling it like it is, how can we then turn around and legitimize these look-alikes with our votes? Bush was so out of that framework that I described him as a "giant corporation running for president disguised as a person" and then provided details of his abysmal record in Texas. As for Gore, who is he on any given day? The master of regular political makeovers. Gore promised to take on "big oil, the big polluters, the pharmaceutical companies, the HMOs" while still taking their money.

Somehow I got it all in that night. The largest applause came when I declared that it was time to join with other nations and secure the abolition of nuclear weapons.

The coliseum event was a few days after the major-party national conventions—where legalized bribery married legalized extortion. The lesson of these super-rallies is that it's important for all of us to think outside the box of narrow reform dialogues. I suggested, for example, that in considering reform of the nation's monstrous federal tax complexities, inequities, and inanities, we press for taxing what we do not like—such as pollution emissions or financial speculation. Why should people have to pay taxes when they go to the stores to buy medicine, furniture, clothing, and often food, but a large investor who buys three hundred thousand shares of General Motors pays no sales tax at all? I recommended a tiny tax on stock and bond transactions as a way to raise large revenues that would then either fund universal health coverage, for instance, or allow reductions in sales and income taxes paid by consumers and workers. Trillions of dollars change hands through the stock and bond markets every week. The more speculative the churning becomes, the more revenues are generated. We should have debates of this kind during election seasons.

Taboos should be lifted. Topics such as legalizing industrial hemp for farmers to grow, which the Portland rally responded to with words and cheers. One of the reasons the rally was so high-energy was that the participants hadn't realized there were so many other people sharing their views.

What really brought those assembled again and again to their feet, and left them so enthusiastic as they streamed out of the arena, was my describing the goals, changing directions so we can move at last to end poverty, advance health care, in addition to health insurance, allow people who work to be able to earn enough to live on, wage peace instead of merely wallowing deeply in armaments, lead the world in renewable energy and sustainable economics, reverse the commercialism of our culture, and preserve the environment of America the Beautiful for their children and for posterity.

Late in the night, our crew drove the 150 miles to Seattle, excitedly envisioning other full arenas in other cities. Perhaps we would not have been so elated had we known that the national media gave scant notice to the rally of more than ten thousand people.

But before we plunged into more super-rallies, and the large organizing and financing efforts they represented, we had a date with Labor.

And where else to campaign on Labor Day than in that grand old union town—Detroit—home of the United Auto Workers and many other trade unions. By the time we flew to Detroit Metropolitan Airport and drove into the city, the Labor Day parade was under way. This was a traditional event and more than twenty thousand marchers were expected. We picked up our UAW friend Dan McCarthy, president of UAW Local 417, and joined the parade. Alas, it was, at that point, a parade of fewer than one thousand workers, mostly with Gore-Lieberman signs, heading for an area where the senator from Connecticut was to speak. Lieberman was no hero of labor. An opponent of the rights of injured people to have full access to the courts, a leading supporter of NAFTA, GATT-WTO, and PNTR, a defender of the HMOs, the drug companies, and continued weak labor laws, he would not seem to invite the raucous enthusiasm of the rank and file. Yet there dutifully onstage were local labor leaders, the head of the United Auto Workers, Steve Yokich, and local Democratic politicians in solidarity with my congenial home-state senator from Aetna, as I describe him.

After a few minutes of boilerplate exhortation and some quick media interviews, Mr. Lieberman was off to his next campaign stop. Steve Yokich came over and warmly welcomed me to Detroit. Three months earlier, he had shaken up the Democratic Party–Union complex by delaying the UAW's endorsement of the Gore ticket.

Following some curbside press conferences and interviews, I went to a rally at the Magic Stick Theater, which was jam-packed with union workers and workers locked out by the *Detroit Free Press* and *Detroit News* management. This dispute was in its eighth year and was one that was very familiar to me. The workers' lawsuit was appealed to the U.S. Supreme Court pro bono by the Public Citizen Litigation Group (which I started with Alan Morrison in 1972), resulting in a 4–4 decision, with one justice recusing himself. This tie gave victory to management, which won approval of its merger in the lower court. Circulation dropped precipitously and has not recovered due to the cancellations by many thousands of Detroit readers. The workers' ire was so intense that they would chase reporters from these newspapers out of their gathering rooms with loud shouts of "Scabs." Now in the Magic Stick Theater, they did just that and out went the forlorn reporter.

I began my address with a recitation of past struggles for labor in order to draw the contrast with the other major candidates. My first contact with migrant farm labor was in California during the summer of 1955, and I wrote about their plight in the late fifties. Our group's intense and continuing efforts on behalf of crucial legislation, including the Coal Mine Safety Act, the black lung compensation law for coal miners, and the establishment of OSHA in 1970, were early and crucial to their passage. (Since 1890 more coal miners have died from coal dust disease and mine collapses than all the Americans who died in World War II—and that was the level of human destruction in just one industry.) In the ensuing years, our groups worked on pension reform and the so-called ERISA law; fought against the Taft-Hartley Act, the chokehold on American labor's ability to form trade unions; pressed the often-moribund AFL-CIO, which in the 1980s flirted with going along with the Reaganite juggernaut to weaken the federal regulatory system in their belief that it was unstoppable (we stopped it); organized the Global Trade Watch, which fought NAFTA and GATT in one labor dispute after another; and stood by workers, most recently in the work stoppages and disputes affecting members of the United Steel Workers in several states during 2000.

All these recountings were greeted with heavy applause, but none greater than when I said that interview requests by the two Detroit newspapers had been turned down on all visits to Detroit even though it meant less coverage in the state to our visits and harm to our campaign. I added that even if we received no support or votes from organized labor, we continued to fight for labor because our stands are civic ones of conviction that transcend political campaigns.

Throughout the spring and summer, the unease over the Gore endorsement—the ranks of the UAW have been devastated by the flight of the auto industry to foreign countries—within several UAW locals was palpable. Dan McCarthy's large local had several internal debates on who to endorse. Yokich himself appeared torn and visited numerous locals to get soundings, and did he ever. The ranks of the UAW have been devastated by the flight of the auto industry to foreign countries. The China trade bill was the outrage of the season. Clinton-Gore pushed it, with the big-business lobbies, through Congress while expecting complete and enthusiastic fealty by the labor unions they undermined. For obviously the Republicans were always worse and labor had nowhere to go, right? Right! The AFL-CIO endorsed the Democratic ticket in late 1999 without securing any labor reform agenda in return. They at least owed their members and the cause of labor some comprehensive proclamation about advancing the economic rights of labor, organized and unorganized, together with commitments to strengthen labor's health and safety laws and enforcement. No matter (except for grumbling by George Becker of the United Steelworkers or Jimmy Hoffa of the Teamsters holding out smartly to exercise leverage), the big unions eventually all went into the fold and started spending their millions of dollars for Gore-Lieberman.

The only national union that endorsed me was, not surprisingly, the one I learned about from one of its longest members, Frank Rosen, the one with the most democratic tradition. After much discussion among the rank and file, the 38,000 United Electric, Radio and Machine Workers (UE) endorsed me at their convention on August 29 in Erie, Pennsylvania. I was there to receive their support and watched unionism in the finest egalitarian tradition. Meetings of different union locals in Michigan raised some hope of official support, but their deliberations did not come out that way, though some votes were close. We fared better on the West Coast with the vigorous California Nurses Association (CNA). CNA is a union's union (see Appendix G), fighting the abuses of the HMOs, putting on a statewide initiative for universal health insurance, collecting data on the harm to patients from HMO restrictive protocols upon physician and nurse judgments, investigating profiteering and waste inside corporate medicine, and taking a strong stand against deskilling hospitals (for example, replacing nurses with untrained "care buddies"). I fought with them on many of these issues in the 1990s, so our campaign was a natural for them to support. A large banner for Nader-LaDuke was placed on their headquarters balcony in Oakland, and they demonstrated for Nader-LaDuke as well. Other endorsing locals were AFSCME Local 1108 (Los Angeles) and the Postal Workers and Teamsters locals in Seattle.

There is something pathetic when a political party, knowing it cannot win without organized labor, keeps catering to corporate demands at the expense of labor justice. There is something sad about how organized labor, nonetheless, rushes to support the party without demanding a turn away from corporatism toward workers' needs. This is the logic of the "lesser of two evils." It tethers labor to a relentless slide deeper into the corporate power pits year after year. Signaling a lack of alternative options, organized labor repeatedly gets rhetoric by the Democrats in Congress and the White House about minimum wage and a ban on permanent replacement of strikers, without real expenditure of political muscle.

When John J. Sweeney and Richard Trumka, leaders of unions both, challenged and defeated the old AFL-CIO regime of Lane Kirkland in 1995, I thought, along with many others, that the new leadership would bring about a resurgence of this largest labor organization in the country. Its member unions counted over 13 million workers in their rank and file. Good things did happen. More money and organizers were committed to starting new unions—but nowhere near the need. The AFL-CIO launched a student summer program during which several thousand college students worked with locals on organizing drives. One result of this overdue initiative was to help galvanize student activism on labor issues such as the anti-sweatshop and living-wage struggles at colleges and universities. As the new president of the AFL-CIO, Sweeney realized that no justice movement can thrive and endure, instead of decay, without appealing to the younger generation. But Sweeney did something that, incredibly, his predecessors avoided. In 1996 he issued a manifesto for working people all over the country. The book was called *America Needs a Raise*—a clarion call for action on matters of economic security and social justice. But the 167-page volume was also an exercise in candor—unheard of for decades in labor circles. His words are worth quoting verbatim:

We all share some of the blame for letting corporate America drive down our living standards and distort our democratic process. For instance, we, the institution for which I've devoted my life—the labor movement—contributed to the crisis by letting our guard down. Too often, we failed to organize workers in the fastest-growing industries. Too often, we let our political efforts degenerate into mere financial contributions to glad-handing candidates. Too often, we kept our heads down, our minds closed, and our mouths shut during the great debates that shaped our nation's social and economic policies. Too often, we refused to reach out to potential allies who could have helped us build a coalition for challenging corporate priorities and offering positive alternatives. . . . The weakness of labor and the absence of a progressive social movement has created a dangerous vacuum.

Only people who have read through the tedious writings of labor leaders and much of their self-laudatory house organ press (with a few exceptions) can appreciate the refreshing recognitions that Sweeney's electrifying words embraced.

I was so taken by Sweeney's book that I bought fifteen hundred copies on remainder and promoted it on radio talk shows around the country. With all its reach, the AFL-CIO could not turn *America Needs a Raise* into a bestseller. Could the problem be more than the declining reading habits of union members? Could it be that lacking a vigorous follow-through, the excellent words remained just that—words? It will take more than new leadership to make the union movement, at its lowest level of membership by percentage of the private workforce in sixty years, into one that is fast-growing and democratically run. It will take a debureaucratization of staff at union headquarters in Washington and the encouragement of reformist activities at local levels. I once noted to Richard Trumka, former dynamic head of the United Mine Workers and presently the number-two man at the AFL-CIO, that the principal occupational hazard at many of these union headquarters was to get caught in the corridors at quarter to five. Trumka, who knows deeply what the union movement needs, smiled.

But Sweeney was not smiling at my candidacy and its "progressive social movement" objectives. When leading Democrats called him to ask what the heck was going on with some of these hesitant member unions, including Yokich's UAW and Hoffa's Teamsters, and their locals, he stepped forward and got most of them back in line. I'll always remember turning on cable TV one day and seeing John Sweeney describe my campaign as "reprehensible." His friend Gerald McEntee, president of the American Federation of State, County and Municipal Employees, then added the memorable comment, "This is no year for a third-party message candidate."

In May I met with steelworkers, or what is left of them, in Gary, Indiana. Ed Sadlowski, now retired, was there. In the seventies, his insurgency slate shook the complacent leadership of the United Steelworkers to their foundations before they narrowly defeated his bid for the presidency. Many of us, who saw in the burly South Chicago steelworker the beginnings of a labor renaissance, supported his widely reported efforts from the outside. I continued to visit and meet with union locals all over the country, but I found those in the Midwest and on the West Coast (Sacramento, Seattle, Los Angeles) more open-minded than those in New York or Boston. Of course, it helped to stand with the Screen Actors Guild in Los Angeles during their negotiations with the movie industry, or picket with the Verizon workers in Virginia during their difficult bargaining following the merger of Bell Atlantic and GTE.

Tony Mazzochi, founder of the Labor Party, and in my judgment the most visionary, accomplished, and steadfast labor leader in the nation, has traveled the most and spoken the most with more union members in small gatherings around the country than anyone else. One of his conclusions is that without a concrete agenda of action for working people, forged, discussed, and backed by them, there will be no turnaround of organized labor. Tony and I have worked together for many years on occupational health and safety, on health insurance, on corporate globalization. This World War II veteran has brought scientists together with workers, as far back as the sixties, blazed the way for the asbestos litigation, pushed for more worker say on the shop floor, brought witnesses from the rank and file to testify before Congress in situations that led to the natural gas pipeline safety law and OSHA, and helped make the Oil, Chemical and Atomic Workers Union one of the most progressive, as OCAW's elected vice president. When Tony speaks, I listen, and someday the

media may discover this honest, selfless, ever curious patriot. Someday may the leaders of the AFL-CIO listen to him. It is not that they
disagree with him. It is that the times never seem ripe for doing
today what should have been done forty years ago.

The second super-rally was on September 22 at the gigantic Target
Center in downtown Minneapolis. The days before, I took part in
a "nonvoter tour" of the upper Midwest. As Michael Moore
started one of his celebrated e-mails to his fans: "Step aside, voters,
I want to speak to the majority in this country." Like all candidates, I am perplexed by the hundred million or so nonvoters in
presidential elections and the much greater number in off-year elections. Why? asked a thousand political scientists spread over half
a century of research. Who are they? asked a hundred polls and
surveys. How can they be drawn to vote? asked many a political
consultant and good government group.

Phil Donahue was so curious about this topic that in New
Hampshire's 1996 presidential primary season he had a show in
the Granite State where the audience was divided in two sections,
with confirmed voters on one side and confirmed nonvoters on the
other. While the voters' arguments were expectedly cogent, the
nonvoters' reasons were not exactly last week's oatmeal. One nonvoter after another stood and gave solid reasons: not enough of a
choice, don't want to participate in a farce, not until they stop
being bought, it doesn't make any difference once they're elected,
been lied to too many times. With this logic, nonvoters remain the
seductive electoral magnet for third-party candidates. If only one
could tap into that huge aggregation of eligible voters.

In his abundantly cogent 1992 book, *The Culture of Contentment,*
John Kenneth Galbraith wrote that the contented classes, with their
influence and their higher voting turnout, were regularly the decisive electoral force, not the lower-income masses. But he too held
out a wistful hope: "It is possible that in some election, near or
far, a presidential candidate will emerge in the United States determined to draw into the campaign those not now impelled to
vote. Conceivably those so attracted—those who are not threat-

ened by higher taxes, and who are encouraged by the vision of a
new governing community committed to the rescue of the cities
and the impacted underclass—could outnumber those lost because
of the resulting invasion of contentment." Galbraith did not think
this to be a "likely prospect."

The customary way the big parties try to reach nonvoters is by
intensive get-out-the-vote registration efforts in demographically
friendly areas. Far more money has been spent on these approaches
than on persuading their fellow state legislators to enact same-day
voter registration laws, as six states have already done. Our campaign did not have the resources for nationwide or even regional
voter registration drives. This was the ulterior genius behind holding these super-rallies: They got out the vote and registered
thousands of new Greens.

With limited fanfare, we announced our nonvoter tour in Madison, Milwaukee, Ann Arbor, Flint, and Minneapolis. Phil Donahue and Michael Moore accompanied us on this trip as speakers.
We had an unusually good press contingent along as well, which
included Eun Kim of the Associated Press, Bill Adair of the *St.
Petersburg Times,* Jim Dao of the *New York Times,* Jennifer Blyer
of NewsforChange.com, and, later on, Gail Collins of the *New
York Times,* David Moberg of *In These Times,* Matt Rothschild
of *The Progressive,* Kerry Lauerman of Salon.com, plus Tom Squitieri of *USA Today.* None of them were at all intrigued by our
nonvoter theme. Their experience had taught them not to inquire
into such elusive quests. They were traveling with our campaign
because of the Portland superrally and the upcoming one in Minneapolis, which they all seemed eager to witness.

Our crew flew out of Washington, Donahue departed New York,
Moore traveled from Flint, and we all arrived in Milwaukee at the
same time. We first went to the University of Wisconsin Student
Union and met with leaders of ethnic communities. Our Milwaukee
friend, activist Robert Miranda, brought these dedicated mobilizers
together. Each of the participants spoke about his or her priorities,
and few, if any, of the dozen persons pressed for Gore as the least
worst. I laid out my platform and noted, as always, the necessity
of emphasizing abuses of class as well as race and their interrela-
tionship. Apolitical activists do not believe in the political system

"giving" them any power. By themselves, they had to figure ways to take it, aggregate it, and direct it toward the injustice.

From Milwaukee to Madison, we plowed through a veritable blizzard of rallies, fund-raisers, and one-on-one press interviews, all made possible by the sure guidance of our field representative, Ben Manski. Donahue and Moore preceded me on each stage, each in his distinctive manner. Moore was particularly jazzed that we would be heading the next afternoon to his job-gutted hometown of Flint. Moore liked to convulse the crowd with laughter by imagining if the revolutionaries of 1776 had been as wishy-washy as the politicians in Washington are now. Donahue more soberly stressed how voters were denied airing of key issues by my exclusion from the debates, that "the corporations have not only hijacked the presidential campaign season, but actually bought it, paid for it, and made sure that there were only two horses in the race. That way they have only two horses to bet on and can't lose."

The next day found us in Ann Arbor at the standing-room-only Michigan Theatre with seventeen hundred people taking in the progressive menu and its theme of a mobilized populace. Civic hopelessness has become a cultural trait, bred into us at an early age when we are taught to believe instead of to think, to accept rather than to reflect. I urged the crowd that day that if we all just gave ourselves some time to engage, we would surprise ourselves with the results.

We arrived in Flint about the same time as President Clinton did on *Air Force One*. Michigan was considered a swing state, and Flint was sore over the loss of tens of thousands of auto jobs exported abroad. Much of this happened under Clinton-Gore, whose NAFTA, WTO, and China trade enactments were bitterly resented by organized labor in Michigan. Clinton came to Flint, which his politics helped strip-mine, and tried to soften his image with an appearance at Mott Community College involving the Disability Network and Career Alliance. The press naturally hastened to his gathering, even though we drew more people (one thousand) to Whiting Auditorium. In his address, the remorseless Clinton declared that his "first objective" as president "was to give work back to the American people." That must have been news in Flint. Later that day, in Livonia, the chronically unabashed Clinton said, "I've got a record in Michigan—if I were trying to cost you jobs, I've done a poor job of it."

Moore was a local hero in Flint, both for his film *Roger and Me* (recounting his frantic attempts to meet with GM's CEO Roger Smith to discuss Flint's economic plight) and for bringing Phil Donahue to Flint to do two shows that brought Flint's devastating plant closings and downsizing to a national audience. Moore was in his element—a great mixture of serious indignation, satire, and rollicking humor. When my turn came, I went after the Democrats for their pro-corporate bias during conflicts between management and labor.

I had with me a pamphlet by Harry Kelber who, in his eighties, continues to edit *The Labor Educator*. A veteran unionist, Kelber, a lifelong Democrat, drew an accurate picture of the mistreatment of labor by the Democratic Party:

> Significantly, in the first six years of the Clinton Administration, even during 1992–94 when the Democrats controlled Congress, it made no effort to promote a worker rights bill or a ban on the permanent replacement of strikers. It stalled on occupational safety and health legislation and on pay equity for women workers. . . . The AFL-CIO must adopt a stiffer stance in its political dealings with Democratic Party leaders. It must insist on greater input into the choice of candidates and issues. The Democrats must stop assuming that organized labor is in their pocket because unions have nowhere else to go.

Not a chance of this happening, Mr. Kelber. Like knowing hostages, the AFL-CIO and its unions march in tandem to endorse the Democratic presidential nominees early in the primary season. They have given up their capacity for negotiation, so frightened are they of the Republicans. Meanwhile, the rank-and-file workers suffer their dwindling status in silence. Predictably, battered Flint went Democrat in November by a wide margin, voting for the very party that pushed policies which helped destroy its economic lifeline.

On to East Lansing, just in time for a rally at another full auditorium. A five-minute video that we made focusing on the campaign and our achievements was played before the trio of Donahue,

Moore, and Nader took the stage in front of a rousing seventeen hundred people.

The next day was September 22, time to see if we could repeat our super-rally success. To ensure a better last-minute outreach to residents of the Twin Cities, I did nonstop press interviews, including live NPR and KUOM radio. At 1:30 P.M. I held a crowded press conference regarding the campaign's agricultural policy. It was decisively different from that of Bush or Gore, first by recognizing the agricultural crisis of the small farmer. Furthermore, I called for a halt to the immense merger wave of giant agribusiness firms, the creation of a farmer-owned grain reserve that could cushion commodity prices, advances in organic farming close to markets, freeing the industrial hemp crop from its chains, and reversing the pronounced bias of the USDA toward big companies. The Organization for Competitive Markets (OCM) had just released a two-hundred-page whole-food report. I urged the reporters, many of whom were knowledgeable about farm issues, to log onto its Web site, competitivemarkets.com.

At five P.M., I joined Winona LaDuke, Phil Donahue, Michael Moore, and Green leader Ken Pentel at a suite in the Target Center for a fund-raiser and met some of the finest Minnesotans one can find. This is a state where earlier in the twentieth century the third party, known as the Democrat Farmer Labor Party, came out of the populist reservoirs to become the leading political force in the state. Hubert Humphrey and Walter Mondale were products of that reform movement.

The super-rally started at seven, and the signs were that the attendance would exceed that of Portland's. A new speaker delighted us with her presence: ninety-year-old Doris Haddock, known to thousands as "Granny D" stemming from her "Believe or Not" walk from Pasadena to Washington, D.C., to publicize and press for genuine campaign finance reforms. All along the way, she met, spoke to, argued with, enthralled, and stimulated people to become more active in rescuing our elections, government, and democracy from the auction block. It took walking with arthritis, ten miles a day—a total of more than three thousand miles—to become a civic celebrity and have the press cover her appearances and statements.

With about twelve thousand vocal people, it didn't do any harm to have some street theater. A couple of fellows in chicken suits pranced around flapping their wings to draw attention to Bush and Gore "chickening out" from letting me into the debates.

Donahue and Moore were no chickens, though, and were in top form for the large, supportive audiences. Donahue, true to his legacy, was Mr. First Amendment, arguing in plain language that the people needed to have me in the debates. That day, campaign volunteers Rob Rafn and Holle Brian brought petitions with the names of eighteen thousand Minnesotans demanding my inclusion in the debates. If I were not included, as the majority of Americans polled on this question wanted, Donahue said "we'll have no real gutsy, so's-your-old-man political discourse that we deserve. Remember," he told Minnesotans, "there wasn't much resonance for Jesse Ventura's ideas until he got into the debates." A sea of LET RALPH DEBATE signs were waved vigorously by hundreds of Green supporters to punctuate Phil's words.

Moore, with his disheveled clothes and trademark baseball cap, had them rolling in their Birkenstocks. He posed uniquely angled imagery. He would bring onstage a potted plant and say that he was trying to place "Ficus" on the ballot in congressional districts where the incumbents have no opposition. He then held up Ficus and declared: "This potted plant can do better than what we've got in Congress right now. Look at it! It's giving you oxygen right now! Has any congressman ever done that?"

Donahue then introduced me. It was another great time to talk—the arena brimming with excitement. The largest sustained applause of the evening came in response to my observations on education:

You hear a lot of talk about education. Oh, yes, education. How long have they been telling us they are going to repair our schools? How long have these two parties been telling us that they are going to have safe schools, repaired schools, with good teachers well paid? Well, the most important educational reform relates to what the students are learning, wouldn't you think? And what they're learning more and more is commercialized education. They're learning memorization. They're not learning how to be independent, critical thinkers who know how to practice democracy.

The Green Party campaign is determined to build the civics

for democracy curriculum in elementary school, in high school, and moving on to higher education. If we do not know the community we live in, if we are moving more and more into virtual reality, looking at computer screens, if we don't connect with real people and real communities to understand the politics and the economics and geography and the environment and the arts and the culture and the city hall, if we do not know how to develop our civic skills, if we do not know how to build a deep democracy, how are we ever going to deal with the problems of today and tomorrow here and around the world?

Fortunately, this time my remarks were reaching far beyond the arena. Not only were the reporters accompanying our tour there, but C-Span had set up its camera. "The most important control system the power brokers have established in our country," I told those who were there and watching on television, "is that we the people will settle for less, that we will settle for the least worst. We have to raise our expectation level. In this resourceful period of American history, we settle for too little." The *Minneapolis Star Tribune* reported that those in attendance were "wildly cheering," something I never take for granted.

I continued on that tack:

> Every vote we get is a vote of rebuke of the corrupt politics of the two-party system and a positive vote for public financing of political campaigns, a clean environment, full Medicare for all, an end to corporate welfare, a crackdown on business outlaws and freeing workers to bargain collectively for better working conditions. And I think these issues resonate all over the country. One's vote is a lasting message to the parties to shape up or shrink down as more votes are denied them in forthcoming elections. That is one reason why we have to build a new political party that comes from the minds and hearts of people and their wishes for a better world.

I then quoted Supreme Court Justice Louis Brandeis, who in the 1930s said, "We can have a democratic society or we can have concentrated wealth in the hands of a few. We cannot have both."

I raised high the September 11 edition of *Business Week* with its cover story "Too Much Corporate Power?" and observed that even *Business Week* was more progressive than either the Democratic or Republican party, despite being loaded with big-business advertisements. In several detailed pages, *Business Week* answered yes, editorialized that "corporations should get out of politics," and published a poll saying that more than 70 percent of Americans agreed that there was too much corporate power over their lives. The roar of thousands that met this magazine display must either have gratified or horrified *Business Week* editor Steve Shepard if he happened to tune in that evening.

If there was any beseeching that evening, it was to ask our backers to leave the Center determined to persuade their friends, relatives, neighbors, and coworkers to think strategically about what they wanted their vote to mean. Did they want to vote for a candidate they do not believe in just because he is not as bad as the other major candidate? Did they want their vote to be taken for granted, ensuring that they would be too? Or did they want to vote for the issues espoused by the Greens and for building a new party? The only message politicians understand is losing an election. Abstaining by staying home may signify a vague rejection, but it does not foster another political pathway. "We will not be taken for granted and we will vote," Winona LaDuke declared to the eager crowd.

This is why I was so pleased the next day to read in the *Tribune* the comment by Peggy Heffner who, with her ten-year-old son, Chris, had come to her first political event in more than three decades. "If my one vote can get some campaign funding into some worthwhile coffers for the next presidential election year, and encourage new individuals to step forward to run for office, then I'll feel that this vote in this election year was the most important that I have ever cast." Ms. Heffner was thinking strategically, knowing that like Rome, a political party cannot be built in a day, and that winning at least 5 percent of the vote nationwide would qualify the Green Party for federal campaign funds in 2004.

Two additional excerpts from the *Tribune* illustrate the different approaches that brought people to our voting column. Joe Horkey, from south Minneapolis, while handing out campaign materials was asked the reason he was supporting my candidacy. "Because he's fun," Horkey reflected. "I enjoy how he's anti-corporate." Then there was Michael Kelly, a onetime DFL activist from St. Paul who told reporter Bob von Sternberg, "I used to support the other guys, but I got tired of wasting my vote on a status quo that keeps the same thing going election after election. And you know this guy can't be bought off—that's a good enough reason alone to vote for him." Mr. Kelly zeroed in on what thousands that night in Minnesota had come together to celebrate.

The next morning, our group split. Donahue headed for Notre Dame to continue his efforts to persuade his alma mater to be tolerant of gays and lesbians. I flew to Seattle for another super-rally that evening at the Key Arena. There was never any time for much contemplation or discussion, and never enough time to thank all the unsung volunteer citizens who did the immense detail work to make these giant Chautauquas happen. This is perhaps the one common experience of all presidential candidates during that Labor Day to Election Day drive. What is uncommon is learning how to keep this frenetic pace from robotizing you into mind-numbing staccato repetition at stop after stop—an affliction that further robotized Al Gore in his last seventy-two hours of campaigning. All imagination, innovation, and intuition can come into a cryogenic freeze as the tempo makes eighteen-hour days seem like a flurry of minutes.

When we arrived in Seattle, our part of town was hopping. The uproar from the Seattle protests against the WTO in November and December 1999 was still reverberating. The Green Party campaign headquarters caught the scrutiny of reporters who wrote about the "Green Forest" toilet paper in the bathroom and the sign on the wall behind the new toilet: "Bush and Gore make me wanna Ralph." Kim Barker of the *Seattle Times* seemed amused by "the little red brick building that appears to be sagging in the middle, between Ms. Helen's Soul Kitchen and Virgie's Beauty Salon." He sensed the momentum. The state party, officially under way just last May, has organizations in thirty-three of Washington's thirty-nine counties.

Something else was happening in Seattle that was almost unheard of for many decades. Two large union locals, the International Brotherhood of Teamsters Local 174 and the Greater Seattle American Postal Workers, separated from their national union endorsements of Gore and instead supported Nader-LaDuke. Postal Workers spokesman Lou Truskoff explained: "On the issues alone, when you compare what the candidates will do for working people, there is no contest."

That evening I met Eddie Vedder for the first time. He had been touring for weeks, saying more nice things about our efforts, and had voter registration tables at all Pearl Jam concerts. Sitting in a small room at the arena, Eddie was still mourning the loss of life in a crowd stampede at their outdoor concert in Copenhagen. He calls the bereaved parents and stays in touch in other ways. Today, he wanted to step out on that stage, tell the people how he felt about our campaign, and play a couple of songs. Eddie is an unassuming and reflective person, which is part of his appeal to his many fans. He is also very sensitive to not having his music overshadow the political purpose of the gathering. He looked out at the crowd and in his terse, tight way told them that they had a "certain look," like "people who give a shit." They loved it. He played a ukulele rendition of "Soon Forget," dedicating the song to Paul Allen and Bill Gates, the cofounders of Microsoft.

> *He counts his money every morning,*
> *It's the only thing that keeps him horny.*

Vedder acknowledged that he had never been to one of these rallies because he had never had "anyone he could believe in before." We did not miss the deep alienation from politicians that lay behind these sentiments.

Jim Hightower, the former elected Texas secretary of agriculture, flew in from Austin and roused the vast crowd with his folksy, factual, and fresh take on the politico-corporate rot in the realm. Jim cannot be paraphrased, so take a moment and enjoy his rendition:

Senator Harry Reid recently came out—apparently had an extra helping of Froot Loops—and said, "Ralph Nader is a selfish person. He has no respect for the process." Well, neither did Thomas Jefferson and Thomas Paine have respect for the process. Neither did Sojourner Truth and Frederick Douglass. Neither did the Populists and the Wobblies and the abolitionists and the suffragists. Neither did Martin Luther King and Cesar Chavez.

We've got an old saying in Texas, "If you've found that you've dug yourself in a hole, the first thing you do is to quit digging." If we don't quit digging in 2000, we're going to be in a hole in 2004, 2008, 2012. We're going to dig deeper and deeper. Let's get out of the hole.

Gore and his corporate Democrats say to us that we're the spoilers. We're in Al's way. But wait a minute. We didn't spoil the Democratic Party with millions of corrupt corporate cash. We didn't spoil the Democratic Party by downsizing the middle class and shutting out more than one thousand farmers a week off the land in this country. We're not the ones who kicked one million low-income moms into the streets saying get a job when we knew there were no jobs with a living wage, no jobs with health care benefits for their children.

I come to you as a Democrat—been elected as such in the state of Texas. They're still laughing about it down there. But I now look up at my party, at the national level, the corporate Democrats, and I see that my party has taken off the old Sears Roebuck work shoes and strapped on the same Guccis and Poochies that the Republicans are running around in.

Some in the Seattle crowd must have given a thought or two to how money made its mark in the Democratic primary race for the U.S. Senate between Deborah Senn and Maria Cantwell. For years, Senn was the best insurance commissioner in the country, with reels of successful consumer protections against overreaching insurance companies. She received good press too. Cantwell, who served one term in the House of Representatives before becoming wealthy as an executive in a computer software company, heavily outspent Senn on television. Because of her money, Cantwell had the support of the Democratic Party apparatus. Senn lost. She was the Greens' favorite. Cantwell then squeaked by Republican Senator Slade Gorton by only 2,300 votes. Our Green turnout in Washington of 103,000 votes in November gave Cantwell the seat (there was no Green senatorial candidate), and her election brought the

Democrats to fifty-fifty with the Republicans in the Senate. This set the stage for Republican Senator Jim Jeffords's switch to independent and the resultant takeover of the Senate by the Democrats in June 2001. At a meeting a few weeks later, Senator Harry Reid, Democratic Majority Whip, told me that both he and Senator Cantwell were "well aware" of the Green voters' impact on her election.

Boston, October 1, was a beautiful autumn day for our rally at the historic Boston Garden. The organizers of the event, led by Jason Kafoury, had just two weeks to meet or break the Minneapolis record. The *Boston Globe* reported that twelve thousand people showed up to "revel in ticker-tape raining down from the ceiling, the giant flashing screens leading the audience in loud chants of 'Let Ralph Debate!'—all of which was decidedly un-Nader-like."

That is correct; I was as overwhelmed by the hoopla as anyone else. If the balloons and ticker tape reminded the reporter of the style of the large parties, any further resemblance came to an abrupt halt as the program of speakers got under way. Donahue was steaming: "The two major political parties, in cooperation with the millions of dollars of contributions by Fortune Five Hundred companies, have formed a company to put on a show and exclude all the folks who would have something to say on this stage except the major-party candidates. This is not what the founders intended. We want a real campaign."

He then listed some major subjects that wouldn't be debated under the auspices of the debate commission: universal health insurance, public financing and free media time on the public airwaves for all ballot-qualified candidates, the prison-industrial complex and the war on drugs, the death penalty and corporate globalization, sovereignty, democracy, and jobs. On this Sunday, a cartoon appeared in the *Washington Post:* There was Gore saying, "Tap the surplus. Burn the oil." And Bush says, "Tear up Alaska. Burn the oil." Nader says, "Conserve oil. Find alternatives." And then the other two say, "That's why no one ever invites you to a debate."

The debate exclusion was a hot-button topic that night for many people at the Garden, commercially renamed the Fleet Center, who took umbrage with a tight clique of a dozen or so men deciding how many debates, where, when, and who transmits them, through the okay of network television executives, to the general public. As I noted, the keys to the gate are held by the very two parties we were trying to challenge.

Donahue was kind enough that night to introduce my mother, Rose, who was sitting in the front row. He told the story of her meeting Senator Prescott Bush (George W.'s grandfather) when the esteemed patriarch was touring his state of Connecticut forty-five years ago. She held his handshake firmly and would not let go until he promised her that he'd push through Congress funds for construction of a simple dry dam a few miles north of our hometown of Winsted, to protect against devastating floods that previously destroyed lives, homes, and buildings along that waterway. He promised. She let go of his hand. Prescott Bush delivered. My mom won, and thousands of people roared with delight all these decades later.

A great favorite in Boston, especially among the many young people in the audience, strode onto the stage. Howard Zinn, former Boston University political science professor, antiwar leader, and author of the bestselling *A People's History of the United States*, laid the essence on the line: "They can give me all the arguments they want about the lesser evils, about being realistic, about being practical, but I refuse to surrender my conscience to the moneyed interests. . . . It seems to me that an election where the candidate needs 150 million dollars or 200 million dollars to run is not a free election." Zinn, a World War II veteran, showed what a vote should not support: "Every month a million children die in the world for lack of food and medicine while these candidates and their parties support this obscene military budget and more and more money for jet bombers and jet fighters and nuclear weapons. They have supported a class war against the poor here and in the rest of the world. And I cannot bear to pull a lever on Election Day in support of that."

Patti Smith at previous rallies had sung her trademark "People Have the Power." This led me to ask the people of Boston, "Do you want more power as a voter, consumer, worker, and taxpayer?" This is not a question that people are accustomed to being asked. But isn't the central question relating to civic motivation for taking power back from the corporate-run political establishment whether the people really want more power, enough to expend some time, talent, and money in that direction?

It is difficult to recall major advances in fairness or living conditions in our country's history that were not struggled over or wrenched from the avaricious grasp of the rulers by the ruled. I am not speaking of charity here. As I said repeatedly at rallies all over the country, a society that has more justice is a society that needs less charity.

A nice aspect of these mega-rallies is that they gave a few minutes to local Green Party candidates and local civic leaders who expressed their concerns and objectives before a mass of media and citizenry that is mostly denied them throughout their years of striving for better communities.

That night I kept coming back to the critical medium called word of mouth which, by the way, made this major outpouring of Bostonians and college students possible. "Replace some of the small talk with exciting political talk about the future of this country," I urged at the end of the rally. And the people streamed out of the Garden in an inspired and reflective mood, judging by the exit interviews. One woman, Carla Herwitz of Fall River, hit the perfect electoral note that we hoped—in vain as it turned out—millions of people would do also, when she said, "I like Ralph Nader a lot, I like what he stands for. I don't want to see the world run by corporations. I think if it seems clear that Al Gore will take Massachusetts, I'll vote for Ralph Nader." There were forty states where either Gore or Bush was the foregone victor. But few voters thought like Ms. Herwitz.

Chicago, October 10, following a labor rally at the Teamsters' 705 Auditorium, we were at the University of Illinois Circle Pavilion rally with ninety-five hundred people. These mega-events were starting to pay dividends in the media. Here was the *Chicago Tribune*'s take:

> Political rallies seldom require the use of earplugs. But when Ralph Nader came to the Chicago campus of the University of Illinois on Tuesday night, with Eddie Vedder of Pearl Jam

fame in tow, more than a few civics-minded Americans who have been following Nader's consumer crusade for more than a generation wondered what they had gotten themselves into.

It was a big place with a small-place atmosphere, which was perfect for hearing that heroic bestselling chronicler of ordinary heroes, eighty-eight-year-old Studs Terkel, tell one of his vintage zingers: "I ride the bus. I was on a bus a few days ago. On this bus, a fellow passenger turned to me and said, 'Studs, Gore or Bush, what's your choice?' And I said, 'Influenza or pneumonia, what's your choice?' Now, there is a difference. Influenza is the lesser of the two ailments." And more from America's great raconteur:

All of a sudden Gore said something un-Gore-like—he took after the malefactors of great wealth. And he spoke of the powerful few getting more powerful at the expense of the many. It was Nader-like. But the fact is that turned the campaign around. I know good, dear friends of mine are worried that Ralph will be taking votes away from Gore. It's precisely the opposite: Ralph put some [guts] in the guy for a moment or two.

Then there was the former Illinois congressman and independent candidate for president in 1980, John Anderson, still a reformist to the bone: "I stood in the streets of Washington, D.C., three weeks ago in front of the office of the so-called Commission on Presidential Debates and said the time has come to give the American people what they want to hear: a new voice in American politics. If we want a new domestic political order that is truly representative, we've got to move to new rules and a new system."

Calling for world peace under law and, at home, for proportional representation and instant runoff voting, Anderson was recalling his own experience. Starting in the 1980 Republican primary with 1 percent voter recognition, he got on the televised primary debates, then on one of the presidential debates with Reagan (Carter boycotted it), and his polls zoomed to 21 percent before settling back on Election Day to a still creditable 7 percent.

By contrast, the same year, environmentalist-scientist Barry Commoner, who started out better known than Anderson, was the candidate of the new Citizens Party, got on no debates, and was shut out by the media.

Young Dan Johnson-Weinberger, a recent University of Chicago law graduate and our field rep in Chicago, made sure that a number of local bands played and several local citizen leaders spoke on behalf of minority and elderly communities. The Chicago medical legend Dr. Quentin Young of Physicians for a National Health Program, told the story of a nation that spends much more per person on health care than other full-coverage nations, excludes tens of millions from coverage, and turns doctor medicine into corporate profiteering medicine. His was a call for universal health care coverage now!

Michael Moore reviewed the recent debates between Gore and Bush and listed the many issues on which they agreed, then made a passionate plea to the students there to vote for the person they believed in: "If you start now, caving in your conscience and not doing what you know is right, you're going to have a miserable life. Because it starts in little tiny increments, doing things that you don't really want to be doing, like voting for Gore instead of who you know you should vote for. And you start chipping away at your conscience and you start settling for less and less and less and less." I had a variation on Michael's point. I asked members of the audience to raise their hands if they wanted their representatives in Washington to vote their conscience. Most put their hands high. Then I asked, "Are you going to vote your conscience?" Thoughtful murmurs of agreement followed.

Jello Biafra dropped by. The musician speaks with few inhibitions. That night he declared, "Look, how many people would rather be part of history than sit on their butts and watch it on TV? The corporations owning the media are not really going to admit we exist. They don't want the rest of America to know that we are everywhere, and we won't go away."

Eddie Vedder strummed on solo guitar. In his low-key way, he told the audience how he'd intended to compose a Nader-specific song but realized he couldn't improve on his second song of the evening, Bob Dylan's "The Times They Are A-Changin'." The crowd went wild.

That day, James Warren, the thoughtful Washington Bureau Chief of the *Chicago Tribune,* wrote a lengthy feature on Phil Donahue, where he drew Phil out on his views over the years of journalism, local television news, and shows such as *Entertainment Tonight.* Phil, in his noncensorious way, is a perceptive critic of the mass media's trivialism, cowardliness, commercialism, conceit, and proprietary sense (of the presidential campaign). Donahue's standard of what a journalist could be is Chicago's famous Mike Royko, the late columnist. This night Donahue hammered home his theme of media concentration and abdication.

I pledged to the people of Chicago that we would not forget what the bipartisan debate commission did in 2000. I promised to sue and expose them until their reputation in this country was lower than that of used-car salesmen. I called for a nonpartisan People's Debate Commission to be formed for 2004 and beyond. The present commission must be put out of its authoritarian business. The audience's response, it must be said, was deafening.

The next morning the *Chicago Tribune* printed a huge picture of the rally and a lead front-page story. Reading it on the way to Midway Airport, I had a three-second tinge of concurrence with old Robert R. McCormick, who modestly coined the front-page mantra of his *Tribune* creation as the "World's Greatest Newspaper."

New York City, October 13, the Big One—Madison Square Garden, which costs a bundle to rent. At first, even our most ambitious rally-maker hesitated. Filling 15,500 seats at twenty dollars each was a tall order, especially when there were only seven days to sell the tickets. Eddie Vedder was the early driving force to do it. Jim Musselman, a public-interest music producer from Philadelphia, and the irrepressible Kafoury-McDougal team then said it could be done. Having received limited media outside the cities where the other rallies were held, they believed that planting our campaign in the Garden in the Big Apple would surely be a big story attracting all the media.

We gave the final go just nine days before the date. The amount of detail and preparation was mind-boggling. We had to arrange for the speakers and entertainers, decide which of the New York

Greens would speak, deal with all the Garden's work rules, prepare the promotional materials, get them distributed, respond to the press calls, and much more. Everybody pitched in and worked together with minimal friction. In what had to be record time, Ani DeFranco (who assented with the phrase "Inaction is not my forte"), Phil Donahue, Professor Troy Duster, Ben Harper, Michael Moore, Bill Murray, Susan Sarandon, Patti Smith, the performers of Company Flo, Tim Robbins, and Eddie Vedder were on board. Two hundred thousand handbills were put up in New York City's five boroughs, especially around the major universities. Radio and TV talk shows relayed the upcoming rally through interviews with the above longtime activists.

It was a magical evening beginning at a raucous six P.M. press conference featuring our entire cast and packed with reporters and cameras. My agent, Jay Acton, told us he'd never seen anything like it—"not even for Ali fights." We were to learn again that having many reporters in attendance does not mean anything close to a multimedia national story the next day or two. The publishers, editors, and producers make the final decisions.

The audience at the rally was, as Salon.com wrote, a "thoughtful" one. This was a progressive political festival. People used to Garden extravaganzas for public crusades of one kind or another told us there was nothing comparable to the good spirit, cheerfulness, and optimism. It was as if a drought over such politics for years had been suspended by a good spring rain and the flowers were sprouting. The deep sense of loss of control of just about everything that mattered was driven back for a few hours by a surge of possibilities about the future of America.

Rolling Stone captured the moment:

> Bill Murray's speech reflected the emotional spirit of the rally. Responding to the idea that a vote for Nader essentially will not count, he said, "You tell the candidate that you're going to vote for to come up to me and tell me, to my face, that my vote is a wasted vote. I don't think anyone who could say that, to my face, or to your face, should be in charge." When he concluded with "I'm going to cry now. I've gotta go," it was clear that the comedian was only partly joking.

Eddie Vedder gazed over the massive assembly, which the *New York Times*'s David Chen described as "fairly diverse in age and ethnicity" and political backgrounds, and called the scene "the most beautiful thing I have ever seen." When master of ceremonies Phil Donahue announced that the Garden was sold out, the crowd thundered. Imagine, people paying twenty dollars to attend a political rally.

Organic farmer and New Yorker Mark Dunau, frustrated by the media ignoring his statewide run as the Green Party senatorial candidate, contrasted his commitments and background with those of the "corporate lawyers—Rick Lazio and Hillary Clinton." Michael Moore counted up the many times that Bush and Gore agreed with each other at the second presidential debate in Winston-Salem. "Where's the debate?" he asked. "All that was missing—other than Ralph Nader—was, at the end, for Gore to go over there and plant one of those Tipper tongue kisses on George Bush. . . . With the lesser of two evils, you still end up with evil. What if we'd said, 'I'm afraid of King George. If we have a revolution, we might get a worse king'? Have some courage and some hope. Follow your conscience. Do the right thing."

Susan Sarandon came on and asked the Garden to turn up the house lights. She then gazed over the crowd and told them, "Look at yourselves. Nobody talks about this." The cheering audience took an exuberant bow.

It was amazing that fifteen thousand people had any lung power left by the time I made the stage. I have a visceral aversion to addressing very large audiences as if they were a crowd. In college, I read books on crowd psychology, how speakers mesmerize masses with tested propaganda cant, verbal incitations, and the more silent language of gestures and voice modulations. I dislike these methods. To address a crowd as if it were one mass with one set of congealed emotions ready to be shaped repels me. It is the antithesis of what my parents and teachers had taught—that reason, fact, context, reflection, challenge, judgment, some satire and humor, and openness of mind are pretty good ways to communicate, while respecting your audience as individuals. Whether I am before a largely supportive or largely adversarial assemblage makes no difference—there has to be a factual predicate to my attempted persuasions and recommendations. That is the only way I can remain true to myself and respect my fellow human beings.

A modified version of crowd manipulation is the pandering by politicians before audiences composed of people already very much behind them. Many Democrats have this pandering down to a science—especially before ethnic or labor groups. It is a way of escaping on the cheap—tell them generally what they want to hear and you won't have to tell them how you are selling them out or how you should be telling them what they don't want to hear but must. I was tired of do-little white politicians like Clinton and Gore pandering in black churches with that rhythmic cadence and told the Garden audience as much.

It was my second time at the Garden. The first time was in 1979, at a No Nukes concert with leaders of the anti–nuclear power movement. There hasn't been a single nuclear plant ordered in the United States since then—the time of the nearly catastrophic Three Mile Island accident in Pennsylvania, when people in New York City were wondering whether a radioactive cloud could be heading their way. This time at the Garden I was at the point in the campaign where I had to go beyond the usual explanations of how the two parties are letting Americans down. I made my own pleas:

- To the 51 percent of adults who do not vote: Realize your power. Don't drop out of democracy. We need you—we even need your skepticism.
- To corporations: You were designed to be our servants, not our masters.
- To the media: Your best exposés of corporate abuses are not resulting in change and you're not asking why.
- For the poor: The major public housing project in this country is building prison cells. The Democrats and Republicans give only lip service to raising the minimum wage. They ignore the crushing burden on ghettos from the corporate crime wave and don't even talk about health insurance for all.
- To the young: You need a party that shuns the cheap rhetoric and replaces it with reality.

After my speech, all the speakers and performers came back on the stage. Led by Patti Smith, and joined by the many in the Garden, we sang "People Have the Power." As Ani DeFranco had looked around and said a little earlier, "How surreal is this? We have a huge American flag, we have a bunch of guys in suits, and it's good. It's good."

During these politically euphoric few minutes, I wondered how to extend the talent, drive, and sensitivity that existed in this largely anonymous assembly. Inside the Garden that night were veterans of many battles for justice in the peace and civil rights movements, in the environmental and political reform drives, in the workplace initiatives for safety, living wages, and the right to organize. Here also were youngsters absorbing speeches about the grave risks and awesome benefits that could loom on the global horizon. There were the high school and college students of immigrant families breathing the fresh air of democratic possibilities as they learned about the grim contradictions and greed of the established powers.

Yes, the people *have* the power, but would the inspiration of this and many other evenings over the months of this campaign nourish the civic energies that are required in the work of a just society? One of my favorite questions to engaged citizens is how they came to their chosen passion. I am impressed to hear over and over again that when they were young they joined a march or attended a large rally with parents or friends or participated in a losing but honorable political campaign.

There should be so many more super-rallies, not only for the Greens but for all the just causes of our country. More than a few sports fans who came to our rallies commented that people cheered just as loudly as did the fans for the Knicks or the Celtics. People want to gather and show their support for a better society.

A post-election survey of our volunteers from the greater Chicago area conducted by University of Chicago senior Katie Selenski found that even these already motivated people often cited the Chicago super-rally as an important event that helped keep them going on the campaign in the face of denunciation.

In my opinion, the best thing to happen that evening occurred after it was over. About thirty-five hundred people registered to vote and carried their registration cards across Eighth Avenue to the U.S. Post Office just an hour or so before the midnight deadline under New York law.

The *Times*'s David Chen scurried around to interview as many as he could. He told his readers that "in conversation after conversation, many of those interviewed offered not a staccato of sound bites and clichés, but rambling and passionate discourses about the issues." That is an important definition of success coming out of a huge audience that could think and cheer at the same time. Syndicated columnist and *NewsHour* TV commentator Mark Shields said that "the Nader super-rallies are the most exciting development of the campaign year."

But Chen, like just about every reporter who covered these super-rallies, took note of the paradox: "For all of the enthusiasm of the adoring crowd, Mr. Nader has not exactly rocked the presidential race, having been stalled for months at about 4 percent in the national polls." Obviously, this disappointed us, as that stall continued during our subsequent successful mega-rallies in Austin, Texas, and in Oakland and Long Beach, California. It also did not help us that the *Los Angeles Times* failed to report the largest area rally of any of the campaigns in their pages the next day.

What's the explanation? In a country without campaign polls—as, say, in the nineteenth century—rallies such as these, if reported, would have led to many more votes than they do now. Political gatherings, conveyed by newspapers and posters, generated the word of mouth. Today, the two major parties start their campaigns by splitting the polls between them, and the two big horses are already far down the track with their tens of millions of hereditary voters.

Our rallies generally received good local print coverage, brief local radio and television coverage, and very little national coverage beyond a few wire service stories. However, and this is crucial, the national television networks did not lead, highlight, or emphasize our rallies in their political coverage. Even the big Garden event did not make major television news.

So we did not have a carrier of any magnitude for these record-setting paid events, featuring prominent speakers, to get word of mouth going among the many millions of voters who never heard of what we brought together. The mass media was our only practical substitute for the major candidates' polls, debates, and massive television ad campaigns. But it did not happen. As large as our arena audiences were, they were precious drops in the bucket, even among the eligible voters in the cities where they took place.

Consider how small is the pool of first-level persuadable voters. Nearly two-thirds of people who actually vote are down-the-line or party-line Republicans or Democrats. Their minds are usually made up before the outset of the campaign. The rest of the voters are either voters of conscience, who vote for the particular candidates or issues they believe in, regardless of the polls, or "practical" voters, who want to be with a winner and look to align themselves with what many other voters are going to do. Voters of conscience are the smallest category. They don't care about polls or pundits, but you still have to reach them with your record and message. Undecided voters looking for a winner are reached by polls and media. No polls, no media. Polls favor party dynasties who receive mass media.

Given the straitjacket enforced by the two-party winner-take-all system, a third party faces exclusion signs everywhere, and this futility gets into the minds of the people themselves. Many people, including political figures such as Clinton's former Secretary of Labor Robert Reich, told us before and after the election that based on our issues and record of seriousness about them, he would have liked to be supportive. But who thinks a third party can break through in our country? There is little elbow room for the underdog party, for the fresh start, for the seeds to flower, for the small innovator to take a large "market share." Any regeneration of politics from a state of decay is difficult under these circumstances.

Nonetheless, the super-rallies are a tremendous start. Someday enough Americans will prove wrong the conventional platitudes, the a priori abdications. These citizens will rise to the challenge of that exhortation: "When the going gets tough, the tough get going." They will overcome the biggest obstacles to help level the political playing field. They will reject barriers that deny challengers a fair chance to have a chance.

Twelve

THE COMMISSION ON PRESIDENTIAL DEBATES— DICTACRATS FOR THE REPUBLICRATS

On the night of October 3, I was with Tarek Milleron and some reporters on a shuttle bus speeding past thousands of vociferous protesters and supporters behind barricades, flanked by hundreds of state police, on our way to the University of Massachusetts. Our eventual destination was a Fox News interview after the completion of the first ninety-minute presidential debate between Al Gore and George W. Bush at the Clark Athletic Center. As the bus slowed, I was spotted by some supporters, and a great rolling cheer preceded us. The bus stopped in what seemed to be a parking lot, and we disembarked thinking that a representative or two from Fox News would be waiting. I had a ticket to get inside not the debate hall itself but the nearby Lipke Auditorium, which was reserved for people to watch the debate on closed-circuit television. On the bus with us was a family heading for the actual debate at the Clark Center, and we marveled at how elaborate and numbered each of their credentials were for that live event. Our plainly printed ticket was one of hundreds distributed by the University of Massachusetts to students in the Boston area to encourage them or their transferees to fill Lipke.

Instead of Fox News reps, we were met by a man who, escorted by a state trooper and two other men in police uniforms, claimed to be representing the Commission on Presidential Debates. He said he had been instructed by the Commission that regardless of whether I had a ticket, I was not welcome and would have to leave. I asked him first to identify himself and reveal who at the Commission instructed him. He said he was John Vezeris, a security consultant to the Commission, and repeated his charge. I asked

him what was the reason, and during our exchange of words—
some in Greek—State Trooper Sergeant McPhail stepped forward
and stated that if I did not leave, he would have to arrest me. A
few reporters were right there. I told the sergeant that he was being
given an unlawful political order and that I had every right with
my ticket in hand to sit in a public university hall to watch the
debate on TV. The trooper became more impatient to get me back
on the shuttle bus, and the sergeant said, "Mr. Nader, is it your
intention to be arrested here?" My immediate thought was: What
the hell? In the United States of America, I have a ticket to a public
function at a public university, and without any cause or disruption, the authorities are throwing me out of the place. A private
corporate power is using the state's police for its partisan political
ends. Sounds like a definition of the corporate state. See you in
court, man.

But as I always prefer to be a plaintiff rather than a defendant,
my associate and I instead repaired to the shuttle and returned to
a Metro train stop several miles away. There, the campaign's deputy press secretary, Laura Jones, contacted the Fox producer, who
said that he'd meet us if we came back to the press entrance. I did
a quick interview with Bloomberg Radio at the bus stop shelter,
then got back onto the shuttle and went back once again past the
barricades and the cheering crowd. No sooner did we get off the
shuttle than we were met again by state troopers. But this time
NBC's *Today Show* had a big camera with a bright light right there
and did an interview with me while we looked for the elusive Fox
people, who, it seems, were intimidated by the CPD and did not
come from their trailer to bring us back for their post-debate interview. All the while, Sergeant McPhail was threatening me with
arrest "for trespass" if I did not leave within three minutes.
Nearby, two Secret Servicemen from the Boston office were observing. They said they had no role regarding this situation, but
they wanted to be helpful, escorting us onto the shuttle and riding
with us back to the T stop. On the bus I had a good conversation
with one of them, Chief Boston Agent John O'Hara, regarding the
abuse of authority without cause that we had just experienced. He
couldn't have been more understanding and at the T stop arranged
for a police cruiser to take us down to a Boston office building
where, though late, we watched the end of the debate and gave

Fox its interview. Although Mr. O'Hara can speak for himself, I received the impression he wouldn't have recommended handling this situation the way the Commission did.

In the following days, there was some public criticism around the country of the Commission's rude and arbitrary exclusion of me strictly for political reasons. Did this diminish the arrogance of the CPD? Paul Kirk, the Democratic co-chair, told a newspaper reporter that the ejection was ordered because I "was the point man for the protest." And this man is an attorney! The Commission must have been gratified at the absence of any expressions of outrage by leading civil liberty advocates in Congress or in the media. The ACLU, which has defended vigorously the constitutional rights of neo-Nazis to demonstrate and the right of tobacco companies to advertise, did not see fit to issue a protest. It was left to Al Hunt of the *Wall Street Journal,* who pronounced my expulsion in Boston as the "outrage of the week" on his weekend panel television program.

Two weeks later, I campaigned in St. Louis, Missouri, and was invited by the student television station (WUTV) for an interview at Washington University, where the third and final presidential debate (one wag called it the "Anheuser-Busch–Gore debate") was to be held. Our advance man had secured perimeter passes to do the interview at the TV studio far from the actual building where the debate was to take place. Arriving at the principal entrance to the university with my associates and a large number of reporters, photographers, and some television cameras, I met the student from the television studio. I was also met by police officers at the outermost checkpoint. Earlier that day, I had called up my former associate and coauthor, Joel Seligman, now dean of the university's School of Law, and asked if there was any time available for a short address to the students—remembering his standing invitation for such a visit. He sighed and said that he had no control over who could enter his law school.

The campus was like an armed fort with the private corporate-funded CPD having the power to use university and city police not only for security but also to enforce its political prejudices. There was no disruption and no indication of any disruption whatsoever associated with our small group. Yet the police were pressed into a highly selective political maneuver. Two of my associates and I each had around our necks the green-and-white perimeter passes as we followed the student through the campus entrance. My path was blocked by a policeman who gripped my arm and pressed me back several yards to the main sidewalk, saying I would not be allowed entry. Meanwhile, my two associates were allowed to go through the guarded checkpoint several times back and forth showing the same perimeter passes. I asked to speak to the officer's superior, who came forward, followed by a snarling public relations representative of the Commission. He shouted that I did not have the proper credentials and had to get out, before quickly slithering back to where he came from. During this back-and-forth, as we were surrounded by reporters and tried to understand how the CPD could sequester the entire campus and use police to exclude anyone with differing political views, two police officers told my associates that they had been given specific orders to bar me, and no one else, from crossing the perimeter.

That day I filed a lawsuit against the CPD in federal district court in Boston for violating my civil rights. The case is pending and at the deposition stage at this writing. No one, candidate or not, should be treated this way in our country. Dictatorial behavior, by a private, partisan, two-party-controlled corporation, using public police power arbitrarily, shouldn't be tolerated in the land of the free and home of the brave. But it has been up to now.

How did this cancer in our democracy get started? How did it become an instrument of the two major parties, which have received millions in taxpayer dollars, to assure that only their candidates reach tens of millions of voters, not any of their challengers, even those whose participation is wanted by a majority of Americans polled?

The nonprofit private corporation that became the CPD was born in 1987, a creation of Republican and Democratic leaders who saw the presidential debate sponsor, the League of Women Voters, as too uppity. The League had a modest mind of its own but the two major parties wanted complete control for their nominated candidates. There would be no more negotiations with the league over having John Anderson–type independents on the debates. No more having to abide by the rules of the League's managers. The dictacrats took over for the republicrats. In retrospect, this amazing coup was overshadowed by the equally amazing lack of vigorous protest from all kinds of groups—the media, political scientists, political reform groups, and at least some members of Congress. It was treated as if it were a housekeeping detail.

Republican Frank Fahrenkopf, the co-chair of the CPD, held a press conference in 1987, and described his new organization as "a bipartisan, nonprofit, tax-exempt organization formed to implement joint sponsorship of general election presidential and vice presidential debates, starting in 1988, by the national Republican and Democratic committees between their respective nominees." The CPD took over from the League when it refused to participate in what its president, Nancy Newman, called "a fraud on the American voter." She was referring to excessive demands made by Dukakis and Bush negotiators regarding the format, the type of questions, and other intrusions into the league's arm's-length stance. Another example of men seizing what little power women assembled in the electoral process.

From then on to the present, the Debate Commission's co-chairs, still Frank Fahrenkopf and Paul Kirk, still serving corporate clients at their law firms, have maintained that the CPD's sole mission is educational, as befits its 501(c)(3) tax exemption from the Treasury Department. Let's examine that assertion. Simply said, bipartisan is not nonpartisan, particularly since the avowed goal, stated in the initial memorandum of agreement between Fahrenkopf and Kirk, was to "strengthen the two major parties." Concentrated power congeals, sustains, defends, and rationalizes itself to a fine point. The CPD has taken this motivation to the level of instinct—a marvelously modulated cabal. Notice how this malignant species has methodically covered its flanks so as to monopolize the simultaneous access by any competitors to the overall electorate. They have the recipe down pat.

First, make sure that the major elements of the two parties are in on the deal. Fahrenkopf, former head of the Republican National Committee and current president of the largest gambling lobby, took no risks. Together with Kirk, former head of the Democratic National Committee and current chairman of the John F. Kennedy Library Foundation, he chose in 1987 a list of who's who in the two parties for the CPD's initial Board of Directors. Former Senator John Culver; Ambassador Pamela Harriman, later to become a veteran Clinton adviser; Vernon Jordan; former assistant to Walter Mondale, Richard Moe; the general counsel to the Republican Party, David Norcross; Governor Kay Orr; Representative Barbara Vucanovich; and Senator Pete Wilson. Two of these board members were replaced later by Representative John Lewis and Senator Paul Coverdale. Of the nine other board members, five are Democratic Party loyalists: Caroline Kennedy Schlossberg, Howard Buffet, Clifford Alexander, Newton Minow, and Antonia Hernandez. Three are Republican Party loyalists: former Senator John Danforth, Treasury Secretary Paul O'Neill, and Representative Jennifer Dunn. To ward off accusations of partisanship following the exclusion of Perot in 1996, the CPD invited Dorothy Ridings as the lone independent board member in 1998. Executive director Janet Brown is a registered Republican.

Second, connect with the corporate money to fund your operations. It helps that eight of the eleven CPD board members serve on major corporate boards. But really that type of overlap is not necessary, just facilitative. Corporations know a good tax deduction when they see it. The CPD spends more than half a million dollars to sponsor a single debate, and for-profit businesses cover most of that bill. Companies like Anheuser-Busch, Philip Morris, AT&T, Ford Motor Co., and Atlantic Richfield relish the opportunity to contribute to this proxy for both major parties and have their top executives rub shoulders with leading politicians at the festive occasions surrounding the debates. They believe that this participation can enhance their civic image and also can provide hospitality to six hundred journalists, many of whom are already predisposed to view these events as entertainment. Dana Milbank, White House correspondent for the *Washington Post,* wrote in his book *Smashmouth* of the Boston presidential debate:

> The whole campus is closed—ostensibly to thwart terrorists, more likely to thwart Nader and Buchanan. Nader gets kicked out of the debate audience, even though he got himself a ticket from a student. He's threatening lawsuits. . . . But I'm not worried about such things. I am inside the debate area, and I am delighted to find an Anheuser-Busch refreshment tent, where there is beer flowing, snacks, Budweiser girls in red sweater (sic), the baseball playoffs on television, ping pong and fusbol.

(Actually, Milbank erred—my ticket was to a nearby auditorium with closed-circuit television.)

If the people at the CPD worried about appearances, they were not showing it. Their stunted sense of propriety can easily overlook the fact that the three candidates excluded by the Commission—Perot, Buchanan, and Nader—all had definite critiques of the very multinational corporations funding the debates. All three had support of the polls to be on the debates. However, these were not the polls that the CPD corporation had in mind.

Third, keep competitors off the debates under the guise of objective criteria. They automatically invited themselves, of course, and from 1988 to 1996 the CPD established the following subjective criteria, the absence of which would justify the exclusion of any competing presidential candidate: evidence of national organization, signs of newsworthiness and competitiveness, and indicators of national enthusiasm and concern. The CPD set up an advisory committee that would determine if any other candidate had these attractions in sufficient density—get this—to have a "realistic chance of winning" the election.

In 1996, Perot, having garnered nineteen million votes four years earlier, was just under 10 percent in the polls and therefore was deemed not to have a chance. So he was cut off at the pass. Since the basic data came down to the standing in the polls, Fahrenkopf and Kirk, after consulting their respective party bosses, decided to establish simple poll-based criteria for the 2000 campaign. In a January 2000 news conference at the National Press Club, these two longtime corporate attorneys dictated the barrier for the next campaign. As I've said before, it would be an average of five major commercial polls in September, which would have to meet or exceed 15 percent voting support for the candidate, along with meeting the constitutional requirements of age, citizenship, and being on enough state ballots to make up a majority of electoral college votes.

In one stroke, the CPD implicated the mass media in the decision. Although we could never obtain the documents to show what exchanges, if any, occurred with these polling organizations, we did know who owned or contracted with them (CNN/*USA Today,* ABC News/*Washington Post,* CBS News/*New York Times,* NBC News/*Wall Street Journal,* Fox News). These news organizations were placed, willingly or unwillingly, in a position of significantly determining much of what the polls would register.

How is it that taxpayers can finance millions of dollars for a candidate's campaign for president if the candidate meets the Federal Election Commission's standard of garnering 5 percent of the popular vote four years earlier, and yet not see or hear him or her on the debates? Simple. The CPD and the two major parties have the power to say nyet because, through their corporations, they fund and dictate the rules. What do you think the privatization and corporatization of the presidential debates means? Certainly not to give seeds a chance to grow and nurture the barren landscape of our eroded democracy. Degenerating big parties are naturally not interested in regenerative open procedures.

The weakest defense of this extraordinary high threshold comes with CPD spokespersons raising the tired excuse that "hundreds of candidates run for president every election." Although Bill Joe Clegg did run for president in 1996, along with 160 others, he was on the ballot in just one state. In 1988 only four candidates, in 1992 only five candidates, in 1996 only six candidates, and in 2000 only seven candidates were on enough state ballots to theoretically be able to win the White House. Canada seemed to have no trouble in November 2000 having its two national debates include five candidates for the office of prime minister. Nor do the major parties believe that it is unwieldy to have seven or more candidates debating one another on the same stage during the primaries.

During 1992, when the criterion was "a chance to win," Ross Perot was included in the debates because both Clinton and Bush, each believing that Perot's presence would help his respective campaign, told the CPD to let him on. Four years later, according to Clinton aide George Stephanopolous, Bob Dole feared that Perot would take votes away from him, and the incumbent Clinton wanted the debates to be nonevents. Presto, the CPD excluded Perot. Further, the two major-party campaign officials, not the Commission, decide who will ask the questions, which gives the candidates a fairly good idea of the possible range of questions asked.

A majority of voters polled in 1999 wanted a viable third party in America to keep the other two parties honest. Independents make up a plurality of voters—reflecting in part the increasing convergence of the two major parties. Historically, third-party candidates introduce new or neglected salient subjects and proposals that both major-party candidates either agree on and don't discuss or avoid so as not to alienate interest groups. All this conformity, self-censorship, protective imitation, and restrictive debate rules make for a gigantic turnoff on the television audience. One reason so many Americans wanted Buchanan and me on the debates was that they wanted to stay awake. Audience levels surged to over 90 million when Perot was on board in 1992. It was through his presidential debate appearances, together with his paid thirty-minute network television presentations, that he thrust the federal deficit, the proposed NAFTA, and the influence of special-interest lobbyists into the forefront of political discourse that year. He also did not talk like a politician—an important sonic spice to the conventional droning between the drab and the dreary.

Some members of Congress have proposed various forms of legislation to broaden the presidential debate process. You probably never heard of them because they received almost no news or editorial notice. Congressman Jesse Jackson Jr. (D-Illinois) proposed lowering the criterion from 15 to 5 percent voter support in the polls or a majority of those polled wanting the candidate's participation in such debates. Congressman Bill McCollum (R-Florida) recommended holding a preliminary debate with candidates on the ballot in all fifty states and then restricting the remaining three debates to candidates polling above 5 percent. Another model, by Congressman James Traficant Jr. (D-Ohio), would invite all candidates who qualify for federal matching funds. Congressman Ron Paul (R-Texas) would prohibit candidates who accept federal matching funds from attending presidential debates that exclude candidates who are on forty or more state ballots. These proposals expose the paucity of imagination in our national discourse when, in the light of so many potential variations of how debates can be structured, scheduled, and covered, we allow ourselves to be cramped inside the CPD's narrow-minded strategic dictates. It is like allowing a corset to define the meaning of underwear.

Fourth, secure the full and exclusive cooperation of the television networks. Getting the networks to play follow-the-leader is simple. The debate negotiations between the two major campaigns are so unpredictable, dilatory, and minute, as they jockey for position, that the networks avoid playing an initiatory role like the plague. Since the two major candidates are the "talent," they can pretty much, given the passivity of the network, write their own ticket with the media—except if they collide with preexisting contractual agreements where, for instance, a network has the exclusive contract to show the World Series. In fact, it did take Gore and Bush a long time to get together on the number of debates and the format.

Throughout 2000, Gore kept saying he would debate Governor Bush every week or more anywhere in the United States. After all, didn't Jim Fallows write a lead story in the *Atlantic Monthly* on how devastating a debater he was? How Gore crushed his primary opponents with rare ruthlessness, such as the job he did on Michael Dukakis in 1988, to set the stage for the Republicans' Willie Horton attack later that year? Bush, on the other hand, was playing coy. In late June, he was not even committing to the proposed three debates, suggesting that he and Gore wait to decide until after their parties' presidential nominating conventions. His candor inadvertently made the point that the debates were subject to tactical considerations, when he was asked whether he would support my presence in the debates. He told Reuters on his campaign plane from New York to Detroit, "I don't know. I haven't figured out the impact yet." The reporter followed up, noting that Bush's answer sounded as if he would be willing to let Nader in only if he believed it would help his own White House bid. Bush replied with a grin, "I am trying to win, aren't I?"

All this didn't sound like the CPD was either nonpartisan or just educational. Instead, it sounded like what the CPD has always been—a servant of duopoly in the high-stakes game of Republican and Democratic presidential politicking. The candidates knew that thinking out loud, as Bush did, was not the appropriate response. At other times when Bush and Gore were asked about minor-party candidates getting on the debates, their standard reply was that they were simply following the CPD's gateway standard of 15 percent poll support. It was not up to them—no, of course not.

Fifth, make sure that you cover your rear with the Federal Election Commission. In 1998, the FEC's chief lawyer, Lawrence Noble, issued a blistering report. He took note of strict FEC regulations that (1) bar corporate contributions to organizations sponsoring debates that do not have pre-established objective criteria that determine candidate participation and (2) prohibit nomination by a particular party as the sole objective criterion to determine whether to include a candidate in a debate.

Noble concluded that the CPD's 1996 criteria for third-party inclusion in the presidential debates were subjective, rather than "pre-established objective." He argued that relying on the "professional opinions of the Washington bureau chiefs of the major newspapers, news magazines, and broadcast networks" and "the opinions of representative political scientists specializing in electoral politics at major universities" was inherently subjective. Moreover, in his legal opinion, the CPD criteria violated FEC debate regulations because major-party candidates were automatically invited to the presidential debates, regardless of their position in the polls.

Then came the blockbuster. Longtime general counsel Noble questioned whether the criteria were applied at all. He suspected that the major-party candidates, not the CPD, had determined Perot's exclusion. Consequently, he requested a full-blown investigation, complete with depositions and subpoenas, of the selection process.

Noble's recommendation was unanimously rejected by all six members of the FEC. It was a considerable convenience to the CPD that by statutory-inspired custom the FEC is made up of three Democrats and three Republicans. The regulatory flank was protected. The cabal was completed. Our year 2000 lawsuit in Boston's federal court to invoke the 1911 law banning corporate contributions to federal candidates was rejected.

As the debate over the debates continued, a surprising number of newspapers and public figures urged my presence on at least one of the debates. In mid-June, the *Christian Science Monitor* denounced the 15 percent hurdle:

> Media which conduct polls that influence the eligibility for the debates also let themselves be influenced by those polls in the amount of coverage given to candidates. . . . A couple of trends argue for giving third parties a guaranteed platform. The media are covering politics less, forcing candidates to rely on TV ads more. And the cost of buying more ads has pushed

the two major parties to become more beholden to well-heeled donors, be they corporations or rich individuals. A pre-election debate that brings in a wide range of views can only strengthen the vibrant dialogue that's needed to inform voters.

The paper argued that any candidate who gets, or whose poll figures indicate he or she will get, public monies should be given room at the debate table.

The *Seattle Times,* also in June, editorialized that Buchanan and I should be allowed on at least one debate. If after the first debate a third party's nominee's polls go up to 8 or 10 percent, the door to the second debate is opened. In the third round, the paper argued, the threshold should go up again, to 15 or 20 percent. "It would add a note of excitement," the editorial concluded, adding that the "15 percent threshold suits the two parties. It unduly restricts the American people." That latter point is the essential one. The prime consideration is the right and need of the American people to have a wide array of information and viewpoints. Perot, noted the editorial, "went into the debates with 7 percent support. He went on to win 19 percent of the vote."

In mid-July, the *St. Paul Pioneer Press* weighed in, calling me a "substantial candidate, one whose issues and priorities are different from Al Gore and George W. Bush" and one who "should be included in this fall's presidential debates." Taking a swing at the CPD, the paper declared that "there must be more reasonable rules for third-party participation." On September 1, the *San Jose Mercury News* urged my inclusion on the first debate and let the subsequent poll numbers decide whether I would be on the next debates. The paper's main argument, however, was not numerical.

He expresses a long and articulate voice of dissent from Republicans and Democrats on important issues that [Bush and Gore] are minimizing or ignoring. . . . Nader takes contrary positions on trade and the North American Free Trade Agreement, corporate "greed" and influence on politics, universal health care and the role of the Federal Reserve. . . . Nader's presence would guarantee that the debate would be lively, with more focus on substance than, for lack of disagreement, on style. . . . The dialogue this fall would be richer and the differences between all of the candidates made sharper and clearer by his presence.

Apart from these editorials boosting our campaign's office morale, they all have a subtext to their judgments. The CPD's presidential debates are not really debates; they are extended, managed press conferences involving highly predictable or bland questions to two candidates whose principal objectives are to avoid slipups, gaffes, and stylistic offenses that can turn off large numbers of undecided voters, and to reiterate, regardless of the question, the well-practiced paragraphs from the rhetoric throughout the campaign. All this bores people. Dan Rather expressed these sentiments right after the second Bush-Gore meeting when he was impelled to describe their debate as "narcolepsy-inducing."

It is telling that when people are asked to remember past presidential debates, what they call up are phrases like "Where's the beef?" (Mondale v. Hart), "I won't hold your youthful age against you" (Reagan v. Mondale), "I paid for this mike" (Reagan v. Republican primary opponents), or "You're no Jack Kennedy" (Bentsen v. Quayle).

Perhaps a yearning for forthrightness, for coming to grips with central matters too long unspoken, and for highlighting solutions upsetting to power structures were some of the reasons why prominent political commentators and figures said publicly or privately that they wanted me in on the debates. Senator Barbara Boxer (D-California) and Russ Feingold (D-Wisconsin), House Budget Chairman John Kasich (R-Ohio), White House Chief of Staff Leon Panetta, and Mark Shields were among those who favored inclusion. Mr. Shields came in late with his October 26 column in quite touching words: "My apology to Ralph Nader for not demanding he be included in the presidential debates. Nader does not let us forget all we owe to our community, our country and to each other. He deserves to be heard beyond the arenas he, alone, can fill."

Many more such expressions by influential people would not have changed the CPD's intransigence. As Temple University law professor David Kairys wrote: "The corporate-funded major parties, which have for many years alienated or bored most of the populace, are literally excluding their principled opposition from the debates. . . . The CPD . . . is completely dominated by the same corporations and two parties and is unaccountable to the government or the people." The Constitution, Professor Kairys might have added, does not apply to such private governments.

And, predictably, the debates were awful—each worse than the one before. Audiences shrank, ranging from sixty-some million to forty-some million. Some of the criticisms for the sheer drowsiness of the events were directed toward Jim Lehrer, the choice by both candidates to ask the questions in the first two debates and manage the audience's questions in the third. If I were Lehrer, I would reply to my critics with a sports metaphor. What if a boxing promoter hired a referee, placed him in a straitjacket, and sent him into a ring where the boxers banged on each other in the corner? Lehrer had to play by the rules the candidates themselves had set forth, as he himself pointed out a couple of times during the debates. Granted those parameters, Richard Berke of the *New York Times* reported on the day of the third debate in St. Louis, there is "intensifying criticism from partisans and analysts who complain that he did not sufficiently probe the candidates in the first two debates and was not particularly aggressive in following up his questions. The result, these critics say, is that the nominees were left off the hook on vital matters and the debates meandered to the point where they verged on being downright tedious." Lehrer told Berke that his job was to foster give-and-take and that "if somebody wants to be entertained, they ought to go to the circus. Or they ought to go to the ballgame. I didn't sign on to entertain people for ninety minutes three times. These have been tremendous exercises for democracy." Tremendous exercises for democracy? Thank you, Pericles.

This is a debate? When Gore and Bush lay down a rule that prohibits them from asking each other direct questions! The two candidates also stipulated that the questions and subjects for the first two debates had to be chosen by Mr. Lehrer. He relayed these and other formats to the television audience at the outset. Then came a terrible downer, and a patronizing one at that, which generated exactly the wrong kind of ambience for what was to follow. Mr. Lehrer stated: "There is a small audience in the hall tonight. They are not here to participate, only to listen. I have asked, and they have agreed, to remain silent for the next ninety minutes. Except for right now, when they will applaud as we welcome the two candidates, Governor Bush and Vice President Gore." How inappropriate. Why bother with an audience at all? Answer? To provide a prop for the instructed applause and a graphic for the television. Unworthy of all involved.

I retrieved a twenty-year-old *New York Times* editorial asking Jimmy Carter and Ronald Reagan to agree to a debate that "enhances face-to-face discussion. Get rid of the clock and the fussy 'Time's up' warnings and get the reporters out of the way. Keep it simple, flexible and open—a moderator, two chairs and maybe a coffee pot. Sparks should fly."

In Boston, Winston-Salem, and St. Louis, the debates were very repetitive; the candidates often brushed aside Lehrer's questions so as to repeat their campaign mantras. From Gore's lockbox and paying off the debt to Bush's educational testing and tax cut ("You can spend your money more wisely than the federal government can"). In the second debate, the two candidates agreed so often that it became the stuff of comedians. It reached authentic hilarity when Bush said and Gore dittoed that he also was not "for command and control techniques either." Gore parroted this two minutes after he rejected the idea that "pollution controls should be voluntary."

It is easy for an onlooker to criticize any political debate and the participants, if one does not empathize with the time limitations, the pressure on the candidates, and the questions they would like to get asked but don't. But because this was their own show and their format, the candidates have no one to blame but themselves. They set the rules whereby they could not ask questions of each other, and Lehrer was severely restricted from asking the searching follow-up questions because he saw himself as a moderator, not an interviewer. For example, Lehrer allowed far too many repetitions over the three debates, which dulled the tempo and content of the event. One way to have dealt with these repetitions would have been to ask Bush, for example, why is giving back tax monies to America as a community (repairing clinics, schools, public transit, drinking water systems, etc.) any less of a return to the people of the alleged surplus than sending out rebate checks to individuals? Or if "testing is the cornerstone" of Bush's education plan, what kinds of tests and standards would he apply and how would he administer and enforce such a top-down structure from Washington to thousands of local school districts? This is an immense logistical undertaking by Bush, and he was allowed to get away with generalities like "accountability" and "consequences."

The role of money in elections and how it affects politicians was—surprise—largely ignored. So were the subjects of corporate welfare, globalization WTO and NAFTA style, the criminal justice system, the drug war, a living wage, universal health care, consumer protection, unions and union building, military budget cuts, housing, energy, public transit, biotechnology, and the civil justice tort system. Wherever Bush and Gore agreed, there were no challenging questions. For example, both nominees claimed that capital punishment deters homicides when studies for more than two generations have contradicted that assertion. Both wanted to increase the military budget, so there were no questions on the perfectly legitimate topic of cutting the military budget in a post–Cold War period.

Anybody can ask his or her favorite questions. But what I am suggesting with these few illustrations is that no moderator should allow such tidal waves of practiced speeches that reflect converging two-party politics and close out windows of information and insight for voters to evaluate the candidates. In response to a reporter's question, I called the Winston-Salem debate "an interminable tedium of platitudinous dittos"—in other words, Bush and Gore became a cure for insomnia.

There was considerable discussion in the second debate, at Wake Forest, about the use of U.S. power overseas. But there was not one fresh proposal from either candidate, such as in launching a major assault on global infectious diseases, which our country is uniquely positioned to lead. In that same debate, Bush said, "We're going to go after all crime." Think what he would have said if Mr. Lehrer asked him whether that includes heavily neglected corporate crime whose widely reported practices take far more lives and produce far more injuries and diseases than does street crime.

During and after the debates there were many comments about which Gore persona appeared at any given debate. He seemed to be into makeovers—a classic example of how hard it is to be all things to all people. Clearly, the Gore who wrote in the book *Earth in the Balance* (1992) that the internal combustion engine was a major threat to the world's environment was different from the Vice President Gore who helped combine a billion-dollar taxpayer subsidy to GM, Ford, and Chrysler over a clean engine project that produced nothing in eight years other than federal regulatory abdication of fuel efficiency improvements. Given the legendary opposition by the auto industry to any regulatory standards or upgrades, why did Al Gore have to say once that "Detroit is itching to build" the new kinds of clean trucks and cars and again that "Detroit is raring to go on that"? This transparent pandering could have invited a penetrating question.

It was not that there were too few subjects mentioned or touched on—I counted about thirty in the three debates, albeit within very conventional ranges. It's how superficial the handling of these subjects was and, most important, how removed they were from the actual record of Bush and Gore in office. The moderator did not see fit to "accentuate the differences," as Senator Bob Kerrey observed. Lehrer left himself with an occasional plea to the candidates to please tell the audience about their differences. The rate of agreement between the major-party candidates in presidential debates increased from 14 percent in 1976 to a whopping 37 percent in 2000.

With the third debate, in St. Louis, came the citizens' turn to present their questions in advance, get selected, and then stand and ask them. Not spontaneous, but more concise. The subjects were the conventional ones—HMOs, price of prescription drugs, national health care, family farms and agricultural policy, paying attention to youth, affirmative action, and others. But they were often asked with an edge that jolted the candidates a little and sharpened their replies.

The last question persuaded me once again that schoolchildren often ask the clearest, most direct questions. Thomas Fischer got up and asked: "My sixth-grade class at St. Claire's School wanted to ask of all these promises you guys are making and all the pledges, will you keep them when you're in office?" There was laughter. Then Gore said "yes," and there was more laughter. Although the question was treated like a softball down the middle by Gore and Bush, the schoolboy was serious. We should be too.

Part of the failure of "sparks to fly" rested squarely on Gore's shoulders. Bush was by far the more testy person. When he wasn't agreeing, he referred to Gore as "he" or "him" or "the man" and came forth with taunts and false figures. Gore must have decided he wasn't going to tangle at those points of interaction. This may have been a mistake, as far as avoiding potentially dramatic moments in your favor. Bush seemed to gain confidence from Gore's aversions and became more folksy and colloquial. He actually had Gore's number with a few simple techniques: "The man is practicing fuzzy math again," "That's totally false for him to stand up here and say that," or ideological bell ringers like, "He'll put liberal activist justices who will use their bench to subvert the legislature, that's what he'll do." When Gore got around to rebutting Bush, he did so in such a cumbersome, patronizing fashion that it was like *he* was imitating Darrell Hammond on *Saturday Night Live*.

When the debates were over, the pundits rendered their various verdicts, but the polls did not change dramatically. This was really a win for Bush, who exceeded expectations and came across as a regular genial fellow while managing to cuff Gore around a bit. On the other hand, Gore received criticism for his body language and his tone—not trivial matters for a television audience.

During all this focus on the question of presidential debates, I noticed increasing frustration and a touch of melancoly among our campaign staff as the absence of any alternatives to the CPD's debates became clear. My letters and calls in early September to major labor unions to sponsor debates in critical midwestern states and to the major networks to invite the four major candidates for a series of debates produced no results. The inevitability of the done deal had afflicted these institutions as well. One former vice president of a large union told me that labor leaders did not want to see Gore challenged by me because they feared Bush more. It gets worse. After the election, Robert Kuttner, the co-editor of *The American Prospect,* told me that he invited an influential labor union chief to write a lengthy article on what labor wants from the Democratic Party and was turned down. He did not want to embarrass Gore by putting him on the spot.

In many ways the debates phenomenon was a critical litmus test for our society's accelerating surrender to the commodification of our elections. The white-gloved managers and consultants have taken over and put the whole election on the tube, and if you don't like it, there is always the "off" button. That's the definition of freedom—if you don't like it, grab the remote control. Under this lifeless, plastic system where you don't have a say, you're going to continue to pay.

In a post-election article in the *New York Observer*, Nicholas von Hoffman saw Janet Brown, the CPD's executive director, as the sour personification of the rigid, passionless

> emptiness of this now thankfully concluded election. . . . As the years have passed . . . all the secondary characteristics of jubilant, out-in-the-open electioneering have shriveled up and gone away. Campaign songs, campaign slogans, displays, barbecues, ox roasts, clambakes, uniformed marching bands—all vanished and gone, and with them the great mass meetings, the parades and processions for party and candidate. No more will there be a Hot Time in the Old Town Tonight. These changes have not made it easy for a candidate to find an audience. If we see them on those low-brow afternoon talk shows and the no-brow late-night comedy hours making mild asses of themselves, it's because the choice is between being seen on *Oprah* or not being seen at all.

Our society has been given its Khyber Pass by the two parties' CPD. It is not surprising that only two candidates can pass through it to the people. It is probably best to view all these dictacrats as an authoritarian result of a serious default among all of us as disserved citizens. In order to break the grip of the Commission there needs first to be a reassertion of civic activity knocking early on the doors of the foundations, the civil society groups, the trade unions, and the media to establish a nonpartisan People's Debate Commission.

By planning now for 2004, before tactical considerations associated with preferred candidates undermine a fundamental strategy of open, numerous, and varied debates with true vigorous formats, an alternative plan that is broadly based and supported can be launched. Why ration debates? Before the primary season, the probable contenders are much more vulnerable to just and fair procedures. If candidates are asked for early commitments and faced with substantial media agreements to carry the debates, a new tradition could start to take hold—a tradition that keeps its options open for fresh ideas and energies from the citizenry.

The Green Party and other reform groups will be working to heighten the demand for a moral reciprocity that flows from the parties and the media to the public. For it is taxpayers' dollars that fund primaries, elections, and conventions, (and it is the people's asset called the public airwaves that the television and radio broadcasters use, free of charge, when they receive their very profitable licenses from the Federal Communications Commission.) The parties and the media should be expected to contribute to a more open and accessible democratic process.

Millions of Americans who have a close interest or stake in one major public policy issue after another should not be told by a private company, controlled by the duopoly, that they will not have these subjects discussed because candidates who would do so are excluded from nationally televised debates.

The Gore-Bush debates were laced with self-censorship and latent taboos against these issues, or their respective records, being raised or debated or challenged vigorously. We need more straightforward questions, such as that asked by the *Business Week* cover story in September 2000: Mr. Gore, Mr. Bush, do large corporations—banks, insurance companies, HMOs, chemical, drug, food, auto, biotech firms, real estate, agribusiness, the prison industries, and military contractors—have too much power in Washington, D.C.? Now, there is the mother of many healthy provocations, the likes of which an experienced Morton Mintz–type interviewer could have engrossed millions of viewers and listeners for one entire debate theme. (See www.Tompaine.com for a sampling of questions Mintz would ask.)

One thing is for sure: After such a debate, in the minds of millions, Gore and Bush would have both shrunk from this red-hot immersion in the crucible of political reality.

Thirteen

WITH COLD FEET AND BIG HEARTS

On October 17, the third and final debate was over without disturbing the drowsy equilibrium between Bush and Gore. Three weeks to November 7, and all that was accelerating was the number of takeoffs and landings of their private jets, as they dashed from one state to another repeating their mantras: "I'm for the people, they're for the powerful," "I trust the people, not the government," "I'll fight for you," and "I'll restore honor and dignity to the White House."

Back in our campaign office, staff members were working around the clock, coordinating with our field staff on getting out the vote in areas where we had Green representatives. Jake Lewis, Laura Jones, Stacy Malkan, and Tom Adkins in our press office were booking me for events around the country and preparing for three days in Washington, D.C., of continuous interviews with the national press, television, and radio. The versatile Theresa Amato, with her associates, the unflappable "no problem" Monica Wilson and a cool Jeanna Penn, kept the whirlwind schedule from dissolving into chaos. Jonathan Dushoff was burning the midnight oil managing our steady stream of position papers.

The morning after the St. Louis debates we flew to Texas, where in two days we visited Dallas, Austin, San Antonio, and Houston. The largest assembly was the rally in Austin at the Tony Berger Center, which we filled with five thousand people. This was, we were told, one of the largest political rallies Austin had seen in many years. And it sure was a memorable one. It opened at 6:15 P.M. with Bill Oliver and His Band, followed by Bill Passalacqua singing "Election Blues." Other musicians sang songs by Dylan and

Guthrie. Then came civic action leaders Charlotte Flynn of the Gray Panthers, Clint Smith, followed by Gary Dugger, son of the populist writer-activist Ronnie Dugger, who along with his ally, Charlie Mauch, was running for the powerful job of Texas railroad commissioner. Doug Sandage spoke on behalf of his Green candidacy for the U.S. Senate. Jim Hightower introduced me ("It takes organized people to fight organized money") and, as always, he had the ralliers jazzed up. After I spoke, the Jimmy LaFave Band closed with everyone singing "This Land Is Our Land."

California was next, and did we ever cover that sprawling state again! In four days we campaigned through fourteen towns and cities from Southern California all the way to Chico State, where we met the California Nurses Association for a news conference and spoke to a full house at the El Rey Theatre. Other highlights included a super-rally with seventy-five hundred people in Oakland, and boisterous assemblies at UC Davis and Stanford. When you travel in California to places like Riverside, Santa Monica, Bakersfield, and Fresno, there is not likely to be any television coverage. Fortunately, Bill Rosendahl had a regular cable program throughout the state that was devoted to red-hot political discussion. Bill had me on his program several times in 2000.

The paucity of California television coverage—sound bite or segment—made reaching people very difficult. When Democrats and Republicans run for the Senate in California these days, they spend almost all their time raising money for television ads that make TV stations richer while using the public's airwaves for free. No matter that we spent more time in California, which from the get-go was going for Gore, not Bush, than all the swing states put together. That, in retrospect, was a mistake. No matter how large the audiences and how many interviews we gave, reaching more than a small fraction of thirty-five million people was a herculean task beyond our resources. Most Californians did not even know we were running. The vote total on November 7 showed we received only 418,707 votes, or 4 percent of the total turnout. Because Gore was so far ahead of Bush, we had expected twice that number, and some early polls indicated that sum was possible. As a volunteer in Los Angeles told us: "You would have gotten more television coverage if you led the LAPD with one hot pursuit at high noon down the Santa Monica Freeway."

On October 22, our campaign staff got a sense of what it means to be overwhelmed. The *New York Daily News* reported that the Republican National Committee (RNC) was set to spend, in just the two weeks leading up to the election, $40 million to $50 million on phoning, leaflets, and door-to-door canvassing, while the Democratic National Committee (DNC) was planning to pay out $10 million to $15 million on similar activities. The DNC's ally, the AFL-CIO, pledged $30 million to $40 million on GOTV (get out the vote) efforts for union workers and their families. Al Gore spent more than $120 million on his campaign efforts and George Bush spent $186 million. We spent about $8 million. The soft-money expenditures by the Democrats and Republicans for the 1999–2000 election cycle are even more staggering. The Democratic Party spent $244 million in soft money and the Republican Party spent $252 million. This up-against-the-big-boys challenge did not discourage our campaign staff but rather served to motivate them even further. Full public financing of public elections was our platform—and someday I hope all campaigns will have the chance to run on their merits rather than on their money.

That the Democrats and Gore possessed very large advantages over us in almost every quantitative category was not enough. Having never faced a challenge for the presidential votes of progressive Americans since the Henry Wallace campaign of 1948, the Democrats had developed a deep sense of entitlement. (See Appendix H.) Those were *their* votes every four years because where else could they go—not to the dreaded Republicans. The "A vote for Nader is a vote for Bush" drumbeat started. Such a strategy was to be expected from the Democrats, but their obvious smugness did not advance their cause. Indeed, through the spring and summer of 2000, the party's line was that it was not losing any sleep over the Green Party candidacy. Ho-hum, wake us when it's over. Inside, though, the party needed to establish a persuasive tactic toward the progressive wing and press its loyal proxies into action. Early on, Toby Moffett, former Nader Raider, former four-term congressman from Connecticut, and former Monsanto lobbyist, counseled the Democrats against direct confrontation. Work both publicly and behind the scenes, he said, to convince voters that Nader will undermine Gore, who, regardless, shares many of the same positions.

Someday I hope someone will conduct a postmortem on the Gore campaign and how it got so many closely affiliated political and citizen leaders all singing on cue—"A vote for Nader is a vote for Bush." The Democratic Party was not saying vote for Gore because we are throwing off our corporate shackles and embracing Green Party policies (most of which were old Democratic Party positions) such as universal health insurance, a living wage as a minimum wage, selective military demobilization in a post-Soviet era, strong health and safety regulations, progressive taxation, consumer protection, or expanding workers' rights to form unions. Instead, the Democratic Party sent out its scary message about how bad the Republicans would be, which is another way of saying that the Democrats are not as bad. Wouldn't it have been better to define the party by its best potential? However, to have gone the high road would have collapsed the similarities between the parties that overwhelmed the shrinking real differences.

The "a vote for Nader is a vote for Bush" bandwagon (one cartoonist pictured Bush looking at such signs and concluding that therefore he should vote for Nader) attracted a variety of adherents. Some were old friends and coworkers now working in government, business, or law firms. One of the more bizarre recruits was Gary Sellers, who worked with me more than thirty years ago to lobby through Congress the Occupational Safety and Health Act (OSHA). He was a delight to work with, in part because he and our ally on the Hill, California Congressman Phil Burton, were very good at sizing up the assets, vulnerabilities, and vanities of various legislators. For more than twenty years, Sellers has operated cherry and apple orchards, volunteered for some bar groups, and generally stayed out of any sustained civic advocacy or political activity. From time to time, recognizing his personal difficulties, his friends, including me, would try to get him going on some project or another, but to little avail. Sellers came to my announcement back in February at the Madison Hotel and in a later telephone conversation was laudatory. Then, at an August fund-raiser at Nora Pouillon's famous organically certified restaurant in Washington, D.C., he stood up and said he was worried about the Greens undermining Gore. I told him we were running a fifty-state campaign to maximize our votes and were not going out of our way to target swing states.

A few weeks later, Sellers started showing up on television representing something oxymoronically called "Nader's Raiders for Gore." But Sellers was one of just a dozen former associates from twenty-plus years ago. Despite extensive calling by Moffett, Sellers, Gore adviser Katie McGinty (who spent a long time on the telephone trying to persuade Peter Gruenstein in Anchorage, Alaska), Harrison Wellford, and the rest of the dozen, well over one thousand former Nader's Raiders did not budge. In the last month or so, Sellers became a Gore servant possessed—mischaracterizing what I had said at Nora's about Gore's record and my fifty-state campaign. He was having a ball, debating Phil Donahue on national television and getting on other media with the expert help of the Democrats. I was more amused than indignant, hoping that such exposure would help relieve the affluent Gary of his stresses and possibly return him later to working in the public interest.

The split between liberals of similar backgrounds and philosophies that occurred over my Green Party candidacy was very revealing for the future of progressive politics in America. The chasm that deepened in the last few weeks of the election to the point of bitterness was not so much over differing policy positions or the preferred direction of the country. What, then, were the differences?

First: expectation levels. Many voters see a very imperfect politics with a choice between a party they are dissatisfied with and another party they abhor. This perception is given further edge by a sharp campaign focus on one or two issues—such as abortion or the Arctic National Wildlife Refuge—where there truly is a distinct difference between the two parties. Attachment to some genuinely progressive Democrats such as Representative Henry Waxman (California) and Senator Paul Wellstone (Minnesota) gives a voter the sense that a few are better than none. Finally, there are friendships and history between these people and elected Democrats that are forged over common issues, get-togethers, political conventions, fund-raisers, and constituent service.

The pro–Green candidacy Democrats are basically saying that the Democratic Party is sick, is decaying, and rejects its internal reformers. These people realize that the party has performed in ways that seriously contradict its progressive past and further entrench the power of corporations and concentrated wealth. Nobody has articulated this condition better than former Secretary of Labor under Clinton, Robert Reich, who was not pro-Green and remains a steadfast Democrat. He is a different kind of realist. As he wrote in the March 11, 2001, issue of the *Washington Post*:

> I know a dead party when I see one, and I'm looking at a dead party right now. Just consider the past eight years: lost the presidency, both houses of Congress, almost all its majorities in state legislatures, most governorships. Will lose additional House seats in the next redistricting. Most of the current justices of the Supreme Court appointed by Republicans, also most current federal judges. And the interminable Bill Clinton scandals. The Democratic Party is stone dead. Dead as a doornail.

> If the Democratic Party's alive, then why doesn't it insist that the budget surplus be spent on health care for the 44 million Americans without it? And child care for the millions who lack it? And good schools for all kids? Why doesn't the party say it's plain absurd to spend $300 billion on the military when the Cold War is over, and tens of billions more on a missile-defense shield that won't work? Why isn't it outraged that most of the benefits of President Bush's tax cut will go to people at the top? Why does it play dead on the environment? Because it's not playing dead. It is dead!

Reich, you will notice, kept emphasizing the party. He knows there are a few individual Democrats who have been fighting for all these objectives, but the party and its fat cat patrons determine the result at the end.

Second, the weighing of rhetoric versus record. Political speech can be mesmerizing, and Clinton-Gore were out front in their conscious ability to have the word confused with the deed. On October 5, President Clinton went to Princeton University and unabashedly proclaimed that he and Al Gore for eight years had been carrying on the progressive tradition of Theodore Roosevelt and Woodrow Wilson. In those eight years, the very corporations that Roosevelt and Wilson repeatedly warned about greatly strengthened their grip on America in manifold ways with the encouragement and active support of Clinton-Gore. So, they both spoke for civil rights, the environment, the small farmer, consumer protection, fair trade. Yet their record belied their speech.

Third: American third-party history. Well-read Democrats would no doubt recognize the pivotal roles played by the little parties that fought early and hard for slavery's abolition, women's right to vote, labor justice, and the small farmers' survival in the nineteenth century. But many believe that today the Democrats can't risk a progressive small party upsetting their claim on the electoral college. It is possible that the Greens may press some better policies onto the Democrats who hold on to their votes and avoid losing more elections. There needs to be some progressive force pulling or jolting the Democrats to counteract to some degree, at least, the opposite pull by the corporations.

What political choice does for galvanizing the citizenry is an important difference as well. Clinton-Gore opened up large areas for drilling in the northern slope of Alaska and proposed six million acres for exploration off the coast of Florida to little vocal opposition from environmental groups. When Bush proposed drilling in the Arctic National Wildlife Refuge and off Florida, there was persistent vociferous outrage from those same organizations, among others, and Bush pulled back and proposed offshore Florida exploration of "only" 1.5 million acres while environmental allies in Congress said they would block ANWR with a filibuster. That's one difference between a do-little anesthetist and a do-nothing provocateur in the White House. Citizen groups slumber with the former and awaken with the latter.

The Gore campaign enlisted as their proxies against the Nader-LaDuke people with a record of progressive commitments who are usually ignored by the Democratic Leadership Council, which spawned Clinton, Gore, and Lieberman. It must have been a delight for these proxies to be so wanted, so often called and beseeched—for a few weeks at least. Off they went on their tours without ever receiving any commitments for their progressive agendas from the Gore people.

Before the October tours by Gore's anti-Nader brigade, columnists and editorial writers were laying the groundwork. Anthony Lewis weighed in on July 8 with an open letter to me in his *New York*

Times column. I'll leave it to you to see his distortion of my words in one charming paragraph: "What is puzzling to some of your old admirers is what you stand for. You say the two major parties are practically Tweedledum and Tweedledee—there are 'few major differences' between them. Sure, they are both awash in campaign money that keeps them close to business. But no major differences? Are you serious?"

From "few major differences" to "no major differences" became the spin. Not only is this an inaccurate transposition, but it takes the public's attention away from the shocking similarities between the two parties. Lewis then went on to draw a legitimate difference between recent and prospective Supreme Court nominees of Democratic and Republican presidents (once again, earlier nominees by Republican presidents were Warren, Brennan, Blackmun, Stevens, and Souter—largely admired by Lewis) but failed to note that the Democrats could have stopped both Scalia and Thomas (confirmed 52–48 with eleven Democratic senators voting for him). Isn't there a similarity of result when one party sends up bad nominees and the other party declines to use its power to defeat them? Lewis then rightly cites the convergence between President Clinton and the Republican Congress on an "abysmal" civil liberties record. He wrongly chides me for paying "little or no attention" to this area. As I told him afterward, I have gone all over the country, making exactly this point dozens of times and specifically referring to his and Nat Hentoff's many articles on the subject. (Lewis printed a correction in a later column.) He included other misstatements, including an erroneous allegation from the *New Republic*, which became a puff sheet for Al Gore. Lewis could have avoided these quality-control problems simply by calling me before he wrote his column—having known me since he was a journalism fellow at Harvard Law School in the mid-fifties.

On August 10 came a *Times* op-ed by Robert F. Kennedy Jr., who leaped into the fray with his "no difference" premise. He is a very forgiving person when it comes to Democrats. Anyone who has heard his earlier tough criticisms of Clinton-Gore on environmental matters has to believe that appraisal. But for his op-ed, Mr. Kennedy did not check his facts. He quoted an erroneous statement attributed to me that, if forced to choose, I would vote for Bush over Gore in order to cause a backlash in the environment's favor.

Again, had he phoned (he called me a friend and mentor in his own column), he might have gotten the record straight. It is always easier to rely on clips.

The anonymous editorial writers of the the *New York Times* resumed their attack with three pieces dated August 20, October 26, and November 3, each escalating in a hysteria that would have been humorous were it not so embarrassing to that paper's history. In 1980, by sober comparison, the earlier editorial writers for the *Times* had a different, more democratic philosophy regarding Carter, Reagan, and Anderson. Here are their words:

> The question is not whether debates are good for the country but how to make them better. There are at least two ways: Let qualified mavericks in. Get media middlemen out. The maverick point is, of course, the political debate question of the campaign. Even the Carter campaigners may not be sure which hurts more, letting John Anderson in or being blamed for keeping him out. But this is not only a political question of Anderson in, Anderson out. It is first a question of principle.
>
> If the United States wants third parties and maverick candidates, and it should, they must have at least a theoretical chance of winning elections. The public will not take seriously Presidential candidates who do not appear in televised debates. To limit participation unreasonably to the two major parties is to eviscerate independents, mavericks and new parties.

All this high road came from a newspaper that favored Carter, believed Reagan to have reactionary views, and thought the election presented a crucial choice.

Now fast-forward twenty years. While conceding that "both parties" were "tranquilizing their activists," the year 2000 *Times* editorial writer asserted that the "biggest difference, perhaps the defining difference, lies in how the two men would distribute the lion's share of a projected budget surplus of $4.6 trillion over the next 10 years. Mr. Bush . . . would use about $1.3 trillion to cut taxes, mainly for affluent families. Al Gore would cut taxes by only $500 billion, mostly subsidies of one sort of another for middle-income families."

So what happens in June 2001, with the Democrats taking over the Senate? The Democrats call a $1.3 trillion Bush tax cut a victory for their side, as indeed numerous Democrats voted with the Republicans. This is just another example of how little skepticism the *Times* displayed, even after eight years of Clinton-Gore casuistry. The October 26 editorial titled "Mr. Nader's Electoral Mischief" hardened into name-calling. Unlike John Anderson, I was on "a self-indulgent crusade," I had "an ego run amok," and my "willful prankishness" would be "a disservice to the electorate no matter whose campaign [I] was hurting." Well, well, that flight into duopolyism comes very close to saying that the Greens had no right to keep the country from "a clear up-or-down vote between Mr. Bush and Mr. Gore." Whatever happened to "mavericks and third parties" in the *New York Times* of 1980? This turn-of-the-century *Times* has the air of inevitability about American politics: "The spectrum has shifted and Mr. Nader cannot jerk it back by demolishing Democratic chances." Then it adds an air of naïveté unbecoming to such worldly editors when it admits that "certainly the candidates and their parties have parallel histories in regard to seeking corporate contributions," but "their approaches to systemic reform of the electoral system are very different." As different as eight years of paying lip service while engulfing all the cash that corporations proffered the Clinton-Gore team for eight years? Take the dough, but say no, no, no—sounds like a display of political prostitution.

The last *Times* diatribe against me came out four days before the election, urging "Mr. Gore to get tougher on Mr. Nader." Setting the standard, the editorial writers got down and dirty. Accusing me of wanting to throw the election to Mr. Bush and damage the Democratic Party, the paper proceeded to accuse me of insensitivity to the poor because of my net worth (which has been used to advance our various civic justice projects), to women because the Republicans would overturn *Roe* v. *Wade*, and, astonishingly, to the makeup of the Supreme Court. What the *Times* ignored was that the Democratic Party, even when it is in the Senate majority, no longer has the will to defeat nominees like Scalia and Thomas the way the Democrats had the mettle to block nominees Haynes-worth, Carswell, and Bork years earlier. What troubled me was the scare tactics used by the *Times* on *Roe* v. *Wade* and other estab-lished policies in our country that breed a clinging defensive atti-tude instead of a tough self-confidence intent on preserving past gains while going on the offensive toward new realms of well-being for the people.

I dwell on these *Times* editorials because they not only provided the polemical background for the Gore proxies as they spread throughout the country in October to counter not Bush but Green Party candidates. They also helped orient, as the *Times* often does, much of the other major media's, which followed in a similar groove. Whenever I recall the *Times*'s stand, Phil Donahue's re-sponse to shock academic Alan Dershowitz's Orwellian comment calling our campaign "antidemocratic" comes to mind: "We've got the free speecher from Harvard, Alan Dershowitz, saying, 'Shut up, already, don't make trouble. This is undemocratic what we're doing.' So I guess that means we should put our hat in our hands, whimper a little bit and wait four years, and then go to these same people and say, 'Can we run this year? Is it okay if we run this year?' " The *Times* editorial opened by praising Marlo Thomas for, as the paper put it, reprimanding her husband, Phil Donahue, on national television and giving him "a civics lesson." It looked like it was Phil Donahue who was giving the *Times* a civics lesson.

Good people who settle for less and less get very upset when reminded of that trait. Unfortunately, it leads them to focus on fear of the Republicans instead of the derelict Democrats and their re-fusal to heed the pleas of their own reformers. It was late in 1998 at a large, annual Irish-American dinner that Jesse Jackson turned to me and, unprovoked, said, "I'm gonna run. We can't leave the party in the hands of Gore and Gephardt." Jesse certainly has paid his dues. No one has brought out more African-American votes for Democratic candidates at all levels. No one has stimulated more voter registration drives. No one has done more to show that po-litical parties need to go where the anguish and injustices reign. He has logged hundreds of thousands of miles of effort. However, his self-restraint toward the manipulative elements of his party is now so extensive that it is affecting him. While he quietly moderated a few of the Clinton administration's calculating moves against principle, his counseling on the Lewinsky affair to the contrary, he no longer sees himself as a singular public force to push the party toward progressive actions. His son, Representative Jesse Jackson Jr. (D-Illinois), already has assumed a more assertive role in this respect. Jesse Sr. now also sees himself as using entrenched corporate power to open doors to African-American businesses. But getting too close to Citigroup and CEO Sandy Weill has made him vulnerable to being used, as when he endorsed prematurely the Clinton-favored bank consolidation legislation in Congress that was very unfriendly to minorities and the poor.

Anyone who has spoken privately to Jackson, or read his writings, knows the difference between what he believes and what he has conceded to the party's rulers. Jackson was not mincing words when, a week after his National Rainbow Coalition meeting in Atlanta, he published an article in the June 4, 1995, edition of the *Los Angeles Times* titled "A Third Party May Be Needed for Progressives." Jackson was clearly very upset with the Democrats' loss of Congress to the Gingrich forces in the previous November elections. "It is not enough," he wrote, "to throw out the conservatives and re-elect traditional Democrats. We need a new direction." He announced that the Rainbow Coalition would explore independent ballot access to run candidates who would stand for a progressive agenda. Citing falling real wages, growing inequality, spreading poverty even for working families, Jackson laid it on the line:

> Why talk about new political options now? Because it is clear that reelecting Democrats to Congress is not enough. We've done that. We registered people and helped bring out the vote. We delivered—and too often we were then ignored.
>
> We don't intend to be exploited anymore. The days of asking us to sow the seeds, cultivate the ground, pick the cotton and then turn it over to others to sell are over.

From his two presidential runs, Jackson knew better than anyone else what it felt like being wooed in the primaries and forgotten in the general election. But the crux of his article came with this unforgettable denunciation of the two-party convergence, which he described as a "bipartisan conservative majority in the Congress":

A bipartisan majority endorsed the supply-side, trickle-down economics of the early 1980s. The rich got richer and working people got stuck with the bill for the massive deficits and S&L bailout. A bipartisan conservative majority blocked efforts to change priorities at the end of the Cold War. A bipartisan conservative majority enforced a trade policy that served Wall Street and multinationals, not Main Street and American workers.

Jackson was thinking like this before the shredding of the federal safety net for the poor, set for 2002, by the phony welfare reform legislation championed by Clinton and especially Gore in 1996. So shocked by the White House's callousness was Clinton's trusted adviser on this subject, Peter Edelman, a top official at the Department of Health and Human Services, that he resigned in protest. The year 1996 brought forth other enacted laws empowering corporations further at the expense of small farmers and telecommunications consumers. If anything, the second Clinton term was even more upsetting to Jackson since he, like many others who share his public philosophy, thought things would get better for a progressive agenda because Clinton would be free from running for reelection. Yet Jackson's support for Clinton-Gore rarely wavered.

So it was with all this background in mind that I accepted Jackson's invitation to appear on his CNN television show *One on One* in late August after the political conventions. Jackson was a very precise interviewer, asking question after question about which team—Democrats or Republicans—would do better on a variety of issues. He could have been Gore interviewing me, except that Jackson does it better. I responded as specifically as he questioned—essentially making the point that one is bad, the other is worse, and the Democrats are much better with the rhetoric that leads to nowhere. Jackson kept saying that the votes we were getting would strengthen Bush. And I countered that supporting the least of the worst, without putting heat on the least of the worst, ends up worsening all every four years—a slide both of us have felt when going up to Congress only to be told no, that we have nowhere to go.

It was to no avail. Jackson portrayed the issue as a choice between the "Gore-Lieberman-Daschle team," or the "Bush–Cheney–Trent Lott–Orrin Hatch team." After the last commercial break, I noted a skeptical twinkle in Jackson's eyes when he heard me say that the Democratic Party used to tell him the same things—that he couldn't win and was only damaging the expected Democratic primary winners with his challenges. The party has even marginalized him, I added. I suggested that Gore was perfectly free to take away the Green Party issues and their voters if he wanted to win. Gore was not entitled to any votes any more than was Bush or I. Jackson, having done his part for the Gore ticket, stressed the "need to democratize the process" and ended by urging everyone to vote, in an ironic twist, "your dreams and not your fears."

Our interview was not in the same room but was remote, with Jackson in Los Angeles and me in Washington, D.C. So I did not have a chance to chat after the program and remind him of the many leading intellectual liberals and politicians who counseled gradualism in the struggle for civil rights. People like Reinhold Niebuhr, William Faulkner, and Hannah Arendt. The great civil rights attorney and later Supreme Court Justice Thurgood Marshall said that when these advisers said, "Go slow," they meant, "Don't go," and Martin Luther King Jr. repeated his belief that "now is the time" for justice. These were more than differences in tactics—they were also a different reading of the public pulse and of their own expectation levels. So it was and so it will be for social justice movements everywhere. For our times, there is no justification for continuing to postpone changes that should have been accomplished in the 1940s and 1950s and were urged on our leaders at that time by leading public figures.

Besides Jackson, Al Gore enlisted the help of Gloria Steinem. Gore, who was part of an administration that sat for years on the FDA and RU-486, who never mentioned the Equal Rights Amendment in his campaign, who voted for Antonin Scalia, who never lifted a finger in the direction of ending scores of economic discriminations against women as consumers of goods and services, called on Steinem to travel from state to state on his behalf. This proud member of the Democratic Socialists of America signed on to coax progressive voters like herself to vote for the hero of corporate globalization and some of the sleaziest big capitalist lobbyists in the nation's capital. During her weeks on the trail for Gore, Steinem became a study in contradictions. Having done many national television talk shows on feminism, including a couple with me, she spent much of her time deprecating and, sad to say, distorting my record on women's rights.

I have known Gloria for many years, attended her fiftieth birthday party at the Waldorf-Astoria, crossed paths with her on subjects ranging from advertising and energy to GATT/WTO, and urged her in vain to have *Ms.* make a bigger deal of how women pay more in the marketplace to their economic and health detriment. At lectures, I must have defended her a hundred times from the mindless slurs of male and some female chauvinists. We were both on the cover of *McCall's* in 1972—she with her picture as Woman of the Year and me as author of an article on discrimination against women as consumers. In turn, she has made many generous public comments about my work. In a note to me five years ago, thanking me for sending her an article where I lauded her very courageous jettisoning of commercial advertising from *Ms.*, she wrote "how grateful I am for your wisdom, clarity, and refusal ever to be still—victory belongs to the long-distance runner." It was dismaying then to see Gloria, without her ever calling me beforehand to discuss what was on her mind, hit the road as a short-distance runner, pushing for Gore by undermining me.

People and reporters who attended her lectures and press conferences heard her say that I have little understanding of feminist issues and then give an example: "The only time that I ever heard from him on an issue concerning women was when he called me about platform shoes. Nader told me, 'They're dangerous. Corporations are selling platform shoes and women are buying them.' " This is a truly desperate distortion. I spoke to her about two books—the first in an important field—called *Women Take Charge* (1983), by Nina Easton, and *Women Pay More* (1995), by Frances Cerra Whittelsey, which documented many ways women are ripped off, overcharged, and harmed in the marketplace because of their gender. From millions of unnecessary surgical operations and tranquilizer prescriptions, to discriminatory treatment by car dealers and home-repair firms and credit providers, women were fair game under an obtuse legal system. The tyrannies of fashion and hurtful beauty regimes and diet fads, together with social sanctions that flow from a male-dominated society and economy, were the subject of our articles, books, and national television shows, like Phil Donahue's show, over the years. Gloria was not the only full-time feminist who was not very interested, but she was one of the most prominent ones unresponsive to my pleas to really take on this deep pattern of sexism. Our Health Research Group has published studies on harm to women from medical and prescription practices. A testing group we inspired documented the bias against female students taking standardized multiple-choice tests some years ago. Had she called me, I would have informed her of my attention to this array of issues as well as my attempts to persuade Democratic senators to vote against the Scalia and Thomas nominations.

Furthermore, had she desired more reassurance, I would have walked her through my efforts at law school, while writing for the law school newspaper in the fifties, to question the deans about their admissions policy, which admitted only about fifteen women in a class of 550 students. (One professor told me that women who take male seats will go on to give birth to babies, not briefs.) I wrote about other issues, including the outrageous laws in several states prohibiting women from serving on juries. In the early sixties I started collecting materials for a book on discrimination against women in the United States only to open the newspaper one day to see that Betty Friedan's *The Feminine Mystique* did it better than I ever could. All this was years before Gloria came upon her life's mission. In the early seventies I urged and initially funded a women's policy institute that is active to this day. So here is Gloria telling people in California, Oregon, and other Pacific Coast states about my belittling *Roe* v. *Wade,* which I see as so well established and so deeply supported (by polls, media, and a very well-connected feminist movement) and which she sees as hanging by one bad judicial nomination.

Well, the Supreme Court justices viewed as antiabortion had three chances to overturn *Roe* v. *Wade* and did not. Republican Party operatives tell people in Washington all the time that they are not about to destroy the Republican Party on this issue but have to promote the rhetoric to keep the support of the party's antiabortion wing. When Tim Russert on *Meet the Press* asked George W. Bush whether as president he would seek to overturn *Roe,* Bush, much like his father and like Ronald Reagan, said, "Not until lots of people in America change their minds."

One of Steinem's forensic forays centered on her "ten top reasons I'm not voting for Nader." It is too easy to take this list at face value and ridicule it. But, to give a flavor, the tenth reason was, "He's not running for president, he's running for federal matching funds for the Green Party." As if there is any conflict among running for president, building a third party and a progressive political movement, and receiving federal matching funds during the primary season—part of a policy for overall public funding of elections that the Greens and I advocate. She treated Winona LaDuke's agreeing to run for vice president as if she were a dupe, unaware of both parties' policies regarding the First Nations. Steinem's third reason was, "If I were to run for president in the same symbolic way, I would hope my friends and colleagues would have the sense to vote against me, too." Building a viable third party, in the American political tradition of major contributions by such parties, including early woman's suffrage, requires long-distance runners, not symbolic gestures, Gloria, through and beyond November 7. (For a detailed rebuttal by feminist Juliana Hu-Pegues of Steinem's Ten Reasons, see www.zmag.org/replysteinem.htm.)

My last communication with Gloria was in 1998, when I sent her a draft article for *Ms.* magazine on the agony young pregnant mothers in West Africa go through after they come down with malaria. She replied with sympathy, but the magazine was not receptive.

During special bus trips in numerous mostly Western and Midwestern states, Steinem made the ludicrous charge that our rallies were "disproportionately male." Another falsehood. Countering her friend, Susan Sarandon urged: "I would ask Gloria to go back to her roots in the sixties and remember how things work . . . to stop being so frightened."

In the closing hours of the campaign, the *Chicago Sun Times* reported, Steinem "will be telephoning about 200,000 households with a tape-recorded message on Gore's behalf. Steinem deleted a line from her original script in which she said that she admired Nader but was voting Gore."

After such a confidence-stricken, mean, and mawkish campaign, against Nader-LaDuke and the Greens, she finally did me a favor.

It was at the completion of my four-day trip through California that I realized how extensive the Gore smear campaign had become. I picked up the October 24 edition of the *New York Times* and read a front-page article by James Dao headlined "Democrats Hear Thunder on Left, and Try to Steal Some of Nader's." The *Times* described a party dispatching its "allies in labor, environmental and women's movements" to the swing states. The roll call for Gore's anti-Nader campaign was quite impressive and included Senator Paul Wellstone (who assured me that while dutifully praising Gore, he never bad-mouthed us); Robert Redford; Elizabeth Birch, executive director of the Human Rights Campaign, who overlooked Gore's anemic stance on gay and lesbian rights; Robert Cox, president of the Sierra Club, who ignored the biting Dorsey memorandum taking Gore apart on fourteen categories of anti-environmental positions or inactions, written by a member of the club's board; Brent Blackwelder, president of Friends of the Earth, who was second to none in denouncing Clinton-Gore during their eight years of abdication or rejection of environmental causes; and former Senator Bill Bradley, whose private contempt for Gore's dirty campaigning was submerged by his party fealty. So terrified were they of the Republican hordes that they did not negotiate any solemn commitments from Gore for their own chosen causes.

Our astute adviser, Steve Cobble, a veteran of many progressive election campaigns, sent a memo titled " 'Pragmatic' Politics" (see Appendix I) to the Sierra Club's Board of Directors just before its meeting to decide on their presidential endorsement in July 2000. He predicted the following Sunday's headline, "As Expected, Sierra Club Endorses Gore," and argued as follows:

> The political result: the Sierra Club will be ignored the rest of the campaign; key environmental issues will be left off the agenda and out of the presidential debates, as Vice President Gore seeks to mollify and attract swing voters, while taking the "base" for granted. . . .

This is not the way to play even the insider game on behalf of the environment, much less the long-term, mass movement to change the anti-environment-corporate-structure-game. After all, in American politics, it's the squeaky wheel that gets the grease, not the go-along-to-get-along liberal interest group—quiet politics only works for those with the big, big corporate money, behind closed doors.

Gore always viewed the Sierra Club endorsement as the most important for his environmental image. In 1996, he went so far as to place personal calls to members of the Sierra board. The club's leaders knew this and still didn't make themselves harder to get. Given the long list in Michael Dorsey's memorandum of Gore's bad moves and the outcry from its members upset with him regarding the Everglades/airport issue, the East Liverpool, Ohio, incinerator reversal (see Appendix K for the details), the salmon-saving dam-breaching indecision, and the coal barons blowing off mountaintops in the Appalachian coal fields—to name a few dives he took—there was ample reason to hold back. Cobble presented an analysis of when Clinton-Gore invoked the Antiquities Act of 1996 in regions where there are special Green Party goals that could swing the result in several western states. Remember also that Clinton was deeply worried about this prospect in conversations with Dick Morris. In June 2000, after polls showed we were running above expectations in the West, Cobble wrote:

> The Clinton/Gore administration invoked the Antiquities Act once again for the Ironwood Forest in Arizona, Hanford Reach in Washington, the Canyons of the Ancients in Colorado, and the Cascade-Sisikyou in Oregon. Notice the pattern: environmental conservation in swing states. . . . Notice the other, more basic pattern: years in which Nader is running, millions of acres saved; years in which Nader is not running, zero acres are saved.

Driving his point home, Cobble summarized it this way: "This is not an accident. Presidential politics in America is not about being nice and polite . . . it's about independent action, swing votes, and leverage. It's also about strength, not weakness."

He recommended several endorsement options—endorsing Nader-LaDuke, or a dual endorsement by targeted state, or deferring an endorsement with a strong urging to have "Nader be included in the presidential debates so that key environmental issues such as the globalization of trade will be heard." Indeed, nothing prevents the Sierra Club from sponsoring its own pre-endorsement presidential debate, Cobble urged. Together with other leading environmental organizations, this could be more than a flight of fancy. As he concluded, "This option would show strength, and force the political system to deal with the environmental issues that the major party candidates would rather just talk about."

Regardless of this clear thinking, the Sierra Club met, endorsed Gore, made no demands, sharply denounced Bush's dismal record, with the help of a chastened Dorsey, and prepared for the thank you call from the vice president to his buddy, Carl Pope, the club's executive director.

Knowing that they have the enviros in their political pocket, Democrats can ignore them and provide the *Wall Street Journal* with material for an article titled "Democratic Leaders Turn Up as Unlikely Allies for Nuclear Power." The *Journal*, on July 27, 2001, listed Senator Jeff Bingaman, chairman of the Senate Energy Committee, Senators Joe Lieberman and John Kerry, and former Interior Secretary Bruce Babbitt, who ignorantly called the case for expanding atomic power plants "absolutely rock solid." The article went on to say that "Al Gore's support for developing safer new reactors went largely unnoticed."

"I don't know what to make of Bruce Babbitt," lamented the Sierra Club's Debbie Bonger. The Greens do. It is not nuclear power versus fossil fuels. Babbitt and the senators failed to contrast nuclear power's liabilities and long-range costs against the truly massive potential of existing technologies and practices for energy efficiency. Every thousand megawatts you save is a thousand-megawatt nuclear power plant you can forgo or close down. But then the many years' work of Arthur Rosenfeld, Amory Lovins, and David Freeman regarding energy efficiencies and renewables does not have the weight with most Democrats that the omnipresent atomic power lobbyists and their campaign cash disbursers do.

But most regrettable for tens of millions of American workers that campaign fall were what the *Times* called "a list of heavy-weight labor leaders" organized by the Democratic Party. These included John J. Sweeney, president of the AFL-CIO, and Andrew L. Stern, head of the Service Employees International Union. For labor, long bearing the brunt of the anti-union Democratic Leadership Council, it was all about avoiding Bush rather than relishing Gore. Though crucial for Gore's chances of winning, the leaders of organized labor received no adequate protections for the working classes. For example, the minimum wage was more than two dollars lower in purchasing power than it was in 1968! This upset one former official in a large union so much that he exclaimed, "It's all about [labor leaders'] visits to the Rose Garden and trips on *Air Force One*." Would it were that simple. It is also about not having the verve to bargain hard for their workers. That is why the Democrats know that no matter how many GATTs, NAFTAs, empty OSHAs, and other betrayals, how many false promises and excuses they heap on these labor leaders, they can be had because, once again, the Republicans are deemed worse. There is no way out of that long tunnel except not to enter it, so that labor can be sought rather than dispatched by an uninspired campaign.

The slams grew stronger and more direct. The *Times* reported that "the Democratic Party has also been asking Gore supporters to flood the Nader campaign with e-mail messages urging him to drop out of the race." As for Gore himself, he was advised to stay aloof from these roadshows; instead, he invited people to look at his record. But he did provide a touch of vintage Gore-the-pendulum when he told KIRO-TV in Seattle, "I don't want to use the argument that a vote for him is a vote for Bush—that may be true."

The most flailing performance was that of Patricia Ireland, president of the National Organization for Women (NOW), who, like Gloria Steinem, questioned my stands on women's rights. Had she checked our Web site, she would have seen my adoption of the entire NOW program, backed by initiatives that started long before she entered this important field. And had she checked NOW's own files, she would have come across a highly publicized letter from her predecessor, Molly Yard, sent to advocates of women's rights, including me, in 1990, announcing an exploratory commission "to examine the failings of our political parties, as well as of our political leadership, and to consider the possibility of a new political party."

What the press did not report was that the Democrats were also making these drives against my candidacy in the states where they were comfortably ahead, such as New York, to drive the Green Party under 5 percent and preclude federal funds in the next election. One can only guess at the price the Democrats paid by diverting millions of dollars in advertisements, both directly and through their proxy organizations, like the League of Conservation Voters, NARAL, and Planned Parenthood, away from use against the Bush-Cheney corporate machine. Their view was that it was better to focus their resources on taking away votes from a small party of conscience than applying their efforts to depress the votes of a large party of contrivance.

There were a number of operational assumptions behind this strategy. One was that the great bulk of Green votes would otherwise be Gore votes. Not true. Exit polls by Democratic pollster Stan Greenberg showed that 25 percent of our voters would have voted for Bush, 38 percent would have voted for Gore, and the rest would not have voted at all. Another was that the conniptions over the Green vote were not stimulating—rather deterring—the Democrats into getting out more of their own votes. This did not happen, as Senator Paul Wellstone concurred when he said that the Green Party was stimulating a greater GOTV by the Democrats. A further assumption—this one correct—was that Gore would not try to take away the Green issues more explicitly so as to deflate the latter's voter turnout. A fourth and final premise under their "sky is falling" alarms was that a Bush election would end "a woman's constitutional right to choose," as Kate Michelman, president of NARAL, stated in its $500,000 ad buy in late October. (Footnote here: Confronted with this charge on ABC's *This Week,* I technically answered like a lawyer that the states would have the jurisdiction in the unlikely event that this occurred. Gore partisans desperately used this to charge that I was belittling *Roe* v. *Wade.*)

George Becker, president of the United Steel Workers of America, wrote me in October saying, "I can say with certainty that as President, George W. Bush would sacrifice the Arctic National Wildlife Refuge and would sign legislation to bring back company unions through a Team Act and wipe out workers' rights to over-time pay through passage of a Comp Time bill—not to mention championing National Right to Work, gutting OSHA, and pushing for Paycheck Deception laws." Was there no confidence that the Democrats, even before they took control of the Senate (due in part to the Green Party spillover vote), could block all these proposals? I wonder whether Mr. Becker also thought that as an outspoken "free trader," President George W. Bush would never impose anti-dumping tariffs on foreign steel imports? But in June 2001, he did. Bush and his fellow Republicans will always place the party's survival ahead of any embedded ideology.

The point is this: It is incumbent on all these liberal groups to stop their "all will be lost" mentality if they are ever to go on the offensive and strengthen their political muscles among an aroused citizenry. Instead, the underlying unspoken premise of their assertions is: Don't you run at all, progressive third parties. We Democrats are entitled to all such votes.

The last to join the "A vote for Nader is a vote for Bush" caboose were the prime vested interests against corporate violence and fraud—the trial lawyers. On October 27, 2000, Fred Baron, a friend for thirty years and president of the Association of Trial Lawyers of America (ATLA), sent an e-mail to their tens of thousands of members urging them and their family, friends, and clients not to vote for me. Baron, who credits an address by me at his law school in Austin, Texas, for changing his mind as a student from becoming a tax attorney to becoming a pioneering trial lawyer of today, now fabulously wealthy, warned his membership that voting for me would help enact Bush's "draconian programs of federal tort 'reforms' that will severely limit every American's legal rights and the authority of citizen juries."

Baron was right on one point—Bush is a mindless pusher for laws that shield corporations from being held accountable. I call this position "tort deform," and for at least fifteen years the trial lawyers and my consumer allies have been fighting a defensive battle with the corporate "tortfeasors" lobby in all fifty states. Not just Republican but often Democratic state legislators and governors have sided with the corporations and insurance industry to slice away again and again portions of this civil justice protective and deterrent system. Their lurid propaganda about out-of-control verdicts contradicts the facts. Civil lawsuits for harm from product defects and medical malpractice have been level or declining in the past decade, and total upheld verdicts and settlements are less than what we as a country spend on feeding and caring for dogs and cats. According to the RAND Institute for Civil Justice, 90 percent of people injured don't even file a claim for compensation. Moreover, 98 percent don't file a lawsuit. And according to the Ernst and Young accounting giant, total liability costs for all businesses are less than $5.20 for every $1,000 in sales and have been declining yearly. Nonetheless, companies are relentlessly pressing to avoid what Bush wants for individuals—"consequences" and "responsibility."

It is, of course, natural for these incorporated giants to make sure they are free to litigate to the skies and, indeed, corporations suing corporations is the fastest-growing form of civil litigation. There have been many defeats and few victories in both state legislatures and Congress for defenders of the civil justice rights of the American people.

For a Democrat to stand on the floor of any legislature, including Congress, and extol the best tort law system (despite its flaws) in the world, honed by thousands of court decisions over a century, is as rare as a sighting of the Australian dodo. Although trial lawyers are their most clinging loyalists, most Democratic politicians think too visible an association with their cause leads to a taint in the minds of business contributors and power players. But having nowhere to go, the trial lawyers have become very forgiving of their national Democrats, while continuing to pour money into their coffers. Eleven times, Bill Clinton signed mini–tort deform bills (e.g., on biomaterials immunity and general aviation planes) into law. In 1998 he was openly prepared to sign the first across-the-board federal preemption of state tort law in several areas, but a fortuitous sharp dispute between two industrial lobbies stalled the bill in the Senate.

In 2000, ATLA received more bad news. Al Gore chose their nemesis, Senator Joseph Lieberman, as his vice presidential running mate over Senator John Edwards, who was a successful trial lawyer from North Carolina. In addition, Gore surrounded himself with an inner circle of longtime advisers and speechwriters right out of a tort deform nightmare. There was Carter Eskew, a lobbyist for tobacco and drug companies, Peter Knight, a lobbyist for the drug industry, Jack Quinn, who after leaving Clinton's White House became a lobbyist for the corporate tortfeasors, and Gore's brother-in-law, Frank Hunger, who had given trial lawyers and consumer advocates fits when as a high official at the Justice Department he helped to preside over the weakening of tort law. There were no environmental or consumer advocates anywhere near Gore's inner circle. And it was significant that Gore insisted that Lieberman change his tune on school vouchers and other neoliberal detours, with one exception. Lieberman was allowed to remain defiant in his view that tort law was a "lottery" and out of control. In public statements and letters, I tried hard to get Gore and Lieberman to go after Bush for his mindless attacks on lawyers, judges, and juries, but to no avail.

Obviously, trial lawyers, when cornered, are a very compliant lot. The Democrats would only have had to remind them that they could be Bushwhacked if their support faltered. So it was natural for Baron and his colleagues to transfer this fear to the Green Party's voters. A few trial attorneys have become immensely wealthy in the past decade, owing to some creative breakthroughs against the asbestos, tobacco, prescription drug, automobile, and chemical industries. With the legislatures and executive branches (the regulatory agencies) pretty much inactive in that period on health and safety enforcement, the courts were the only outlet left for justice. Even with that door still open, it was no mean feat to persuade a mostly conservative judiciary at trial and appellate levels to recognize the ancient principle: For every wrongful injury there must be a remedy.

These lawyers are risk-takers. They invest a great deal of their money in these cases without a guarantee of any recompense, because their fee is contingent on securing compensation for their clients. Losing these cases brings the lawyers nothing. Indeed, it might even backfire. Over the history of American common law, attorneys have brought cases that on appeal produced a wholly unexpected decision that established a precedent damaging to the rights of the aggrieved across the board. Further, attorneys sometimes miscalculate, to the detriment of their clients, by urging rejection of a settlement offer and then losing everything in court. So it was surprising that these regular risk-takers with other people's legal fates, and that of the law generally, would not understand that a progressive political movement, at a time when their preferred candidate, Al Gore, was running against a bumbling governor from Texas with a horrible record and should have defeated him handily, was a sensible way to give the Democrats a wake-up call.

A political jolt was needed on behalf of millions of Americans who lose life, limb, or their health to reckless or worse misbehavior. Unfortunately, that was not the way many prominent trial lawyers saw the scene. Along with the rest of them, ATLA would not only settle for less from the Democrats as long as the Republicans were worse (with few exceptions), but had developed a bad habit over the years of almost never fighting back whenever they lost a legislative battle to recover their clients' rights. This signaled to the industry bosses that they did not have a second-strike capability. Instead, the ablest, most experienced attorneys were usually able to readjust their practices to new fields of litigation as they were driven away from previous areas of practice.

Letters from several other attorneys urged me to drop out before Election Day. Interestingly, none of them ever suggested that Gore-Lieberman be asked to stand strong against tort deform. Not that Gore-Lieberman would ever have made such a commitment. Nor would I have believed them had they done so. But it did reflect just how depleted the bargaining power of the trial lawyers had become.

After the election, a number of trial lawyers decided to inflict collective punishment on several citizen action groups, which I founded but no longer ran, by ceasing their charitable contributions. It wasn't the amount that did damage—their entire donations did not reach much more than 1 percent of all these groups' budgets. It was the stupidity of rupturing their relationships with consumer groups that the arch tort-deform corporate attorney Victor Schwartz believed saved them from more than a few defeats. To a reporter for *Legal Times*, Schwartz figuratively rubbed his hands with glee and said he was looking forward to attacking "the turtle without its shell on it. That's Nader. They're abandoning a man who stood with them for thirty-two years through thick and thin."

I have yet to hear any of these indignant trial lawyers, who were so quick to blame us for Gore's defeat, credit us for making it possible for the Democrats to reach fifty-fifty with the Republicans, which set the stage for the Republican Senator Jim Jeffords's switch to Independent and the control of the Senate and its committees to the Democrats. They can now stop any Bush tort deform.

Finally, I would contend that for their issues, trial lawyers, as I write this, are better off with a Democratic Senate than with a wobbly Gore and a defiant Lieberman in the White House facing a Republican-dominated Congress. And as for judicial nominees, if Senator Patrick Leahy, chairman of the Senate Judiciary Committee, chooses to exert as much influence over Bush's proposed nominations as Senator Orrin Hatch, his predecessor, did over Clinton's, the results should not be anywhere near as troubling as some Democrats fear.

The fissure opened by this modest Green Party campaign proved to be a much deeper fault line between liberals who believed there were no alternatives and liberals who had endured enough of the commercialized politics of concessions and broken promises in election cycle after election cycle. There is little disagreement on major policy issues, only on different kinds of urgency and expectations for the country. This schism was illustrated by the different approaches of two businessmen and two distinct constituencies.

For years, Sol Price, the founder of Price Clubs, and Bernard Rapoport, founder of the American Income Life Insurance Company, have been supporters of our projects. They are both in their eighties, major donors to Democratic Party candidates, often critical of the Democratic leadership, very liberal, and active philanthropists. Mr. Price believes in a tax on wealth, including his own large fortune. Mr. Rapoport is a stickler on breaking up big business under our antitrust laws. They are humane people with a similar worldview of "liberty and justice for all." When it came to the Nader-LaDuke campaign, however, they had distinctly different opinions. Sol Price was so upset that he placed a quarter-page open letter to me in the *Los Angeles Times* listing about a dozen differences he saw between the Democratic and Republican parties. After some words of praise for my past work, he ended with the message, "A vote for you is a vote for the Republican position on these issues." Alone among all my friends who publicly took this position, he made a courtesy call telling me what he was about to do. I responded by pointing out major similarities and antidemocratic positions adopted by both parties. I noted that his list did not weigh the difference between rhetoric and action. He would hear none of it.

Mr. Rapoport, on the other hand, could not have been more pleased with our campaign. His explanation was simple. "My father," he related, "used to tell me that he voted for Norman Thomas for president every time because every vote for Thomas was a push for Franklin Delano Roosevelt and the Democrats to be more progressive." By denying FDR his vote, he was sending his signal that the president must stand for the people's needs.

Then the ads against me started to run. One was printed November 6, released to avoid rebuttal just one day before the election, by a self-described collection of thirty-four "concerned scholars, writers, artists, and activists 2000." This ad won the prize for 100 percent false or wildly distorted charges. It erroneously accused me, among other examples, of saying, "If given a choice between Bush and Gore, I would vote for Bush," that "the repeal of *Roe* v. *Wade* would be of little consequence," that I was "never a champion of women's rights," and on and on. It is one thing for the signers themselves to make the charges. It is more disreputable for these professors and writers to attribute to me these false statements. I pity their students and TAs.

Among the signers were Professor Benjamin Barber (Rutgers University), John B. Judis (*The New Republic*), Harold Meyerson (*Los Angeles Weekly*), Sean Wilentz (Princeton University), and, of course, Gloria Steinem. These and other signers must have treated this advertisement as a standard form contract—don't even check the large print, just sign on the dotted line. Intellectuals becoming lemmings for a day. Possibly the most surprising name was Barber's, as he was known to be an independent thinker. Here is a man who, sitting next to me on a plane trip, made an incisive critique of the Clinton-Gore administration. Mentioning that he was a friend and sometime adviser to Bill and Hillary Clinton, Barber was slated to be appointed director of the National Endowment for the Humanities shortly after the 1996 election. At least he thought so. But the man who cut and ran from his nominees

Lani Guinier (Justice Department Civil Rights Division) and Peter Edelman (for the U.S. Circuit Court of Appeals) the moment Senator Orrin Hatch and some right-wing "think tanks" bellowed decided to buckle to political pressure and nominate someone else to that post.

Compare this fallacious eleventh-hour tirade to a political statement released on October 25, 2000, titled "Labor for Nader," endorsed by some 250 union activists and leaders. Our candidacy, it stated, would "present voters with clear policy alternatives and would offer the possibility for working people to register their disgust with the way in which money determines the choice of candidates." The Green ticket, the unionists wrote, presented "the most comprehensive and reasoned critique of the continuing inequities in our society and offered a humane alternative direction for our country." Moreover, they viewed our candidacy as the only one that was "talking about how unrestrained corporate power affects our political institutions, economy, media, culture and democracy." They followed these general observations with a lengthy list of our positions that were "of critical importance to working people and for the quality of life for all of our people." The final words address the "A vote for Nader is a vote for Bush" argument: "A strong showing by Ralph Nader will have a positive effect long past November. We have a chance to break with the past and raise the standard of political debate and decision-making in our country. A vote for Ralph Nader is not a vote for anyone else. It's a vote for the best candidate in the race. It's a vote against big-money politics as usual. It's a vote for our future." The political statement was paid for by the California Nurses Association, which had earlier endorsed our candidacy, and was signed by members of about twenty-four unions. Most of their union leaders already had endorsed the Gore-Lieberman ticket.

There you have it: good people on both sides, coming from different backgrounds and incomes, to be sure, and seeing the politics of their country from different perspectives. One is a politics of fear, the other is a politics of hope and democratic renewal. There is another difference in consequence. The liberal reverters or apologists for Gore were regaled and praised by the party establishment. The progressives who supported our ticket had much more to lose—risking ostracism, isolation, friendships cut off, loss of

opportunities, cessation of grants or contracts, and a general closing of doors. Sometimes these rejections materialized, sometimes
they did not. Who were some of these people?

I thought of the courageous Ralf Hotchkiss, a paraplegic from a
motorcycle accident as a teenager and now, in his fifties, a leader
in teaching Third World peoples how to build flexible, durable
wheelchairs with local resources. He was with us at the Oakland
rally, knowing that some grantors to his center at the University
of San Francisco might look askance.

I thought of Nicholas Johnson, the former very young chief of
the National Maritime Administration and a federal communications commissioner under Lyndon Johnson, who introduced me to
fifteen hundred people at the University of Iowa with a short history of progressive politics and his own personal rationale:

> I have worked for the election of Democratic presidents since
> Harry Truman in 1948. I have received three presidential ap-
> pointments from two Democratic presidents. I have run for
> Congress from Iowa as a Democrat. I have served the Dem-
> ocratic Party at every level, from local precinct chair to a
> Democratic National Committee task force. So it's not easy
> for me, this endorsement of a Green Party candidate. But the
> corporate corruption that engulfs both major parties has now
> reached the stage when we cannot afford to wait any longer.

You don't think he took brickbats after that declaration?

Or I thought of author Jeff Gates, a former staff director for
Democratic Senator Russell Long, chair of the Senate Finance
Committee, who ran on the Green Party ticket for the Senate from
Georgia. He not only burned his political bridges but also had to
endure being physically thrown out by a TV station manager from
a debate between Zell Miller and Mack Mattingly for standing up
in the audience and politely asking why he had been excluded.

The uncensorable Jim Hightower found his small progressive
media operation, which relentlessly and colorfully spoke for America's working families ("Dave Jones instead of Dow Jones"), cut
off from funding by Andrew Stern, president of the Service Employees International Union (SEIU). Questioned about this at a
public session after the election, Stern murmured, "Hightower is

my friend. We'll be talking soon." Even Tony Mazzochi, founder of the Labor Party, who stayed neutral, soon saw his group's funding cut by the Paper, Allied-Industrial, Chemical and Engineering Workers (PACE). Why? Because in his newsletter to blue-collar workers he displayed the precise positions on health care of Bush, Gore, and Nader. PACE's leaders were upset because on the comparisons Gore did not come out very well.

Life is full of the least worst choices or options. But politically there is no discernable end to that logic—it just goes on and on for one election cycle after another, as automatic fealty induces endemic manipulation. For Nick Johnson, the United Electrical Workers, and others who drew a line, there is a depth to the party's sinkhole that will no longer be tolerated. There comes a tipping point at which the probability of past established gains being weakened or rolled back by Republicans is far less likely than the probability of the Democrats continuing to adhere to policies and alliances that ignore or worsen mounting injustices and devastations, here and around the world. Most Democratic and independent critics of the party have displayed for many years extraordinary patience, but in 2000 some could no longer abide being taken for yet another cycle made by a party that shows no remorse for its decay and no promise for its resurrection.

There will be more citizens coming to this tipping point in future elections, if the Democrats don't wake up. The widespread feeling among younger Americans that politics is irrelevant to them cannot always be assumed to be immutable. It could transform itself into a political mobilization that leaves the Democrats behind, as the apathy of the 1950s turned into the activism of the 1960s. Seattle and its successors portend a challenge to the politics of corporatism, oligarchy, and exclusion that will not be content to remain on the streets protesting. The tired whine of "But the Republicans are worse" will fall flat as more young Americans take charge of their future and move, with their reenergized elders, toward the Green Party and parallel civic and political movements.

Back at our campaign headquarters, these contrasts between the proxies and the protesters were being mirrored in letters, calls, and e-mails that were streaming in. There was little time to handle this influx, so much was there to do in the closing days of the campaign. What our campaigners enjoyed were stories from around the countryside, and none more than schoolchildren persuading their chums about the Greens through debates and mock elections. We learned of a grizzled World War II veteran in New Jersey telling his neighbor half jokingly that he wouldn't fix the latter's leaking roof unless he voted for Nader-LaDuke. Youngsters and adults created poems and songs and designed clever buttons and postcards. Artists fashioned posters and colorful T-shirts ("Don't waste your vote on the wasters") with pithy exhortations about voting one's conscience.

And what further galvanized our campaign workers were the spontaneous initiatives of support from hometown USA. John Nichols, a writer for the Madison *Capital Times* and *The Nation*, told his readers about one event that warmed our hearts:

> In the crucial swing state of Wisconsin, the village of Belleville took a pre-election break for its UFO parade, an annual commemoration of a supposed Halloween visit by aliens some years back. Bush and Gore backers were no-shows. But there, between the Brownies and the Belleville Dairy Queen, were forty Nader supporters, almost all of them from nearby farm towns. They carried a banner reading RALPH NADER IS OUT OF THIS WORLD and handed out packets of seeds with a reminder to "plant a seed for democracy on November 7."

Better than all the pithy phrases of our cooperative minds in Washington, from rural Wisconsin came the quintessential point of the Nader-LaDuke campaign: "Plant a seed for democracy."

Fourteen

THE ELECTION STRETCH DRIVE

For all the experience that the Republicans and Democrats had in previous campaigns, the last four weeks before Election Day were dull boilerplate. With the polls as their dim searchlight, the standard operating procedure was to increase the number of stops per day, repeat the few sentences that your consultants say are hitting the bells, also don't try anything new or impromptu that may result in gaffes, be alert to any surprises or dirty tricks from the other side, and as the days become fewer, step up the pace to somewhere between frantic and frenzied. The final days are a whirligig heading for the final thirty-six-hour roller coaster. To the millions of people casually watching these rapid peregrinations and the thousands who showed up at airports or city squares to see the candidates, it must have had all the political substance of a beauty pageant. After all, didn't Gore appear on *Oprah* and discuss the "big kiss" between him and Tipper at the Democratic National Convention? Gore did try to speak about health care and education, but Oprah cut him off. This had to be up close and personal.

Eight days later, an anticipating Bush meshed with Oprah's motif and embraced her with a kiss. Observers thought Bush scored points over Gore's visit, because he discussed giving up alcohol at age forty, told viewers that he wasn't running on his father's name, and brought tears to his eyes when he remembered the birth of his twin daughters. Bush perfected this regular-guy image—a fellow you'd like to have a beer with—with his practiced statements that warded off potentially damaging criticisms. In answering charges of drunkenness and drug use, he would say, "When I was young and irresponsible" and "I made mistakes and I'm proud to say that

I've learned from them." The latter response worked, even when on November 2, 2000, the story broke that he had been arrested in 1976 for driving under the influence of alcohol near his parents' house in Kennebunkport, Maine. It worked like a charm, even obscuring the more damaging point: that he kept it secret all these years and might not have answered any questions about any prior record accurately. The disclosure, thought at the outset to be a last-minute disaster, had no legs and petered out with a shrug of Bush's shoulders.

Appearing with Gore on *Saturday Night Live* on November 4, Bush made much fun of his verbal stumbles. He referred to himself as initially "ambilavent" when he was first invited on the show, since he considered some of its comedy "offensible." Sometime in the middle of the year 2000, George W. Bush had become Teflon-Reagan redux. Nothing that Gore hurled against him stuck, but the vice president used little of the devastating contents of *Shrub*, Molly Ivins's bestselling book on Bush's business and political deficiencies.

Gore did not make more of Bush's dismal record in Texas, so ably depicted in Ivins's report, because doing so would have required him to be specific, naming company names and offending his own contributors in the business community. It would have also exposed his own administration's lackluster performance, such as its weak antipollution enforcement and the toxic border mess in the state of Texas, among other jurisdictions. So Gore, ever the policy wonk, hewed to the arcane assault on Bush's proposals. The elder Bush succeeded in 1988 by taking apart, however distortedly, Michael Dukakis's boast of the "Massachusetts Miracle." People remember Bush charging that Dukakis allowed the pollution of Boston Harbor. This is a memorable image that people can relate to in their own community. In contrast, watching Gore on television, in that flat voice, say that his plan on prescription drugs does this, but Bush's plan does not do that, simply does not connect well, given that Bush blurred the issue just by having any plan at all.

The nonpartisan Rand research group released a report on October 24, which declared that "student gains on standardized tests may overstate educational progress in Texas," adding that "the immense test-score gains by black and Latino students in Texas appear to be the result of intensive drilling (i.e., teaching to the test) in order to pass the tests" and that the "massive" number of Texas dropouts "misleadingly shrinks the test score gap." One might have expected this nationally publicized report to expose both the educational record of Bush's governorship and his plan to take this intensive testing to the rest of America. "Shrub" shrugged it off, saying the timing of the report was "suspect." Massive television advertising by the Gore campaign against Bush's positions on Social Security, his tax cut that will lead to deficits again and jeopardize Medicare, and his unreadiness to lead the country did not score with many undecided voters.

Bush, on the other hand, really got under Gore's skin with his "values" attack ads. Two new ads on television in twenty swing states said that Gore could not be trusted and reminded the voters of improprieties, sexual and fund-raising, of the Clinton-Gore regime. Bush also made much of Gore's frequent exaggerations. This message was coming from a man who admitted being a wastrel until the age of forty, who was renowned for fumbling the facts beyond "young and irresponsible," and who sold his entire primary campaign to corporate-interest contributors by rejecting federal matching funds.

In late October, Gore allowed Bush to put him on the defensive. Campaigning at a rally in Little Rock, Gore denied Bush's accusation that he was a "big-spending, big-government candidate." Instead, Gore promised to "promote choice and change, while making government smaller and smarter than ever before." On the defense again. How much better it would have been to remind his audience of what the federal government had succeeded in doing for this country over the past century—from public works in their communities to Medicare, from safer cars and drugs to lifesaving medical breakthroughs. The conservative Brookings Institution had recently released a report documenting fifty major contributions that have improved our country from the federal government in the twentieth century—in case Gore did not have the research.

On November 2, the Gore campaign bought television time for a spot that went after Bush's record in Texas in a general way (pollution, poverty, etc.) and ended with the line, "Is he ready to lead America?" I wonder which Gore adviser found historical precedent to persuade them that the "readiness" charge ever worked.

George Will was overheard on Sunday in ABC's *This Week* Green Room saying, "Hell, I don't think he's [Bush] prepared, and I'm voting for him." On the same day, Clinton went on the Tom Joyner nationwide radio show and, in a comment that must have chilled the Gore crowd, said that by electing Gore, Americans "can get the next best thing" to a third Clinton term.

In late October, Pat Buchanan, on the Reform Party ticket, captured the conservative populist sentiment with a new ad titled "Auction." It showed George W. Bush and Al Gore being auctioned off to the wealthiest bidder, including a Buddhist monk, a Chinese general, a Hollywood couple, and a Texas oilman. Even *Washington Post* cartoonist Herblock couldn't resist conveying his sense of how unpersuasive Gore and Bush were. He drew two men, one with a "For Bush" button and one with a "For Gore" button, saying to each other, "I [the Bush button man] made my decision after listening to Gore" and "I [the Gore button man] made mine after listening to Bush."

Political advertisements on television have been studied by many academics and consultants for their effects. Books have also been written about "how political advertisements shrink and polarize the electorate" (the actual subtitle of the 1995 book *Going Negative* by Stephen Ansolabehere and Shanto Iyengar). In my opinion, these wall-to-wall television buys can lull the candidates away from the need to engage the citizenry so they can participate in elections instead of being spectators at the passive political parade.

On a trip to South Florida to support the many Floridians striving to preserve what was left of the great Everglades, I met many activists who had been begging Gore for months to come out against the real-estate interests bent on converting Homestead Air Force Base into a commercial airport. They had strong arguments. The proposed new airport would be located in an environmentally sensitive area, eight miles from the Everglades, two miles from Biscayne National Park, and ten miles from the Florida Marine Sanctuary. The airport would be expected to handle 230,000 flights per year and emit tons of air pollutants daily. In March 2000, the EPA announced that it had "serious environmental objections" to the airport. The Interior Department found that it "could have a series of negative consequences" on the fragile coral reefs and waterways of nearby parks. Even with his own administration's two pertinent agencies warning about this development, Gore repeatedly refused either to support or oppose the airport conversion, claiming that he was waiting for the Air Force's environmental study.

The Everglades were not remote from Gore's knowledge. He spoke often about the need to rehabilitate them with large infusions of federal money. In 1992, Gore wrote in his book *Earth in the Balance* that "the destruction of the Everglades is being actively subsidized by taxpayers and consumers through artificial price supports for sugarcane, a crop that otherwise would never be grown in that area." Nevertheless, when the chips were down, he typically threw indecision and procrastination at the large numbers of South Floridians who wanted more than a Green Party candidate to support their prudent conservation of the Everglades, a critical ecological oasis in the midst of gigantic sprawl. Gore could have drawn a bright line between him and Bush. This was another "what if" that might have brought Gore the state of Florida and the White House. And this is a rather small example of how people who wanted responses to their participation were ignored. This is the way campaigns often incite cynicism and turn off voters.

I had my own misgivings about buying television spots. First, we had so little money that whatever we could buy would reach only a fraction of the population. Bill Hillsman, who came up with the Priceless Truth ad, naturally differed. He believed if the ad was really fresh and compelling, the news media would pick it up as a news story and reach far more people than the original ad could. That was really the only rationale for trying to break through the blizzard of commercials by the major parties and their candidates, from the national to the local, that were flooding the airwaves. So the Hillsman team came up with a message portrayed by child actors who were paid union scale, with the permission of their parents.

At first I rejected the ad, clever as it was. It was October and I went down the list. Why couldn't we use the money instead for campaign vans visiting communities? Too late to find and train the people to staff them, and we have several on the road already, was the answer. Why can't we find a thousand people and pay them for a week to get out the vote in selected precincts? An enormous undertaking given the shortness of time and staff was the reply. So the children's ad played on television and radio in a few markets such as California and New York. It received some news coverage, but nothing like the MasterCard parody.

The Internet ushered in a vote-swapping network in October designed to encourage Gore voters in Gore landslide states such as New York to promise to vote for Nader if a Nader voter in a swing state such as Wisconsin would agree to vote for Gore. As one entry touting this idea said: "This is legal, and has the advantage of letting both candidates end up with the same totals. . . . It depends of course on personal honesty to be successful." In a few states it may not be technically legal, but who would know about any violations? Indeed, who would know whether this swapping occurred much at all? There is a secret ballot in the country. When asked about this suggestion, I described such exchanges as diverting people from voting for the person they believe in and urging others to do the same. The polls will prejudge outcomes; vote swapping shouldn't turn such predictions into practice. Nonetheless, there were well-intentioned people, like law professor Jamin Raskin, supporting vote swapping who wanted both Gore to win and Nader-LaDuke to receive as many votes as possible.

During the last ten days before November 7, I had to decide how to divide my time between field campaigning and mass media in Washington. Unlike Gore and Bush, who had private jets, I couldn't do fifteen cities in thirty hours. The experts told us that only 15 percent of those who voted would make up their minds in the last week. So it made sense to spend time in Washington, D.C., to appear on *This Week* with Sam Donaldson and Cokie Roberts, followed by a very well-attended news conference at the National Press Club on October 30 for the foreign media. Reporters from other lands where Americans work and vote absentee showed a keen interest in my campaign, in part because of growing and established Green Parties in their countries.

My opening remarks at the Press Club focused on the successful propaganda of U.S. multinationals peddling their ideology in Western Europe and elsewhere—that the preconditions for the booming U.S. economy were deregulation, selling public assets to companies, less corporate taxes, and reducing public services. It was axiomatic then that these were also prerequisites for these countries, if they wished to be on the road to greater prosperity. I pointed out that this was a trap that should be uncovered and avoided.

That afternoon was spent on telephone conference calls with our field constituencies, covering culture and gender diversity, globalization, labor, environment, youth vote, agriculture, health care, senior citizens, and independent voters. That night I was picked up for an interview with Larry King. Larry King's media career is a textbook study of the differences between radio and television when it comes to discussions of issues and selections of guests. Larry had the largest late-night syndicated radio show in the country. They were feasts of vigorous dialogue and arguments between authors, politicians, civic leaders, actors, athletes, and other achievers with Larry's many callers. The sessions would go on for three hours. Then Larry switched to CNN television. Celebrities and the scandal of the week took over. If you were Hollywood, you were on. Flash, glitz, fluff, and personalities. I felt sorry for Larry, an old acquaintance, although he seemed to be having a great time and was making great money. However, apart from a few news coups, as with Ross Perot, he was not often astride the significant debates of our times, as he had been on radio. This evening, however, I was part of the pre-election cliffhanger.

Arriving at the studio, I met some of the other guests. Paul Begala was somber, saying only that if the Greens "get five percent, Gore loses." Senator John Kerry, who visited me right after he came back from Vietnam in the late sixties as an articulate protester against the war, mentioned the Supreme Court issue, and then explained the Scalia vote as senatorial deference to the president. And Larry's interview centered on how the Green Party candidacy would take votes away from Gore and help Bush. How did I feel about that possibility, should Bush become the next president?

As usual, I replied that we were building a long-term reform movement and that takes time. I noted briefly a number of our positions that neither Bush nor Gore would touch: renegotiating NAFTA and GATT into pull-up, rather than pull-down, international trade agreements, repealing the antiworker Taft-Hartley law, and reducing the influence of the munitions companies that are shaping defense policies in a post–Cold War period. When asked the same question about our campaign run, Senator Kerry and Paul Begala said it was unfortunate because the differences between Gore and Bush on the environment, women's rights, civil rights, foreign policy, campaign finance reform, and the Supreme Court were clear. Of course, there was no time for any of us to discuss whether there were actually sufficient differences or too many similarities or to talk more about the Greens' differences from both parties. Welcome to television, where the sound bite dominates.

The next day, after events in Dearborn and Minneapolis, I taped Ted Koppel's *Nightline* in the Twin Cities with Jesse Ventura. Koppel started out auspiciously by asking, "How important can third-party candidates be, since they rarely ever seem to win any elections?" I said to myself, Great, this program will be about what subjects we are advancing. Koppel then answered his own question by continuing, "Well, let's take the issue of Social Security. You don't win the White House without supporting Social Security— not these days, anyway. But when the issue first appeared as a major plan in the political platform of a presidential candidate, it was denounced as pure socialism, which was fair enough, since Norman Thomas was, after all, the presidential candidate for the Socialist Party. That was back in 1928. Thomas would run in every subsequent election through 1948. While he never came close to winning the presidency, he had an enormous impact on someone who did: Franklin Delano Roosevelt, who later made the notion of Social Security his own. So, there's one third-party candidate who never won an election but who changed our political landscape forever."

By this time, I have to say I was smiling. Imagine, a national television audience and a readiness by the esteemed host to entertain "major planks" in our platform. The large audience at the University of Minnesota was visibly stirring—no yawns. So then Koppel's first question was to Governor Ventura, and it was whether he thought I was going to cost Gore the ten electoral votes in Minnesota. Here we go again. Ventura astutely brought his answer back to how he came from nowhere to win the governorship in 1998. Turning to me, Koppel recited the polls on my candidacy and asked whether I thought they were accurate. We sparred a little, and before long it was time for questions from the audience. A local high school teacher asked whether after "women are con-

fined to back-alley abortions, our tax money is diverted to parochial school vouchers, our Bill of Rights perhaps replaced by a
police state—all because President George W. Bush has appointed
a few more Clarence Thomases, a few more Scalias to the U.S.
Supreme Court—would [I] look back with pride in what [I] have
accomplished this election?"

After informing her about the Democrats letting Scalia and Thomas through the Senate—nominations that I strenuously opposed
at the time—I cautioned against turning George W. Bush into a
Genghis Khan and asked what good is Gore if he can't beat Bush's
terrible record. I could have added, had there been time, that last
I heard the Republican Party didn't want to commit political suicide. The teacher, whether she was a plant or a concerned citizen,
showed just how successful the Democrats' scare tactics were.

Jesse Ventura was becoming upset with Koppel's questioning
and he told the host so during the commercial break. Back on the air,
sensing a little drama, Koppel asked him to repeat his complaint
about how tough Koppel and other interviewers are on third-party
candidates compared to their interviews with the major-party candidates. Koppel took amused exception in the exchange with Ventura, and then time ran out. So much for the promising Norman
Thomas/Franklin Delano Roosevelt opening. The audience was left
with Koppel emitting the words "often from the fringe . . . but
sometimes the spoilers" while the background pictures showed me
and our supporters. How bizarre! Most of our stands and positions
are supported by most Americans. Moreover, the majority in this
country support having more than two political parties and for me
to be part of the presidential debates. Some fringe, some spoiler. As
one woman nonchalantly told me while we were boarding an air
plane together, "You're trying to improve the country and they call
you a spoiler." Clearly, political astigmatism sees things through
different lenses.

We started November with a rousing gathering on the capital
steps in Madison and a super-rally in Milwaukee. The Madison
trip was memorable for being one of the two (the other at historic
Cooper Union in New York City) most intense and exciting audiences—mostly University of Wisconsin students attending an
hour-long taping of *Hardball* by Chris Matthews. The pace of the

repartee was supersonic and the sheer sound level of the students' reaction even stunned Matthews himself.

November 2 began at O'Hare and ended in Denver with a rally at the Paramount Theater. Phone interviews with local and distant talk radio were conducted all day long. The interviewers were going ballistic on Gore and the Green factor. The next day we flew to Los Angeles, where we were organizing the next-to-last super-rally, this one to be held at the Long Beach Arena. If you ask anyone who attended the Long Beach rally what they most remember from the event, it would probably be the stirring remarks of Ron Kovic, the Vietnam War veteran who returned home as a paraplegic and became a peace activist (remember the movie *Born on the Fourth of July?*).

To thunderous cheers, Ron Kovic drove his wheelchair to the microphone. "Thank you for coming to this historic gathering tonight," he started.

> We are going to change America. Never doubt for a moment that you are part of an important turning point in the history of this country. Not only does your vote count in this election, but because you have decided to have the courage to step forward and to tell America what you really feel, you have begun the process like a gigantic wave that is going to sweep this country into an entirely new time and era.
>
> Thirty-two years ago I was paralyzed in the Vietnam War. Millions were wounded and hurt on both sides, both American and Vietnamese. We learned about a policy that did not care about lives. We are gathered here tonight to say that we believe in the preciousness of life. We believe that this country can be more caring, more compassionate, more beautiful, more sensitive. We know . . . I want to know someday that the sacrifice I made in Vietnam was not in vain.

great!

Ron Kovic's words only begin to convey the intense passion and gravity of his presentation and what the thousands of people knew he had endured during and long after the Vietnam War—the pain, the torment by others for crossing over to help lead the antiwar movement, the personal agony of his paraplegia, the immense inner drive to make his life one of meaning, inspiration, and a lasting focus on humanity, his capacity for love and caring. His introduction was both prologue and Promethean. He reflected those precious intangibles of character that float into the minds of those who listen to him.

Leaving California we were on our way to Florida—our most neglected large state. We had spent only two and a half days there since February, and our supporters were not happy, especially in the Miami area where this would be our first visit.

We arrived around four P.M. and went quickly to a series of one-on-one interviews with newspaper and television reporters, including one by a ten- or eleven-year-old boy whose questions, predictably, were the most thoughtful of all. The rally afterward at the Radisson Center was for only one hour, but that was time enough to hear two additional issues on people's minds: the Homestead Air Force Base conversion and the compulsory uprooting of citrus trees due to a citrus canker. During this quick trip people kept asking us why Gore wouldn't take a stand on Homestead—"he would receive so many more votes," one middle-aged woman kept repeating. Little did we know how razor-thin the result would be.

We landed back in Baltimore just after ten o'clock that night. The next day—Sunday—I appeared on *Meet the Press* with John McCain and Ross Perot. Perot took the occasion to repeat his very recent support of George W. Bush. We chatted briefly in the Green Room. When asked by Tim Russert about me, he said a kind word but declared, "This horse isn't in the race." McCain, fresh from his losing battle over the proposed criminal penalties amendment, in the aftermath of the many Ford Explorer/Firestone tire crash fatalities, said, with some revulsion, that the vote was made into a "litmus test" for members of Congress by the auto industry.

The event that evening was the last super-rally, at the cavernous and very expensive MCI Center. It was also a subject of controversy inside our campaign. The previous ten days devoted to planning and attracting people to this large gathering took away, in the minds of some staffers, from time and resources needed for getting out the vote nationwide. I favored the rally for two reasons. First, I was under the impression that the field representatives in the various states already had their roles defined and would not be affected other than possibly to have another national story to buttress their efforts. Second, I wanted to have the final super-rally in the most heavily African-American city in our country to publicize its disenfranchised status and miserable neglect before the large turnout of national and international media. As the only capital district of any democratic nation in the world to deprive its residents of voting representation, the District of Columbia bears the brunt of presidential campaigns. Washington, D.C., is treated as the whipping boy and pilloried as a nest of officious bureaucrats.

Congress essentially rules the District in spite of a locally elected government. Congress controls the purse strings, can and did replace the elected D.C. governmental authority with an appointed Financial Control Board, can overturn popular referenda, and is the ultimate veto on just about everything done by public authority there.

This was not an event that we expected would attract black voters to the Green ticket. From the beginning, I knew that the Democratic Party, having made its mark with civil rights advocacy in the sixties, had the allegiance of all but a few black voters. Still, from the beginning of our campaign, I made every effort to show how the Democratic Party should stop lunching off its past and get moving on subjects dear to the hearts and minds of African Americans and Hispanics nationwide. Because people in low-income areas vote Democratic, the Republican presidential candidates don't bother campaigning there, while the Democratic presidential hopefuls take them for granted. For years, the Democrats, led by Clinton, would refer repeatedly to helping "the middle class" as if the poor did not exist.

The point is that the goal of campaigning should be more than seeking votes. It is an opportunity to connect with people who have been ignored, who see in politics nothing for them, who are never asked for their insights and worries and aspirations. I did that all over the country, where presidential candidates are seldom seen or heard. I conversed on black talk radio—local and syndicated—and on the Monday before Election Day accepted the Reverend Al Sharpton's invitation, which he had extended to other presidential candidates, to meet with neighborhood people, local leaders, and media at the National Action Headquarters in Harlem. There, I urged the transition from chants of "We Shall Overcome" of the civil rights movement and "We Are Somebody" of the past twenty years to "We Want Power." Freedom is participation in power— the necessary expansion of democracy to include the dispossessed and the voiceless. The devastation of community, I said, guarantees bad schools, unlawful police violence, the failed war on drugs, and a criminal injustice system with its sharply discriminatory prosecution. It also guarantees another kind of pervasive violence—the silent cumulative type that comes from lead-based paint poisoning of little children by the tens of thousands yearly in rotting apartments, the pollution that feeds an epidemic of asthmatic illness, the contaminated food that distributors dump into ghettos, the obstacles that block access to equitable health care, the infant mortality, the inequities in the delivery of municipal services such as fire fighting, community policing, and law enforcement of building safety codes in low-income neighborhoods, and the environmental racism that exposes poor families to incinerators and other intensely polluting facilities and toxic dumps. The discrimination inherent in "breathing while black" deserves at least equal attention to "driving while black."

A meticulous understanding of rebuilding community has to be consciously revived or originated. The old saying "Without community there is crisis" is very apt. Community health clinics, food and other cooperatives, such as community development credit unions and repair shops, bind the neighborhood together. Ending redlining by banks and insurance companies breaks the vicious cycle of decay that undermines home ownership. That takes law enforcement. Community policing is a proven way to stabilize a fearful community, reduce the animosity toward the police, and diminish police brutality because the police live where they work. All this nourishes a climate for attracting private capital that doesn't have to be so heavily subsidized by the taxpayers because there are needs to be met for people who can afford to pay for them in a safe environment. All this comes together in a larger framework embracing a comprehensive effort to abolish poverty and destitution through community building and community self-reliance and self-sufficiency.

Instead of presenting this social symphony, many Democratic politicians who address the underclasses avoid facing these necessary prospects by playing up the fear of Republicans who, they say, would take away what little these people now possess. There are always enough grants, patronage, and get-out-the-vote money to secure the political loyalties of many local leaders. This pattern has been resisted by African Americans like <u>Lawrence Hamm</u>, who, *Kusp?* since he was nineteen years old, with a stop at Princeton University's graduate school, has been organizing neighborhoods in Newark, New Jersey. There are hands-on leaders like Hamm in other cities, but there are far too few of them to turn the political dynamic away from sweet talk by the Democrats who have dominated the central cities for so many years, a few Republican mayors notwithstanding.

Too many black leaders are prone to this politics of fear. The summer annual convention of the NAACP in Baltimore invited Gore and Bush to address their members. I was not invited, despite the groundbreaking work we have accomplished in the areas of redlining, consumer fraud, environmental racism, health care discrimination, and biased educational standardized testing. Randall Robinson made calls on my behalf to his friends at the storied civil rights organization to have me make a presentation. When Bill Clinton had to postpone his appearance for two days, Julian Bond and Kweisi Mfume gave that afternoon slot to me. Then, suddenly, Hillary Clinton's people called and asked if she could fly down from New York and speak. We met in the holding room. She was pleasant enough, exchanging a few words about her having been on a committee with my sister years ago and our common interest in reducing global infectious diseases. She spoke before me and went beyond her allotted time, thereby pushing me further away from any news coverage. Whatever the motivation behind Hillary Clinton's last-minute arrival, it worked for her party. The next day's newspapers featured her appearance and ignored my substantive speech. The NAACP leadership was polite and cordial but clearly they were not into anything other than to defeat Bush and elect Gore without demanding a comprehensive agenda from the vice president. The next day, Gore gave his evangelical speech and told them, "I'll fight for you."

At the same time, Congressman John Conyers was releasing a statement praising Gore beyond hyperbole and dismissing my efforts on "issues critical to progressives." An example: "While Nader was fighting for a safer bus," Conyers wrote, "Gore was fighting so that Rosa Parks could get a seat on the bus." There is a "Gore-like" calendar problem here. Rosa Parks refused to go to the back of the bus in Montgomery, Alabama, in December 1955. I was in law school then, where I wrote and spoke about civil rights violations. Al Gore was seven years old at the time. Twenty years later, well after the major civil rights laws were enacted, Gore was a twenty-seven-year-old newspaper reporter in Nashville.

All the same, thousands of people poured into the giant MCI Center that Sunday afternoon. Diverse bands were playing, and local speakers, including Jamin Raskin of American University Law School and the D.C. Greens, were making their views clear, as was Annie Goeke of the Association of State Green Parties. Tom Tomorrow, the nationally syndicated cartoonist, showed his political video and said a few words sharing his pictorial passion for justice through satire. There was a Chuck D video, and Adam Yauch of the Beastie Boys spoke, while Phil Donahue assumed the master of ceremonies role.

It was one great speaker after another. The Reverend Graylan Hagler was such a community force in Boston that when he left to work in Washington, D.C., it was front-page news in the *Boston Globe*. He quickly established focus when he led others to picket the D.C. headquarters of Fannie Mae (one of the world's largest corporations at the asset level), which received tax exemption from D.C. taxes through congressional enactment. Fannie Mae has a good deal. It escapes roughly $300 million in annual D.C. taxes, and through its tax-exempt foundation grants a tenth of that sum back to District charities. Hagler rose to speak: "Everybody keeps coming to me and saying, 'What do you think of these elections?' And I have to respond, 'What election?' My issues are not being addressed. The issues of working people in America are not being discussed. Nobody is addressing the issues of where I live, where my community lives, except for Ralph Nader."

Danny Glover held the audience spellbound as he spoke of his own struggles before and after his years as a community organizer. He declared that a Green vote was one that "means our vision of the world we want to see matters, that we are prepared to be participants in our own rescue, participants, not onlookers." He proceeded to recite the beautiful, poignant Langston Hughes poem "Let America Be America Again."

Jim Hightower and Michael Moore—our era's most evocative populist communicators—brought tears of laughter. And 1980 independent presidential candidate John Anderson raised our sights once again. However, it was up to Randall Robinson and Cornel West to speak to the African-American community about why it was time to leave the Democrats. Drawing on history, law, and the precedent of reparations for other ethnic groups, Robinson recently authored the compelling case for restitution from those who profited from a long and massive unpaid labor of black slaves, including businesses like Aetna, and state treasuries and the U.S. government. These reparations would take the form of institutional payments for the alleviation of conditions flowing from the destructive legacy of slavery and its de facto aftermath. "This is not about cash to individuals," wrote Robinson. And before anyone reacts in knee-jerk fashion, they should read his incisive book _The Debt: What America Owes to Blacks_.

But on that Sunday at the MCI Center, his impassioned, low-key words were intended to erase the myth of the day:

> For the better part of the century, the Republican Party has been hostile to the fundamental interests of America's black community. Consistently, Democratic Party candidates for the presidency have sought and received our support, only to turn their back to us upon assuming office. Nonetheless, for all my adult life, I voted for Democrats seeking the presidency. I cannot do that again.
>
> This is the course to be taken by one hundred million Americans who, on Tuesday, will choose to not vote at all. Were Ralph Nader not running for the presidency, I would be, for the first time in my life, among their ranks. They are not homogenous, though largely young and poor. They proportionately include women and men, black and white, Asians and Hispanics. They have dropped out because they intuit that their vote means nothing, that deals have been cut, that public policy has been bought, that jobs have been peddled, that favors have been traded, that big money has made folly out of our democratic exercise, fools of our citizenry.

Robinson's words have a way of sinking into one's recollections long after you hear them. When Cornel West completed the event, he drove home his belief, which he has conveyed directly to many of his friends in and outside of Congress, of where the line must be drawn:

> We will not be deterred by frightened liberals. We will not be deterred by short-sighted Republicans. We will not be deterred by mean-spirited neoliberals. We are on the move. Why? We are on the move precisely because we believe we are at an historic juncture. We are wrestling with a fundamental question: What are the conditions under which progressives will break from the two-party system?

Then it was my turn. The first twelve minutes of my address focused on the continuing denial to residents of the District of Columbia of rights held by all other Americans in the fifty states. Some in the audience later told me that it was a side issue that took away from the finale. However, I believed it was important to illuminate the colonial mentality of Congress, the affront to a largely African-American population that faithfully gives over 90 percent of its vote to the Democratic presidential candidates. I was also persuaded by the dedicated work of civic leaders Sam Smith, Ambrose Lane, Gail Dixon, Jennifer Ellingston, Scott McLarty, and many others who have fought so long for democracy in the District. How appropriate it was to conclude the event with all the speakers joining Patti Smith in singing with the audience "The People Have the Power."

The hallways outside the arena were filled with activists staffing tables that advanced D.C. statehood, living wage, health care, eliminating child poverty, an end to the death penalty, revoking the cruel life-destroying sanctions on innocent Iraqi people, protecting the global environment, free Tibet, and sustainable self-sufficient economies. The turnout, estimated at ten thousand by the *New York Times,* was gratifying. Amazingly, this rally was organized by our energetic campaign staff and volunteers in just a few days.

There was one major disappointment. Although our community volunteers distributed more than three thousand free tickets to black churches, union locals, and numerous neighborhood nonprofits only a few blocks away, there were not many African Americans in the audience. It will take much more effort by Green Party workers and supporters from black and Hispanic neighborhoods to encourage minorities to run for the many local, state, and national offices as Greens. For our efforts, we received 5 percent of the vote on November 7 in the District. Bush got 9 percent and Gore, without campaigning there, garnered 85 percent. Taken once again. No change foreseeable.

Here was my take on that day, as reprinted in the *New York Times*:

> The Green Party recognizes that every major social-justice movement in our history was made possible by a shift of more power to the people, away from the power that the few control. And it's way past time for a shift of power today from big business to the people.
>
> When slavery was abolished, shift of power from the plantations. Women's right to vote installed, that was a shift of power. Freedom to form trade unions by workers, shift of power from the industrialists to the workers. When the farmers started the progressive political movement, shift of power from the banks and the railroads to the farm areas and gave us political reforms for all Americans to enjoy to this day 100 years later. Power is the central contention of politics; that's what it's all about.
>
> If we don't have a more equitable distribution of power, there is no equitable distribution of wealth or income. And people who work hard will not get their just rewards. And the main way to shift power, if you had to have one reform, it's public funding of public elections. Clean money, clean elections.
>
> Clean money and clean elections to stop the nullification of your votes by special interest money. Just think about it: you go down to vote, you expect it to count, and the votes are cut off at the pass by fancy fund-raising dinners all over the country where fat cats pay off politicians for present and future favors and the politicians shake down the fat cats in a kind of combined symbiosis of legalized bribery and legalized extortion.

On Monday November 6, the ABC News/*Washington Post* poll, conducted between Friday and Sunday, showed voters supporting George W. Bush slightly more than Al Gore—48 percent to 45 percent, with a margin of error of plus or minus 2.5 percent. That morning I was back at the National Press Building taping short interviews with television stations in various cities through satellite hookups. There was no guarantee that these segments would actually be used on the noon or evening news, but we had to give it a try. Then it was off to New York and Harlem for a community meeting and a press conference.

Candidates and their associates are really on automatic in the last days of a campaign, trying simply to reach as many people as possible while the field representatives work to get out the vote. These reps from California to Massachusetts were telling us that the Gore forces were taking back the Gore voters who were thinking of voting for Nader-LaDuke but got cold feet when the race tightened. This was true even in the landslide states, whether for Gore or Bush. Voters, by and large, do not think about the electoral college; they vote as if the popular vote determines the outcome. Although we cautioned voters for months about this confusion—we wanted to receive more votes from the nearly forty states in the landslide category—it did not sink in for the most part. Carl Mayer tells the story that on Election Day in Princeton, New Jersey, he was passing out literature at a voting precinct. Along came a graduate student who chatted with Carl and heard his message that Gore had New Jersey locked up. The student nodded, said he was voting Green, and went inside and voted. Emerging from the building, the student met Carl again and said that although he voted for local and state Green candidates, he voted for Gore for president because the race with Bush was so close. Carl was left shaking his head in disbelief. Unfortunately, there were many people like that graduate student. This explains perhaps why polls conducted weeks after the election had 6 to 10 percent of the people saying they voted for us.

From New York City, it was up to Boston for an 8:30 P.M. overflowing rally at Boston University. My able and enthusiastic advance men, George Farah and Andy Goldman, were always one step ahead of us. We traveled to Portsmouth, New Hampshire, for a 10:30 P.M. rally and finally ended this marathon in Portland for a midnight gathering of 250 cheering Mainers. There greeting me was the grand old man of the Green Party, retired professor John Rensenbrink. A hardy veteran of hundreds of Green Party meetings and conferences in the United States and Europe, he is a very committed proponent of Ten Key Green Values: grassroots democracy, ecological wisdom, social justice and equal opportunity, nonviolence, decentralization, community-based economics, feminism, respect for diversity, personal and global responsibility, and present and future focus for sustainability

Wind-up political speeches are usually reduced to a series of one-liners. I compromised with my remarks, reducing the means and goals of our long-term reform movement to short paragraphs. These words were very well received and, I hope, remembered, for the gratifying road up the mountains of justice is long, and the trip is not for the weary but for the long-distance runners.

On Election Day I flew from Portland to Philadelphia. Theresa Amato thought it would be an appropriate symbol to end the campaign at eleven A.M. outside the Liberty Bell in front of Independence Hall. It was a terrific occasion for some serious words about the accomplishments of the campaign and the call for people to give us their votes if they believed in enhancing their common causes after the election. "The Green Party, coming in third, could be a watchdog party," I said, "holding the other major parties' feet to the fire, the more so, the more votes received. That is what your vote can mean with the votes of other Americans."

After a quick but delicious lunch at Judy Wick's White Dog Cafe, we took the train back to Washington and caught a couple of hours of rest in preparation for the Election Night celebration at the National Press Building's main ballroom.

Just before the start of the evening, I learned that America's most indefatigable environmentalist, naturalist, mountaineer, Bronze Star recipient in World War II, and institution builder, David Brower, age eighty-eight, had passed away. His family said that shortly before he died he sent in an absentee ballot for Nader-LaDuke. I had spoken with him last in mid-October when the environmental groups, some of which he founded (Friends of the Earth and the California League of Conservation Voters) or reinvigorated (Sierra

Club), were pursuing their zero-sum pro-Gore, anti-Greens treks across the country. Brower had long experience with the tendency of leading environmental organizations to concede and recede before the forces of reaction. After building them, he had a parting of the ways and each time he reacted by starting a new group—the last being the Earth Island Institute. Where there were rivers to be preserved, mountains and forests to be saved, parks to be created, air to be cleansed, and devastating technologies to be confronted, David Brower was there on site, networking, writing, and mobilizing. I remembered fondly how he would bring people together on Sundays for his famous strawberry waffle brunches at his Berkeley home. That is where I last saw him with Ross Mirkarimi, Danny Moses, Peter Camejo, and Tarek Milleron in June with his stalwart though ailing wife, Anne, and two of his four children. Brower mastered the facts, lifted the horizons for nurturing Planet Earth, and brought thousands into environmental action here and abroad. What was best about Brower was his extraordinary backbone and the enduring legacies of such stamina.

There were many people with backbone at the Press Club that Green Party evening. People who had lost friends, career opportunities, and business contacts. The prospect for such retaliation was high, all for daring to support a progressive third-party candidacy that challenged the dormant imperious Democrats and Republicans. They held firm.

(After the election, James Carville, the number-one apologist for Bill Clinton's frolics and detours, announced on television that he was going to "shun" me if I came into the same room where he was. "Shunned by Carville!"—it sounds like the trade name for a cheap line of clothing! Only weeks after the election was decided by the Supreme Court, Carville and Paul Begala wrote an article chastising the Democratic Party and urging it to become more aggressive—i.e., more progressive.)

With seven hundred people crowded into the ballroom chatting vivaciously and a variety of print and electronic media situated in the balcony trying to interview me and other key shapers of the campaign amid the din, the evening wore on without any confirmation of Gore or Bush winning, though there were many embarrassing projections by the networks. It was a very informal gathering. People were milling around, snacking, renewing old acquaintances and making new ones. I had a conversation with Greg MacArthur, who ran his own ads supporting our campaign, about strengthening the citizen movement. Lois Gibbs, the grand organizer of thousands of local groups against toxic environments, spoke, along with Todd Main and Theresa Amato. Winona La-Duke called in from the White Earth Reservation in Minnesota and was greeted with enthusiastic applause. There were pictures of the campaign's high points, such as the 450 new Green Party locals, on the large projection screen and posters lined along the walls. From seven P.M. to two A.M. they stayed, and still no one knew who won several of the swing states, including Florida.

Leading Democrats, gathering for their late-night election parties, were nervous. As the returns were coming in from the close states, where Greens were seen as affecting the outcomes, Hillary Clinton in New York City and Michael Dukakis in Boston delivered crude and violent remarks that repelled some of their close supporters and friends.

During the hectic network television coverage of the election results, Mike Wallace of CBS was trying to elbow his way between the Gore-Bush Ping-Pong announcements and projections to render his opinion on our election run:

Well, Dan, as I was saying when Al Gore's victory in Florida interrupted us, I've not heard the name of Ralph Nader until just a couple of minutes ago when Ed Bradley and Bob Schieffer were talking about it. This despite the fact—you know, they've spent up to one billion dollars, according to John McCain, during this campaign on television commercials, local and national. Well, despite all these commercials, that have assaulted and bored the dickens out of us the past few months, there were just two ads that caught my fancy. Take a look. [Footage shown of our two political messages done by the Hillsman firm.] They wouldn't let Ralph Nader into the debates. He charged ten dollars for a seat at his crowded rallies. He played it earnest and angry, mainly, in his speeches. And for millions of Americans, he managed to raise the questions and the doubts and to underline the disillusion that lots of us feel about how we wage our political campaigns.

Two days before the election, David Broder, dean of the *Washington Post* political reporters, gave his take on our election run. He wrote, "Who's put on the best campaign? Who's made the most of his available resources and opportunities?" He answered, "I think the answer has to be Ralph Nader."

Two days after the election, we had a farewell dinner with the campaign staff, about fifty of them. Many were leaving shortly to all points north, south, east, and west, so it was a sentimental parting between mostly young people who had become friends under the daily pressures of their tasks. I said a few words of gratitude and recognition at what they had accomplished and how enduring would be the memories as they looked back on campaign 2000 years hence. It was a lot of on-the-job training for many of them, even though they, like Stacy Malkan (journalism), Jonah Baker (computers), Megan Case (finance), and Darci Andresen (fundraising), brought relevant skills or transferable accomplishments to their responsibilities. I regretted not being able to spend more time with them at the campaign headquarters, but being on the road so much made my time back at the base one of rushing between responding to media and attending to pressing details with our manager, Theresa Amato. Throughout the dinner it was enjoyable chatting with each of them personally. I felt blessed by their idealism, enthusiasm, dedication, and self-reliance, but mostly buoyed by the thought that the coming decades would bring out their leadership qualities for the benefit of the society.

Our candidacy did not do as well as the polls indicated a week or two prior to Election Night. We expected that deflation because of the historic cold feet or "can't win" syndrome that afflicts most third parties especially given our exclusion from the debates. Those facts did not make it any easier to take. Nonetheless, in my remarks I summarized what we had achieved. The Greens now had the third-largest party in the county. We ran nearly three hundred local and state candidates and won nearly a third of them—a pretty good percentage for a tiny young party. Five towns in California, led by Santa Monica, have Green mayors. Thousands of people, young and older, had come into the political arena, and millions of conversations were sparked about serious issues confronting our country and what can be done about them. We brought out more than one million nonvoters, according to the exit polls. The campuses came alive with a new post-election organization, Campus Greens, establishing hundreds of chapters at universities and colleges around the country. From this campaign involvement and this new post-campaign organization will come a new generation of leaders.

Idealism took a stand in 2000, facing squarely the least worst malady of two-party politics. We got some progressive Democrats thinking out loud and more boldly to put their party on a reform track. We exposed the corporation known as the Commission on Presidential Debates as the rigged mechanism whereby the Republican and Democratic parties could exclude third-party candidates from reaching tens of millions of Americans on the same stage. This laid the groundwork for an entirely different, nonpartisan debate process in the future. We held the largest progressive political rallies in decades, bringing to the attention of many Americans what this campaign would mean for their daily lives and well-being. Finally, we gave heart to many committed Americans from a wide variety of backgrounds that there is a springtime party ready for them to grow at the local, state, and national levels in future elections and ready soon to be a watchdog party over the corporate uniparty. Then, of course, there are the intangibles of Americans, seeing the Green Party effort, deciding to engage their community in various ways. If the Greens keep expanding and stay closely aligned between elections with local and national community improvement or justice efforts, they will convey to an increasing number of Americans that new parties are important. They require the determination and patience of people over several election cycles.

Before calling it a day, I turned on the television at 3:30 A.M. to see Wisconsin Governor Tommy Thompson emphatically state that Bush had won Wisconsin and would be the next president of the United States. As it turned out, Bush lost Wisconsin by a few thousand votes and nobody knew who was going to be president until December 13, 2000, when Gore conceded and Bush declared victory.

Fifteen

CONCEIT AND CONFUSION

Following the November 7 deadlock came a torrent of recriminations and "what ifs." Amid all the arguments there emerged one
consensus: The election machinery is a mess—and not just in
Florida. It is prone to confusion by the voters, mistakes by the
counters, manipulation by the parties, and outright violations of
civil rights of voters who just happen to be poor, minorities, or
disabled.

Europeans are amazed that we have our own parties in charge
of state and county election commissions. Brazil, having recently
modernized its voting mechanisms, offered to send observers and
advisers to the United States. Our neighbor to the north shook its
collective head. In Canada, no precincts cover more than 350 voters. Every eligible voter is already registered to vote. Voting is by
writing an X on a paper ballot, and the nation finishes its counting
by eleven P.M. on Election Night. Former President Jimmy Carter,
who often is invited by foreign nations to serve as an election observer, says that the Carter Center in Atlanta requires three criteria
to be met before he agrees. One is that voters are able to understand the ballot procedures and the ballots themselves. Two, voters
have equal rights to have their votes counted. And three, there is
a central commission in the country to resolve election disputes.
Carter says that none of these conditions prevail throughout the
United States and that Florida violated all three.

The test of any democracy is whether after a national trauma
significant reform follows. The Democrats believed that not all the
votes were counted in Florida and that the election was stolen from
them even before the starkly partisan Supreme Court decision

CONCEIT AND CONFUSION 297

ended their misery. The Republicans know that the administration of the elections is a mess in other states as well and has and will haunt them in future elections. Even in 2000, Republicans were making similar allegations in New Mexico to those the Democrats were making in Florida. Chicago was in its usual questionable mode, where over 120,000 votes were not counted and would have been challenged had Illinois been close. From obstacles to registration to incomplete or erroneous voting lists (note the miscues regarding ex-felons in Florida), to machine errors, to confusing ballot designs, to poorly publicized changes of precinct locations, and on and on, millions of voters are not having their votes counted or counted accurately.

State laws and rules differ over what constitutes a valid vote or recount. Federal elections should call for federal uniform standards. Adequate funds need to be allocated to upgrade and modernize existing antiquities.

So what has occurred since the debacle of November? Florida passed a law that its backers claim will avoid similar failures in the future. That remains to be tested, however. The federal Civil Rights Commission report seems to indicate that Florida's problems are deep and resistant. But for the most part, despite two formal commission reports—one headed by Jimmy Carter and Gerald Ford and the other composed of state and local election administrators—and some congressional hearings, there have been no enactments of any reforms. Nor are any near the top of the agenda for either party. Should we be surprised? Probably not. But we should be outraged. A deep democracy with strong citizen organizations would not have tolerated such abuses in the first place. The responsibility for an enduring democracy starts with its everyday citizens, while the accountability for overriding and damaging our democratic processes starts with the concentrated controllers of power and wealth. Thus, elections should always embody a vigilant concern with the nature and distribution of power structures, as they affect serious necessities and injustices by their course and impact.

The very purpose of elections has been debased by both parties. Voting is supposed to be about the citizenry expressing its will with wide-angled hopes, views, proposals, revisions, and energetic participation in shaping the future through the robustly contested choice of delegated local, state, and national representatives. It is time for people to ask themselves how badly they want a democracy in which they actually have this deliberative power that is so critical to their well-being. Is it worth a few hours or a few days of their time in an election year? Can they be bothered to take time out from powerless routines with which they are so often displeased? The sins of politicians are in blurring, blunting, and blocking such encouragements and opportunities. They accomplish this largely by tightly connecting their reelection with the commercialization of the process. Accepting vast monies from corporate interests in return for granting plenary power to giant business is a deeply embedded political institution in our country.

Given the sources of their financial nourishment, neither Al Gore nor George W. Bush strayed from the blurring tunnel that they knowingly entered and remained in for the entire campaign. With the practical potential range of the stands they could have taken, they appeared to me to be very eager to tread the same ground in order to minimize any risks of being distinct. After the closest election in more than a century, I was by no means a unique observer of this "protective imitation" phenomenon. Consider the conclusions on this point by commentators who are not of common political background. Senator Daniel Patrick Moynihan told the *New York Times* on November 12: "There is no great ideological chasm dividing the candidates—each one has his prescription drugs plan, each one has his tax cut program—and the country obviously thinks one would do about as well as the other." From the far right a few days later wrote columnist Holmes Jenkins in the *Wall Street Journal*: ". . . in a duopoly market the competitors gravitate toward strategies of 'minimal differentiation.' When the vote splits 50–50, it tells you voters didn't see any large reasons to distinguish between the candidates, only small reasons (mostly cultural). . . . On the 'role of government,' an issue beloved by ideologues but of more situational interest to voters, the candidates agree to disagree, slightly."

On December 1, the African-American independent columnist for the *Washington Post* William Raspberry expressed his view: "Even this incredible mess of an election we are still trying to sort out is, at bottom, over fairly minor differences. . . . There just wasn't that much difference between them—which may be why half the American people voted for one and half the other."

Roger Simon has written two perceptive eyewitness accounts of the 1996 and 2000 presidential elections. In his book on Gore and Bush, *Divided We Stand,* he wrote, "Why was this the closest election in American history? Not because the candidates were so different, but because they were so similar." He cited exit polls showing that 55 percent of voters said they had reservations about the vote they had just cast.

Writing in the *New York Times,* Michiko Kakutani thought that "Citizen Clinton's tenure in the Oval Office helped shape the tone of the 2000 presidential campaign—a campaign uncommonly focused on personalities and character flaws, on sighs and smirks and spousal kisses." Clinton's own pollster, Stan Greenberg, said that "in the end, almost half the electorate threw up its hands, unable to differentiate the proposals of the two candidates." Even though Gore won the popular vote, his own campaign chairman, Bill Daley, still managed to tell Simon, "To tell you the truth, I think they [the people] never really liked either one of them."

Clearly, powerful adherents of either party thought this similarity analysis to be nonsense. Some pro-choice leaders believed that a Republican administration surely would take away the reproductive rights of women. And as Jenkins noted, the "NRA hears the midnight knock on the door every time a liberal gets elected."

Forty years ago, the Harriman doctrine (named after W. Averell Harriman, the very wealthy Democratic governor of New York) held that when liberals have no place to go, they do nothing. This was not true when it came to our Green Party candidacy. Some liberals in influential positions decided to shout, curse, boycott, blame, and retaliate against any groups, projects, or well-known people closely or remotely related to my campaign. Bill Maher, Susan Sarandon, Phil Donahue, Tim Robbins (see Appendix J), Ani DeFranco, and Michael Moore, among others, took real heat. Jim Musselman, a Pennsylvania music producer of folksingers whose proceeds are given to civic causes, was told explicitly by people in the industry that memories of his helping our Madison Square Garden rally will remain fresh. Public Citizen and the Center for Auto Safety, which I founded thirty years ago but do not run, lost contributions from rattled Democrats who believed that collective punishment was more important than helping the lifesaving causes in which they still believed.

Collective punishment reached a new low when pioneer New York aviation trial attorney Lee Kreindler, about whom I wrote articles in the 1950s, withdrew his pledge of ten thousand dollars to the Aviation Consumer Action Project (ACAP), which I founded in 1970. ACAP is the only consumer group in Washington, D.C., pressing the Federal Aviation Administration to advance safety, security, and service for air passengers. Paul Hudson lost his daughter in the Pan Am 103 crash over Lockerbie. He gave up his small real-estate law practice in Albany to devote his time to heading ACAP in memory of the loss of his child. Kreindler is the senior partner in a wealthy law firm that has dozens of Pan Am 103 cases. Even this tragic connection meant nothing to that firm when it came to helping a small, hard-pressed aviation safety advocacy organization.

Bob Cooper, when he headed HBO films, commissioned a made-for-television movie on my struggle with General Motors, later dropped by his successors, but wanted to take another look at getting it produced now that he had his own production company. In mid-2001, he sadly returned the screenplay to my colleague Wesley Smith, saying that people in Hollywood no longer liked me and he couldn't get it financed. Another Los Angeles production company that had been very interested in the movie told Wesley the same thing.

An idealistic, youngish CEO of a computer company visited the *Washington Post* in early 2001 to interest the paper in covering a conference the next day on Internet privacy—problems and solutions—where I was to be the keynote speaker. A consumer reporter heard him out, then she irrelevantly said: "People around here don't like Ralph Nader now." There was, one might expect, little chance of any coverage the next day.

Just as there were other loyalists in Congress and around the country unwilling to declare any conditions under which a progressive third party should ever challenge the Democrats, there was a large number of leading liberals who admired our efforts, even if they could not also support them. Sniffing the personal question, many reporters asked me how "did I feel" being rejected or ostracized as persona non grata. In a variety of verbal modes, my answer in essence was "my cup runneth over with pity" over the limitless tolerance these liberal Democrats have for their party's dominant swing away from its roots. I recalled an article written in the July 1970 issue of *Harper's* magazine by John Kenneth Galbraith titled "Who Needs Democrats? And What It Takes to Be Needed." He was wrestling with a question that today's Democrats should return to their frontal consciousness to ponder. Galbraith's words are worth recounting:

> The function of the Democratic Party, in this century at least, has, in fact, been to embrace its solutions even when, as in the case of Wilson's New Freedom, Roosevelt's New Deal, or the Kennedy-Johnson civil rights legislation, it outraged not only Republicans but the Democratic establishment as well. And if the Democratic Party does not render this function, at whatever cost in reputable outrage and respectable heart disease, it has no purpose at all. The play will pass to those who do espouse solutions. . . . The system is not working. . . . The only answer lies in political action to get a system that does work. To this conclusion, if only because there is no alternative conclusion, people will be forced to come. Such is the Democratic opportunity. Oddly, I do not think the prospect entirely bleak.

Not "entirely" but only interminably bleaker, it can be said thirty-one years later. There are today Galbraithian voices within the Democratic Party. They frequently write for *The Nation, The American Prospect,* or *The Progressive.* But their words are not listened to by the congealed powers that hold decisive sway over the party's downward drift. In an early June 2001 appearance before the National Press Club, I suggested some questions that Democrats should put to their party.

1. Are your differences with the Republicans tweaking at twigs or going to the trunk or roots of the issues? The Citigroup banking legislation of 1999 comes to mind. So do the so-called Freedom to Farm Act and the notorious Telecommunications Act of 1996.
2. Are your basic differences in position papers or party planks backed up by an intensity of advocacy, an expenditure of political capital, a willingness to turn off funders?

Here the widely reported tepid efforts by Clinton on behalf of campaign finance reform for eight years comes to mind.

Similarly, Congressional Democrats bewailed what they believed to be the horrendous consequences of Bush's tax bill—future deficits, undermining Social Security, Medicare, and the environment—yet declined to use their voting power to stop it.

3. Does the party work to strengthen its presumed constituencies? For twenty years, party leaders have declined to introduce the Consumer Protection Agency (CPA) bill. This was a major priority of President Jimmy Carter but was narrowly defeated by an extraordinary business lobbying effort in the House of Representatives in 1978. A CPA challenging misbehaving or inert regulatory agencies may well have anticipated and reduced the size of the savings and loan fiasco by exposing early the federal bank regulatory agencies' derelictions. The Democratic Party has not been serious about reforming anti–worker labor laws. Even in the ghettos, whose residents vote overwhelmingly Democratic, the party has never launched a major drive to deal with the street-level economic and higher-level corporate crimes that eat away low incomes and damage health and safety. The party has no counter to this daily erosion of people's lives, this daily mockery of the rule of law in those tormented neighborhoods. The Democrats know they cannot win without the votes of organized labor and the minorities. Still, the Democrats made corporate power ever more dominant during Clinton's eight years in office.

4. Can the party defend the country against the extreme wing of the Republican Party? The events of the 1990s would seem to answer a resounding no, as Robert Reich and other Democrats have shown to be the case at the local, state, and federal level.

5. Does the party have a clear commitment, by its actions, to a pro-democracy agenda? Beyond the very modest McCain-Feingold campaign finance reform bill, it has nothing in action, very little in rhetoric. Even the Progressive Caucus of some fifty members of the House cannot organize itself

around this agenda, cannot introduce the legislation around which people throughout the country could rally.

6. How does the party react to its own progressive wing? The Democratic Leadership Council (DLC) still believes Gore lost because of his progressive rhetoric. It could be that Mark Russell, the political comedian, had the best reason why Gore lost when, in one of his acts, Russell urged Gore to stop vacillating and "pick one of yourselves." The DLC's idea of recovering the House of Representatives has been to run right-wing Democrats against right-wing incumbent Republicans. The *Washington Post* on October 16, 2000, highlighted its page-one story with "Party Energetically Aids Conservative Candidates." Dana Milbank asked in the June 15, 1998, *New Republic*: "What Differentiates the Newest Democratic Candidates from Their Republican Rivals? Not Much." Milbank quotes the political director of the Democratic Congressional Campaign Committee, Paul Frick, as saying, "The only real litmus test we have is 'Who are you going to vote for for speaker?' " Milbank then adds: "And so, to pick up the eleven seats, separating them from majority status, they have embraced a group of conservative Democrats who are, to varying degrees, pro-life, pro-gun, pro–death penalty, pro–term limits, pro–school prayers—and, in everything but party affiliation, pro-Republican." One might expand the list to include pro-corporate, anti-consumer, anti-environmental, anti-labor, and pro–larger military contracts for more weapons systems. In short, more corporatist than conservative.

The conservative strategy failed for the Democrats in 1998 and 2000. Harry Truman observed long ago that faced with a choice between two conservatives, the voters will always opt for the real thing. Suppose it had won— the party would not have had a governing majority. Its right wing would have unseemly leverage over the party, joining Republicans on many votes, and hinting that it could switch to the Republicans if unduly provoked, as several blue-dog Democrats have done already. Without a well-formed philosophy of its historic role and roots, the party will always be giving the backhand to its progressive members, without whom, one must stress again, it cannot win national elections and not a few state ones.

7. How does the Democratic Party as a whole react to a challenge from the Green Party or other progressive third parties? With pouting animosity, visceral indignation, and petty retaliation. Notice what is left out—adopting long-overdue progressive agendas and taking away these issues, not in rhetoric but in deed, from these parties. Well, no more. The Democrats will have to start earning those progressive votes, instead of taking them for granted.

   For a while, the Green Party spillover vote should help some Democrats on Election Day, where there are no Green Party candidates on the ballot line. Greens bring out new voters as well. Senator Maria Cantwell is one of several elected Democrats who is well aware of what many of the 103,000 Green spillover votes meant to her 2,300-vote victory over Senator Slade Gorton in 2000.

Because both the Republican and Democratic parties are delivering our elections and our government to the highest bidders at the expense of our democratic processes, the trend toward independent candidates and third parties is likely to continue, as predicted in an August 2001 report by the Committee for the Study of the American Electorate. This will occur in spite of the formidable barriers erected by the DemReps in state legislatures and debate commissions. There is just too much to be accomplished, too many new horizons to be reached by the United States domestically and around the world. More voters will conclude in the future that both parties are unworthy, that both parties flunk, that the dwindling differences between the two parties are not different enough, and that the similarities between them are increasing to exclude real people and surrender to artificial persons (called corporations) the authority in which they are invested under our Constitution.

The transition from the Clinton-Gore to the Bush-Cheney administration agitated the D.C. real estate market more than the permanent corporate government that so pervasively controls the departments and agencies. The munitions industry and its consultants spent the intervening weeks trying to figure out which of their executives would journey to Washington, walk through the Pentagon's revolving doors, and take up their positions. The new regime will declare that bureaucratic waste reduction and military reform are coming, and what President Eisenhower called the military-industrial complex will yawn once again. They know that the game of exaggerating foreign perils (pointed out by General Douglas MacArthur in 1957) and exploiting the desire of the armed services each to have their own distinct overlapping weapons systems will relentlessly expand growth of the customary military budget in a post–Soviet Union era.

Meanwhile, the bankers barely looked up from their perch over the Treasury Department, Federal Reserve, and cosmetic bank regulatory agencies. Executives at Cargill, ADM, Monsanto, and Novartis fixed the names—not the numbers—on their Rolodexes of people at the top of the U.S. Departments of Agriculture and Commerce. This was basically the adjustment of the food and drug industry, the auto, railroad, and aviation companies, and all the rest of the many trade associations, law firms, and public relations firms. For them it meant new names about the same routines—get the government contracts, get the government giveaways, subsidies, and bailouts, and keep the government's cops off our backs. After a while, these routines become so automatic as to be tedious. So the more exciting frontier for companies and their lobbyists is breaking new ground in actively turning the government against its own people. That way, they can get the pliant John Stossels of the global media world to report to ordinary citizens on how rotten, wasteful, and corrupt the federal government is.

But there was one unique wrinkle in the transition. Along with his controversial last-minute pardons, Clinton cleverly issued a flurry of regulations designed to advance environmental, consumer, and worker interests. Most of them could have been issued in the first half of Clinton's second term. The celebrated arsenic in drinking water standard and the ergonomics standard were ready to be issued years ago. Western Europe had its arsenic standard in place long ago. Actually, the carpal tunnel syndrome proposal was ready for OSHA to issue in 1995 and when it was not, the principal physician working on it resigned.

Clinton wanted to both burnish his historical image and lay a

political trap for the incoming Bush administration. So in the last
hours of his term, Clinton had these regulations issued, though
knowing that it makes them seem vulnerable to expedient Republican charges of being prepared in an unsound, hasty manner. But,
by waiting until after the election, he avoided jeopardizing campaign contributions flowing to the Democrats, and other uncer-
tainties associated with taking explicit stands against powerful
commercial interests, such as the U.S. Chamber of Commerce and
the National Association of Manufacturers with their own well-
endowed media propaganda machines. Had Gore become president, it is not likely that Clinton would have released these rules.
In all likelihood, he would have let Gore continue their administration's policy of putting off such decisions. Bush fell into Clinton's trap and started suspending some of these rules with the
approval of the vocal pack of corporate lobbyists. This callousness
about arsenic and other safety precautions became the stuff of ridicule by cartoonists, editorial writers, and television reporters. It
surely was not an auspicious start for a self-styled "compassionate
conservative."

Bush made other bad moves. He shelved the Kyoto Protocol on
global warming, which Clinton had sat on inside the White House
rather than send to a hostile Senate for ratification. Bush explained
his jettison of this essentially modest expression of goals by saying
it was far too costly for the U.S. economy. In reality, energy efficiencies that reduce greenhouse gases mean a more efficient economy, less health-damaging pollution, and more energy per dollar
for the family budget. Clinton-Gore mildly lauded Kyoto but con-
signed it to a limbo as so much parchment, when they could have
used it as an instrument of leadership to transform the global
warming debate to focus on one demonstrating greater energy savings to a safer global environment. In any event, environmental
groups escalated their clamoring for Bush to come out with his
own promised reduction policy. They were inhibited from such
vociferous demands during the Clinton era, even when the Democrats were indicating that counting tree cover and restarting nuclear power missions would be ways to comply with Kyoto's
modest schedules. After all, Clinton and Gore, who refused to campaign for lower carbon dioxide levels, did favor Kyoto. Bush: acts

of commission. Clinton-Gore: acts of omission. Result: continued technological and policy stagnation in Detroit, Houston, and Washington.

By midsummer, Bush was backtracking on many of his remaining challenges to Clinton's last-hour rules, treating them as faits accompli, and relatively harmless at that. As for arsenic, carbon dioxide, and ergonomics, the White House has promised some decisions shortly—a public recognition that it is unwise politically to reject outright these widely supported issues. Some benefits may emerge from the interplay between Clinton's political trap and Bush's fumbles, but it's hardly a way to enact critical government functions. But that is what passes for action by commonly, if unevenly, indentured politicians.

During a meeting I had with House Democratic leader Congressman Dick Gephardt in February 2001, the Missourian observed that he has not seen the party's key constituencies—labor, minorities, and environmentalists—so mobilized in years. Maybe that is an indirect and consequential difference between Clinton-Gore and Bush-Cheney. So often the former did nothing but said the right things, while the latter do nothing and say the wrong things. The former anesthetized progressive civic forces. The latter make them indignant and more tenacious. That energy could represent an important shift in the balance of power, with longer-term benefits. This is by no means the entire comparative landscape, though. There are many critical policy areas where both parties are saying and doing the same thing—a type of ditto political discourse where corporations shape much domestic and foreign, military and economic policy.

Progressive Democrats who are deeply critical of their party during off-election years and then march to the drumbeat of the party's rulers in a campaign because of the Republican specter are subjects of manipulation, narrow perspectives, or diminished expectation levels. They would do well to embrace the whole continuum of party performance, direction, and concession, not just their favorite issue or admired incumbents. If your party does not have the votes to be in charge, then it should use its many votes to stop the Republicans' agenda—what William Greider calls demonstrating an "intensity of purpose."

Demanding more of our alleged political representatives means demanding more of ourselves. This is fundamental. Consider a few unlikely actions taken by Bush early in his administration. He backed down on continuing the decades-long practice bombing on Vieques Island in Puerto Rico by the navy. He reduced offshore oil drilling near Florida from Clinton's proposed 6 million acres to 1.5 million acres. He scrapped a proposed survey of offshore oil prospects off the coast of New Jersey. His EPA administrator Christine Todd Whitman surprised New York's environmentalists when she decided to take action to require General Electric to pay for the dredging of the upper Hudson River contaminated for years by GE's dumping of PCBs.

All this activity went against Bush's ideology, his corporate supporters, and the powerful oil and gas industry, whence he came. How come? He and his advisers heard the growing rumble of the people. Enough people became vocal, wrote letters, sent e-mails and petitions, attended rallies, passed group resolutions, and promised marches and lawsuits. They turned George W.'s words back on him that "actions should have consequences."

When Bush came into the White House swearing that his government would not restrain gouging, monopolistic wholesale electric prices in California (up to ten times the usual price without any increased costs of production), the rumble became louder, and the promise of a statewide referendum by Harvey Rosenfield's consumer rights group on electricity prices in 2002 was becoming more likely. So Bush's Federal Energy Regulatory Commission (FERC) did what it refused to do under Clinton—it established the beginning of a regulatory regime for wholesale prices.

Of course, these are only a few pullbacks by an administration that continues and expands Clinton's corporate supremacy just as Clinton expanded it after Reagan-Bush.

Both parties are locked into a deep trend of contributing to the imbalance of power between corporate systems and civic systems, which shortchanges the nation, drains revenues, resources, and control from the many to the few, and, most important, renders people ever more defenseless to fight back. So the more election campaigns become about us as a people—both individually and as a community—and less about the candidates and their monied patrons, the more our elected officials will run in our direction and away from the corporate maw of temptation and surrender.

The challenge is clear and urgent.

Several months after the election, we formed a new group called Democracy Rising to organize super-rallies in cities around the country to bring together a large variety of local and national social justice associations to focus on building a deeper democracy, with new synergies and civic engagements. Also established at the same time was Citizen Works, whose purpose is to expand public participation in arenas of power by providing the materials, training, and tools for such endeavors. Democracy is always under assault by the forces of plutocracy and needs regular renewal not just with ideas and strategies but also with greater numbers of participants of all ages and backgrounds, but especially the younger generation. This is why an important event, flowing out of our Green Party campaign, was the Campus Greens' Founding Convention of more than two thousand students in Chicago on August 10, 2001.

Three of our college undergraduate interns—Tom Adkins of Carleton College, Corey Eastwood of New York University, and Shelly Fite of New College (Florida)—and Duke University graduate Jacob Harold started working on the Campus Greens project right after the November election. The effort moved to Madison, Wisconsin, in early 2001, where Ben Manski, a local organizer, joined them. By the time of their founding convention in Chicago, they and others who volunteered had chartered nearly one hundred Campus Green chapters at colleges and universities, with the hope of reaching up to one thousand chapters by the end of the 2001–2002 academic year within sight.

Campus Greens are organized independently of the Green Party but share most of the same platforms for change and reform. This is the future. This is one answer to my call for a new generation of astute leaders putting their arms to the wheel of global justice as did their predecessors on whose shoulders they are standing.

The night of their convention, at the Classic Congress Theater, I had the privilege of giving the first keynote address. Winona LaDuke, Medea Benjamin, and Professor Cornel West were among the speakers who sharpened the resolve and robust spirits of the assemblage. Patti Smith and Ani DeFranco thrilled the gathering with their songs and their support. For the better part of the next two days, the students attended rigorous workshops on how to proceed from discussion to decision to action. I advised them to study the successes and failures of prior student movements to understand both what worked and what produced the ups and downs that eventually withered away these initiatives. This promising endeavor must be stable, yet it must adjust, change, grow, and put down deep roots for renewal and sustainability, just like the sustainable economies and democracies it strives to help build into the future.

Sixteen

LOOKING AHEAD

So where does that leave us? The revered principle of government of, by, and for the people requires more citizen involvement and, for those able to do so, assigning a certain amount of time, talent, and tenacity to our civic responsibilities. We have to believe that, should we make the effort, our convictions will count for something. This is where a reading of American history becomes so energizing in forming a personal political philosophy. For, in our past, when our democracy has been overridden or too weak, an aroused citizenry took our democracy and nation to a higher level of humanity. Although these struggles were often intense and painful for the most part, great advances were achieved with remarkably few active people making it happen for women, minorities, workers, farmers, consumers, debtors, the physically disabled, and many others. Too many people mistakenly believe either that it is not possible for any degree of civic energy to affect the powers that be, or that it takes multitudes and a great disruption of regular living practices to do so.

Still, an appreciation of our greatly achieving forebears provides only some of our motivation. There are also our contemporary issues and empathies, and the ethical and religious principles that Americans live by. Moreover, the personal experiences of tragedy and mistreatment drive our civic self-respect to engage the necessities of corrective action and not stand by idly rationalizing our futility. As a university student one summer, I had occasion to see and feel a little of what migrant farm workers endure every day. I never forgot that those who do the backbreaking work to harvest our foods are paid the least, treated the worst, and harmed the most. That motivated me to speak, write, and act on behalf of these laborers.

Almost everyone sees, hears, or experiences zones of gross unfairness, violence, or grievous displays of short-term thinking, but they need ever more refined tools to help them communicate, mobilize, and act together without losing their civil rights and civil liberties. In this way, they can stem the erosion of our democracy by the perpetrators and holders of excessive power over government or indirectly by adversaries abroad.

What Justice Louis Brandeis called control over "other people's money"—and one might add "other people's wealth and commonwealth"—remains one of the more important ways that large business firms allow the symbols of representative politics and the reality of legal ownership by the people to remain intact while taking over the show. As I have already noted, the public airwaves, the public lands, the giant pension funds, the public's research and development assets, and the public works are all reflections on this clever separation between ownership and control. For it is control, not ownership, that companies see as more flexible, less risky, and therefore far more profitable.

Were we the people to control what we already own—that enormous portion of our overall wealth that authors Jonathan Rowe and David Bollier have re-called (from early American history) the "commons"—then we as shareholders, investors (directly and through workers' pension trusts), taxpayers, and voters would give reality to ownership. Authors Peter Drucker, Jeff Gates, and other advocates of grassroots capitalism have written volumes about ways and means to achieve what Gates calls "The Ownership Solution." He says the trouble with corporate capitalism in the United States is that there is a lot of capital but very few capitalists, by which he means that very few Americans reap any significant returns from capital that for years has reaped higher returns compared with returns for labor.

A shift of economic power is critical for the workings of any political reforms. But enough people have to be willing to spend the time and energy. Oscar Wilde once said that socialism could never work because it requires too many meetings. Perhaps to a lesser degree the same can be said of economic democracy or a people's capitalism, or cooperatively owned economic institutions such as food co-ops. Complex, changing societies need more public or citizen time for a more just society if our private time is to be enjoyable, peaceful, safe, and productive. Each person has a contribution to make. It is sometimes useful to evoke a metaphor from the natural world. The great natural asset of our country which is the Mississippi River starts with a drop of water in northern Minnesota. One drop joins with other drops to form a tiny rivulet that joins with other rivulets to form a brook, which together with other brooks makes a stream that with other streams makes a river, which together with other rivers swells the mighty Mississippi. So, too, is the case with millions of citizens, watering the life-expanding potential of a functioning democracy open to fresh ideas and replenishing initiatives.

Fifty-two years ago, Harvard anthropologist Clyde Kluckhohn wrote some words of wisdom in his book *Mirror for Man*. America's chief claim to greatness, he observed, is not in its illustrious writers or in its outstanding scientists or thinkers. It is in being the "first country to dedicate itself to the conception of a society where the lot of the common man would be made easier, where the same opportunities would be available to all, where the lives of all men and women would be enriched and ennobled. This was something new under the sun." He went on to a deep insight: "Ideals of flourishing freshness that adapt to changed conditions and to what is sound and creative in the distinctive American Way are the only sure antidote for our social ills. Only those ideals will spread and be accepted which correspond to the culturally created emotional needs of the people." He believed that "visions" must offer men and women that "common nobility of purpose, which is the vitalizing energy of any significant culture." While "ventures," he added, will "be proved only if diminished anxiety and greater gusto in day-to-day living transform the lives of us all."

It is simply not possible to convey these sensibilities over the mass electronic media, even assuming the media barons agreed to program them. What Kluckhohn was suggesting to us is that we can be informed from a distance about these opportunities, but we can incorporate them only by the intangible he calls our "total philosophic attitude" rooted in the commitment that "the basis of social life is the sensitivity of human beings to the behavior of other human beings." The function of democratic politics is to put forth the forms of societal action that arise from a sense of common pursuits concerning matters of common concern. In a phrase, people to people, all of us pulling our oars in the boat of life where we all find ourselves. The task of an authentic democracy is to make sure that these journeys are accomplished with the informed consent of the governed in a vibrant civil society.

Our country's independence was declared in 1776 by patriots, many of whom would be considered very young by contemporary standards. Thomas Jefferson was thirty-two, James Madison was thirty-five, John Hancock was thirty-nine, and John Adams was forty-one. Their leader, George Washington, was only forty-four. Today our society is borrowing heavily from future generations, and debts of all kinds are mounting. As history conveys to us, it is again up to the young to give new character to their times, to forge the civic personalities that will bring old wisdoms, new thinking, and new democratic institutions to bear upon the torments of our world.

It is always the young who can give the people and their collective judgments that "new birth of freedom," in Lincoln's words, who can constrain greed and power—those classical Molochs—by civil society's motivation and action. It is always the young who break through the shams and frauds and raise our expectation levels beyond our eroded horizons. It is always the young who see the "impractical and the impossible" as entrenched excuses by the established interests to avoid realizable caring futures. When three hundred of the richest people on Earth have wealth equal to the bottom three billion people on Earth, extreme affluence is built on the backs of extreme mass poverty.

In the forward march of history, it will always be the young who look at the conventional "can't be dones" and demand that "they can be done, they must be done, and they will be done." The questions remain: Are our younger generations in America up for establishing the democratic sovereignty of the people? Or will they continue to grow up corporate and let ever larger global corporations increasingly plan our futures—economically, culturally, politically, militarily, environmentally, and genetically right into their obedient brave new world?

The civic personality, in contrast, sees through the politically dominant ideology of commercial supremacy and evaluates what it is doing by the measure of civic values. The tobacco industry works ceaselessly to addict kids and sell its products to ever more people. That millions die every year around the world from tobacco-related diseases does not deter this industry. The processed-food companies want to sell ever more fat and sugar to a population, young and older, suffering serious diseases and disabilities from such diets. The drug companies then push their pills onto children and adults with ever less restraint and ever more overwrought marketing mania. A serious published study in the American Medical Association's journal estimated that more than one hundred thousand hospitalized patients die from adverse drug reactions each year. The military weapons companies search the world to sell, with taxpayer subsidies, more and more of their lethal armaments to whoever can pay, regardless of their customers' intent or uses. When companies commercialize childhood, accelerate sprawl, imperil the environment with contaminating fuels and chemicals (the EPA estimates that sixty-five thousand Americans die each year from air pollution), block sustainable technologies, encourage more debt, own politicians, skew public tax dollars in their favor, oppress labor, and gouge defenseless consumers, they are simply following their commercial imperative without limits. Civilization as if people are first is not just about opportunities; it is about limits and boundaries around antisocial, criminogenic behavior whose limitless logic eventually would spell omnicide for this very limited home we call Mother Earth.

The British philosopher Alfred North Whitehead once wrote that a society is great when its businessmen think greatly of their calling. The young are very adept at searching out or creating such models, and a good place to start is the Social Venture Network, which consciously strives to inject civic values as the framework for their successful midsize businesses. Reading, learning, and thinking in a time of megamedia obfuscation and confusion are a prerequisite for the civic personality. Just what are the proper functions of an accountable government that is not paid to play favorites and forfeit its trust and integrity? What is meant by the commons or commonwealth of public property and public assets that the American people own together but do not control? How did our forebears motivate their fellow citizens to organize person to person, reaching levels that organizers today, with all their communications technology, view with unalloyed awe? Just how did the power of creeping corporatism over the past two hundred years take an artificial legal entity chartered by the state, called the corporation, and have it endowed with the rights of real human beings plus privileges and immunities denied human beings?

There are also distinct elements of courage to the civic personality. Thousands of men and women each year in our country blow the whistle on abuses in business and government, universities, unions, and other institutions to the detriment of their jobs, careers, and livelihood. Civic values drive them to expose avarice and wrongdoing. Keeping an open mind to revisit positions and policies is part of the way civic personalities maintain touch with reality and other people's wishes. When I held a news conference with New Mexico's Republican governor, Gary Johnson, a former businessman, during the campaign, he again spoke out, urging a rethinking of the self-defeating and cruel war on drugs. Johnson is the only sitting governor to open such a taboo subject, even though he told me that other governors privately agree with what he says but think it too politically delicate to raise similar questions in their states.

A civic personality possesses a keen awareness of how large corporations have institutionalized the shifting of their avoidable costs to police, soldiers, taxpayers, consumers, workers, and the environment, and how governments waste or redirect tax dollars to wealthy recipients who make up the corporate government. Being sensitive to how some other democratic nations essentially abolished poverty, as we know it, years ago and provided other safeguards and services for workers, children, and needy citizens informs the civic personality to be more insistent. Similarly, such a commitment is strengthened by an expanding grasp of available solutions or achievable ones shelved not because of any technical objections but because of the resistance of the entrenched powers that be. Solar energy in all its historic and modern active and passive forms remains a prominent illustration of the penalties society pays for not democratizing technology.

During the nineties when a new generation came of age, the United States exhibited a dominance that Clinton and Gore called "peace and prosperity." Apart from the sweeping veneer over real conditions that this phrase obscured domestically and internationally, it does raise the central question: What did we do with all this peace and prosperity? Did we regenerate our culture, strengthen our democracy, and launch a drive to abolish poverty? Did our rulers keep a majority of workers and families from falling behind? Did we meet long-delayed public needs? Did we improve industrial efficiencies that reduce environmental degradation and enhance the productivity of natural resource inputs? Did we strive for world stability by reasonably demobilizing following the demise of our traditional adversaries and instead vigorously waging peace and justice to help humanity and the genius of other societies to join in common efforts for sustainable living standards? Did we move to a new way of thinking and acting apropos of William James's notion of "the moral equivalent of war" back in the late nineteenth century? Why didn't we ever wonder about what we missed? Are we a society stuck in traffic?

What does this decade-long respite from the conventional excuses and red herrings tell us about our political economy's unwillingness to rise to such wonderful occasions and beckoning opportunities? It tells us what happens when power is too concentrated and when the dreams of avarice supplant the dreams of justice—the great work, as Daniel Webster put it, of human beings on Earth. The remarkable persistence of these human frailties throughout centuries and millennia, despite dramatic secular changes, technologies, and pretensions, is one reason why people can relate to ancient plays from Euripides to Shakespeare. It is why the sayings of the ancients remain so relevant today in an otherwise dramatically different world. It is why the civic personality—to be true, resilient, productive, and respectful of itself—cannot ignore these personal failings and insecurities that can remain apart from but dominant over intellect, knowledge, or one's desired contribution to higher priorities in our world and community.

Five hundred years before the birth of Christ, the Greek philosopher Heraclitus said that "character is destiny." One might add that "personality is decisive" for the capability of people building civic cultures. It is character and personality that spell the steady sense of commitment, that give recognition to others in similar endeavors, that enable growth and development of civic skills, perspectives, and frames of reference, that provide the necessary pauses for reevaluation, for improved strategies and modes of self-renewal, for keeping alert and alive the public's imagination of life's possibilities for human beings everywhere.

It is indeed the young who take the risks, who break new ground, who locate or create solutions to widespread needs, who think the unthinkable, who show how prevailing ideologies regularly lie to themselves through phony symbols and images. However, it is also the young who can be most dissuaded by a sensual, tempting corporate culture, who can be seduced into trivializing their lives and postponing their potential. As I have said to many college undergraduates, you have about fifteen thousand days or a little over two thousand weeks before you turn sixty-five. Whether you wish to relax and smell the roses after that age or continue making this a better world, there is little time to lose. Put your knowledge and your vision to work. Keep thinking of the valiant efforts from the past and the children of the future. Put your beneficent mark on your world. Become good ancestors. Let it never be said by future generations that, during *your* days in the sun, your generation declined to give up so little in order to accomplish so much.

FIRST-STAGE GOALS FOR A BETTER AMERICA

1. Enact legislation that mandates publicly financed public elections and broad reforms of the electoral process. Strengthen citizen participation in our political economy.

2. Enact living-wage laws, strengthen worker health and safety laws, and repeal Taft-Hartley and other obstructions to collective bargaining and worker rights.

3. Issue environmental protection standards to systematically reduce damaging environmental toxins and to promote sustainable technologies.

4. Provide full Medicare coverage for everyone and revamp our national programs for prevention of disease and trauma.

5. Launch a national mission to abolish poverty, as other Western democracies have done, based on proposals made long ago by conservatives, liberals, and progressives.

6. Design and implement a national security policy to counter violence and the silent mass violence of global diseases, environmental devastation, and extreme poverty. Reduce waste and corporate domination of defense budgets—a wasteful defense is a weak defense. Wage peace and advance nonviolence by education and by foreseeing and forestalling global perils.

7. Renegotiate NAFTA and GATT to be democratic and to be "pull-up," not "pull-down," trade agreements that subordinate labor, consumer, and environmental standards to trade matters.

8. End criminal justice system discrimination, reject the failed war on drugs, and replace for-profit corporate prisons with superior public institutions.

9. Defend and strengthen the civil justice system, apply criminal laws against corporate crime, and fully prosecute consumer fraud and abuses. Expand consumer, worker, and children's health, safety, and economic rights.

10. Strengthen investor-shareholder rights, remedies, and authority over managers and officers and boards of directors so that those who own the companies also control them. End the massive corporate welfare schemes that distort and misallocate public budgets. Reintroduce the historic function of corporate chartering as an instrument of ensuring corporate accountability and the sovereignty of the people.

APPENDIX A: CITIZENS' COMMITTEE FOR NADER-LaDUKE

(AFFILIATIONS PROVIDED FOR
IDENTIFICATION PURPOSES ONLY)

Co-Chairs
Phil Donahue, former talk-show host
Jim Hightower, author and radio commentator
Randall Robinson, TransAfrica Forum
Susan Sarandon, actor and activist

Members
John B. Anderson, third-party presidential candidate in 1980
David Barsamian, author and radio interviewer
Juliette Beck, Global Exchange
Elaine Bernard, Harvard Trade Union Program
Herbert Bernstein, Professor of Physics at Hampshire College
Thomas Berry, historian and author of *Dream of the Earth*
Wendell Berry, farmer and writer
Jello Biafra, former member of the Dead Kennedys
Norman Birnbaum, professor at Georgetown University
Grace Lee Boggs, human-rights activist
Blase Bonpane, Office of the Americas
Theresa Bonpane, Office of the Americas
Eric Brakken, United Students Against Sweatshops
David Brower, founder and chair of the Earth Island Institute
Ira R. Byock, physician, author, and advocate for Improved End of Life Care
Edgar Cahn, Time Dollar Institute
Peter Camejo, CEO of Progressive Asset Management
John Cavanagh, Director of the Institute for Policy Studies

Noam Chomsky, author and professor at Massachusetts Institute of Technology

Yvon Chouinard, owner of Patagonia

Robert Clark, General Secretary of the United Electrical Workers

Steve Cobble, former political director of the Rainbow Coalition

Ben Cohen, cofounder of Ben & Jerry's

Barry Commoner, scientist and 1980 Citizen's Party candidate

Peter Coyote, actor and writer

Ronnie Cummins, National Director of the Organic Consumers Association

Herman Daly, professor at the University of Maryland

Iris Dement, folk musician

Rose Ann DeMoro, Executive Director of the California Nurses Association

Mark Dowie, journalist and former editor of *Mother Jones*

Barbara Dudley, former president of Greenpeace and the National Lawyers Guild

Ronnie Dugger, founder of the Alliance for Democracy

Troy Duster, professor at New York University

Barbara Ehrenreich, political essayist and social critic

Richard Falk, Center of International Studies, Princeton University

Robert Fellmeth, Director of the Children's Advocacy Institute

Jeff Gates, president of the Shared Capitalism Institute

Lois Gibbs, Love Canal Homeowners

Danny Glover, actor and activist

Jim and Rebecca Goodman, Organic Dairy Farmers

Kevin Gray, former ACLU National Board member

Arlo Guthrie, entertainer

Doris (Granny D) Haddock, Campaign Finance Reform activist

Dan Hamburg, former member of Congress

Stewart Harris, executive producer of WebWorks

Paul Hawken, author and economist

Randy Hayes, Rainforest Action Network

Tim Hermach, Native Forest Council

Wes Jackson, The Land Institute

Nicholas Johnson, former commissioner of the Federal Communications Commission

David Kairys, law professor at Temple University and author

Casey Kasem, radio broadcaster

Mel King, founder of the Massachusetts Rainbow coalition

Ynestra King, ecofeminist author

John Kinsman, Family Farm Defenders

Philip M. Klasky, director of the Bay Area Nuclear Waste Coalition

David Korten, author of *The Post-Corporate World: Life After Capitalism*

Frances Korten, director of the Positive Futures Network

Ron Kovic, Vietnam veteran and peace activist

Al Krebs, Corporate Agribusiness Research Project

Saul Landau, California State Polytechnic University

Rabbi Michael Lerner, editor of *Tikkun* magazine

Theodore Lowi, historian and author

Howard Lyman, former rancher and vegetarian activist

Joanna R. Macy, author and teacher

Jerry Mander, president of the International Forum on Globalization

Dr. Manning Marable, director of Columbia University's Institute for Research in African American Studies

Dave Marsh, writer and editor of *Rock & Rap Confidential*

Redwood Mary, Plight of the Redwoods Campaign

Arno Mayer, Dayton-Stockton Professor Emeritus at Princeton University

Dan McCarthy, UAW Local 417

Robert McChesney, professor at the University of Illinois

Kay McVay, president of the California Nurses Association

Carolyn Merchant, Professor of Environmental History, Philosophy, and Ethics at UC Berkeley

Peter Montague, Environmental Research Foundation

Michael Moore, filmmaker and journalist

Willie Nelson, country musician

Gus Newport, former mayor of Berkeley, California

Ruth Ozeki, novelist, filmmaker, and author of *My Year of Meats*

Jan Pierce, former vice president of Communication Workers of America

Frances Fox Piven, City University of New York

Anthony Pollina, candidate for governor in Vermont

Nora Pouillon, chef

Bonnie Raitt, blues singer/guitarist

Sheldon Rampton, coauthor of *Toxic Sludge Is Good for You*

Marcus Raskin, author, political theorist, and cofounder of the Institute for Policy Studies

John Rensenbrink, Bowdoin College

Mark Ritchie, Institute for Agriculture and Trade Policy

Tim Robbins, actor

Vicki Robin, New Road Map Foundation

John Schaeffer, CEO of Real Goods Trading Company, Inc.

Pete Seeger, musician

Andy Sharpless, vice president of Interactive Media, Discovery Enterprises Worldwide

Michelle Shocked, musician

Cora Lee Simmons, Round Valley Indians for Justice

Gerry Spence, Spence, Moriarity & Schister

John Stauber, coauthor of *Toxic Sludge Is Good for You*

Andrew Strauss, Professor of International Law at the Widerner University School of Law

Charlotte Talberth, Max and Anna Levinson Foundation

Meredith Tax, feminist author and human-rights activist

Studs Terkel, radio personality and historian

Tom Tomorrow, cartoonist

Jerry Tucker, former regional director of International UAW

Sarah van Gelder, editor of *YES!* magazine

Eddie Vedder, musician, *Pearl Jam*

Harvey Wasserman, author of *The Last Energy War*

Cornel West, professor and author of *Race Matters*

Sheldon Wolin, Professor Emeritus at Princeton University

Howard Zinn, author

APPENDIX B: SOME ORGANIZATIONS RALPH NADER FOUNDED OR HELPED START

American Antitrust Institute
Appleseed Foundation
Arizona Center for Law in the Public Interest
Aviation Consumer Action Project
Capitol Hill News Service
Center for Auto Safety
Center for Insurance Research
Center for Justice and Democracy
Center for Science in the Public Interest
Center for Study of Responsive Law
Center for Women's Policy Studies
Citizen Advocacy Center
Citizen Utility Boards
Citizen Works
Clean Water Action Project
Congress Project
Connecticut Citizen Action Group
Corporate Accountability Research Group
Democracy Rising
Disability Rights Center
Equal Justice Foundation
Essential Information
FANS (Fight to Advance the Nation's Sports)
Foundation for Taxpayers and Consumer Rights
Freedom of Information Clearinghouse
Georgia Legal Watch
Multinational Monitor

National Citizens' Coalition for Nursing Home Reform
National Coalition for Universities in the Public Interest
National Insurance Consumer Organization
Ohio Public Interest Action Group
Organization for Competitive Markets
Pension Rights Center
Princeton Project 55
PROD (truck safety)
Public Citizen
    Buyers Up
    Citizen Action Group
    Congress Watch
    Critical Mass Energy Project
    Global Trade Watch
    Health Research Group
    Litigation Group
    Tax Reform Research Group
    The Visitor's Center
Retired Professionals Action Group
The Shafeek Nader Trust for the Community Interest
Student Public Interest Research Groups nationwide
Telecommunications Research and Action Center
Trial Lawyers for Public Justice

APPENDIX C: ANNOUNCEMENT SPEECH

Speech Announcing Ralph Nader's Candidacy for the Green Party's Nomination for President, Washington, D.C., February 21, 2000

Today I wish to explain why, after working for years as a citizen advocate for consumers, workers, taxpayers, and the environment, I am seeking the Green Party's nomination for president. A crisis of democracy in our country convinces me to take this action. Over the past twenty years, big business has increasingly dominated our political economy. This control by the corporate government over our political government is creating a widening "democracy gap." Active citizens are left shouting their concerns over a deep chasm between them and their government. This state of affairs is a world away from the legislative milestones in civil rights, the environment, and health and safety of workers and consumers seen in the sixties and seventies. At that time, informed and dedicated citizens powered their concerns through the channels of government to produce laws that bettered the lives of millions of Americans.

Today we face grave and growing societal problems in health care, education, labor, energy, and the environment. These are problems for which active citizens have solutions, yet their voices are not carrying across the democracy gap. Citizen groups and individual thinkers have generated a tremendous capital of ideas, information, and solutions to the point of surplus, while our government has been drawn away from us by a corporate government. Our political leadership has been hijacked.

Citizen advocates have no other choice but to close the democracy gap by direct political means. Only effective national political leadership will restore the responsiveness of government to its citizenry. Truly progressive political movements do not just produce more good results, they enable a flowering of progressive citizen movements to effectively advance the quality of our neighborhoods and communities outside of politics.

I have a personal distaste for the trappings of modern politics, in which incumbents and candidates daily extol their own inflated virtues, paint complex issues with trivial brushstrokes, and propose plans quickly generated by campaign consultants. But I can no longer stomach the systemic political decay that has weakened our democracy. I can no longer watch people dedicate themselves to improving their country while their government leaders turn their backs, or worse, actively block fair treatment for citizens. It is necessary to launch a sustained effort to wrest control of our democracy from the corporate government and restore it to the political government under the control of citizens.

This campaign will challenge all Americans who are concerned with systemic imbalances of power and the undermining of our democracy, whether they consider themselves progressives, liberals, conservatives, or others. Presidential elections should be a time for deep discussions among the citizenry regarding the down-to-earth problems and injustices that are not addressed because of the gross power mismatch between the narrow vested interests and the public or common good.

The unconstrained behavior of big business is subordinating our democracy to the control of a corporate plutocracy that knows few self-imposed limits to the spread of its power to all sectors of our society. Moving on all fronts to advance narrow profit motives at the expense of civic values, large corporate lobbies and their law firms have produced a commanding, multifaceted, and powerful juggernaut. They flood public elections with cash, and they use their media conglomerates to exclude, divert, or propagandize. They brandish their willingness to close factories here and open them abroad if workers do not bend to their demands. By their control in Congress, they keep the federal cops off the corporate crime, fraud, and abuse beats. They imperiously demand and get a wide array of privileges and immunities: tax escapes, enormous corporate welfare subsidies, federal giveaways, and bailouts. They weaken the common law of torts in order to avoid their responsibility for injurious wrongdoing to innocent children, women, and men.

Abuses of economic power are nothing new. Every major religion in the world has warned about societies allowing excessive influences of mercantile or commercial values. The profiteering motive is driven and single-minded. When unconstrained, it can override or erode community, health, safety, parental nurturing, due process, clean politics, and many other basic social values that hold together a society. Abraham Lincoln, Theodore Roosevelt, Franklin Roosevelt, Supreme Court Justices Louis Brandeis and William Douglas, among others, eloquently warned about what Thomas Jefferson called "the excesses of the monied interests" dominating people and their governments. The struggle between the forces of democracy and plutocracy has ebbed and flowed throughout our history. Each time the cycle of power has favored more democracy, our country has prospered ("a rising tide lifts all boats"). Each time the cycle of corporate plutocracy has lengthened, injustices and shortcomings proliferate.

In the sixties and seventies, for example, when the civil rights, consumer, environmental, and women's rights movements were in their ascendancy, there finally was a constructive responsiveness by government. Corporations, such as auto manufacturers, had to share more decision making with affected constituencies, both directly and through their public representatives and civil servants. Overall, our country has come out better, more tolerant, safer, and with greater opportunities. The earlier nineteenth-century democratic struggles by abolitionists against slavery, by farmers against large oppressive railroads and banks, and later by new trade unionists against the brutal workplace conditions of the early industrial and mining era helped mightily to make America and its middle class what they are today. They demanded that economic power subside or be shared.

Democracy works, and a stronger democracy works better for reputable, competitive markets, equal opportunity, and higher standards of living and justice. Generally, it brings out the best performances from people and from businesses.

A plutocracy—rule by the rich and powerful—on the other hand, obscures our historical quests for justice. Harnessing political power to corporate greed leaves us with a country that has far more problems than it deserves, while blocking ready solutions or improvements from being applied.

It is truly remarkable that for almost every widespread need or injustice in our country, there are citizens, civic groups, small and medium-size businesses, and farms that have shown how to meet these needs or end these injustices. However, all the innovative solutions in the world will accomplish little if the injustices they address or the problems they solve have been shoved aside because plutocracy reigns and democracy wanes. For all optimistic Americans, when their issues are thus swept from the table, it becomes civic mobilization time.

Consider the economy, which business commentators say could scarcely be better. If, instead of corporate yardsticks, we use human yardsticks to measure the performance of the economy and go beyond the quantitative indices of annual economic growth, structural deficiencies become readily evident. The complete dominion of traditional yardsticks for measuring economic prosperity masks not only these failures but also the inability of a weakened democracy to address how and why a majority of Americans are not benefiting from this prosperity in their daily lives. Despite record economic growth, corporate profits, and stock market highs year after year, a stunning array of deplorable conditions still prevails year after year. For example:

- A majority of workers are making less now, inflation adjusted, than in 1979.
- Over 20 percent of children were growing up in poverty during the past decade, by far the highest among comparable Western countries.
- The minimum wage is lower today, inflation adjusted, than in 1968.
- American workers are working longer and longer hours— on average an additional 163 hours per year, compared to twenty years ago—with less time for family and community.
- Many full-time family farms cannot make a living in a market of giant buyer concentration and industrial agriculture.

- The public works (infrastructure) are crumbling, with decrepit schools and clinics, library closings, antiquated mass transit, and more.
- Corporate welfare programs, paid for largely by middle-class taxpayers and amounting to hundreds of billions of dollars per year, continue to rise along with government giveaways of taxpayer assets such as public forests, minerals, and new medicines.
- Affordable housing needs are at record levels while secondary mortgage market companies show record profits.
- The number of Americans without health insurance grows every year.
- There have been twenty-five straight years of growing foreign trade deficits ($270 billion in 1999).
- Consumer debt is at an all-time high, totaling over $6 trillion.
- Personal bankruptcies are at a record level.
- Personal savings are dropping to record lows and personal assets are so low that Bill Gates's net worth is equal to that of the net assets of the poorest 120 million Americans combined.
- The tiny federal budgets for the public's health and safety continue to be grossly inadequate.
- Motor vehicle fuel efficiency averages are actually declining and, overall, energy conservation efforts have slowed, while renewable energy takes a backseat to fossil fuel and atomic power subsidies.
- Wealth inequality is greater than at any time since World War II. The top 1 percent of the wealthiest people have more financial wealth than the bottom 90 percent of Americans combined, the worst inequality among large Western nations.
- Despite annual declines in total business liability costs, business lobbyists drive for more privileges and immunities for their wrongdoing.

It is permissible to ask, in the light of these astonishing short-comings during a period of touted prosperity, what the state of our country would be should a recession or depression occur? One import of these contrasts is clear: Economic growth has been decoupled from economic progress for many Americans. In the early 1970s, our economy split into two tiers. Whereas once economic growth broadly benefited the majority, now the economy has become one wherein "a rising tide lifts all yachts," in the words of Jeff Gates, author of *The Ownership Solution.* Returns on capital outpaced returns on labor, and job insecurity increased for millions of seasoned workers. In the seventies, the top three hundred CEOs paid themselves forty times the entry-level wage in their companies. Now the average is over four hundred times. This in an economy where impoverished assembly line workers suffering from carpal tunnel syndrome frantically process chickens that pass them in a continuous flow, where downsized white- and blue-collar employees are hired at lesser compensation, if they are lucky, where the focus of top business executives is no longer to provide a service that attracts customers but rather to acquire customers through mergers and acquisitions. How long can the paper economy of speculation ignore its effects on the real economy of working families?

Pluralistic democracy has enlarged markets and created the middle class. Yet the short-term monetized minds of the corporatists are bent on weakening, defeating, diluting, diminishing, circumventing, co-opting, or corrupting all traditional countervailing forces that have saved American corporate capitalism from itself.

Regulation of food, automobiles, banks, and securities, for example, strengthened these markets along with protecting consumers and investors. Antitrust enforcement helped protect our country from monopoly capitalism and stimulated competition. Trade unions enfranchised workers and helped mightily to build the middle class for themselves, benefiting also nonunion laborers. Producer and consumer cooperatives helped save the family farm, electrified rural areas, and offered another model of economic activity. Civil litigation—the right to have your day in court—helped deter producers of harmful products and brought them to some measure of justice. At the same time, the public learned about these hazards.

Public investment—from naval shipyards to Pentagon drug discoveries against infectious disease to public power authorities— provided yardsticks to measure the unwillingness of big business to change and respond to needs. Even under a rigged system, shareholder pressures on management sometimes have shaken complacency, wrongdoing, and mismanagement. Direct consumer remedies, including class actions, have given pause to crooked businesses and have stopped much of this unfair competition against honest businesses. Big-business lobbies opposed all of this progress strenuously, but they finally lost and America gained. Ultimately, so did a chastened but myopic business community.

Now, these checkpoints face a relentless barrage from rampaging corporate titans assuming more control over elected officials, the workplace, the marketplace, technology, capital pools (including workers' pension trusts), and educational institutions. One clear sign of the reign of corporations over our government is that the key laws passed in the sixties and seventies that we use to curb corporate misbehavior would not even pass through congressional committees today. Planning ahead, multinational corporations shaped the World Trade Organization's autocratic and secretive governing procedures so as to undermine nontrade health, safety, and other living standard laws and proposals in member countries.

Up against the corporate government, voters find themselves asked to choose between look-alike candidates from two parties vying to see who takes the marching orders from their campaign paymasters and their future employers. The money of vested interests nullifies genuine voter choice and trust. Our elections have been put out for auction to the highest bidder. Public elections must be publicly financed, and it can be done with well-promoted voluntary checkoffs and free TV and radio time for ballot-qualified candidates.

Workers are disenfranchised more than any time since the 1920s. Many unions stagger under stagnant leadership and discouraged rank and file. Furthermore, weak labor laws actually obstruct new trade union organization and leave the economy with the lowest percentage of workers unionized in more than sixty years. Giant multinationals are pitting countries against one another and escaping national jurisdictions more and more. Under these circumstances, workers are entitled to stronger labor organizing laws and rights for their own protection in order to deal with highly organized corporations.

At a very low cost, government can help democratic solution

building for a host of problems that citizens face, from consumer abuses to environmental degradation. Government research and development generated whole new industries and company start-ups and created the Internet. At the least, our government can facilitate the voluntary banding together of interested citizens into democratic civic institutions. Such civic organizations can create more level playing fields in the banking, insurance, real estate, transportation, energy, health care, cable TV, educational, public service, and other sectors. Let's call this the flowering of a deep-rooted democratic society. A government that funnels your tax dollars to corporate welfare kings in the form of subsidies, bailouts, guarantees, and giveaways of valuable public assets can at least invest in promoting healthy democracy.

Taxpayers have very little legal standing in the federal courts and little indirect voice in the assembling and disposition of taxpayer revenues. Closer scrutiny of these matters between elections is necessary. Facilities can be established to accomplish a closer oversight of taxpayer assets and how tax dollars (apart from social insurance) are allocated. This is an arena that is, at present, shaped heavily by corporations that, despite record profits, pay far less in taxes as a percent of the federal budget than in the 1950s and 60s.

The "democracy gap" in our politics and elections spells a deep sense of powerlessness by people who drop out, do not vote, or listlessly vote for the "least worst" every four years and then wonder why after another cycle the "least worst" gets worse. It is time to redress fundamentally these imbalances of power. We need a deep initiatory democracy in the embrace of its citizens, a usable brace of democratic tools that brings the best out of people, highlights the humane ideas and practical ways to raise and meet our expectations and resolve our society's deficiencies and injustices.

A few illustrative questions can begin to raise our expectations and suggest what can be lost when the few and powerful hijack our democracy:

- Why can't the wealthiest nation in the world abolish the chronic poverty of millions of working and nonworking Americans, including our children?

- Are we reversing the disinvestment in our distressed inner cities and rural areas and using creatively some of the huge capital pools in the economy to make these areas more livable, productive, and safe?
- Are we able to end homelessness and wretched housing conditions with modern materials, designs, and financing mechanisms, without bank and insurance company redlining, to meet the affordable housing needs of millions of Americans?
- Are we getting the best out of known ways to spread renewable, efficient energy throughout the land to save consumers money and to head off global warming and other land-based environmental damage from fossil fuels and atomic energy?
- Are we getting the best out of the many bright and public-spirited civil servants who know how to improve governments but are rarely asked by their politically appointed superiors or members of Congress?
- Are we able to provide wide access to justice for all aggrieved people so that we apply rigorously the admonition of Judge Learned Hand, "If we are to keep our democracy, there must be one commandment: Thou Shall Not Ration Justice"?
- Can we extend overseas the best examples of our country's democratic processes and achievements instead of annually using billions in tax dollars to subsidize corporate munitions exports, as Republican Senator Mark Hatfield always used to decry?
- Can we stop the giveaways of our vast commonwealth assets and become better stewards of the public lands, better investors of trillions of dollars in worker pension monies, and allow broader access to the public airwaves and other assets now owned by the people but controlled by corporations?
- Can we counter the coarse and brazen commercial culture, including television that daily highlights depravity and ignores the quiet civic heroisms in its communities, a commercialism that insidiously exploits childhood and plasters its logos everywhere?

- Can we plan ahead as a society so we know our priorities and where we wish to go? Or do we continue to let global corporations remain astride the planet, corporatizing everything, from genes to education to the Internet to public institutions, in short, planning our futures in their image? If a robust civic culture does not shape the future, corporatism surely will.

To address these and other compelling challenges, we must build a powerful, self-renewing civil society that focuses on ample justice so we do not have to desperately bestow limited charity. Such a culture strengthens existing civic associations and facilitates the creation of others to watch the complexities and technologies of a new century. Building the future also means providing the youngest of citizens with citizen skills that they can use to improve their communities.

This is the foundation of our campaign, to focus on active citizenship, to create fresh political movements that will displace the control of the Democratic and Republican parties, two apparently distinct political entities that feed at the same corporate trough. They are in fact simply the two heads of one political duopoly, the DemRep Party. This duopoly does everything it can to obstruct the beginnings of new parties, including raising ballot access barriers, entrenching winner-take-all voting systems, and thwarting participation in debates at election times.

As befits its name, the Green Party, whose nomination I seek, stands for the regeneration of American politics. The new populism that the Green Party represents involves motivated, informed voters who comprehend that "freedom is participation in power," to quote the ancient Roman orator Cicero. When citizen participation flourishes, as this campaign will encourage it to do, human values can tame runaway commercial imperatives. The myopia of the short-term bottom line so often debases our democratic processes and our public and private domains. Putting human values first helps to make business responsible and to put government on the right track.

It is easy and true to say that this deep democracy campaign will be an uphill one. However, it is also true that widespread reform will not flourish without a fairer distribution of power for the key roles of voter, citizen, worker, taxpayer, and consumer. Comprehensive reform proposals from the corporate suites to the nation's streets, from the schools to the hospitals, from the preservation of small farm economies to the protection of privacies, from livable wages to sustainable environments, from more time for children to less time for commercialism, from waging peace and health to averting war and violence, from foreseeing and forestalling future troubles to journeying toward brighter horizons, will wither while power inequalities loom over us.

Why are campaigns just for candidates? I would like the American people to hear from individuals such as Edgar Cahn (Time Dollars for neighborhoods), Nicholas Johnson (television and telecommunications), Paul Hawken, Amory and Hunter Lovins (energy and resource conservation), Dee Hock (on chaordic organizations), James MacGregor Burns and John Gardner (on leadership), Richard Grossman (on the American history of corporate charters and personhood), Jeff Gates (on capital sharing), Robert Monks (on corporate accountability), Ray Anderson (on his company's pollution and recycling conversions), Johnnetta Cole, Troy Duster, and Yolanda Moses (on race relations), Richard Duran (on minority education), Lois Gibbs (on community mobilization against toxics), Robert McIntyre (on tax justice), Hazel Henderson (on redefining economic development), Barry Commoner and David Brower (on fundamental environmental regeneration), Wendell Berry (on the quality of living), Tony Mazzochi (on a new agenda for labor), and law professor Richard Parker (on a constitutional popular manifesto). These individuals are a small sampling of many who have so much to say but seldom get through the ever more entertainment-focused media. (Note: Mention of these people does not imply their support for this campaign.)

Our political campaign will highlight active and productive citizens who practice democracy often in the most difficult of situations. I intend to do this in the District of Columbia, whose citizens have no full-voting representation in Congress or other rights accorded to states. The scope of this campaign is also to engage as many volunteers as possible to help overcome ballot barriers and to get the vote out. In addition it is designed to leave a momentum after Election Day for the various causes that committed people have worked so hard to further. For the Greens know that political parties need also to work between elections to make elections meaningful. The focus on fundamentals of broader distribution of power is the touchstone of this campaign. As Supreme Court Justice Louis Brandeis declared for the ages, "We can have a democratic society or we can have great concentrated wealth in the hands of a few. We cannot have both."

Thank you.

APPENDIX D: WOULDN'T PRESIDENT GEORGE W. BUSH AND VICE PRESIDENT DICK CHENEY HAVE DONE THE SAME?

What the Clinton-Gore administration did:

1. Promoted legislation for welfare reform that ended the federal safety net and put many children at risk.

2. Lobbied, with big business, NAFTA and GATT into law against labor, consumer, environmental, and human-rights groups.

3. Expanded corporate welfare programs.

4. Approved dozens of giant mergers in the chemical, oil, drug, defense, agribusiness, media, HMO, hospital, auto, banking, and other financial industries.

5. Encouraged larger military weapons exports by the private munitions companies using taxpayer subsidies and approved many costly, redundant weapons programs.

6. Supported a bloated military budget, post–Soviet Union, driven more by defense industry greed than national defense needs.

7. Failed to enforce laws against corporate crime, fraud, and abuse.

8. Gave away to corporations massive taxpayers assets in natural resources, scientific, health, space, and other R&D areas.

9. Bailed out, with taxpayer billions, reckless foreign governments and oligarchies through the IMF.

10. Opened up large areas of Northern Alaska for oil and gas drilling and supported the destruction by coal companies of mountaintops in Appalachia.

11. Gave the auto companies an eight-year holiday from higher fuel efficiency and auto safety standards.

12. Signed legislation eroding civil liberties and produced a record that commentators called "abysmal."

13. Under-enforced the civil rights laws while orating for them.

14. Backed large corporate prison expansions and failed to address discriminatory patterns of criminal justice enforcement.

15. Supported dictatorships and oligarchies that have suppressed their people.

16. Continued the deep sleep of the regulatory agencies at the expense of health, safety, and economic assets of consumers and workers.

17. Favored big agribusiness over the family farmer.

18. Subsidized and gave the biotechnology industry insulation from regulation.

19. Raised large amounts of money from almost every corporate interest and let big money continue to nullify honest elections.

20. Opposed ways and means to facilitate consumers, workers, taxpayers, and investors banding together for self-defense.

APPENDIX E: THE NADERHOOD 2000

Tom Adkins
Theresa Amato
Darci Andresen
Michael Avey
Mike Avitzur
Jonah Baker
Jessica Berger
Vanessa Bliss
Byron Bloch
Keight Bloeser
Jerry Bloomer
Adrienne Boer
Rita Bogolub
Al Brooks
Matteo Burani
Alan Bushnell
Vergil Bushnell
Peter Byer
Amy Carberg
Laquetta Carpenter
Megan Case
Michael Caudell-
  Feagan
Anthony Cimino
Mark Clarke
Steve Cleary
Christopher Cloud

Steve Cobble
David Cobb
Bryan Conley
Steve Conn
Stacy Cordeiro
Charlie Cray
Kevin Crisp
Jana Cutlip
Pete D'Allessandro
Ericka Dana
Carolyn Danckaert
Paul DeMain
Dave DeRosa
Alan Dicara
James Diokno
Masada
  Disenhouse
Jonathon Dushoff
Matt Duss
Brian Duss
Josh Edelman
Karen Elenich
Khalid Elhassan
Hugh Esco
George Farah
Jill Farmer
Jan Ferland

Katie Fisher
Shelly Fite
Scott Foster
Nathan Foster
Erin Frisby
Jeff Gates
Marnie Glickman
James Goettler
Andrew Goldman
Raj Goyle
Gwendolyn Griffin
Winston Grizzard
Joshua Gronsbell
Max Guzman
Martha Guzman
Jacob Harold
Roberta Harper-
  McIntosh
Nancy Harvey
Woody
  Hastings
Laird Hastay
Howie Hawkins
Linda Henry
Andrew Hinkel
Alan Hirsch
Lydia Holden

Rob Holzapfel
Greg Jan
Dan Johnson-
  Weinburger
Laura Jones
Tonya Jordan
Greg Kafoury
Jason Kafoury
Partick Keaney
Smita Khatri
Susan King
Lauren Klepac
Kevin Kniffin
Tyesha Kobel
Alan Kobrin
Regina LaBelle
Rebecca Leamon
Kenneth Leija
Matt Leonard
Mark Lewis
Mark Lewis
Rita Lombardo
Bob Lyon
Todd Main
Lowell MacGregor
Stacy Malkan
Ben Manski
Amy Marshak
Mark McDougal
Scott McLarty
Benjamin
  Meiklejohn

Andrew Mercer
Dean Meyerson
Tarek Milleron
Elizabeth Mims
Ross Mirkarimi
Jason Morgan
Greg Mullen
Martha Murray
Faramarz Nabavi
Peter Noerr
Isaac Opalinsky
Mike Palmedo
Natalie Paravincini
Jeanna Penn
Dennis Perrin
Jan Pierce
Richard Pinner
Andrea Plant
Bernard Pollack
Nick Raleigh
Annette Ramos
Jim Reed
Sandi Rizzo
Ken Rogers
Scott Royder
Bonnie Rubenstein
Belvey Russ
Ken Sain
Anthony Schinella
Joe Sexauer
Arlen Slobodow
Aaron Smith

Leslie Smith
Dan Sockrider
Bryan Spoon
Peter Stair
Alex Stewart
John Stith
Doug Stuber
Jennifer
  Thangevalu
Lori Theis
Martin Thomas
Dru Tidwell
Jeff Toste
Tom Unzicker
Andrew Van Iter-
  son
Juscha Vannier
Philip Varner
Marcia Vottero
Richard Wachs
Jaclynn Cavis
  Wallette
Elizabeth Wasson
Kevin Webb
Mark Weber
David Weiss
Rich Weiss
Branden Willman
Monica Wilson
Gary Wolf
Nathan Wolf
Alex Zwerdling

I also thank the following people for their pro bono and professional services:

Pat Alia
Harvey Jester
Jean Highland

Carl Mayer
Wesley J. Smith
Greg Kafoury
Mark McDougal
Michael Trister of Lichtman, Trister, Singer & Ross
Scott P. Lewis of Palmer and Dodge
John Bonifaz, Gregory Luke, Bonnie Tenneriello, and Brenda
  Wright of the National Voting Rights Institute
Glenn Moramarco and Elizabeth Daniel of the Brennan Center for
  Justice at New York University School of Law
Howard Friedman
Jason Adkins
Anthony Fletcher
Stacy Grossman
Mark Lemley
Lawrence Kolodney

And to the tens of thousands of volunteers, donors, supporters, and those we have inadvertently not listed—you know who you are—my deepest gratitude for all your efforts.

APPENDIX F: THE GREENS' TEN KEY VALUES

1. Grassroots Democracy

Every human being deserves a say in the decisions that affect their lives; no one should be subject to the will of another. Therefore, we will work to increase public participation at every level of government and to ensure that our public representatives are fully accountable to the people who elect them. We will also work to create new types of political organizations that expand the process of participatory democracy by directly including citizens in the decision-making process.

2. Ecological Wisdom

Human societies must operate with the understanding that we are part of nature, not separate from nature. We must maintain an ecological balance and live within the ecological and resource limits of our communities and our planet. We support a sustainable society that utilizes resources in such a way that future generations will benefit and not suffer from the practices of our generation. To this end we must have agricultural practices that replenish the soil; move to an energy-efficient economy; and live in ways that respect the integrity of natural systems.

3. Social Justice and Equal Opportunity

All persons should have the rights and opportunity to benefit equally from the resources afforded us by society and the environment. We must consciously confront in ourselves, our organizations, and society at large barriers such as racism and class oppression, sexism and heterosexism, ageism and disability, which act to deny fair treatment and equal justice under the law.

4. Nonviolence

It is essential that we develop effective alternatives to our current patterns of violence at all levels, from the family and the streets to nations and the world. We will work to demilitarize our society and eliminate weapons of mass destruction, without being naive about the intentions of other governments. We recognize the need for self-defense and the defense of others who are in helpless situations. We promote nonviolent methods to oppose practices and policies with which we disagree, and will guide our actions toward lasting personal, community, and global peace.

5. Decentralization

Centralization of wealth and power contributes to social and economic injustice, environmental destruction, and militarization. Therefore, we support a restructuring of social, political, and economic institutions away from a system that is controlled by and mostly benefits the powerful few, to a democratic, less bureaucratic system. Decision making should, as much as possible, remain at the individual and local level, while assuring that civil rights are protected for all citizens.

6. Community-Based Economics

We recognize that it is essential to create a vibrant and sustainable economic system, one that can create jobs and provide a decent standard of living, for all people, while maintaining a healthy ecological balance. A successful economic system will offer meaningful work with dignity, while paying a "living wage" that reflects the real value of a person's work. Local communities must look to economic development that assures protection of the environment and workers' rights, broad citizen participation in planning, and enhancement of our quality of life. We support independently owned and operated companies that are socially responsible, as well as cooperatives and public enterprises that spread out resources and control to more people through democratic participation.

7. Feminism

We have inherited a social system based on male domination of politics and economics. We call for the replacement of the cultural ethics of domination and control with more cooperative ways of interacting, which respect differences of opinion and gender. Human values such as equity between the sexes, interpersonal responsibility, and honesty must be developed with moral conscience. We should remember that the process that determines our decisions and actions is just as important as achieving the outcome we want.

8. Respect for Diversity

We believe it is important to value cultural, ethnic, racial, sexual, religious, and spiritual diversity, and to promote the development of respectful relationships across these lines. We believe the many diverse elements of society should be reflected in our organizations and decision-making bodies, and we support the leadership of people who have been traditionally closed out of leadership roles. We acknowledge and encourage respect for other life forms and the preservation of biodiversity.

9. Personal and Global Responsibility

We encourage individuals to act to improve their personal well-being and, at the same time, to enhance ecological balance and social harmony. We seek to join with people and organizations around the world to foster peace, economic justice, and the health of the planet.

10. Future Focus and Sustainability

Our actions and policies should be motivated by long-term goals. We seek to protect valuable natural resources, safely disposing of or "unmaking" all waste we create, while developing a sustainable economics that does not depend on continual expansion for survival. We must counterbalance the drive for short-term profits by assuring that economic development, new technologies, and fiscal policies are responsible to future generations who will inherit the results of our actions. Our overall goal is not merely to survive, but to share lives that are truly worth living. We believe the quality of our individual lives is enriched by the quality of all of our lives. We encourage everyone to see the dignity and intrinsic worth in all of life, and to take the time to understand and appreciate themselves, their community, and the magnificent beauty of this world.

A VOTE FOR OUR FUTURE

RALPH NADER FOR PRESIDENT

"Every major social justice movement in our nation's history was made possible by more power to the people and it is way past time for a shift of power from big business to the people" –Ralph Nader.

We, union activists and leaders, have carefully reviewed the candidates and issues in this election and have decided we will vote for Ralph Nader for President and Winona LaDuke for Vice President and urge others to do so as well.

We believe Ralph Nader has been barred from the Presidential debates because his participation would mean a break in politics as usual, would present voters with clear policy alternatives and would offer the possibility. for working people to register their disgust with the way in which money determines the choice of candidates.

The Nader candidacy presents the most comprehensive and reasoned critique of the continuing inequities in our society and offers a humane alternative direction for our country.

Nader is the only candidate in this campaign who is talking about how unrestrained corporate power affects our political institutions, economy, media, culture and democracy.

Nader is the only candidate offering a comprehensive program to improve the quality of life for all of our people. It includes eradicating poverty, narrowing the income gap, enhancing labor rights, establishing a universal healthcare system, ending the death penalty, halting the current misguided and repressive "drug war," ending discrimination in our criminal justice system, protecting our environment, and democratizing our elections.

Here's where Ralph Nader stands on just a few issues of critical importance to working people:

- A living wage for all workers, repeal of the anti-labor Taft-Hartley Act, triple back pay for workers fired illegally in organizing drives, expanded power for the National Labor Relations Board to stop unfair anti-union practices and a ban on permanent replacement of strikers.

- Opposition to the unfair trade treaties and institutions such as the North American Free Trade Agreement (NAFTA) and the World Trade Organization (WTO).

- Tougher penalties for corporations that pollute or make (or withhold information about) defective products.

- Elimination of unneeded weapons systems, reduction of our nuclear arsenal and a cut in Pentagon spending.

- Ending corporate welfare, subsidies, and bailouts. Redirection of these funds for public education, healthcare, renewable energy, childcare, public transit, clinics, libraries, drinking water systems, and public works.

- A publicly funded, administered, and accountable universal healthcare system with comprehensive preventive, diagnostic, and therapeutic services without co-payments or deductibles, including full prescription drug coverage for everyone.

- Genuine enforcement of affirmative action, opposition to police violence, equal rights for Lesbians and Gays, including civil unions and ending the military's "don't ask, don't tell" policy.

- A Constitutional guarantee of equal rights for women and full abortion rights.

A strong showing by Ralph Nader will have a positive effect long past November. We have a chance to break with the past and raise the standard of political debate and decision-making in our country. A vote for Ralph Nader is not a vote for anyone else. It's a vote for the best candidate in the race. It's a vote against big-money politics as usual. It's a vote for our future.

To join Labor for Nader call 510 273-2240

Paid for by CNA Federal Pac. FEC number# C00360438

APPENDIX H: FDR LETTER TO THE DEMOCRATIC CONVENTION

Here is the text of the letter that FDR drafted to read to the Democratic Convention in 1940 when he thought they would deny him Henry Wallace as a running mate.

July 18, 1940
Members of the Convention:

In the century in which we live, the Democratic Party has received the support of the electorate only when the party, with absolute clarity, has been the champion of progressive and liberal policies and principles of government.

The party has failed consistently when through political trading and chicanery it has fallen into the control of those interests, personal and financial, which think in terms of dollars instead of in terms of human values.

The Republican Party has made its nominations this year at the dictation of those who, we all know, always place money ahead of human progress.

The Democratic Convention, as appears clear from the events of today, is divided on this fundamental issue. Until the Democratic Party through this convention makes overwhelmingly clear its stand in favor of social progress and liberalism, and shakes off all the shackles of control fastened upon it by the forces of conservatism, reaction, and appeasement, it will not continue its march of victory.

It is without question that certain political influences pledged to reaction in domestic affairs and to appeasement in foreign affairs have been busily engaged behind the scenes in the promotion of discord since this Convention convened.

Under these circumstances, I cannot, in all honor, and will not, merely for political expediency, go along with the cheap bargaining and political maneuvering which have brought about party dissension in this convention.

It is best not to straddle ideals.

In these days of danger when democracy must be more than vigilant, there can be no connivance with the kind of politics which has internally weakened nations abroad before the enemy has struck from without.

It is best for America to have the fight out here and now.

I wish to give the Democratic Party the opportunity to make its historic decision clearly and without equivocation. The party must go wholly one way or wholly the other. It cannot face in both directions at the same time.

By declining the honor of the nomination for the presidency, I can restore that opportunity to the convention. I so do.

———

Political Broadcast Paid for by Americans for Democratic Action 1948

Let's get one thing perfectly clear. You're not wasting your vote if you vote for Wallace, you're not just throwing it away. Far from it—a vote for Wallace is a vote for Dewey. A vote for Wallace is a vote for Dewey. Almost every vote for Wallace reduces the number of votes Truman will get and every vote take from Truman is given to Dewey. . . .

APPENDIX I: STEVE COBBLE MEMO

To: The Sierra Club
From: Nader 2000
Date: July 21, 2000
Subject: "Pragmatic" Politics

This was Wednesday's headline, front page:
"Clinton/Gore Administration will not breach dams to save salmon."
Will this be Sunday's headline, inside page?
"As expected, Sierra Club endorses Gore."
The political result: the Sierra Club will be ignored the rest of the campaign; key environmental issues will be left off the agenda and out of the presidential debates, as Vice President Gore seeks to mollify and attract swing voters, while taking the "base" for granted; and the Sierra Club will gain the image of a special interest group that will subsume its core principles at the behest of the Democratic Party. In addition, of course, the Sierra Club will snub perhaps the greatest consumer, environmental, and anti-corporate activist in American history.

This is not "practical" politics. It is certainly not practical politics only three days after a major public insult, which the salmon decision is.

This is not the way to play even the insider game on behalf of the environment, much less the long-term, mass movement, change the anti-environmental-corporate-structure game. After all, in American politics, it's the squeaky wheel that gets the grease, not the go-along-to-get-along liberal interest group—quiet politics only works for those with the big, big corporate money, behind closed doors.

Contrast that possible outcome of this weekend's meetings with the recent actions of President Hoffa and the Teamsters Union. When the Clinton-Gore administration rammed PNTR (Permanent Normal Trade Relations) with China down the throats of the labor and environmental movements, the Teamsters (along with the UAW) did not take this double-cross lightly.

Instead, President Hoffa announced that the Teamsters would reconsider their 1996 support of the Democrats. He then held a press conference with Ralph Nader, and announced that he supported Nader's inclusion in the presidential debates, as the only way to get fair trade issues discussed in front of the voting public.

The result: reams of press, lots of media attention, an enhanced reputation for independent action and standing up for their members of the Teamsters Union, and more focus on the trade question. That's practical politics.

The sad fact is that in modern politics, only when a candidate is fearful of losing your vote does he pay attention. We have a recent illustration of this principle—the Clinton-Gore administration's late discovery of the Antiquities Act of 1906, when faced with an independent campaign by Ralph Nader and the Greens.

First used by Teddy Roosevelt, to save some of the most precious sites in the United States, the Antiquities Act of 1906 has since been used by president after president to set aside threatened lands.

In 1978, the last Democratic president, Jimmy Carter, saved 56 million acres in Alaska, by invoking the Antiquities Act seventeen times after Congress refused to set aside these lands from development.

Yet for the first three-and-three-quarters years of the Clinton-Gore administration, the Antiquities Act of 1906 was never applied. In 1993, zero acres were saved. In 1994, zero acres were saved. In 1995, zero acres were saved.

Yet in late 1996, just before the election, Bill Clinton appeared on the edge of the Grand Canyon, to announce his first-ever use of the Antiquities Act of 1906 to preserve the Grand Staircase–Escalante in Utah—a staged event obviously aimed more at neighboring California, Arizona, Colorado, and New Mexico than at Utah, where Democratic chances were nil.

Some noticed that there were Green Parties in those four states. And some noticed that Bill Clinton blamed Ralph Nader for losing Colorado in 1996, after winning it in 1992.

Still, in 1997, after the election, zero acres were saved. In 1998, the Antiquities Act was again never invoked. In 1999, zero acres once again.

Then Nader began to make it known that he was going to run in 2000, this time seriously. In January, the Clinton-Gore administration rediscovered the Antiquities Act of 1906, setting aside the Grand Canyon–Parashant and Agua Fria in Arizona, and the coast off California's shore.

In late February, Nader made an official announcement, promising to raise several million dollars, campaign in all fifty states, and qualify for the ballot in almost all the states. In April, the Giant Sequoia area became the latest land set-aside.

Nader broke the all-important 5 percent barrier in the national polls, the level that would make the Green Party a national political party, and began to poll very well along the West Coast. And then in June, the Clinton-Gore administration invoked the Antiquities Act once again for the Ironwood Forest in Arizona, Hanford Reach in Washington, the Canyons of the Ancients in Colorado, and the Cascade-Siskiyou in Oregon.

Notice the pattern: environmental conservation in swing states, personified by announcing the Utah set-aside in Arizona.

Notice the other, more basic pattern: years in which Nader is running, millions of acres are saved; years in which Nader is not running—zero acres are saved.

This is not an accident. Presidential politics in America is not about being nice and polite; it's not about nice rhetoric; it's about independent action, swing votes, and leverage. It's also about strength, not weakness.

To endorse Al Gore, alone, while snubbing Ralph Nader, only three days after the Clinton-Gore administration committed its most recent environmental breach of trust would show weakness. (And how's that Ohio incinerator doing these days?)

Instead of defending salmon, the Sierra Club would be protecting Al Gore.

What other options are there?

- An endorsement of Ralph Nader. Obviously, Nader 2000 would prefer this option. Nader's work on Clean Air and Clean Water, consumer safety, fuel efficiency, and global

trade has earned him the unparalleled respect of environmentalists around the world.

- A dual endorsement of Nader and Gore. This action would
  make it clear that voters who care about the environment
  have two champions in the race.
- A dual endorsement, by targeted state. In this option, the
  Sierra Club would recognize the value of a new political
  party founded on environmental principles, and led by a
  lifelong environmental leader. The Sierra Club would endorse both candidates, and then suggest to its membership—
  by state, in late October—which candidate to support. So,
  in California, where Gore is leading, the Sierra Club could
  suggest a Nader vote in November, to build the Green Party
  and create environmental leverage in the future. In Ohio,
  however, if the race is very close, the suggestion could be
  that Sierra Clubbers vote for Gore, to insure that the state's
  electoral votes do not go to Bush. Given the very sophisti-
  cated nature of the Sierra Club's polling and direct mail
  operations, this is not that difficult to do.
- A deferred endorsement, with a passionate public argument
  that Nader be included in the presidential debates, so that
  key environmental issues such as the globalization of trade
  will be heard. (This is essentially the Teamsters' action.) The
  Sierra Club could then decide on an endorsement after the
  debates, when it will be much clearer whether Nader's candidacy has caught on (like Ross Perot's), or not.

We would respectfully argue that the minimum response of the
Sierra Club to this weekend's deliberations is a public declaration
that Ralph Nader should be included in the presidential debates.
Nader's four decades of public interest work on behalf of the earth
and its people have earned him at least that amount of respect.

*Indeed, there is nothing preventing the Sierra Club from holding a
national debate of its own, inviting all the candidates, and at a minimum refusing to endorse any candidate who is afraid to show up and
debate environmental issues in front of an environmental audience.*

This option would show strength, and force all the political system to deal with the environmental issues that the major party
candidates would rather just talk about.

APPENDIX J: WHAT I VOTED FOR BY TIM ROBBINS

The Nation, August 6, 2001

In mid-June 2001 Tim Robbins spoke at the annual dinner of the Liberty Hill Foundation, which funds grassroots organizing in Los Angeles. In recognition of his politically engaged films and his activist commitments, the foundation gave him its Upton Sinclair Award. Following is an edited version of his remarks.

—*The Editors*

About a month ago in a New York theater, I was approached by an agitated older couple. "We hope you're happy now," they said. "With what?" I said, suspecting the answer they gave. "Your Nader gave us Bush." Now, this wasn't the first time since the election that I had been attacked by irate liberals who saw my support of Ralph Nader as a betrayal, as blasphemy, as something tantamount to pissing on the Constitution. Before the election, Susan [Sarandon] and I had been attacked in the op-ed pages of the *New York Times*; we'd received intimidating faxes from a leading feminist admonishing us for our support for Nader. A week before the election we'd gotten a phone call from a Hollywood power broker, who urged us to call Nader and ask him to withdraw from the race. If he did so, this mogul said, he would contribute $100,000 to the Green Party. I told him that no phone call from us would sway this man, that this was not a politics of personal influence and deal-making, and that the Green Party probably wouldn't take his contribution. After the election I read an article in which a famous actor criticized supporters of Nader, calling them limousine liberals of the worst kind, unconcerned with the poor.

It was not easy to support Nader. In no uncertain terms the message sent to us by colleagues and business associates was that our support of Nader would cost us. Will it? I don't know. After the election one of our kids was admonished in public by the aforementioned Hollywood mogul. And who knows what fabulous parties we haven't been invited to.

So, what to make of all this? As someone who has voted defensively in the past and at one time recognized all Republicans as evil incarnate, I completely understand the reactions of these people. I like these people. Eight years ago I would have said the same thing to me. But a lot has happened that has shifted the way I think. After talking with friends in Seattle after protests there, after going with Susan to Washington, D.C., and talking with activists at the IMF–World Bank protests, after talking with thirteen-year-olds handing out pamphlets on sweatshops outside a Gap on Fifth Avenue, after watching the steady drift to the right of the Democratic Party under Clinton, I have come to the realization that I would rather vote my conscience than vote strategically.

There is something truly significant happening today. A new movement is slowly taking hold on college campuses, among left-wing groups in Europe, and human rights groups throughout the world. The protests in Seattle in 1999, the IMF–World Bank protests in Washington, D.C., in 2000, and the continuing presence of agitation wherever corporate entities gather to determine global economic and environmental policies do not, as the media portray them, merely reflect the work of fringe radicals and anarchists. Such events arise out of a broad-based coalition of students, environmentalists, unions, farmers, scientists, and other concerned citizens who view the decisions made in these cabals as the frontline in the battle for the future of this planet. This is a movement in its infancy that I believe is as morally compelling as the early abolitionists fighting to end slavery in the eighteenth century; as important as the labor activists advocating workplace safety and an end to child labor in the early 1850s; as undeniable as the scientists who first alerted the American public to widespread abuse of our environment by corporate polluters. All of these movements met with overwhelming condemnation by both political parties, were ignored and then criticized by the press, while their adherents were harassed, arrested, and sometimes killed by police and other agencies of the government. But because of their tenacity, we were eventually able in this country to create laws that ended slavery and established a minimum wage, Social Security, unemployment insurance, environmental responsibility, and workplace safety.

Despite years of progress in our own country on all these issues, we now face a resurgence of child and slave labor, of unsafe working conditions, of sweatshops, and of wanton environmental destruction in the Third World wrought by the very same corporate ethos that resisted for years the progressive gains in the United States. In the interest of profit margins and economic growth, our corporations have reached out to the global economy and found a way to return to 1850 on all of these issues. Enabled and emboldened by free trade and the protections granted by NAFTA, GATT, and the WTO, we have farmed these problems out to other countries. Amid our booming economy this is an uncomfortable concept to embrace. It certainly is not being written about in our official journals. But it is being shouted on the streets, and the protesters' arguments bear an incontrovertible moral weight. Ralph Nader was the only candidate to talk about these issues and to embrace this new movement as his own. That is why Susan and I voted for him.

Last year's election brought us to an important crossroads. The closeness of the race lifted a rock to expose the corrupt, manipulative, and illegal way in which elections are run in this country. Indeed, the election year's most surreal and humorous moment was when Fidel Castro offered to send observers to monitor our election. Aside from the obvious voter fraud in Florida, a brief spotlight was focused on the racist practices that have accompanied elections for years. Whether it's the roadblocks outside polling places in African-American voting districts or the disappearance of African-American names from voting registers, the ineffective and antiquated voting machines in low-income voting districts or the exposure of the Supreme Court as a partisan political institution, the picture is the same. Powerful people in the American ruling class fear democracy.

There was a time when I would have said that it is the "evil" Republicans who fear democracy. But the sad realization I have come to after the 2000 election, and after experiencing the reactions to our support for Nader, is that you can count the Democrats in that bunch, too. Not only do they fear democracy, but many in the Democratic Party elite fear, if not outright despise, idealism. I have lost a great deal of respect for a party that admonished its progressive wing, that had no tolerance for dissension in its ranks, and sought to demonize the most important and influential consumer advocate of the past fifty years. But we shouldn't be surprised. A similar reaction occurred earlier in this century when another leading advocate, Upton Sinclair, was running for governor of California. The power brokers of the Democratic Party did everything they could to isolate him. If they gave any support at all to his candidacy, it was halfhearted, while some even endorsed his Republican opponent, Frank Merriam. And the press? They demonized him, said he was anti-business, said he was an egomaniac. Sound familiar?

Most of the Nader supporters I met were the real deal, people who have dedicated their lives to advocacy. These were the people at the center of the struggle around controversial, difficult issues; their political engagement was way beyond and deserving of much more respect than that of many people who would wind up criticizing them.

The judgmental and patronizing attitude of those in the generation that fought to end the Vietnam War and work for women's rights is disappointing and discouraging, but understandable. But I am not of the opinion that Bill Clinton was the best this generation had to offer, and I would like to believe there is a dormant power still left in these progressives who have yet to acknowledge the importance of the new movement growing around them. I would like to believe that the children of the Vietnam era who protested that unjust war were concerned with more than self-preservation, with issues beyond not losing their lives to the war. I would like to believe that feminists—recognizing which gender works predominantly in sweatshops and which gender is predominantly sold into slavery—would acknowledge these issues as their own, and begin looking beyond reproductive rights as the only litmus test for a candidate. I would like to believe that higher ideals drive all of us, ideals that have to do with the world at large.

The young people who have helped launch a quest for an alternative party, one that will not compromise this planet's future for campaign donations from corporate sugar daddies, believe the Democratic and Republican parties are united on the major issues of our time. This new movement is a rejection of politics as usual, a rejection that has frightening implications when you consider the progressive community's reaction to it. Have we become our parents? Are we the Establishment? Are we now the status quo that so cynically rejects those with ideals and dreams, that says to the idealist that there is no room for that in this election, that one must vote strategically, that we can't afford our dreams, that we must accept the lesser of two evils? The couple in the theater, the op-ed columnist, the Hollywood mogul, and the actor beat their drums once every four years for their candidate and talk about their opponents as if their election will end civilization as we know it. This is a gay op-ed columnist who would not vote for the one candidate who unashamedly supported same-sex marriage; this is a mogul who would not be having any more sleepovers and private screenings in a Republican White House; this is an actor professing to care about the poor who couldn't seem to find his way to the picket line to support his own union's strike.

I don't respect armchair activists. I respect the kids outside the Gap who don't compromise. I'm not ready to cede their idealism and passion and vision, to compromise their integrity for a Democratic Party that aspires to be centrist, for a Democratic Party that supports the death penalty, that dismantled the welfare system while increasing corporate welfare, that helped create the economic system that tears at the heart of the labor movement.

How embarrassing it must be for Democratic senators that the embodiment of political courage in this country is now a Republican from Vermont. Maybe it's time to stop demonizing people for their political affiliations and to follow the example of the man who risked his political future to follow the voice inside him. To reject politics as usual and follow our grassroots hearts; to form alliances in unlikely places.

It's a long struggle for justice. It is grassroots movements that create real change, and no grassroots movement ever got anywhere compromising its ideals. Real change won't happen at Washington cocktail parties or in the Lincoln Bedroom. It is arduous and messy, and takes relentless agitation. It took over a hundred years of advocacy to eliminate slavery, over a hundred years to put an end to child labor, and over a hundred years to establish the minimum wage. This movement is in its infancy, but it is alive and it's not going away. Its door is wide open to you. It's a frightening threshold to cross but an essential one.

APPENDIX K: EAST LIVERPOOL MEETING

On September 27, we went to meet with citizens at East Liverpool Ohio's junior high gymnasium who had a community experience with Al Gore's environmental record.

For Terri Swearingen, a registered nurse and organizer with the Tri-State Environmental Council, Al Gore's double-talk regarding the location of the giant WTI incinerator provoked dozens of demonstrations and litigation starting in 1992. That was the year when Al Gore campaigned in East Liverpool by the Ohio River and lambasted the incinerator, then under construction. He said it was "unbelievable" to have such a polluting facility in a flood plain, only four hundred yards from an elementary school. "We'll be on your side for a change," he declared, adding that "the Clinton-Gore administration is going to give you an environmental presidency to deal with these problems."

To Swearingen and many residents of East Liverpool, who don't want their families living with daily levels of dioxin, mercury, lead, arsenic, and other toxins, Gore gave them the clear impression that this incinerator would not be given an operating permit. We have supported the people of East Liverpool for several years and understood their subsequent indignation at what they believed was an outright betrayal by Clinton-Gore. It started with Clinton's environmental adviser, Katie McGinty, who met on January 8, 1993, with President George Bush's environmental chief, William Reilly, to discuss transition matters. According to Swearingen, who spoke with him in 1997, Reilly later told McGinty about a number of pending decisions that he, as a courtesy, offered to hold over until the new administration came into office. The test burn permit application by WTI was one of them. McGinty gave him to understand that he could to ahead and issue it. He did and the Clinton administration would soon be saying that their hands were tied by the previous Bush decision.

As Swearingen kept saying, "A lot of days we see the plumes blowing right into the school."

At the junior high gathering, I called on Gore to honor his commitments of 1992 and the subsequent mass of evidence that made his early incredulity over the incinerator's site more urgent. Although I preceded this call with a letter to Gore, there was never any answer, other than a staffer saying to the press that Gore was waiting for a report from the EPA's independent ombudsman. Lo and behold, in mid-October, the ombudsman, Robert J. Martin, reported that the Swiss-owned incinerator was "neither protective of human health and the environment nor of public safety" and recommended that it be shut down for a minimum of six months to allow more reliable testing of health risks. Still, there was no support by Gore for the exposed people of East Liverpool right through Election Day.

The politically-well-connected WTI corporation, which has escaped accountability for its violations and hazards, has a debt to pay the people and children who have had to breathe its emissions. A shutdown order should include, I added, a two-year severance pay for its employees, on whose backs and health it has made sizable profits.

Alonzo Spencer, a retired steel worker and head of the group Save Our Country, opposing the incinerator, said of Gore: "I don't think it's too much to ask to hold a politician to his promise. A man is as good as his word." Well put, about a man who every day told Americans that he "will fight for the people, not the powerful."

SUGGESTED READING

Alinsky, Saul D. *Rules for Radicals: A Practical Primer for Realistic Radicals*. Vintage Books, 1971.

Baker, Dean, and Mark Weisbrot. *Social Security: The Phony Crisis*. University of Chicago Press, 1999.

Berman, Daniel M., and John T. O'Connor. *Who Owns the Sun?: People, Politics, and the Struggle for a Solar Economy*. Chelsea Green Publishing Co., 1996.

Birnbaum, Norman. *The Radical Renewal: The Politics and Ideas in Modern America*. Pantheon Books, 1998.

Black, Charles L., Jr. *A New Birth of Freedom: Human Rights, Named and Unnamed*. Grosset/Putnam, 1997.

Bollier, David, and Joan Claybrook. *Freedom from Harm: The Civilizing Influence of Health, Safety and Environmental Regulation*. Public Citizen, Democracy Project, 1986.

Brown, Lester. *State of the World 2001* (Worldwatch Institute Books). W. W. Norton & Company, 2001. Also published in thirty other languages.

Bullard, Robert D. *Unequal Protection: Environmental Justice and Communities of Color*. Sierra Club Books, 1994.

Burnham, David. *Above the Law: Secret Deals, Political Fixes and Other Misadventures of the U.S. Department of Justice*. Scribner, 1996.

Cahn, Edgar S. *No More Throwaway People: The Co-Production Imperative*. Essential Books, 2000.

Carnoy, Martin, and Derek Shearer. *Economic Democracy: The Challenge of the 1980s*. M. E. Sharpe, Inc., 1980.

Chomsky, Noam. *Necessary Illusions: Thought Control in Democratic Societies*. South End Press, 1989.

Commoner, Barry. *Making Peace with the Planet*. Pantheon Books, 1990.

Derber, Charles. *Corporation Nation: How Corporations Are Taking Over Our Lives and What We Can Do About It*. St. Martin's Griffin, 2000.

Derickson, Alan. *Black Lung: Anatomy of a Public Health Disaster*. Cornell University Press, 1998.

Drew, Elizabeth. *The Corruption of American Politics: What Went Wrong and Why*. Overlook Press, 2000.

Durnil, Gordon K. *The Making of a Conservative Environmentalist*. Indiana University Press, 1995.

Edelman, Peter. *Searching for America's Heart: RFK and the Renewal of Hope*. Houghton Mifflin, 2001.

Ehrenreich, Barbara. *Nickel and Dimed: On (Not) Getting By in America*. Metropolitan Books, 2001.

Frank, Thomas. *One Market Under God*. Doubleday, 2000.

Friere, Paulo. *Pedagogy of the Oppressed*. Free Press of Glenco, 1963.

Gardner, John W. *On Leadership*. Free Press, 1990.

Garfinkel, Simson, and Deborah Russell. *Database Nation: The Death of Privacy in the 21st Century*. O'Reilly & Associates, 2000.

Garland, Anne Witte. *Woman Activists: Challenging the Abuse of Power*. City University of New York Press, 1988.

Gates, Jeff. *Democracy at Risk: Rescuing Main Street from Wall Street*. Perseus Press, 2000.

Geoghegan, Thomas. *Which Side Are You On?: Trying to Be for Labor When It's Flat on Its Back*. Plume, 1992.

Goodwyn, Lawrence. *The Populist Moment: A Short History of Agrarian Revolt in America*. Oxford University Press, 1978.

Green, Mark, Michael Calabrese, et al. Introduction by Ralph Nader. *Who Runs Congress?* Viking Press, 1979.

Green, Mark, and Robert Massie. *The Big Business Reader: Essays on Corporate America*. Pilgrim Press, 1983.

Greider, William. *Who Will Tell the People: The Betrayal of American Democracy*. Touchstone Books, 1993.

Harrington, Michael. *The Other America: Poverty in the United States*. Macmillan & Co., 1997.

Hawken, Paul, Amory Lovins, and Hunter L. Lovins. *Natural Capitalism: Creating the Next Industrial Revolution*. Back Bay Books, 2000.

Herman, Edward. *Corporate Control, Corporate Power*. Cambridge University Press, 1981.

Hertsgaard, Mark. *Earth Odyssey: Around the World in Search of Our Environmental Future*. Broadway Books, 1999.

Hock, Dee. *The Chaordic Organization*. Berrett-Koehler, 2000.

Isaac, Katherine. *Civics for Democracy: A Journey for Teachers and Students*. Essential Books, 1992.

Jacobson, Michael F. *Marketing Madness: A Survival Guide for a Consumer Society*. Westview Press, 1995.

Kim, Jim, et al. *Dying for Growth: Global Inequality and the Health of the Poor*. Common Courage Press, 2000.

King, Martin Luther, Jr. *Why We Can't Wait*. Harper & Row, 1963.

Klein, Naomi. *No Logo: Taking Aim at the Brand Bullies*. Picador, 2000.

Korten, David C. *When Corporations Rule the World*. Kumarian Press, 2001.

Kotz, Mary L., and Nick Kotz. *A Passion for Equality*. W. W. Norton, 1977.

Kwitny, Jonathan. *The Crimes of Patriots*. Simon & Schuster, 1988.

LaDuke, Winona. *All Our Relations*. South End Press, 1999.

Lappe, Frances Moore. *World Hunger: Twelve Myths*. Grove Atlantic, 1986.

Lekachman, Robert. *Greed Is Not Enough*. Pantheon, 1982.

Levy, Jacques E. *Cesar Chavez: Autobiography of La Causa*. W. W. Norton, 1975.

Lewis, Charles. Center for Public Integrity. *The Buying of the Congress: How Special Interests Have Stolen Your Right to Life, Liberty, and the Pursuit of Happiness*. Avon Books, 1998.

Lindblom, Charles. *Politics and Markets: The World's Political-Economic System*. Basic Books, 1980.

Loeb, Paul R. *Soul of a Citizen: Living with Conviction in a Cynical Time*. St. Martin's Press, 1999.

Lynd, Alice, and Staughton Lynd. *Rank and File: Personal Histories by Working Class Organizers.* Monthly Review Press, 1989.

McChesney, Robert. *Rich Media, Poor Democracy: Communication Politics in Dubious Times.* New Press, 2000.

Mills, C. Wright. *The Power Elite.* Oxford University Press, 2000.

Mintz, Morton, and Jerry S. Cohen. *Power, Inc.: Public and Private Rulers and How to Make Them Accountable.* Viking Press, 1976.

Mishel, Lawrence, et al. *The State of Working America, 2000–2001.* Cornell University Press, 2001.

Mokhiber, Russell. *Corporate Crime and Violence: Big Business Power and the Abuse of Public Trust.* Sierra Club Books, 1988.

Mokhiber, Russell, and Robert Weissman. *Corporate Predators: The Hunt for Mega-Profits and the Attack on Democracy.* Common Courage Press, 1999.

Monks, Robert A. G. *The New Global Investors: How Shareowners Can Unlock Sustainable Prosperity Worldwide.* Capstone Publications, 2001.

Nader, Ralph. *Unsafe at Any Speed.* Twenty-fifth Anniversary Updated Edition. Knightbridge, 1991.

Nader, Ralph, ed. *The Consumer and Corporate Accountability.* Harcourt Brace Jovanovich, 1973.

Nader, Ralph, Mark Green, and Joel Seligman. *Taming the Giant Corporation.* W. W. Norton, 1976.

Nader, Ralph, and William Taylor. *The Big Boys.* Pantheon Books, 1986.

Noble, David. *America by Design: Science, Technology and the Rise of Corporate Capitalism.* Oxford University Press, 1977.

Phillips, Kevin. *The Politics of the Rich and the Poor: Wealth and the American Electorate in the Reagan Administration.* Random House, 1990.

Phillips, Peter. *Censored 2001: 25 Years of Censored News and the Top Censored Stories of the Year.* Seven Stories Press, 2001.

Piven, Frances, and Richard A. Cloward. *Poor People's Movements: Why They Succeed, How They Fail.* Random House, 1977.

Pollin, Robert. *The Living Wage: Building a Fair Economy.* New Press, 2000.

SUGGESTED READING   367

Rasor, Dina. *The Pentagon Underground.* Times Books, 1985.

Rensenbrink, John. *Against All Odds: The Green Transformation of American Politics.* Leopold Press, 1999.

Ritz, Dean. Program on Corporations, Law & Democracy. *Defying Corporations, Defining Democracy: A Book of History and Strategy.* Apex Press, 2001.

Robinson, Randall N. *The Debt: What America Owes to Blacks.* Plume, 2001.

Rosoff, Stephen M., Robert Tillman, and Henry Pontell. *Profit Without Honor: White Collar Crime and the Looting of America.* Prentice Hall, 1997.

Schlosser, Eric. *Fast Food Nation.* Houghton Mifflin, 2001.

Schmidt, David. *Citizen Lawmakers: The Ballot Initiative Resolution.* Temple University Press, 1989.

Schumacher, E. F. *Small Is Beautiful: Economics As If People Mattered.* HarperCollins, 1991.

Soros, George. *The Crisis of Global Capitalism: Open Society Endangered.* PublicAffairs, 1998.

Sparrow, Malcolm K. *License to Steal: How Fraud Bleeds America's Health Care System.* Westview Press, 2000.

Stauber, John, and Sheldon Rampton. *Toxic Sludge Is Good for You!: Lies, Damn Lies and the Public Relations Industry.* Common Courage Press, 1995.

Teitel, Martin. *Genetically Engineered Food: Changing the Nature of Nature.* Inner Traditions International, 2001.

Terkel, Studs. *Hard Times: An Oral History of the Great Depression.* Pantheon, 1970.

Wachsman, Harvey F., and Steven Alschuler. *Lethal Medicine: The Epidemic of Medical Malpractice in America.* Henry Holt, 1993.

Wallach, Lori. *Whose Trade Organization?: Corporate Globalization and the Erosion of Democracy.* Public Citizen Inc., 1999.

Wasserman, Harvey. *The Last Energy War: The Battle over Utility Deregulation.* Common Courage Press, 1999.

West, Cornel. *Race Matters.* Vintage Books, 1994.

Whittelsey, Frances Cerra, and Marcia Carroll. *Why Women Pay More: How to Avoid Marketplace Perils.* The New Press, 1993.

Wolfe, Sidney M. *Worst Pills, Best Pills: A Consumer's Guide to Avoiding Drug-Induced Death or Illness.* Pocket Books, 1999.

Wolff, Edward, and Richard C. Leone. *Top Heavy: The Increasing Inequality of Wealth in America and What Can Be Done About It.* New Press, 1996.

Woolhandler, Steffie, Ida Hellander, and David Himmelstein, M.D. *Bleeding the Patient: The Consequences of Corporate Healthcare.* Common Courage Press, 2001.

Wylie, Jeanie. *Poletown: Community Betrayed.* University of Illinois Press, 1989.

Zinn, Howard. *A People's History of the United States.* HarperCollins, 1995.

A variety of worthwhile information can be found on the following Web pages:
www.citizenworks.org
www.citizen.org
www.essential.org

Magazines/Publications
The Amicus Journal
The Atlantic Monthly
Consumer Reports
Harper's
The Hightower Lowdown
In These Times
Mother Jones
Multinational Monitor
The Nation
The Progressive
The Progressive Populist
Rachel's Environmental & Health News
The Washington Monthly
The Workbook

The following two publications regularly have numerous feature articles on corporate abuses:
Business Week
Wall Street Journal

INDEX

WTO (World Trade Organization), 13, 89, 112, 124, 205. *See also* trade issues; GATT

Yard, Molly, 260–61
Yauch, Adam, 286
Yokich, Steve, 105–6, 127, 191–93, 196
Young, Don, 131

Young, Quentin, 67
youth, 1–2, 115, 129, 152, 216, 236, 271, 294, 314, 318

Zero, Jerry, 70
Zimbalist, Andrew, 81
Zinn, Howard, 209, 323
Zogby surveys, 103, 164